THE U. S. ARMY IN THE GULF WAR

CERTAIN VICTORY

Brig. Gen. Robert H. Scales, Jr., USA
The Desert Storm Study Project

BRASSEY'S
Washington•London

Brassey's Five-Star Paperback 1997
First Brassey's Edition 1994

This work was originally published in a slightly different form by the Office of the Chief of Staff, United States Army, in 1993.

Grateful acknowledgement is made to Pocket Books, a division of Simon & Schuster, Inc., to reprint excerpts from *Iron Soldiers* by Tom Carhart. Copyright © 1993 by Tom Carhart. Reprinted by permission of Pocket Books, a division of Simon & Schuster, Inc.

<table>
<tr><td>Brassey's Editorial Offices:</td><td>Brassey's Order Department:</td></tr>
<tr><td>22883 Quicksilver Drive</td><td>P.O. Box 960</td></tr>
<tr><td>Dulles, Virginia 20166</td><td>Herndon, Virginia 20172</td></tr>
</table>

Brassey's books are available at special discounts for bulk purchases for sales promotions, premiums, fund-raising, or educational use.

Library of Congress Cataloging-in-Publication Data

Scales, Robert H.
　　Certain victory: the U.S. Army in the Gulf War/Robert H. Scales, Jr.
　　　　—1st Brassey's ed.
　　　　p.　cm.—(AUSA book)
Originally published: Office of the Chief of Staff, United States Army, 1993.
　　Includes biblioographical references and index.
　　ISBN 0-02-881111-9 (hardcover)　　ISBN 1-57488-136-1 (paperback)
　　1. Persian Gulf War. 1991—United States.　2. United States—Army—History—
Persian Gulf War, 1991.　I. Title.　II. Series: Ausa Institute of Land Warfare book.
DS79.724.U6S3　1994
956.7044'2373—dc20
　　　　　　　　　　　　　　　　　　　　　　　　　　94-1263
　　　　　　　　　　　　　　　　　　　　　　　　　　CIP

10　9　8　7　6　5　4　3

Printed in the United States of America

FOREWORD

During World War II, General George C. Marshall, Army Chief of Staff, introduced a series of short books by writing:

> *American Forces In Action* is a series prepared by the War Department especially for the information of wounded men. It will show these soldiers, who have served their country so well, the part they and their comrades played in achievements which do honor to the record of the United States Army.

In the same spirit, General Scales and his team wrote *Certain Victory* to provide both the public and the military a clear picture of the Army's role in the Gulf War. The breadth and speed of Desert Storm operations left many participants unaware of the larger context in which they acted. This book is for them. To capture their story, General Scales essentially interweaves three distinct themes, each of which stands apart.

First, *Certain Victory* tells the story of the young men and women who, in the heat and blowing sand of Iraq and Kuwait, took the fight to the enemy and won a compelling victory.

Second, that victory vindicates the tireless and often unheralded work of a generation of Army leaders who forged a new Army from the dispirited institution that emerged from Vietnam.

Third, *Certain Victory* provides a window on the future as well as a chronicle of the past. The reader, reflecting on the overarching sinews that General Scales extracts from the story, will gain insight into how future American wars might be fought.

We leave it to scholars with broader perspectives to write the definitive history of the entire period from summer 1990 to summer 1991. This account shows but one facet of a complex, interdependent effort, over many years, by Saudi, American, and other nations' forces who formed the Coalition. Together they shouldered the responsibility for defending against naked aggression, and together planned and conducted operations in Iraq and Kuwait. Although these pages are filled with US Army exploits, "certain victory" was predicated on many nations' ground forces working together and teamed with similarly combined air and naval elements.

The ability to develop such joint and combined teams rapidly and far from home was never tested so dramatically as it was in August 1990. We should remember that "certain victory" was not assured for long, worrisome weeks in the autumn of 1990. In the future, we must maintain the training and the readiness of every aspect of our nation's capability to meet a similar challenge whenever and wherever it may be thrust upon us.

Washington, D.C.
1993

GORDON R. SULLIVAN
General, United States Army
Chief of Staff

THE DESERT STORM SPECIAL STUDY GROUP [1]
Brigadier General Robert H. Scales, Jr., Director

PRIMARY AUTHORS

Brigadier General Robert H. Scales, Jr.
Chief of Staff, US Army Field
Artillery Center and School,
Fort Sill, Oklahoma

Lieutenant Colonel Terry L. Johnson
11th Aviation Brigade, VII Corps,
Germany, KTO

Major Thomas P. Odom
Office of the Deputy Chief of Staff
for Military Intelligence, The
Pentagon, Washington, DC

EDITORIAL/PRODUCTION TEAM

Mrs. Bonnie K. Nealon
US Army Training Support Center
Fort Eustis, Virginia

Mr. Stan Erwin
US Army Training Support Center
Fort Eustis, Virginia

Ms. Jean Cerve
US Army Aviation Logistics School
Fort Eustis, Virginia

Mrs. Linda Christensen
Headquarters, TRADOC
Fort Monroe, Virginia

ADMINISTRATIVE TEAM

Captain Paul Darragh
Headquarters, TRADOC

Captain Miles Williams
Headquarters, TRADOC

Specialist Valorie Johnson
US Army Reserve, Saudi Arabia

Mrs. Amye Stephenson
Headquarters, TRADOC

RESEARCH/WRITING TEAM

Colonel James G. Scott
US Army Combined Arms Support
Command, Fort Lee, Virginia

Lieutenant Colonel John D. Hathcock
Headquarters, VII Corps,
Germany, KTO

Lieutenant Colonel Terry L. Johnson

Lieutenant Colonel George F. Oliver, III
101st Airborne Division
(Air Assault), Fort Campbell,
Kentucky, KTO

Lieutenant Colonel Michael R. Quirk
Headquarters, VII Corps,
Germany, KTO

Lieutenant Colonel Henry S. Tuttle
US Army Command and General
Staff College, Fort Leavenworth,
Kansas

Major Stephen B. Finch
Headquarters, XVIII Airborne Corps,
Fort Bragg, North Carolina, KTO

Major Thomas P. Odom

VIDEO PRODUCTION TEAM

Lieutenant Colonel Bryant B. Hamaker
Headquarters, 22d Support
Command, Saudi Arabia

Lieutenant Colonel Terry L. Johnson

Captain Jack J. Pagano
US Army Reserve, Joint Information
Bureau, Saudi Arabia

---

[1] Desert Shield/Storm units of assignment.

PREFACE

Certain Victory is a unique report of the Army's performance during Desert Shield and Desert Storm. It was researched and written under my direction by a group of eight officers drawn from many different combat specialties and backgrounds. Most are veterans of the Gulf War.

Our only instructions from the Army leadership as we did our research for this book were to uncover what soldiers term "ground truth." As such, *Certain Victory* is the first depiction of the war built exclusively on combat interviews and reports from units returning from the theater. The frankness and candor, as well as the color, derived from these sources have been carefully preserved.

In order to reach the widest possible audience, the study group went to extraordinary lengths to declassify intelligence and after-action reports as well as operations orders and overhead photography. We have also expunged as much of the Army jargon and acronyms from the book as possible. Many observations and insights are presented as part of personal stories or combat narratives. We hope this will help readers to better understand the issues and draw their own informed conclusions.

The focus of *Certain Victory* is the operational and tactical level of war. The political and diplomatic decision making that resulted in the Army's deployment to Southwest Asia is mentioned incidentally and only to the degree that it sets the stage for the war-fighting aspects of the conflict. *Certain Victory*'s treatment of other Services and other nations' contributions to the defeat of Saddam Hussein intentionally focuses on those Services and countries that most directly and immediately impacted on the Army's mission. Regretably, time and space did not permit us to include all units and key personalities. For example, Colonel John Sylvester's 1st Brigade of the 2d Armored Division, the "Tiger" Brigade, receives very little coverage for its outstanding exploits, although its place in history is no less important than the other units we have covered. I hope to see the joint warfare aspects of Desert Storm taken up more thoroughly in another work.

No single Service or nation won the Gulf War on its own. The Army recognizes its dependence on the other Services and other nations in this and any future conflict. As early as 1958, President Dwight D. Eisenhower, explaining that separate ground, sea, and air warfare is gone forever, stated, "...we will fight with all Services, as one single, concentrated effort. Strategic and tactical planning must be completely unified, combat forces organized into unified commands, and each equipped with the most efficient weapons systems science can develop, singly led and prepared to fight as one...." Eisenhower's vision, vindicated in the Gulf, continues to be an important historical legacy.

My special thanks to General J.H. Binford Peay III, the former Deputy Chief of Staff for Operations and Plans, US Army, for the latitude he gave my team to pass on the ground truth as we saw it to the public. The work could never have been assembled in such a limited time without the exceptional work done by Major General (Retired) Thomas Tait and the officers of his Desert Storm After-Action Report Study Group, who followed the Gulf War from initial deployment during Desert Shield to redeployment after Desert Storm. General Tait's team amassed thousands of documents and lessons learned that tell the story of Desert Storm with more detail and candor than any war in history.

The precision and focus of *Certain Victory* were enhanced significantly by an editorial board that conducted a detailed and objective review of the final draft. Lieutenant General Ronald Griffith and General Peay chaired the board. Members included Major Generals Jay Garner, Daniel Christman, and William Stofft; Brigadier General Hal Nelson; Colonels Robert Doughty, Michael Harper, Thomas Leavitt, and Jack LeCuyer; Colonel (Retired) Raoul Alcala; Dr. Roger Spiller; and our three principal authors, Lieutenant Colonel Terry Johnson, Major Tom Odom, and myself. Major Eli Alford from General Peay's staff also participated in the board and in clearing the book for publication.

The writing and publication of *Certain Victory* was accomplished by a very small but extremely dedicated staff. Mrs. Bonnie Nealon was the lead editor and all graphics were done by Mr. Stan Erwin. Mrs. Amye Stephenson typed much of the manuscript and assisted with copyediting. Ms. Jean Cerve assisted in editing and proofing the final manuscript. Mrs. Linda Christensen typeset the entire book. Specialist Valorie Johnson assisted with typing and filing. The quality of their work is evident in the pages that follow. Most of all, the Army is indebted to a group of eight officers, ranging in grade from major to colonel, who put their souls into these pages. These men came to the project as combat officers, not writers or historians. The quality of their work is just another testament to the exceptional body of talent that comprises the American Army today.

ROBERT H. SCALES, JR.
Brigadier General
United States Army

TABLE OF CONTENTS

LIST OF ILLUSTRATIONS

Chapter 4

Chapter 5

In war, then, let our great object be victory,
not lengthy campaigns.

Sun Tzu, *The Art of War*

An AUSA Book

The Association of the United States Army, or AUSA, was founded in 1950 as a not-for-profit organization dedicated to education concerning the role of the U.S. Army, to providing material for military professional development, and to the promotion of proper recognition and appreciation of the profession of arms. Its constituencies include those who serve in the Army today, including Army National Guard, Army Reserve, and Army civilians, the retirees and veterans who have served in the past, and all their families. A large number of public-minded citizens and business leaders are also an important constituency. The Association seeks to educate the public, elected and appointed officials, and leaders of the defense industry on crucial issues involving the adequacy of our national defense, particularly those issues affecting land warfare.

In 1988 the AUSA established within its existing organization a new entity known as the Institute of Land Warfare. Its purpose is to extend the educational work of the AUSA by sponsoring scholarly publications, to include books, monographs, and essays on key defense issues, as well as workshops and symposia. Among the volumes chosen for designation as "An AUSA Institute of Land Warfare Book" are both new texts and reprints of titles of enduring value that are no longer in print. Topics include history, policy issues, strategy, and tactics. Publication as an AUSA book does not indicate that the Association of the United States Army and the publisher agree with everything in the book, but does suggest that the AUSA and the publisher believe this book will stimulate the thinking of AUSA members and others concerned about important issues.

CERTAIN VICTORY

Chapter 1

FORGING A NEW ARMY

By late afternoon on February 26, Captain H. R. McMaster had been at war for 72 hours. His tank, Eagle 66, led a nine-tank formation as it moved across the featureless Iraqi plain like a squadron of miniature warships gliding through a glass-calm sea. Inside the steel body of Eagle 66, three other soldiers peered intently into a swirling sandstorm searching for the lead tanks of the Iraqi Tawakalna Division.

Isolated in the driver's compartment in front, Specialist Christopher "Skog" Hedenskog lay supine on his "lazy boy" couch. Skog's greatest fear was that his tank, the one that carried the troop commander, might stumble over a mine and miss the war. As he peered intently ahead, he nudged his T-bar left and right to steer smoothly around every piece of suspicious metal or slight imperfection in the ground ahead.

Staff Sergeant Craig Koch, the gunner, sat in the right of the turret, wedged between the gently moving gyro-stabilized gun and a densely packed jumble of white boxes and black telescopes illuminated periodically by blinking red, white, yellow, and green computer lights. The sandstorm, which limited visibility to 900 meters, made Koch very tense. He knew that in a tank battle, victory goes to the gunner who sees the other guy first.

Koch pressed his head tightly against the vinyl rest of his thermal-imaging sight, his right hand gently turning the "cadillac" handgrips left and right to maintain a constant, rhythmic slewing motion of the turret. His left hand nervously flipped the toggle that changed his sight picture from 3 to 10 power and back and forth between a "black hot" and "white hot" thermal image. He strained to discern from the desert horizon any telltale point of light that would be his first indication of Iraqi armor.

To Koch's left sat Specialist Jeffrey Taylor, youngest and newest of the crew. Taylor had mastered the gymnastics of loading a 54-pound projectile into the pitching breech of the main gun. Less proficient loaders were known to ride with a round cradled in their arms for faster loading. Not Taylor; he could routinely load from the racks in a second and a half. At any rate, McMaster didn't allow free rounds in the turret...too dangerous. He wanted them kept safely isolated behind the inch-thick steel plate of the ballistic shield to prevent secondary explosions if they should take an enemy round. Taylor's job on the move was to steer the tank using a satellite position-locating device mounted on a bracket over the gun breech. Every few seconds he would crouch forward, read the digital display, correct Skog's heading, and drop back into his seat.

The crew's senses were muted inside the combat vehicle crewman helmets that each wore. The whine of the tank turbine was faded and distant. With his head outside, McMaster could hear, faintly, the staccato beat of the tank tracks as they churned through the desert, throwing behind a mud-sand plume. Above Koch, the thermal-sight cooling motor rattled continuously. The sound, coupled with the continuous motion of his sight, gave him the sensation of looking at a slow-moving, ghostly, black-white panorama through an old-time nickelodeon.

McMaster sensed intuitively that he was closing on the Iraqis. He ordered his vulnerable Bradleys, scouting to the front, to slip behind the protective line of tanks. Endless battle drills allowed the troop to shift formation immediately without further instruction. McMaster, centered now among eight other tanks, broadcast a clipped "Follow my move," and each tank fell behind in formation, four tanks echeloned on either side.

The shooting war began for Eagle 66 at 1618 hours and lasted exactly seven seconds. As he crested a slight rise, Koch spotted not one, but eight thermal hot spots. He could only make out a series of thin lines through his sight because an earthen berm masked the image of each Iraqi tank. Eagle 66 was loaded with a high-explosive antitank round, or HEAT, not the optimum choice for taking on the Soviet-made T-72 tanks. Should Koch's first shot hit the berm, the HEAT round would explode harmlessly. Koch screamed, "Tanks, direct front." McMaster spotted the tanks. "Fire, fire sabot," he yelled as he kicked up the metal seat and dropped inside to look through his own thermal imager. McMaster's clipped command was a code that automatically launched his three crew mates into a well-rehearsed sequence of individual actions. To Jeff Taylor,

"Fire, fire sabot" meant that once the loaded HEAT round was gone, he must reload sabot, known to tankers in the desert as the "silver bullet."

Skog looked up and began immediately to "follow the tube" with his steering bar as he drove the tank briskly forward at 20 miles per hour. By aligning the tank body with the turret, Skog kept the 2-foot-thick frontal armor pointed toward the enemy. Koch, the gunner, knew what "fire" meant. He hit the button on his laser range finder. The red digital figure "1420" appeared just below the target reticle in his sight. "Jesus," Koch thought, "this sucker is close, practically a 'gunfight at the OK Corral' at tanker ranges." Red dot centered, Koch squeezed the trigger on the "cadillac," and the steady rocking motion of the moving tank was momentarily interrupted by a slight jerk and a muffled boom. Outside, the blast was deafening. Inside, the crew, working now on automatic, barely noticed any sensation other than an acrid smell of burned cordite and a discernable drop in air pressure as the HEAT round sucked out turret air on its way to the target.

Koch's HEAT round found an Iraqi tank less than one second later. It cleared the berm by 6 inches and struck a spot 4 inches above the base of the turret ring. Four pounds of Composition A3 exploded in a narrow 3,000-degree jet of burning gas, transforming the armor plate underneath into a white-hot, viscous fluid. The jet penetrated and continued to burn inside the tank, spewing gas and liquid turret metal in a deadly cone back toward the bustle of the turret. Two milliseconds later, gun propellant charges stored exposed in the bustle ignited. Half a second later, the turret separated from the tank body, spinning lazily 20 feet into the air like some cylindrical box lid that had been carelessly flipped open by an unseen hand. Sheets of white sparks, blue-white flame, and black smoke erupted from the now shapeless hulk.

A half-second after the first three Iraqi crewmen died, Taylor pushed himself back in the seat and kicked his right knee against a padded switch. With a smart clang, a shiny steel plate slammed open beside him, exposing two rows of deadly silver bullets ready to load. Taylor's right hand hit a release button and a round popped forward. Continuing the motion, he reached for the steel base of the projectile with his left hand and jerked it into the crew compartment. Like a twirler with an enormous baton, he spun the round nose forward and flicked it into the gun breech. As his knee left the switch, the safety door closed, instantly shutting off the crew from the volatile ammunition. Taylor's fluid motion took two seconds... about average for the fastest loader in the regiment.

Koch had another target. He pushed the illuminated sabot button on his computer to index a different round. Imperceptibly, the computer dropped the gun's point of aim half an inch and automatically refined the aim further to compensate for other ballistic variations in range, crosswind, temperature, and velocity at the muzzle. The gun's stabilizer kept it locked automatically on the target even as the tank gently pitched and swerved. The range finder read 600... a chip shot. With sabot, berms were no problem. Koch couldn't miss. He squeezed the trigger on the "cadillac." The second round was gone. The battle was now three seconds old.

The slender, yard-long, depleted uranium dart of the sabot round crossed the killing zone in a fifth of a second. It tore through the berm and hit the T-72 with the force of a race car striking a brick wall at 200 miles per hour, but with all of its energy compressed into an area smaller than a golf ball. One millisecond later the dart broke through just above the track and a foot below the turret ring. Two milliseconds later it had gone through to the right side of the tank, then the berm again, and off into space. The dart's impact caused what ballistics scientists tactfully term a "pyrophoric effect," the result of thousands of tiny bits of dense uranium material, sheared off and turned white hot, flashing throughout the crew compartment. One piece of metal torched through the combustible cardboard of the propellant charges in the autoloader. A second Iraqi tank erupted in grisly pyrotechnics.

Koch aligned his gun with a third tank; range—400 meters. The enemy turret filled his telescope. Taylor had the round "up," and a third sabot streaked to its mark. The exploding T-72 was so close that McMaster felt a blast of hot wind against his face and watched, transfixed, as a shower of pyrophoric sparklers flew backward from the sabot impact and arched lazily over his head.

Suddenly other enemy tanks started to come alive, twisting their turrets to and fro like a herd of confused Paleolithic monsters searching for some unseen predator. The remaining tanks of Eagle troop closed on Eagle 66 and joined the gunfight in a disciplined, sequential pattern of engagement constantly practiced by the troop in peacetime. In 10 seconds, the five remaining Iraqi tanks erupted in flames. The battle lasted barely half a minute. In 23 minutes of combat, Eagle troop "killed" 30 more armored vehicles. Two platoons—nine lone American tanks—had cut a 3-mile swath of destruction through Iraq's most capable armored force and had virtually destroyed a tank force four times its size.

The crew of *Eagle 66* from left to right, Captain H. R. McMaster, Staff Sergeant Craig Koch, Specialist Christopher Hedenskog, and Specialist Jeffrey Taylor.

The example of these four cavalrymen from the 2d Squadron, 2d Armored Cavalry Regiment, in the Battle of 73 Easting dramatically illustrates the transformation of the American Army from disillusionment and anguish in Vietnam to confidence and certain victory in Desert Storm. Only 100 ground combat hours were necessary for the Army to reestablish itself convincingly as a successful land combat force. During that brief period, mechanized forces moved more combat power faster and farther than any similar force in history. They averaged 95 kilometers per day, more than twice as many as the Wehrmacht's best blitzkrieg effort. Helicopter-borne forces conducted history's greatest aerial envelopment by placing the combat elements of an entire division 160 miles deep behind enemy lines. As part of the Coalition, the American Army decisively defeated the fourth largest field army in the world. It did so at the lowest cost in human life ever recorded for a conflict of such magnitude.

The 100-hour victory was all the more extraordinary because the American Army had seldom done remarkably well in the opening battles of past wars. America's traditional disdain for large standing armies has usually prompted a rapid demobilization at the end of a major war. Whether lulled by the euphoria of victories like those in the two World Wars or relieved by the end of an indecisive conflict like Korea, the nation wanted to believe that there would never be another war. As a result, military preparedness declined drastically so that, almost without exception, from the War of 1812 to Task Force Smith in Korea, American soldiers found themselves overmatched, outsmarted, and undergunned in the first battles. Victories came eventually, but at great cost: green American soldiers learned the art of war the bloody way, on the job. After Vietnam, the Cold War prevented a wholesale demobilization, despite the country's distinctly antimilitary mood, and the American Army committed itself to a revolutionary program of reform. The result was a peacetime army that was better prepared for war than any American Army in history.

To be sure, history tells us that disaster is often the surest catalyst to reform, particularly among armies, which tend by their conservative nature to resist change. Napoleon's Grand Army emerged from the defeated citizen mobs of the Directory. In turn, Napoleon's obliteration of the once-mighty Prussian army at Jena induced reformers such as Scharnhorst and Gneisenau to construct from the ashes of defeat an army capable of brilliant victories against Austria in 1866 and France in 1870. Subsequent defeat on the Western Front in 1918 reinvigorated reform in Germany and gave the world blitzkrieg 20 years later.

THE POST-VIETNAM ARMY

The American Army emerged from Vietnam cloaked in anguish. In the early seventies it was an institution fighting merely to maintain its existence in the midst of growing apathy, decay, and intolerance. Forty percent of the Army in Europe confessed to drug use, mostly hashish; a significant minority, 7 percent, was hooked on heroin. Crime and desertion were evident in Germany, with at least 12 percent of soldiers charged with serious offenses. In certain units, conditions neared mutiny as soldier gangs established a new order in the barracks through extortion and brutality. Barracks became battlegrounds between blacks and whites. Racial violence spread into the streets of garrison communities from Fayetteville, North Carolina, to Bamberg, Germany. Soldiers assaulted noncommissioned officers, officers, and their families. In Vietnam, the practice of "fragging"—attacking unpopular leaders with grenades— remained a problem even after American soldiers ended active combat operations. Between 1969 and 1971, Army investigators recorded 800 instances of attacks involving hand grenades in which 45 officers and noncommissioned officers were killed.[1]

Soldiers rebelled for many reasons. In part, their ill-discipline reflected a concomitant decline of order within American society. Whether right or not, many in American society took out their collective frustration with Vietnam on the most visible American presence there—the Army.

Few young men wanted to be among the last to be drafted into an institution that promised to end the draft, and fewer still were willing to join voluntarily. As a result, the Army reluctantly accepted markedly lower-quality soldiers. Forty percent had no high school diploma and 41 percent were Category IV soldiers, a mental aptitude grouping of the lowest order. The lower standards for induction forced the Army to lower its standards for discipline and training. Yet even with lower standards, the ranks of young men willing to wear the uniform continued to thin. By 1974 the Army was 20,000 soldiers below authorization and missed its reenlistment target by 11 percent. The combat arms were short 14 percent. Manning and training shortfalls combined to make only 4 of 13 Active component divisions combat-ready. One frustrated young major, when interviewed by Drew Middleton of the *New York Times*, said, "You ought to see them, babied, pampered, dumb. Hell, they couldn't even lick the Cubans."[2]

Noncommissioned officers and officers, particularly the younger ones, found themselves trying to lead an army in purgatory. They were caught between soldiers they were unable to discipline and an "all-volunteer army" that had yet to take recognizable form. The job was thankless as well as frustrating. A 1973 Harris Poll revealed that the American public ranked the military only above sanitation workers in relative order of respect. Faced with no support inside or outside the institution, tens of thousands voted for the future with their feet.

FIRST ATTEMPTS AT REFORM

Many stalwart leaders remained, however, and resolved to turn things around. General Creighton Abrams, a protégé of General George Patton, was determined to wrench the Army out of its lethargy and set it on a course toward reform. Like Patton, Abrams was also known for his bluntness and honesty. As Army Chief of Staff from 1972 until 1974, Abrams concentrated on ensuring that the Army was prepared to fight. In a speech repeated time and again during his tenure as Chief of Staff, Abrams told his audience with great passion: "You've got to know what influences me. We have paid, and paid, and paid again in blood and sacrifice for our unpreparedness. I don't want war, but I am appalled at the human cost that we've paid because we wouldn't prepare to fight." He was equally determined to restore a sense of values to the Army. In a time of growing cynicism, the craggy-faced, "fireplug" Chief constantly reminded dispirited leaders of the ideals that had brought them into the Army: patriotism, integrity, honesty, and devotion to duty. His tenure as Chief was tragically cut short by cancer in 1974, but before he gave up the stewardship of the institution to General Fred Weyand, he had instilled a new spirit of renewal among the professionals. He had convinced them that reform was not only possible, but had already begun. [3]

First evidence of Abrams' tough, uncompromising, but caring push toward reform began to appear in Europe as leaders there faced the tough issues of crime, racial strife, and professional lethargy head-on. General Michael Davison, the commander in Europe, instituted a series of programs to wrest control of the barracks back from unruly soldiers. Crime statistics actually increased somewhat in 1972 as gang leaders were rounded up and court-martialed. The authority to test randomly for drugs and the "expeditious discharge program" begun in 1973 were essential weapons in the battle to win back the barracks. Soldiers found to be habitual users or just troublemakers and malcontents could be immediately released from service without lengthy court-martial proceedings. Within four months, the Army in Europe discharged 1,300 gang members, drug users and dealers, and other criminals.[4] Davison also began a top-to-bottom racial awareness program that brought black and white soldiers together to confront the growing racial mistrust and polarization that so nearly brought the Army in Europe to its knees. Noncommissioned officers, sensing a return of trust and authority, responded by restoring the proven chain of command for dealing with soldier grievances. Without fanfare, the so-called "enlisted men's councils," intended to allow soldiers to petition directly to battalion commanders, gradually disappeared. Funds were tight and the 1973 Arab oil embargo significantly limited large-scale maneuvers, but by year's end the Army was largely out of the barracks and focused on relearning the basics.

Davison could garner only enough money, resources, and public support to conduct a rear-guard action against erosion of soldier welfare and morale. By the mid-seventies, one-third of the soldiers in the four lowest grades had families, a fivefold increase over the pre-Vietnam drafted Army. Europe in particular found it very difficult to assimilate this new social order into a crumbling infrastructure originally constructed for single soldiers. High housing costs were devastating to the 21,000 families of young first-term soldiers forced to live on the local European economy. Soldiers often had to rely on a second job or, in the States, food stamps to provide adequate support to their families. One financially beleaguered soldier, after spending only for food, clothing, housing, and other essentials, came up $60 per month short. He lamented, "I like being a soldier and serving my country, but when you have to go home at night and hear your stomach growl and there's no money for food, then you wonder why you're doing it."[5]

Herculean efforts by Weyand, Davison, and other leaders restored order in the worst units, an essential first step toward institutional reform. However, substantial improvements in soldier quality and the quality of soldiers' lives would require an equally substantial increase in the Army budget that would not come until the late seventies.

THE OCTOBER '73 WAR

The fourth major Arab-Israeli War, which began on October 6, 1973, jolted the Army out of its doctrinal doldrums and forced it to face the reality that its method of fighting, if not changed, risked obsolescence. On that day, the Egyptian Second and Third Armies forced their way across the Suez Canal, penetrated the Israeli Bar Lev Line, and pushed deep into the Sinai in a stunningly successful operation. Concurrently, five Syrian divisions rushed the Golan Heights and locked themselves into a hellish tank-on-tank battle with the Israelis. For 16 days Americans watched transfixed as the Israelis fought to restore their defenses and regain the initiative.

The war influenced the Army's effort toward reform for two reasons. First, it was the first large-scale confrontation between two forces equipped with modern weapons representative of those found in NATO and the Warsaw Pact. As such, the battle was a propitious window on the future. Second, the battle was so bloody, intense, and close-run that policymakers outside the Army began to seriously question the ability of a seemingly moribund American Army to fight a war of similar intensity. The war prompted a compelling argument for sweeping modernization and reform.

The Israeli experience made it clear to the Americans that the modern battlefield had become enormously more lethal. The terrible destruction that US Army investigating teams observed in the Sinai and on the Golan Heights was the first evidence of the precision revolution in warfare applied to ground combat. American pilots in Vietnam first took advantage of precision technology in bombing raids over North Vietnam. In the air as well as on the ground, two distinct methods delivered ordnance with precision. The first was to instrument and computerize the delivery platform so that it greatly reduced the radial error, or circular error probable (CEP), of its unguided, or "dumb," bombs. The Navy A-7, later purchased by the Air Force, was the first close air support aircraft to be so equipped. With computerized bombing, the average CEP for fighter aircraft decreased from 300 meters to fewer than 30 meters. The second technique was to make the bomb or projectile itself "smart" by engineering a method of precision guidance. Using reflected laser energy or internally mounted "fire-and-forget" seekers, projectiles could be guided (or guide themselves) directly into a target with virtually no error.

In the October '73 War, the precision revolution was most apparent in the tank and infantry direct firefight. Range finders, analog ballistic computers, and rapid improvements in main-gun ammunition technology gave tanks an enormous advantage in long-range precision gunnery. A World War II tank required an average of 17 rounds to kill another tank at a maximum range of approximately 700 meters. By 1973 tanks required

9

only two rounds to kill at 1,800 meters. Both the Israelis and the Egyptians possessed precision weapons in the form of wire-guided antitank missiles. The Soviet Sagger, available in large numbers to the Egyptians, was a primitive but effective first-generation missile. The American TOW used by the Israelis could kill with almost a 90 percent probability out to a range of 3,000 meters. To a small-unit tank or infantry commander, the realities of the precision revolution applied to the direct firefight meant, in soldier parlance, "what can be seen can be hit, and what can be hit can be killed."

The Israelis still believed the tank to be the dominant weapon on the battlefield, but the presence of lethal antitank missiles and rockets made the battlefield too lethal for tanks to go it alone. All battlefield systems had to be balanced and employed in synergy if a unit were to survive. Direct fire or artillery suppression of enemy systems was essential if platoons and companies were to maneuver against a force liberally supplied with wire-guided missiles.

The Israeli experience also made it clear that, at least for the foreseeable future, the Americans would not be able to rely solely on superior technology to win against the quantitatively superior Soviets. Tank-on-tank combat showed the Soviet T-62 tank to be a match for the older M60, particularly at close range. The Soviet BMP infantry fighting vehicle proved a particularly nasty surprise because it was the first true infantry fighting vehicle. The proliferation of antiaircraft missiles and guns greatly complicated close air support, long considered by the American Army as essential to offset the firepower imbalance of direct and indirect fires posed by superior Soviet numbers.

If the future enemy were Soviet, how could the Army hope to win when the Soviets possessed not only greater numbers of weapons but ones of equal or better quality? The answer seemed to lie in harnessing the intangibles: to optimize the fighting qualities of limited numbers by training each soldier to fight to his full capacity and to create a superior war-fighting method through progressive doctrinal reform. Evolutionary changes in training and doctrine would not be enough to close the gap on the Soviet army. Ten years had been lost wandering in the jungles of Vietnam. What was needed was not change, but revolution.

TRAINING REFORM

The powerful personality of General William DePuy, who at the establishment of the Army's Training and Doctrine Command (TRADOC) in July 1973, became its first commander, dominated the process of institutional metamorphosis in the early years in training, doctrine, and leader development.[6] DePuy's experience as an infantry officer in Europe during World War II profoundly affected his vision of how a future army should fight. He had witnessed poor-quality soldiers, sent into battle by poorly prepared leaders, waste themselves in poorly conceived and executed operations against an enemy often better led and better prepared for the harsh realities of combat. Thirty years later DePuy retained a pervasive respect for the fighting skill of the German army, as well as an often critical view of the leadership and fighting ability of American soldiers. His fixation on the European battlefield remained steadfast, and he sought from the start of his tenure at TRADOC to redirect the Army's focus from jungle warfare to a possible ground war with the Soviets on the plains of central Europe. He emphasized the value of the indirect approach in battle and stressed the importance of suppressing an objective with direct fire before assaulting a prepared defense. Nevertheless, his combat focus remained, as it had in World War II, on the "how-to" of unit-level training, battle drills, and coordinating tanks, artillery, and infantry.[7]

As with so many of his ideas, DePuy derived his vision for a revolution in training from his experience with the 90th Division in World War II. The 90th trained a full two years in the United States and England prior to D-Day. DePuy recalled with dismay how the division trained for combat *by the numbers*, devoting each day to endless field firings, road marches, and classroom lectures. "Learning and relevance," he noted, "were secondary to scheduling."

The division learned to fight for real against the Germans in Normandy—the Germans did the instructing. In six weeks, the 90th Division lost 100 percent of its strength in infantry soldiers and 150 percent of its infantry officers. Years later, DePuy blamed the slaughter on inept leaders at the division level who were unable to train infantry companies and platoons to take ground against skilled resistance.[8] Some officers were reasonably well trained in the scholastic art of "drawing arrows on a map." Yet these same officers had no idea how to make soldiers perform at the points of the arrows. DePuy watched them march soldiers against well-defended hedgerows after a few rounds of preparatory fire when battalions of machine guns, tanks, and artillery should have been used to suppress the enemy. He watched countless soldiers die in unnecessary frontal assaults because impatient commanders ignored obvious soft spots in the enemy's defenses.

In time the 90th Division would fight better. In Normandy a lieutenant's life expectancy was two weeks; five months later, during the Battle of the Bulge, it was 10 weeks. Yet the price paid for improvement was too high. In DePuy's analytical terms, "the casualty curve was too steep and the seasoning curve too flat." When he took command of TRADOC, DePuy determined to steepen the seasoning curve, preferably without paying in blood.

Post-Vietnam training methods had changed little from World War II. Huge training centers continued to crank out soldiers en masse. Teaching was by the numbers and learning was by rote. The most realistic peacetime battlefield for infantrymen and tankers was still the firing range. The Army school system was bloated with overhead and infused with a similar obsolete approach to learning. Officers were sequestered in classrooms to learn the outdoor activity of war. Equally disturbing, the Army had seriously neglected noncommissioned officer training.

As its first order of business, TRADOC began a fundamental reformation of Army training. It adopted a simple and direct slogan: "An army must train as it fights." Training reform began by pushing young officers out of the classroom and into the field. Instead of studying the art of war, lieutenants learned the intricacies of maintenance and gunnery. The Army refocused from its fixation on training schedules to training to a standard—preferably one based on necessary combat skills. The "systems approach to training" was based on the proposition that even the most complex combat endeavor could be subdivided into a series of discrete individual tasks. Each task would have set conditions and a measurable standard by which soldiers' skills would be evaluated and to which the soldiers would be held accountable. The Army Training and Evaluation Program, or ARTEP, appeared in 1975 and became the principal vehicle for measuring training readiness among companies, battalions, and brigades. The objectivity of the ARTEP system did in fact expose units that looked good in garrison but failed to meet the standard in the field. But the ARTEP fell short of providing a realistic yardstick for predicting how units would perform in combat. While sums of individual skills might provide a reasonably accurate assessment of crew and section proficiency, battalion and brigade performance depended more on intangibles. Qualities like leadership and decision making, as well as the intuitive ability of leaders to sense terrain and synchronize the employment of men and weapons, were more important indicators but were difficult to measure objectively. More to the point, combat experience in previous wars indicated that a scripted, one-sided exercise like the ARTEP, no matter how objectively measured, could not adequately replicate combat conditions. Soldiers could be seasoned and tested only by subjecting them to a reasonably close approximation of real war.

DOCTRINAL REFORM

General Depuy was a practical soldier. As such, he viewed with a healthy skepticism those who looked at the development of doctrine as a scholastic exercise. "Doctrine, or the method of war an army employs," noted DePuy, "doesn't work unless it's between the ears of at least 51 percent of the soldiers who are charged to employ it."[9] DePuy also had an almost obsessive desire to break the Army from its Vietnam malaise and "get it moving again." As TRADOC commander, he had little influence over the budget, nor did he command units in the field. But his charter made him the conductor of a huge orchestral body that was obliged to play according to the doctrinal score he devised. DePuy's challenge was to compose a symphony bold enough to snap the orchestra out of its lethargy and credible enough for at least 51 percent to play in tune. During his tenure, DePuy's symphony, Field Manual 100-5, *Operations*, served as a wake-up call to the Army. But this keystone manual for Army doctrine fell far short of achieving the harmony he sought.

Intending FM 100-5 to stimulate reaction in the Army, DePuy went to great lengths to avoid sterility. Beginning in late 1973, he hosted a year of meetings with branch commandants, allies, and the Air Force. He demanded that the manual be written in simple English. Instead of the traditional tan bound publication, he published a camouflage-covered manual in loose-leaf format, both to facilitate future changes and to send a message to the field that even though it had the DePuy stamp, he intended the manual to be the first iteration of a continuing doctrinal dialogue.

DePuy personally wrote much of the 1976 version of FM 100-5, which sought to define the fundamentals of land warfare. Not surprisingly, the manual mirrored his personal experiences and prejudices. Above all, it reflected his fixation on practical soldiering. He wanted to give the field a practical guide on "how to win the first battle of the next war." The Fulda Gap region of the inter-German border became a familiar prospective battlefield. The manual told soldiers how to fight using weapons then in their hands. It included a detailed tutorial on the lethality, accuracy, and range of weapons on both sides to graphically impress prospective users with the precision revolution in direct fire that had made the battlefield tremendously more destructive. The October '73 War became the model for the first battle: short-lived, exhausting, and terribly destructive to both sides. If, like the Israelis, the American Army expected to fight outnumbered and win, it had to exploit every advantage accruing to the defender in order to hit the enemy first and with great precision. FM 100-5 reflected the value that both the Israelis and the Germans placed on the liberal use of suppressive firepower to paralyze an enemy momentarily before maneuvering against him.

The manual accepted from the Germans the value, if not the primacy, of the defense—but defense of an unconventional kind. The so-called "active defense" emphasized economy of force and the need to strike a penetrating enemy force with surprise and with carefully husbanded combat power at the critical place and time. The objective of the active defense was to halt the Soviet advance as close to the inter-German border as possible. Since the Soviet operational concept was to attack in successive armored waves or echelons, the task at hand was to kill enough Soviet tanks in each echelon to give the defenders time to regroup and prepare to face the next echelon before it came within range.

As soon as it was published, FM 100-5 became the most controversial doctrinal statement in the history of the American Army. The chorus of disharmony came principally from outside TRADOC, the most discordant from outside the Army. Criticism centered on the manual's preoccupation with weapons effects and exchange ratios and the perceived return to the American fixation on *firepower-attrition* warfare rather than the maneuver-centered focus traditionally attributed to European armies, particularly the Germans.

Within the Army, criticism tended to be more introspective and conceptual and began, albeit subtly, while DePuy was still commander of TRADOC. The light Army—those raised in the airborne and air assault family—criticized the manual for focusing on Europe to the exclusion of other theaters and other methods of war. Parochialism aside, they had a point. In Vietnam the Army had developed a method of warfare in airmobility as unique and revolutionary as German blitzkrieg had been in its day. Light Army proponents argued that future victories would increasingly be decided in the third dimension, and they saw in Vietnam the prospect of future Third World battlefields in which the helicopter would continue to predominate.

Opposition to the maestro's tactical method centered on the active defense. Many detractors perceived it as a tactic intended to avoid defeat rather than to attain victory. Lieutenant General Donn Starry, a DePuy protégé, co-wrote much of this doctrine. However, after taking command of the Army corps charged with defending the Fulda Gap, he was among the first to publicly question its utility. Starry particularly did not like the math. Facing him across the inter-German border were at least four Soviet and East European tank armies arrayed in three enormous echelons of armor, infantry, and artillery. Active defense doctrine would be helpful in disposing battalions and brigades to defeat the first echelon, but Starry had neither the forces nor the time to reset the defense before being overwhelmed by the second and third. To avoid defeat, he would have to find a way to slow and weaken follow-on echelons before they arrived within direct-fire range of the main line. Starry's elevation as DePuy's successor at TRADOC in 1977 sparked the renaissance that would eventually lead to the rediscovery of operational art within the Army and the creation of AirLand Battle doctrine.

Despite the criticism, the 1976 version of FM 100-5 brought about a fundamental change in the way the Army viewed itself. Expressing that view led to a subordinate body of doctrinal literature called the "how to fight" series of field manuals, which energized the entire training and education system. As DePuy intended, FM 100-5 was a transition step that opened an intellectual dialogue throughout the Army. It set the stage for later revisions in 1982 and 1986 that introduced and refined the AirLand Battle concept which underpinned the way the Desert Storm campaign was planned and fought. Reforms that improved discipline, training, and doctrine without addressing how to attract and retain a quality force, however, were only partial solutions.

THE HOLLOW ARMY

After a brief period of public support prompted by the end of the draft, the American public and Congress's interest in the volunteer Army quickly dissipated. To induce recruitment, the Nixon administration raised soldier salaries 61 percent in 1973. But in spite of large-scale inflation, salaries remained essentially frozen for seven years thereafter. Earlier pay raises were targeted toward first-term enlistees, while non-commissioned officers, considered already hooked by the system, received proportionately less. The consequent pay compression meant that an experienced sergeant earned only 30 percent more than the newest private. In real terms, purchasing power for sergeants dropped from $20,000 per year in 1973 to $14,000 by 1979. Entitlements, which military families considered essential for economic survival, lost value in proportion to pay. Moving allowances for a family of four remained at 10 cents per mile—unchanged since the Eisenhower administration. Young sergeants, in the best of circumstances barely able to make ends meet, found themselves thrown hopelessly into debt with unexpected movement orders. By 1979, the salary of junior enlisted soldiers had dropped so low that a corporal with a small family was officially below the prescribed government poverty level. In that same year Army commissaries accepted almost $10 million in food stamps.[10] The soldiers' plight grew considerably worse in Europe. As large numbers of wives streamed overseas to join their soldier husbands, the problem of poor or nonexistent housing was compounded by poverty wages. With no money to spend, soldiers and families had little to do but try to survive.

In the lean years following Vietnam, the Army created the conceptual outline for a future force fundamentally different from any American Army of the past. Accepting the mantle of steward from Weyand in 1976, General Bernard Rogers embraced Abrams' goal of creating a force consisting of 16 Active and 8 Reserve component combat divisions. At the same time, he continued to work on ways to improve soldiers' quality of life. However, while Rogers paved the way to improved readiness and worked on long-term sustainability in an effort to pull the Army out of the intellectually and physically stagnant period of the volunteer Army, his task was severely hampered by budget woes.

In the late seventies, the Army witnessed drastic cuts in funding for maintenance and training. By 1979, 6 of 10 Stateside Army divisions were, by the Army's own liberal standards of measurement, not combat-ready. Even though Europe was the Army's front line, one of the four divisions stationed there was not combat-ready. Serious shortages of qualified soldiers, spare parts, and replacement equipment grew alarmingly. The Commander in Chief, US Army Europe, General Frederick Kroesen, long noted for his frankness, confessed publicly that the European Army had become obsolescent. Kroesen and other senior officers began to speak openly of a "hollow army." Although the Army could boast 16 divisional flags, the content and quality of those divisions was diminishing rapidly.

Soldier quality, never particularly high during the early years of the volunteer Army, started another precipitous drop after 1976. The numbers recruited in mental Categories I, II, and IIIa, which measure the upper half of mental aptitude among American youth, shrank from 49 percent in 1973 to 26 percent in 1980. Only 50 percent of those recruited in 1980 had graduated from high school.[11] Statistics for drug addiction, unauthorized absences, and crimes, while still below the immediate post-Vietnam War figures, were still alarmingly high. The Army recruited so many poor-quality soldiers during the late seventies that it dismissed 40 percent for indiscipline or unsuitability before they completed their first enlistment.

Meanwhile, in late 1979, the Islamic fundamentalists' removal of the Shah of Iran and the Soviet invasion of Afghanistan began to shake the American public from its lethargy.

CRISES OPEN THE COFFERS

The failed attempt to rescue American hostages held in Iran in 1980 marked one of the lowest points in American military performance since the end of the Vietnam War. The spectacle of broken Marine helicopters and crashed Air Force C-130 aircraft and the tales that emerged from Desert One of confusion, overcentralization, poor communication, and botched planning brought to light publicly what the pros had foretold for some time. As so often happens in American military history, a military debacle was necessary to wrench the Services back from the brink of ruin.

The furor following Desert One alerted the American public to chronic institutional problems that had remained shrouded since Vietnam. The Army realized that reduced budgets had left equipment inoperative, shortened training exercises, and delayed the arrival of new weapons. The Army leadership also recognized that the Army could not achieve real combat readiness unless it could, as a first priority, populate itself with good soldiers. In the wake of Desert One, the cry grew more shrill for a return to the draft. A volunteer army, so the argument went, would only draw from the poorest and most poorly educated segment of the population. In time the Army would consist only of the socially disenfranchised. While ostensibly volunteer, the Army was still "drafting," but using economics rather than the Selective Service System to force enlistments.[12] Some pro-draft sentiment could still be found within the Army, but by and large, most Army leaders favored the all-volunteer concept. The flaw, they believed, was in how the volunteer system was implemented. The draft was over. Simply opening doors was not enough to induce quality men and women to enlist. America's youth had to be convinced that service in the Army was right for them. Needing a marketeer to sell itself, the Army found its salesman in the person of Major General Maxwell "Max" Thurman.

Thurman began his tenure as head of the Army Recruiting Command by selecting only the best soldiers to be recruiters. Instead of long-term recruiting professionals, he brought in officers and noncommissioned officers from the field for short-term assignments. Their job was to recruit the same soldiers that they would later have to train. The recruiting market moved from the streets to high schools. High school students were harder to recruit, but research proved that a diploma was the most reliable indicator of future success as a soldier.[13] Each of Thurman's subordinate commanders negotiated a contract with him to produce a certain quality of soldier in a certain number, balancing the demands of the Army against the particular demographic and economic circumstances of the region. Thurman recognized the power of advertising. With the enthusiastic support of Vice Chief of Staff General John Vessey, he convinced Congress to appropriate approximately a half-billion dollars to finance Army recruiting and bonuses. The "Be All You Can Be" campaign achieved instant recognition among American youth. Thanks to positive image-making and the improving quality of life within the Army, the "Willie and Joe" image inherited from the drafted Army gave way to the Army's new image as a caring, challenging, high-tech outfit.[14]

A Congress increasingly alarmed by the Army's declining readiness and sympathetic to the plight of soldiers and their families responded by increasing soldiers' salaries 25 percent between 1981 and 1982. Army research found that the most important reason for the smartest soldiers to enlist was money for college. After Congress reinstated the GI Bill and initiated the Army College Fund, the quality gap began to close.[15]

While Army recruiting continued to experience occasional growing pains, the quality of young men and women recruits steadily climbed, keeping pace with the public's increasingly favorable image of the Army. By 1991, more than 98 percent of the applicants were high school graduates. Seventy-five percent scored in the upper mental categories, less than one percent in the lowest. Fully 41 percent chose to enroll in the Army College Fund. As quality increased, traditional indicators of indiscipline dropped off the charts. Desertions and unauthorized absences dropped 80 percent and courts-martial 64 percent. Positive indications of drug abuse dropped from 25 percent in 1979 to less than 1 percent a decade later.[16]

As defense budgets increased, the temptation grew to expand the size of the Army to meet the growing Soviet threat. However, with end-strength capped at 780,000 soldiers, meeting the goal of 16 Active divisions was difficult enough, let alone trying to expand the force. General Edward "Shy" Meyer, Chief of Staff from 1979 to 1983, chose to hold the line on total numbers. He reasoned that any large increase, given the limited number of available high-quality prospective recruits, would substantially lower overall quality. The most glaring shortage would be made up by the Reserves.

The political argument for greater integration of the Reserves had its roots in Vietnam. President Johnson chose to rely on the draft alone to prosecute the war in order to cause as little disruption on the home front as possible and thereby dampen popular opposition. While successful during the early years, Johnson's policy created an army in the field made up largely of the very young, the poor, and the disaffected. As the war dragged on and casualties mounted, a rift was inevitable between the people and this unfamiliar, unrepresentative body of men fighting an unpopular war. For that reason, General Abrams, during his short tenure as Chief of Staff, had insisted that the Army could not go to war again without the involvement and tacit approval of the American people. A call-up of the Reserves would bring home to Americans from the beginning that they had a personal stake in the conflict. Therefore, Abrams had sought to weave Reserve forces so inextricably into established deployment schemes that no force would be able to fight a major war in the future without them.

The creation of what was to become the Total Force Policy began gradually during the mid-seventies as the Army shifted combat support and combat service support necessary to sustain the Active Army in a large-scale European conflict into the National Guard and Army Reserve. The plan was to increase the total number of Active divisions to 16 while staying within mandated end-strength ceilings by "rounding out" selected Army divisions so that they consisted of two regular and one Reserve component brigade. A number of separate Reserve component battalions were also included in the roundout program. Roundout brigades were expected to join their parent division after a period of muster and postmobilization training, which was originally postulated to require at least 30 days. By the late eighties, the Total Force Policy had been so firmly embedded in the Army's structure that 52 percent of combat forces and 67 percent of other forces were Guard or Reserve. Seven Reserve component brigades—six from the National Guard and one from the Army Reserve—rounded out Active Army divisions, while 10 separate battalions, all in the Guard, served additionally as roundout augmentation to the Active Army. [17]

THE BIG FIVE

While General Abrams committed the Army to producing world-class soldiers, he also sought to develop first-class materiel. Following Vietnam, the obstacles to achieving that commitment were seemingly insurmountable. The Soviets had exploited the Army's Vietnam diversion to close the gap in weapons technology. Popular opinion at the time did not appear to favor significant funding increases for new weaponry. Since the Army traditionally spent proportionately more than the other Services on people programs, not enough developmental money was available to buy every weapon the Army needed. The Army was fortunate to have Abrams at the helm. He was an officer who continued to maintain the trust and respect of Congress and the public through the Army's troubled times. He had a congenital distrust of Pentagon bureaucracy. Perhaps his obvious discomfort with Washington was one reason Congress listened to him so attentively. Abrams drew copiously from this wellspring of political credibility to rebuild the Army, but first he had to deal with the bureaucracy.

Clockwise from top left, the Big Five weapons systems are the UH-60 Blackhawk, the M1 Abrams tank, the AH-64 Apache, the Patriot, and the M2/3 Bradley.

The Army materiel development community consisted of dozens of constituents, all of whom believed that their particular weapon or program deserved funding priority. Legions of young officer-analysts labored intently to produce tightly argued, amply documented justifications to prove the worth of their particular systems. However, even within each community, opinions varied. To Abrams, the Army seemed reluctant to make up its mind or to keep to an established course once it made materiel decisions and only he could discipline the process. He began by selecting five weapons the Army had to have: a new tank, an infantry fighting vehicle, two helicopters—an attack helicopter and a utility transport to replace the ubiquitous Huey of Vietnam fame—and an air defense missile. Other programs would be proposed and some would ultimately survive Congressional scrutiny, but having put his reputation on these Big Five, Abrams would tolerate no further dissention within the Army.

As the development of the Big Five weapons systems began during the period of constrained military budgets, Abrams' successors continued to fight to keep the programs alive. With the efforts in recruiting, training and doctrinal reforms, and new weapons systems all running concurrently, Army leaders continued to seek better ways to bring all of these improvements together.

BIRTH OF THE COMBAT TRAINING CENTERS

Studies of combat experience in World War II, Korea, and Vietnam revealed a disturbing propensity for units to suffer very high casualties in their first exposure to direct combat. The problem was particularly perplexing because the human cost in first battles did not seem to be lessened by the time spent in training prior to deployment. Some divisions like the 90th prepared for war in Europe for more than two years, yet suffered more than 100 percent casualties in the hedgerows of Normandy. A method was needed in peacetime, as DePuy had noted, to steepen the seasoning curve without paying in blood. Curiously, the Navy showed the Army how to practice fighting for real. In early air-to-air combat over Vietnam, Navy pilots achieved a kill ratio against North Vietnamese MiGs of only two to one. A careful study showed a seasoning curve increase for pilots after combat as dramatic as Army studies had found for ground soldiers. Forty percent of all pilot losses occurred in their first three engagements. However, 90 percent of those who survived three engagements went on to complete a combat tour. In 1969 the Navy began a program that sought to provide a pilot his first three missions risk-free. *Top Gun* pitted novice airmen against a mock aggressor skilled in North Vietnamese aerial tactics. Combat was bloodless yet relatively unfettered. Uncompromising instructors recorded and played back every maneuver and action. The results were dramatic. From 1969 until the end of the air war, the Navy's kill ratio increased sixfold.

A similar method of battle seasoning was needed for Army training, and General DePuy handed the task to his TRADOC deputy chief of staff for training, Major General Paul Gorman. However, technological problems in creating a ground-based *Top Gun* were daunting. Aircraft came equipped with their own on-board radars and computers. Aircraft instruments could easily be linked to ground-based sensors to track and record every aerial track and maneuver for later playback and critique. But how do you keep track of thousands of soldiers shooting at each other among the folds and foliage of normal terrain? Gorman again got the answer from the Navy. In 1973, he discovered a young technician who was experimenting with a method for sailors to practice marksmanship indoors. The technician simply attached a laser to a pistol and fabricated a laser-sensitive target to record hits. Gorman expanded the "laser pistol" idea into what eventually became the Multiple Integrated Laser Engagement System (MILES) with devices that could be attached to all weapons from rifles to tank guns. MILES was a sophisticated version of the "laser pistol" concept that used coded signals to record kills and to discriminate among the types of weapons firing so that rifles "killed" only soldiers and not tanks. To replicate the Navy's successful program, planners had to devise an instrumentation system capable of tracking units, vehicles, and individuals and linking them all together through a master computer. The Core Instrumentation System (CIS) that evolved for the National Training Center utilized state-of-the-art technology with video cameras and multiple radio monitoring stations.

To exploit the promise of MILES and CIS, Gorman pursued an Army version of *Top Gun,* which was ultimately created at Fort Irwin, California. The exercise area was vast, and MILES permitted combat units to be pitted against each other in relatively free-play, force-on-force engagements. An observation center equipped with CIS near Fort Irwin kept track electronically of MILES kills, individual vehicle movement, and radio transmissions from the evaluated units. The center resembled a dimly lighted video arcade with monitors and television screens depicting real vehicles engaged in mock combat. Elaborate data-processing equipment provided instantaneous information on unit locations, troop concentrations, heavy weapons positions, the number of shots fired by caliber, and hits and misses. Remote-control cameras located on mountaintops provided total video coverage of the battle area. Observer-controllers accompanied every unit throughout the rotation, unobtrusively recording actions that were then combined with electronic data for the after-action reviews (AARs).

The resounding success of the National Training Center was the result not so much of its technology, but of the effect of its real-world, real-time, no-nonsense combat simulation on how the Army prepared for war. Each successive iteration or rotation of a unit through the NTC experience increased that unit's ability to survive and win in combat. The experience was grueling indeed and often, at first, very humbling. The opposing force, or OPFOR, regiment that daily hammered the novice commander was finely practiced in Soviet tactics and offered no quarter. Four hours after each instrumented engagement, leaders of the evaluated unit faced the harsh realities of watching their performance played back during an AAR. The conduct of an AAR embodied, perhaps more than any other single event, the commitment of the Army to no-nonsense training. In silence, each commander watched on video as the observer-controller dispassionately explained, vehicle by dead vehicle, how the OPFOR took the unit apart. The observer-controllers did not intend the AAR to be cruel. Units that did not do well were not necessarily bad units; the more numerous and highly skilled OPFOR was tough to beat. The AAR simply brought home to every leader the realities of combat. Lieutenant General Frederick Brown, former deputy chief of staff for training at TRADOC, saw the AAR process as the "truly revolutionary characteristic of the NTC." There was no precedent for exposing a unit's chain of command to a no-holds-barred battle against an OPFOR where a leader's failure was evident in exquisite detail to his subordinates. "No army—including the Israeli army—has dared to do this," Brown said.[18] After leaving the briefing van, the commander knew whether his skill at drawing arrows on the map was equaled by his ability to infuse his soldiers with the confidence, leadership, and combat skills necessary to make his battle plan work in the harsh, unforgiving world of real combat. Almost a decade of continuous exposure to NTC and other derivative exercises at the Joint Readiness Training Center at Fort Chaffee in Arkansas and the Combat Maneuver Training Center at Hohenfels in Germany infused in field commanders an institutional obsession to train realistically for combat. With each successive rotation, the Army moved inexorably and bloodlessly a notch higher along the combat learning curve.

In 1984, *America's First Battles,* a volume produced under the auspices of the Army Command and General Staff College (CGSC), Fort Leavenworth, Kansas, appeared and caused an instant stir among senior leaders throughout the Army. The final chapter concluded what American soldiers had known intuitively for some time. The American Army performed poorly in the opening battles of all its wars not so much because of poorly prepared soldiers but because senior leaders—division and corps commanders—were not up to the task of commanding and controlling large units in the field. Lieutenant General Jerry Bartlett, then commander at the the Combined Arms Center and CGSC, believed that this problem could be substantially solved by applying the learning curve to generals as well as privates. What the Army needed was an NTC-like experience for generals and their staffs. Divisions and corps were too large to be routinely placed in the field to conduct realistic force-on-force combat. Therefore, the Army created a computer-driven OPFOR to be manned by experienced controllers capable of electronic force-on-force interaction. To put as much of the fog of battle as possible into the Battle Command Training Program, or BCTP, the simulation was taken to units in the field so that the war game could be played using the tested division's headquarters staff and communications equipment. Whenever possible, Bartlett's controllers would exercise the division's existing war plans.

BCTP would provide the same realism, stress, and harsh, objective reality for generals and their staffs as NTC provided for colonels. The problem was the dreaded AAR. Holding colonels accountable for their errors in front of troops was difficult enough, but what about generals? The Army solved the dilemma by bringing in three retired four-star generals, each known and respected throughout the Army as experienced war fighters, to supervise the exercise. Initially, the Army in the field balked at such frank exposure. However, General Carl Vuono, then Chief of Staff, insisted that the BCTP continue.[19]

Unit-level training is the focus of the NTC, the ARTEP, and the BCTP. Units and their leaders perform mission-essential tasks that can be observed and evaluated against measurable standards under specific conditions. Within units, the leadership skills required by increasingly sophisticated weapons systems and training tools called for a simultaneous revamping of the Noncommissioned Officer Education System (NCOES).

THE NONCOMMISSIONED OFFICER EDUCATION SYSTEM

In late November 1990, Command Sergeant Major of the Army Julius Gates accompanied General Vuono to the Soviet Union at the invitation of General Valetin Varennikov, the Soviet Ground Forces Commander-in-Chief and a hero of the battle of Vilnius in World War II. Near Kiev, Vuono, Gates, and another Soviet General, Boris Gromov, stood together as they watched two young Soviet officers lead a platoon of trainees through a demonstration of close-order drill. Soviet officers did not quite know what to make of Gates. A master paratrooper and a Ranger, Gates' many years with light infantry units had kept him trim and fit. Yet the sight of a sergeant purported to be a personal advisor and confidant to the highest-ranking officer in the Army seemed incongruous to them, to say the least. Gates was not terribly impressed with what he saw. As the soldiers wheeled about in intricate evolutions, Gates turned to Gromov, pointed to the officer drillmasters, and remarked dryly, "You know, in our army sergeants would be doing that—junior sergeants."

"Yes, I know," the Soviet replied through an interpreter. "That's what makes your army so good. We use officers because we don't have sergeants like you."

Soldiers have long recognized that sergeants are the backbone of an army, particularly the American Army, which has traditionally given noncommissioned officers a great deal of authority and responsibility. But 10 years of war in Vietnam damaged the NCO Corps physically, morally, and psychologically—more than any other segment of the institution. The strain imposed by back-to-back combat tours in Vietnam exacted a terrible toll on young NCOs. Tens of thousands died or were wounded, and many more left the Army frustrated and fatigued as soon as their hitch was up. Morale continued to plummet after the war. NCOs found themselves in an unfamiliar army where the message to new volunteer soldiers was not one of discipline and combat readiness but rather "the Army wants to join you." Pay compression made NCOs almost as poor as their privates. Those who remained stood by and watched anxiously as their authority steadily eroded in a progressively more permissive and ill-disciplined environment.

The near ruin of the NCO Corps during Vietnam caused the Army leadership to take a careful look at how the Army developed noncommissioned officers. Without a comprehensive schooling system, NCOs were expected, for the most part, to learn on the job. In 1969 General William Westmoreland, at the urging of his Vice Chief, General Ralph Haines, had instituted a system of NCO training and selection that in many respects paralleled the officer system. The concept called for four levels of training. The primary level was similar to the old NCO academies. Basic and advanced levels required board selection for attendance and included advanced skill development balanced with a strong dose of leadership and training evaluation. The fourth and highest level was the Sergeants Major Academy founded at Fort Bliss, Texas, in 1972. The Academy curriculum paralleled that of the Army War College, and selection became as highly prized among senior NCOs as the War College has traditionally been among officers. The NCOES added rigor to NCO career development. A sergeant had to prove himself to his leaders in order to advance to each level, and at each level he learned the skills necessary to succeed at the next higher grade.

As the NCOES produced better sergeants, the trust of officers in their NCOs returned in full measure and then began to grow. With trust came increased responsibility and in turn confidence began to reappear among the "new breed" of well-trained and well-educated NCOs. As pay and quality of life for NCOs improved, so too did the quality of the NCOs themselves. Of the SMA's first graduating class in 1973, fewer than 8 percent had attended college. Of the soldiers who joined the Army that year and who rose through the ranks to attend the academy 18 years later,

88 percent had attended college; nearly half had earned degrees.[20] In addition to education, the NCO Corps maintained with equal strictness standards for job performance, personal conduct, physical fitness, and, most importantly, demonstrated leadership ability. By the time units deployed for Desert Shield, the transformation of the NCO Corps was virtually complete. Sergeants performed in the desert with unequaled initiative, professionalism, skill, and concern for soldier welfare. Brighter, better educated NCOs also required the best possible officer leaders.

AIRLAND BATTLE DOCTRINE

Most of the Army's senior leadership, with General Starry in the lead, had grown increasingly uncomfortable with the 1976 version of FM 100-5. In 1977, a year after taking command of V Corps, Starry stood on the Golan Heights looking east toward Damascus as Israeli General Rafael Eitan explained how, in the desperate hours of October 6, 1973, he watched as waves of Syrian tanks formed successive echelons as far as the eye could see.[21] Although force ratios clearly called for the Syrians to win, they lost because of *intangibles*. To Starry, the battle of Kuneitra proved conclusively that the side that seized the initiative and demonstrated superior fighting skill and determination would prevail.

The Soviet invasion of Afghanistan in 1979 underscored to General Meyer that Europe might not be the only probable future battlefield. Meyer was particularly concerned that fixation on the active defense, whether intended or not, might affect the morale and fighting spirit of young officers. General Richard Cavazos had a heightened respect for unquantifiable aspects of warfare that FM 100-5 tended to ignore. Commander of Forces Command (FORSCOM) at the time, Cavazos spoke about the value of leadership, courage, endurance, and will as principal determinants of combat effectiveness: "What's important is how soldiers, not systems, fight."

The 1982 version of FM 100-5, for the first time, moved decisively away from force ratios to intangibles as predominant factors on the battlefield. It listed leadership as an element of combat equal to firepower and maneuver and went on to underscore the validity of training, motivation, and boldness—the ability to perceive opportunity, to think rapidly, to communicate clearly, and to act decisively. The success of AirLand Battle depended on four basic tenets: *initiative, depth, agility,* and *synchronization,* each demanding as much from the intellect of the commander as from the physical power of his force.

The 1982 manual also introduced AirLand Battle doctrine. General Glenn Otis, Starry's successor as TRADOC commander, recognized that the size and complexity of the air and land battlefield had outgrown the narrow tactical focus that DePuy had imposed on Army operations in FM 100-5. Otis chose, therefore, to introduce the operational level of war in the

1982 version as an intermediate level between tactics and strategy. By the time the Army developed the 1986 edition, AirLand Battle had become synonymous with the operational level of war. [22]

AirLand Battle doctrine sought to find a method for defeating second- and third-echelon forces. A defending force waiting passively for the enemy to appear would be swept aside by successive Soviet echelons. In order to have any chance of winning against such unfavorable odds, the defender would have to seize the initiative by attacking follow-on echelons before they appeared. The manual proposed two methods of attack. The first was to use distant fires and electronic warfare to slow, confuse, and damage as many early arriving forces as possible, executing distant strikes in a carefully conceived pattern. The object was to create gaps in the enemy's battle array that could then be exploited with the second means of attack: lightning-fast offensive maneuver using mechanized forces supported by tactical air power and attack helicopters. Fires became, therefore, not merely a means to attrit the enemy, but also a mechanism for setting the terms of battle. Fires would freeze the enemy and stun him long enough for maneuver forces to strike deep to destroy following echelons.

The imperative to strike deep forced the writers of FM 100-5 to observe the battlefield from a higher perspective. In the 1976 version, the view from the division commander's perch, essentially a tactical view, was high enough to observe the direct firefight at the point of collision between two opposing forces. But to see and strike echelons not yet committed demanded a higher-level perspective. In terms of time and space, three echelons attacking in column formation occupied ground to a depth of 150 kilometers and required about three days to close on the point of contact. In 1982 the maneuver commander had few weapons or means of observation capable of reaching that far. The Air Force, however, did have a deep capability, so the need to extend the battlefield and strike deep gave the corps commander an even greater interest in how air power was employed. Since World War II, the Air Force had considered aerial deep attack, or interdiction, to be an essential mission, but they had not, in the past, so closely linked the interdiction effort to the corps commander's maneuver scheme. However, the Air Force did accept the Army's contention that success on the ground depended on deep strikes to shape the battlefield. Beginning in 1979, the Tactical Air Command at Langley Air Force Base, Virginia, and TRADOC headquarters, just 20 minutes away, began to develop a joint doctrinal vision that included a system for Army fires to suppress enemy air defenses and air interdiction (AI) to attack the second echelon.

In 1984 General John Wickham and General Charles Gabriel, the Army and Air Force Chiefs of Staff, announced the acceptance of 31 initiatives specifically designed to enhance joint employment of AirLand Battle doctrine. The initiatives resulted from a year of discussions, war-gaming, and intellectual free-for-alls by members of a joint force development group. The group's charter, simply stated, was "to create a means to design and field the best affordable AirLand combat force."[23] A focal point of their effort was to reach an agreed method for using air interdiction as an integral part of combat power. As a result, the group redefined air interdiction as an attack on targets beyond the corps commander's area of interest and established a new category, battlefield air interdiction (BAI). Initiative 21 stated in part that BAI was:

> *Air action against hostile surface targets nominated by the ground commander and in direct support of ground operations. It is the primary means of fighting the deep battle at extended ranges. BAI isolates enemy forces by preventing their reinforcement and supply and restricting their freedom of maneuver. It also destroys, delays, or disrupts follow-on enemy units before they can enter the close battle....* [24]

Operational art and the increasing importance of joint operations demanded more from commanders and their staffs than ever before. As these demands increased, so would the need for educating officers more capable of understanding and applying the new concepts.

SCHOOL OF ADVANCED MILITARY STUDIES (SAMS)

General William Richardson was commandant at the Command and General Staff College during the period when the 1982 version of FM 100-5 was being written. He lamented the Army's system of officer education, which had not adequately provided the intellectual rigor necessary to grapple with the complexities of the operational level of war. The intellectual ferment surrounding the birth of the new doctrine rekindled interest throughout the Army in military history as the most practical laboratory for learning the art of war and applying intangibles to its execution. The result was a concept, first offered in 1981, to create an advanced second-year course for a small, select group of perhaps 50 first-year graduates of CGSC. They would study the art of war in an intensive program of reading military history, practicing computer war games, and writing extensively. Recitations in class would be scrupulously critiqued by their peers and a faculty selected for their own intellectual acumen and knowledge of military history.

Instituted in 1983, SAMS was so rigorous that it initially overwhelmed its students. Long hours of concentrated study and intense pressure to perform led some students to wonder if this "academic Ranger school" was really worth the effort. To avoid any appearance of elitism, graduates received no special favors other than a guaranteed position in division- or corps-level staffs. As its motto SAMS adopted the unofficial maxim of the

German general staff, "Be more than you appear to be," and the director admonished graduates that they must be an elite with a humility that bears no trace of elitism.[25] The intention of the program to infuse a common body of thought—a common *cultural bias*—throughout the Army by means of its graduates worked beyond anyone's expectation.

By the time the Gulf War began, SAMS graduates had established a reputation as some of the best staff officers in the Army. They were present on all planning staffs and were heavily involved in the conception, development, and execution of the strategic and operational plans that would win the war so convincingly.

LIGHT FORCES RENAISSANCE

Despite the focus on armor and mechanized forces fighting on the Central European plain, which had been sharpened by the October 1973 Arab-Israeli War, the Army could not ignore light and Special Operations forces. General Abrams recognized the value of highly trained and disciplined light infantry when he instituted the formation of two Ranger battalions in 1974. He intended to create a core of light fighters that would set the standards for the rest of the Army. The 1-75th Infantry (Ranger) was formed at Fort Stewart, Georgia, and the 2-75th at Fort Lewis, Washington. Many Ranger-qualified soldiers actively sought assignment to these tough units that they knew to be bastions of discipline and pride.

As the seventies progressed and terrorism increased, the Rangers and other Special Operations forces received more attention. The Army described a spectrum of conflict that compared the likelihood of engagement in combat to the risk or magnitude of danger. The high risk of total war up to and including nuclear holocaust seemed less likely than terrorism and brush wars at the low-risk end. This model argued for balance at both ends.

The Ranger battalions did indeed set the standards throughout the Army for training, physical fitness, and discipline. Parallel to the resurrection of the Rangers, the Army's Special Forces also underwent a renaissance to throw off the lethargy of Vietnam. Expanded several times over during that conflict, the Special Forces had lost the professional edge that had made them such an elite force. Like other elements of the Army, the Green Berets returned to basics—in their case, teaching indigenous forces to fight unconventional wars. After Desert One, the role of Special Forces expanded considerably to include counterterrorism and difficult direct-action missions that required specialized equipment and training.

In 1980 General Meyer established the High-Technology Test Bed in the 9th Infantry Division at Fort Lewis. Meyer's idea was to increase the mobility and firepower of the division while simultaneously making it smaller and lighter. Technology would cover the combat power gap created by smaller size and greater deployability. During its early years, the 9th Infantry Division under Major General Robert Elton, and later under Major General Robert RisCassi, tested emerging equipment in the midst of its development cycles, bought off-the-shelf items, and restructured itself to test Meyer's concept. Shortly after becoming Chief of Staff in 1983, General John Wickham carried Meyer's initiatives one step farther with the creation of light infantry divisions. Driven by the shortage of airlift, the high likelihood of conflict at the lower end of the risk spectrum, and the constrained end-strength of the Army, Wickham foresaw an ascending role for light divisions. These divisions would not replace the heavy force, but would increase responsiveness and provide a complementary force optimized to fight where heavy armor and mechanized units could not go.

URGENT FURY

The first signs of progress in the long climb back from the abyss of Desert One occurred three years later with the airborne coup de main in Grenada, code-named Urgent Fury.[26] Many of the structural problems that plagued the Iranian rescue operation also plagued Urgent Fury preparations. Useful intelligence was practically nonexistent. No agents were on the island, and hastily dispatched electronic and photographic collection platforms provided very little tactical information. To command the operation, US Atlantic Command, headquartered in Norfolk, Virginia, quickly created a joint task force. This arrangement placed the fighters—Army, Air Force, Marine, and SEAL combat elements—under a naval command equipped with incompatible communications and largely inexperienced in Army-Air Force planning and operational methods. In addition, the physical separation of the joint command from ground combat on Grenada would inevitably lead to numerous miscommunications and delays.

Tens of thousands of sailors, marines, soldiers, and airmen were ultimately involved in the Grenada operation. Nevertheless, as so often happens in war, responsibility for victory fell almost exclusively to a small body of fighters: five companies, each consisting of 50 to 80 Army Rangers, a few Army Special Operations commandos, and a handful of Air Force AC-130 Spectre gunships.

On the evening of October 24, 1983, Lieutenant Colonel Wes Taylor, commander of the 1-75th Infantry (Ranger), took off from Hunter Army Airfield, Fort Stewart, Georgia, with four MC-130 aircraft en route to Grenada. A late departure left Taylor with, at best, only 30 minutes of darkness over the objective, the airport at Port Salines. His only reference to the battlefield was a vaguely legible black-and-white photocopy of a British Ministry of Overseas Development map. His mission was to clear the runway at Salines to allow follow-on forces to land. At takeoff, the situation at Salines was so poorly developed that he could not tell his soldiers what resistance to expect. He could not even tell them whether they would parachute into the objective or land on the runway. Not until he was in the air an hour out did Taylor learn that the Cuban defenders at Salines had scattered barrels and road-grading equipment across the runway. The Rangers would have to jump. Flying in the dark and stuffed 45 to each aircraft, the Rangers began harnessing parachutes and snapping 150 pounds of parachute, kit bags, rucksacks, and weapons containers onto their bodies.

A mile short of the island, a searchlight illuminated Taylor's aircraft, which was flying at only 500 feet. The C-130 was so low that guns emplaced on the heights above Salines airstrip fired red and green tracers at it horizontally. Taylor's planeload jumped out into the pyrotechnics and seconds later slammed onto the airstrip only to endure a crescendo of automatic weapons fire from angry Cubans entrenched in the hills all around them.

During the next two hours, a handful of Rangers set about clearing obstacles from the runway and assaulting the Cuban defenses. Captain John Abizaid, commanding Taylor's A Company, charged the heights to the east of the runway. Rangers shouted in Spanish to the Cubans to surrender; the Cubans replied with bilingual obscenities and increased fire. To reach the high ground, Abizaid needed a tank. Sergeant Manous Boles provided one in the form of a Cuban bulldozer that he found on the runway and hot-wired on the spot. Boles raised the blade for protection, slouched in the driver's seat, and charged his unlikely armored vehicle toward the enemy. Other Rangers crouched behind the blade and fired in every direction. When they reached the top, the Cubans were gone. By midmorning the airfield was secure.

Two days later, Rangers rescued American medical students trapped by the insurgents at the Grand Anse campus some distance up the coast. This time the mission fell to the 2-75th Infantry (Ranger) commanded by Lieutenant Colonel Ralph Hagler. Major General H. Norman Schwarzkopf, at the time the Army advisor for operations, suggested a joint heliborne operation using Marine helicopters aboard the *USS Guam*—the surest way to reach the students quickly with the least risk. While Marine and Navy staff officers argued the wisdom of this course of action, Hagler and Colonel Granville Amos, commander of the Marine helicopter squadron, sat down on concrete blocks in the hot sun at Salines and developed a simple plan of assault. They coordinated preparatory fires by Navy A-7 fighters and Air Force AC-130 aircraft placing 105mm cannon fire into buildings surrounding those that sheltered the students. The operation went exactly as Amos and Hagler had planned. Marine helicopters landed the Rangers while CH-53 helicopters followed immediately and rescued the 233 medical students and American citizens.

The complete operation, from first arrival to last departure, required only 26 minutes.

The next day Hagler's Rangers conducted a second successful airmobile assault against a Cuban barracks complex at Calivigny. In all, the Rangers accomplished most of the combat tasks on Grenada at the cost of 8 killed and 69 wounded. Grenada succeeded, thanks to the bravery and competence of ground soldiers and in spite of flawed operational planning and an incomplete integration of land, sea, and air forces.

From the deck of the admiral's flagship, General Schwarzkopf watched the operation unfold with mixed emotions. On the one hand, he grew increasingly frustrated—and at times furious—with the difficulties inherent in conducting such a complex operation on such short notice with Services so little acquainted with each other. On the other, the performance of the infantry soldiers at Salines and Grand Anse reinforced his lifelong belief that great soldiers were the single most important ingredient in victory. "We need to focus on the fundamentals, the values of the battlefield, and the standards and discipline of our soldiers," Schwarzkopf remarked after the battle, "because Grenada, once again, proved that even though higher headquarters screws it up every way you can possibly screw it up, it is the initiative and valor on the part of the small units, the small-unit leadership, and the soldiers on the ground that will win for you every time."[27]

CHANGES BEGIN TO TAKE HOLD

Urgent Fury gave the Army a renewed sense of pride and accomplishment. Rangers appeared on national television at the Army-Navy football game halftime show at the Rose Bowl in December 1983 drawing thunderous applause and well-deserved respect. Abrams' Ranger battalion idea had not only taken root but had grown into a fighting force vindicated in battle. The 82d Airborne Division shared the spotlight along with the Army's 160th Aviation Battalion (Special Operations). This sense of well-being came at a time when the ground was ripe to replant the fundamentals and values referred to by General Schwarzkopf.

General Wickham put a distinctive stamp on this effort when he and Secretary of the Army John Marsh instituted a series of yearly themes that emphasized such subjects as leadership, the soldier, and the family. By emphasizing a different theme each year, the Army kept values in front of everyone's eyes as programs and policies were implemented to strengthen that theme. Direct measurement of progress was difficult, but the emphasis on ethics and soldierly values like courage, competence, candor, and commitment became bywords in the lexicon of leadership in the mid-eighties.

The infusion of defense dollars and the renewed focus on values needed at least three years of gestation before they began to produce clearly recognizable results in the field. Arthur Hadley, a syndicated reporter and long-time observer of the military, began to notice the turn-around as early as 1982. Often, indicators were subtle. A group of German civilians in Bad Mergentheim noted that American vehicles no longer drove across planted fields and orchards or knocked corners off buildings. In 1984 a German panzer colonel noted an "unbelievable" jump in combat proficiency by an American tank battalion attached to his regiment. Hadley noted that vehicles no longer littered German roadways during exercises. He met tank crewmen with as many as eight years' experience and these crewmen knew their jobs: "In 1985 most of the tanks one saw broken down beside the road had soldiers with tools working on them, while others directed traffic. Four years before, there were far more broken-down vehicles and soldiers were sitting on them smoking."[28]

More tangible indicators demonstrated improvements in combat readiness. In 1987 an American tank crew from the 4-8th Cavalry won the Canadian Army Trophy for the first time in 24 years. The superior fire control of the M-1 tank, combined with imaginative use of simulators for training, gave Americans the advantage in this NATO competition.[29] That same year, a team from the 11th Armored Cavalry Regiment broke German dominance of the Boeselager reconnaissance team competition for the first time. At the National Training Center, units on their third or fourth rotation began to beat the OPFOR—consistently. Some units, in fact, became famous throughout the Army for their skill at "fighting outnumbered and winning."

JUST CAUSE

After 15 years of reform, the Army considered its transformation from a mass conscripted force to one of long-service professionals virtually complete. In the interim since Urgent Fury, the Congress had taken a hand in military reform with the passage of the Goldwater-Nichols Act in 1986. The new law was intended to improve the conduct of joint operations, strengthening the positions of the Chairman of the Joint Chiefs of Staff (JCS) and the operational CINCs. The first test of the new law came with the invasion of Panama on December 21, 1989. Tensions in the region had mounted rapidly in late 1989 with assaults on American soldiers and civilians and growing evidence of dictator Manuel Noriega's support of drug traffic. In response, the President decided to execute Just Cause, an operation that would dramatically showcase the Army's growing professional competence. The brief campaign against Manuel Noriega and his band of thugs is important to the story of Army reform because it demonstrated the operating techniques and military principles that would be proven again on a greater scale in Desert Storm.

The President retrieved General Thurman, former chief of Army recruiting and later Army Vice Chief of Staff and TRADOC commander, just short of retirement to be his man-on-the-spot in Panama. Immediately after arriving at his headquarters in Quarry Heights, the new Commander-in-Chief, Southern Command, made it absolutely clear that he was in charge. Thurman arrived prepared to fight a campaign. A veteran paratrooper himself, he placed responsibility for executing a military option on his friend, Lieutenant General Carl Stiner, commander of XVIII Airborne Corps at Fort Bragg, North Carolina. Stiner was the right man for the job. Any action against Noriega would be a joint operation; Thurman would command regular and special operations forces from four Services. Stiner, who had extensive experience in joint commands and had accumulated more practical knowledge of special operations than any general in the Army, became commander of Joint Task Force South.

Thurman and Stiner planned an enormously intricate joint coup de main—the most detailed, complex assault of this sort since World War II. It included simultaneous airborne operations against 27 objectives spread across the country—and all conducted at night. Many of the assaulting units would fly directly into battle, almost 1,500 miles from garrisons in the United States. The plan was a complex and compressed "takedown" operation intended to smother the Panamanian Defense Force (PDF) and wrest control quickly. That way, civilian and military casualties and collateral damage would be minimized.

The medley of available forces included Army Rangers, Special Forces, and troops from three divisions: the 82d Airborne from Fort Bragg, North Carolina, the 7th Infantry (Light) from Fort Ord, California, and the 5th Infantry (Mech) from Fort Polk, Louisiana. The 193d Infantry Brigade permanently garrisoned in Panama provided a substantial portion of the Army's combat strength. The Air Force provided airlift as well as fire support from F-117 Stealth fighters and AC-130 Spectre gunships. The Navy provided special SEAL teams and the Marines stationed in Panama would act as a blocking force.

All players would be tied together through the use of a single, compact list of communications frequencies and call signs. Units in Panama would conduct repetitive rehearsals in full view of the enemy, both to hone their troops to a sharp edge and to "cry wolf" so many times that they would not alert the Panamanians when the real operation began.

By the time the President authorized Just Cause, many of the soldiers tagged for the operation had been through real or simulated versions of the exercise many times. They were accustomed to operating autonomously, and they were trained to take charge even when left virtually alone. Finally, the joint command had good intelligence. It knew where each enemy unit was located and infiltrated US Special Operations forces ahead of the main assaults to keep an eye out for unexpected movements.

Operation Just Cause played out almost exactly as planned. Prior to H-hour, midnight, December 20, 1989, Special Forces soldiers infiltrated key facilities in and around Panama City. One team blocked a mechanized task force crossing the Pacora River bridge to the city to join the fight. This team engaged the task force with AT-4 antitank rockets and called in fires from Spectre to hold the bridge against heavy odds. Task Force Bayonet, consisting of the 193d Infantry Brigade reinforced by the 5th Infantry and by light tanks from the 82d, attacked Noriega's headquarters, the *commandancia*, with a phalanx of armored infantry carriers supported again by Spectre gunships circling overhead.

Three minutes after H-hour, two battalions of Rangers dropped out of the night to seize Rio Hato Airfield some 50 miles west of Panama City and to neutralize two companies of PDF. After three minutes of assault fire by Spectre gunships, another Ranger battalion dropped on Tocumen International Airport to seize the control tower and capture PDF forces nearby. Fifteen minutes after H-hour on the Atlantic side, a task force of paratroopers secured key facilities, including vulnerable canal locks and machinery. A small force secured Madden Dam in the center of the Canal Zone and, after a brief firefight, rescued 20 political prisoners Noriega had locked up nearby in Renacer Prison.

Forty-five minutes after H-hour a brigade of the 82d Airborne Division began parachuting into Tocumen International Airport to assault Pana-manian army and air force elements defending there. An ice storm at Fort Bragg hindered loading and takeoff, delaying the arrival of follow-on troops three hours. However, after landing, the follow-on paratroopers quickly transferred to 18 waiting Blackhawks, escorted by Apaches, to conduct three coordinated air assaults on Panama Viejo, Fort Cimarron, and Tinajitas army barracks. The three hours' delay transformed a rela-tively safe night landing into a daylight combat assault against the elite PDF Tiger Company occupying Tinajitas barracks. The Blackhawks took numerous hits as they dropped soldiers into the landing zone some 400 meters from the barracks complex. In stifling heat, the paratroopers pushed forward. When they arrived at the garrison walls, the enemy soldiers had fled, leaving most of their equipment behind. The PDF command and control structure and most PDF units were neutralized by H-plus-10 hours. The PDF were simply smothered by unseen attackers from every direction and in every dimension. While they had expected battle, they did not expect to be confronted with such a simultaneous display of overwhelming force.

The Army would repeat the success of Just Cause again in the Iraqi desert barely more than a year later. Just Cause presaged Desert Storm in several important respects. First was the growing confidence among the Army leadership that the newly minted generation of high-quality soldiers could be relied upon to execute even the most dangerous and difficult missions. Second, Just Cause indicated to field commanders that the President and his national security advisors would give them wide latitude to conduct the operation. The operation demonstrated again the imperative that victory must be won quickly with overwhelming force to ensure minimum casualties.

From the tactical perspective, Just Cause demonstrated that joint operations were not only possible but imperative in future wars so long as all units involved could talk to each other and operate together under a single chain of command. Precision weapons proved worthy of the extra cost in Panama because of their unique ability to take out military targets discretely while reducing collateral damage to surrounding civilian facilities. Night operations are the most difficult to execute, but when executed with competence, achieve the most decisive results at least cost. The soldiers' performance in night combat vindicated the Army's commitment to, and substantial investment in, expensive night vision technology for ground soldiers and aviators. Just Cause showed what a combat multiplier psychological operations (PSYOP) can be when fully integrated into the tactical plan. PSYOP induced bloodless surrenders and prevented needless casualties on both sides.

Just Cause also foretold the problems that the Army might have after Desert Storm in supervising humanitarian assistance, restoring order, and rebuilding damaged infrastructure. In fact, postconflict headaches in both wars would last considerably longer and would require a great deal more effort than generals ever imagined. Before the shooting stopped, soldiers in Panama found themselves guarding prisoners of war, distributing food, and walking the beat in Panama City as surrogate policemen. Soldiers ran a displaced persons camp as well as 20 food distribution sites and contributed free medical assistance to more than 15,000 Panamanian citizens. As in Grenada, the transition from warrior to humanitarian was made smoothly by superb young soldiers, many of whom had been standing on the freezing tarmac at Fort Bragg just a few hours before. Only the very best could have pulled off what was "the largest, most sophisticated contingency operation conducted over the longest distances in the history of the US armed forces. It succeeded because of tough young soldiers, sailors, airmen, and marines."[30]

EVOLUTION NOT REVOLUTION

Shortly after the Gulf War, the Senate Armed Services Committee asked Major General Barry McCaffrey, commander of the 24th Infantry Division (Mech), how the war was won in only 100 hours. He replied, "This war didn't take 100 hours to win, it took 15 years." McCaffrey's sentiments reflects those of his generation who as young soldiers watched the Army fracture in Vietnam and who devoted most of their adult lives to the task of reforging the institution through a remarkable process of evolutionary reform.

All of the Services regenerated themselves during the Reagan years, but Army reform differed from the other Services in two important aspects. First, at the time of greatest institutional crisis immediately after Vietnam, the Army was obliged to fundamentally change its character from the mass conscripted army of World War II, Korea, and Vietnam, to a small body of high-quality, long-service professionals. Second, Army reform centered primarily on ideas and people rather than machines. To be sure, the Army went to war with first-class weaponry. But it was the quality of the young soldier and his leaders and the excellence of their operational method that proved so overwhelmingly decisive in the Gulf.

A visionary cohort of soldiers who stayed with the institution during the difficult years following the war in Vietnam was responsible for launching the Army on its path to reform. They saw in the volunteer Army concept the opportunity to create a new-style Army capable, for the first time in its history, of winning the first battle at the lowest possible cost in human life. The small professional Army they created would be able to maneuver with unprecedented agility and speed. Its leaders would possess the independent spirit to make decisions on their own initiative. This new Army would seek to outthink rather than outslug its opponents. It would be peopled by a new style of soldier whose intelligence, skill, and esprit would allow him to take on and defeat a more numerous foe. Thanks to these soldiers and their successors, the Army that met Saddam Hussein was fundamentally different from the Army that emerged from the jungles of Vietnam 20 years before.

Notes

1. Dr. Thomas Barn, "Fragging: A Study," *Army*, April 1977, p. 46, and Eugene Linden, "Fragging and Other Withdrawal Symptoms," *Saturday Review*, January 8, 1972, p. 12.

2. Drew Middleton, "Armed Forces' Problem: Finding Good Volunteers," *New York Times*, April 17, 1974, p. 21.

3. Lewis Sorley, *Thunderbolt* (New York: Simon and Schuster, 1992), pp. 333-384.

4. Larry Carney, "USAREUR Boots Out 1300 Troublemakers," *Army*, March 1974, p. 6.

5. Jay Finegan, "Washington Viewed as a Hardship Tour," *Army Times*, September 12, 1977.

6. Major Paul Herbert, "Deciding What Has To Be Done: General William E. DePuy and the 1976 Edition of FM 100-5, *Operations*," Leavenworth Paper No. 16, 1988, pp. 11-13.

7. *Ibid*. p. 14.

8. Paul F. Gorman, *The Secret of Future Victories* (Alexandria, VA: Institute for Defense Analyses, October 1991), p. 86.

9. *Ibid*.

10. Orr Kelly, "The Crippling Squeeze on Pay in the Services," *U.S. News & World Report*, March 31, 1980, p. 49.

11. William Bowman, Roger Little, and G. Thomas Sicilia, *All-Volunteer Force After a Decade: Retrospect and Prospect* (Washington, DC: Pergamon-Brassey's, 1986), p. 270.

12. Senator J. James Exon as quoted in "Navy Chief Breaks with Carter, Urges Return to Military Draft," *Washington Post*, June 20, 1981, p. A1 (UPI, September 4, 1981).

13. Interview with General (Retired) Maxwell Thurman, February 25, 1992.

14. Bowman and Little, pp. 266-286, and interview with General Thurman, March 7, 1992.

15. *Ibid*.

16. Major General Jack C. Wheeler, "In Recruiting, Quality Is All," *Army*, September 1991, pp. 35-43.

17. US Army Center of Military History Policy Paper, "US Army and the Total Force," August 1992.

18. Lieutenant General Frederick J. Brown, letter to Ms. Ann Chapman, TRADOC historian, January 2, 1991.

19. Interview with Colonel David Blodgett, March 24, 1992.

20. Interview with Sergeant Major John Whitten, US Army Sergeants Major Academy, March 24, 1992.

21. John M. Broder, "The Army Does an About Face," *Los Angeles Times*, April 20, 1991, p. A1.

22. John Romjue, "From Active Defense to AirLand Battle: The Development of Army Doctrine 1973-1982," *TRADOC Historical Monograph Series* (June 1984), p. 61.

23. Richard Davis, *The 31 Initiatives: A Study in Air Force-Army Cooperation* (Washington, DC: Office of Air Force History, 1987), p. 38.

24. *Ibid*. pp. 58-59.

25. Interview with Colonel Richard Sinnreich, February 16, 1992.

26. Major Bruce R. Pirnie, *Operation Urgent Fury: The US Army in Joint Operations* (US Army Center of Military History, 1986).

27. 44th MHD interview with Major General H. Norman Schwarzkopf, November 21, 1983.

28. Arthur T. Hadley, *The Straw Giant: Triumph and Failure, America's Armed Forces* (New York: Random House, 1971), pp. 246-7.

29. 3d AD and V Corps Crisis Action Team, "On Track with CAT," *Armor*, November-December 1987, p. 17.

30. Lieutenant General Carl W. Stiner, December 29, 1989, as quoted in TRADOC Just Cause briefing, May 4, 1990.

Chapter 2

DESERT SHIELD

After Highway 127 from Chattanooga tops Signal Mountain, it begins a steep, winding descent into the emerald green Sequatchi River Valley and turns sharply east into Dunlap. Although Ken Stephens made the trip nearly every week, he never tired of driving down the rugged ridge lines thick with birch, oak, and pine. Once over the Sequatchi Bridge, just into Dunlap, he usually grabbed a biscuit and coffee at the Win-Bob Drive-In (two places to eat—here and at home) before passing completely through town and pulling into the old glass-fronted automobile dealership that served as home to the 212th Engineer Company, Tennessee National Guard.

Staff Sergeant Ken Stephens' call to active duty came as no surprise. He had quietly resigned himself to that reality some time ago. His wife and friends remarked that he never seemed to get excited about much of anything, even war. He anticipated hardships because he was fairly sure his electrical and plumbing business was not healthy enough to make it through his absence. But if he were lucky, he might find a permanent place in the Signal Mountain police force when he returned. Stephens' brother had been tragically killed in Cambodia in 1970, so he really didn't have to go. But 67 percent of his company were Vietnam veterans, many of them wounded in that conflict, and the town still looked to soldiers, past and present, with a special sense of belonging and pride. He never seriously considered staying back.

His vertical construction squad assembled in the armory on October 11, 1990. The 212th was a close outfit. Stephens had spent seven years as an artilleryman in the regular Army, serving in Texas, Oklahoma, and Germany, but he had never been around men more tightly drawn together than this bunch. Steve Brady, a draftsman from Nashville, was also a staff sergeant and his assistant. The others were all highly skilled: an ironworker, a truck driver, a water well driller from Tip Top over in Bledsoe County, and a student from Tennessee Tech who felt somewhat out of place surrounded by so many skilled tradesmen who knew each other so well. All were fiercely independent and, like Stephens, quietly confident. They were used to working for themselves and to working out problems without a great deal of supervision, especially from the top. Stephens was convinced that, collectively, his squad had the experience and practical savvy to build anything. Within 30 days, they would get the chance to prove themselves in the heat and blowing sand of Saudi Arabia.

The peculiar thing about the 212th in Saudi Arabia was that nothing in the outfit seemed to break. The Guardsmen in Stephens' squad had been trained as carpenters and plumbers, but they spent most of their time operating well-used graders, bulldozers, and dump trucks, doing road work. A closer look at the company's night laager would reveal enough disassembled machinery, all scattered out over tarpaulins and greasy plywood sheets, to fill Barker's Garage on Rankin Avenue. Truck headlights illuminated the scene as squad members worked late into the night rebuilding engines, transmissions, and other major assemblies. Radiators that ruptured in the desert heat were a constant problem, but a sergeant in the second platoon who owned a Midas shop in Chattanooga had no trouble jury-rigging the company's arc welder to braze broken radiators. Hydraulic seals ruptured constantly, but Sergeant "Mutt" Mills had less problem fixing those than he did keeping his ancient water well-drilling rig in action back in Bledsoe County.

A few days before the war began, Stephens and his squad carved their way through the border berm and continued to build a six-lane road 6 miles deeper into Iraq. Mistaking them for Iraqis, a combat patrol from the 101st Airborne stumbled on the squad nonchalantly working away in enemy territory. The Guardsmen were stripped to the waist, with handkerchiefs and goggles fixed to their faces. They had neither the time nor the inclination to explain their presence over the berm. Nor were they terribly disturbed to discover that they were among the first American soldiers to drive into enemy territory—in dump trucks and graders.

In less than half a year, tens of thousands of soldiers like those in the 212th Engineer Company transformed a relatively undeveloped region in Southwest Asia into a combat theater capable of sustaining two Army corps. The soldiers from Dunlap were essential elements in a process that, over the course of Operation Desert Shield, picked up the equivalent of the city of Atlanta, with all its population and sustenance, and moved it

Staff Sergeant Ken Stephens, 212th Engineer Company, Tennessee National Guard.

more than 8,000 miles to Saudi Arabia. Accomplishment of this feat required the unloading of 500 ships and 9,000 aircraft that carried through Saudi ports more than 1,800 Army aircraft, 12,400 tracked vehicles, 114,000 wheeled vehicles, 38,000 containers, 1,800,000 tons of cargo, 350,000 tons of ammunition, and more than 350,000 soldiers, airmen, marines, sailors, and civilians. Within the theater, 3,568 convoys of supply trucks covered 35 million miles, traversing 2,746 miles of roadway in Saudi Arabia and Kuwait.[1] Many of these roads were carved out of barren desert or improved by highly skilled soldiers like the citizen-soldiers from the 212th. More than 70 percent of the manpower dedicated to building the combat theater in Saudi Arabia came from the Army National Guard and the Army Reserve.

AMERICAN MILITARY INVOLVEMENT IN THE GULF

The United States Army acquired an active operational interest in the Persian Gulf after the fall of the Shah of Iran in 1979 precipitated a series of unsettling events that threatened the world's oil supply. No one at the time could foresee how the Ayatollah Khomeini intended to carry out his threat to punish "the Great Satan" for its role in supporting the Shah. Equally disturbing was the growing truculence of the Soviets in the region. Since the days of the tsars, the Russians had sought expansion through Iran to a warm water port on the Indian Ocean. Suspicions became more acute with the Soviet invasion of Afghanistan that same year. Suddenly, a nightmare scenario took shape for the Carter administration. What if the Soviet adventure were just the opening round of a more ambitious scheme to encircle and absorb Iran by invasion from Soviet and Afghan territory? The subsequent Carter Doctrine, which declared any invasion in the region to be a threat to vital United States' interests, was a symbolic first step to counter Soviet expansion. A physical expression of new American resolve came with the formation of the Rapid Deployment Force in 1979.

The forces the Joint Chiefs initially allocated to the Persian Gulf mission were more symbolic than real. The Rapid Deployment Joint Task Force consisted mainly of a planning staff headquartered at MacDill Air Force Base just outside Tampa, Florida. While the Navy had maintained a presence in the Gulf since 1948, plans for committing Army forces in Southwest Asia were not made until Iran was threatened with a Soviet invasion. On January 1, 1983, the task force became one of six United States multi-Service commands and was renamed Central Command, or CENTCOM, with specified theaters of operation in the Persian Gulf and Northeast Africa. Although designated a joint command, CENTCOM had no troops stationed in its area of responsibility. The regional nations, led by Saudi Arabia, were willing to accept assistance in the form of equipment and training, but only Bahrain was willing to allow the stationing of American forces on its soil. Tiny Bahrain welcomed American presence, permitting the Navy to maintain its Middle East Task Force Headquarters at Manama.

Two debilitating and seemingly intractable wars served to lessen the immediate threat to the Gulf oil supply. Saddam Hussein's surprise attack against Iran in 1980 put on hold any inclination by Khomeini to cause mischief. Likewise, any latent Soviet designs on Iranian oil and ports became secondary to the more pressing military challenge posed by

Mujahadeen freedom fighters in Afghanistan who fanatically and skillfully fought the Soviets to a stalemate. Both wars created a tenuous, yet convenient, strategic impasse in the region and made further expansion by any of the three major warring powers unlikely.

Late in the Iran-Iraq War, however, Iranian attacks against Gulf shipping grew more intense, particularly against Kuwaiti tankers in response to the Emirate's support of Baghdad. The United States' response was Operation Earnest Will, the reflagging and limited escort of Kuwaiti tankers in the Persian Gulf, supported by United States Army helicopters. Slightly more than two years later, the United States would again come to Kuwait's assistance, this time against Saddam Hussein.

ANTICIPATION

General Schwarzkopf became Commander in Chief of CENTCOM on November 23, 1988. Burly, emotional, and brilliant, Schwarzkopf earned the handle "Stormin' Norman" early in his career primarily because of his outspoken personality and his volcanic outbursts. Most often he lost his temper in response to the frustrations that any commander encounters when dealing with the sometimes glacial pace of military bureaucracy. To those unfamiliar with his unique style, he had a dreadful "shoot-the-messenger" reputation. Those who knew him well, however, understood that underneath his awesome exterior was a deeply compassionate soldier who always considered the welfare of his soldiers his first priority.

Schwarzkopf was one of the first to see how the changing world environment might shift the Army's strategic focus from Europe back to his particular corner of the world. Iran and Iraq chose to end their mutually exhausting war in 1988 after more than eight years. Shortly thereafter the Berlin Wall came down, signalling both an end to the Soviet Union as a threat in Europe and a decline of Soviet influence in the Middle East. With a huge, well-equipped Iraqi military at loose ends, Schwarzkopf realized that the Iraqis had replaced the Soviets as the most serious threat in the Persian Gulf. In November 1989 Schwarzkopf directed that the plan addressing a possible Soviet invasion of Iran, OPLAN 1002-90, be revised as soon as possible to reflect an Iraqi invasion of Kuwait and Saudi Arabia. In December the JCS granted him permission to shift the geographic focus of the biennial Joint Chiefs' war game from Iran to Saudi Arabia.

To test how the command might deploy to blunt such an Iraqi invasion, the CENTCOM staff put together in record time a remarkably fortuitous and prophetic exercise, INTERNAL LOOK 90, which ran from July 23 through 28 concurrently at Fort Bragg, North Carolina, and Hurlburt Field, Florida. The exercise postulated an Iraqi attack into Saudi Arabia with six heavy divisions. In the plan's scenario, XVIII Airborne Corps was given sufficient time to deploy to the region and to establish a defense in eastern Saudi Arabia before the attack began. The corps defended northern Saudi Arabia by blocking the Iraqis with the 82d Airborne and the 24th Infantry Divisions. The 101st Airborne Division (Air Assault) became the corps' covering force. While just a battle on paper, INTERNAL LOOK proved to be a sobering exercise. Iraqi armor, though badly mauled by helicopters and tactical aircraft, continued to advance as far south as al-Jubayl, nearly 200 kilometers deep into Saudi Arabia. The airborne corps succeeded in holding Dhahran, ad-Dammam, and the Abquaiq refineries, but at a cost of almost 50 percent of its fighting strength.

INTERNAL LOOK was a joint exercise with all Services and component commands represented and thoroughly integrated. For example, the corps battlefield coordination element (BCE) deployed to the Ninth Air Force Tactical Air Control Center at Eglin Air Force Base, Florida, and coordinated air and ground operations just as it would later in Desert Storm. INTERNAL LOOK provided an essential common framework to participants during the war. When actual deployments began during Desert Shield, planners would routinely remark, "We did this on INTERNAL LOOK."

INTERNAL LOOK underscored for logisticians the idea that any intervening force in the region would heavily depend on Saudi support for survival. The main tactical lesson from the exercise was that no matter how much Air Force and attack helicopter reinforcement the allocated forces had, they would have a tough time confronting Iraqi armored formations. Most important, INTERNAL LOOK emphatically demonstrated what CENTCOM planners had known for some time, that a serious shortage of sealift posed the greatest single element of risk associated with such an operation. Should the United States move to check an Iraqi invasion, the decisive advantage would rest with the side that managed to arrive at the critical point in the theater first with the most combat power. After the exercise, Schwarzkopf resolved to give ground combat units first priority for deployment by sea.

THE IRAQI INVASION

In mid-July 1990 Saddam summoned Lieutenant General Ayad Futayih al-Rawi, commander of the Republican Guard Forces Command, to his palace. The Iraqi president ordered al-Rawi to begin preparations to invade Kuwait. While al-Rawi was a Shia in an inner sanctum of Sunni thuggery, he gave Saddam the unquestionable loyalty typical of a grateful interloper. Al-Rawi realized full well that his future in the regime, not to mention his life and the lives of his family, rested on his performance in the coming war against Kuwait.

Al-Rawi had commanded the Republican Guard in its most successful offensive against Iran. In a quick series of battles between April and July 1988, al-Rawi's elite corps made the difference between continued stalemate and victory. He applied the offensive lessons of those attacks to his plan to conquer Kuwait. His first principle was to apply overwhelming force. Al-Rawi would be killing a flea with a sledgehammer.

At 0200 on August 2, 1990, the Hammurabi Armored and the Tawakalna Mechanized Divisions, two of al-Rawi's elite heavy units, rushed across the border in tightly disciplined formations and quickly overran a single Kuwaiti brigade deployed along the frontier. The Kuwaitis, equipped with only Saladin and Ferret armored cars, had little hope of checking the onslaught of nearly 1,000 T-72 tanks. Al-Rawi coupled the mass of the assault with a rapid ground advance that swept south, capturing most Kuwaiti forces in garrison and reaching Kuwait City by 0500. Meanwhile, three Republican Guard special forces brigades launched a heliborne assault into the city, closing the back door on Kuwaiti withdrawals. Seaborne commandos deployed farther south and cut the coastal road. By early evening the city was reasonably secure despite some sporadic resistance from a few die-hard Kuwaitis. To the west, al-Rawi's third heavy unit, the Medina Armored Division, screened the main attack against the unlikely event that the Gulf Cooperation Council's Peninsula Shield Brigade in northern Saudi Arabia might intervene. Al-Rawi committed four Guard infantry divisions behind the lead armored forces to begin mopping up. All three of his heavy divisions then moved hastily south to establish a defensive line along the Saudi border. Saddam's military machine had conquered Kuwait in fewer than 48 hours.

THE RESPONSE

On August 2 at 0230 Washington time, General Colin Powell phoned the JCS operations director, Lieutenant General Thomas Kelly, and told him to find General Schwarzkopf and immediately order him back to Washington. Schwarzkopf and Powell met the President and other National Security Council members at the White House at 0800. In the meeting, Schwarzkopf laid out preliminary military options to respond to the invasion and a summary of Iraqi military capabilities. At the regular morning National Security Council meeting on August 3, the President agreed with other members that some force might be needed. Powell told the President that Schwarzkopf and Kelly were working on options and would brief him shortly. At Camp David on August 4, Schwarzkopf expanded his briefing to the President on details for deployment of a defensive force to Saudi Arabia. Shortly after the meeting, King Fahd asked the president for a briefing on the situation from American officials. National Security Advisor Brent Scowcroft hurriedly began to assemble a briefing team to travel to Saudi Arabia in an effort to convince the Saudis to ask for help.

During the evening of August 4, 1990, Lieutenant General John Yeosock, commander of CENTCOM's Third Army, was dining at a neighbor's house at Fort McPherson, Georgia, when the phone rang. Schwarzkopf was on the line and he wasted few pleasantries before telling Yeosock of the requirement to brief King Fahd. Schwarzkopf wanted Yeosock with him on this key Saudi trip and directed Yeosock to report to CENTCOM headquarters at MacDill Air Force Base as quickly as possible. They had no time to waste; if Yeosock could not get a flight out immediately, Schwarzkopf would dispatch his own plane from MacDill to pick him up.

THE SHIELD'S FOUNDATION

General Yeosock would prove during the Gulf War to be a necessary calming and introspective counterpart to his emotional and extroverted boss. Yeosock's deep, craggy features and measured, methodical way of choosing when to speak gave him a grave appearance and manner. He possessed a keen intellect and a prodigious capacity for work. Often overshadowed in the company of his peers, he exuded a compulsive desire not to take credit or elbow into the limelight. He exercised an indirect approach to decision making by allowing others to posture and vent their frustrations in the highly charged and structured atmosphere of the CENTCOM briefing room. He reserved his time for quiet, one-on-one discussions where he could fully exploit his particular skill at measured debate and logical persuasion.

Yeosock's selection as CENTCOM's Army commander was just as fortuitous for Gulf War planning as INTERNAL LOOK had been. As project manager for the Saudi Army National Guard (PM-SANG) some seven years before, he had been responsible for training and equipping much of the Saudi ground force. That experience, combined with his empathetic personality, suited him well for his new position as the Army's first point of contact with the Arabs. The Saudis, in particular, placed great value on personalities and personal relationships. When faced with impending disaster, they would not relinquish authority to anyone who had not first earned their trust. Yeosock had that essential commodity well in hand.

As soon as he finished talking to Schwarzkopf on August 4, Yeosock called Major General William "Gus" Pagonis who had recently been assigned as the chief logistician in FORSCOM. The men had come to know each other well during numerous REFORGER exercises in Germany. REFORGER was like a national training center for logisticians. The exercise realistically tested logisticians' ability to assemble and transport large bodies of troops and equipment from the United States to Europe. The requirement for 10 divisions in 10 days stressed planners and logistics systems to their maximum. Old REFORGER hands maintained that in

Lieutenant General John Yeosock, commanding general, US Third Army.

spite of detailed plans and extensive automation, the secret of survival once the operation began was the ability to anticipate and react to the unexpected. Logisticians who did well in REFORGER managed from docks and warehouses. Just as the National Training Center experience would prove to be the supreme preparation for desert war, REFORGER would provide an equally realistic training exercise for the movement of American forces to Saudi Arabia.

Pagonis was a systems analyst by training and inclination who had a reputation for breaking down the most complex logistical problems into their component parts to implement logical, sequential solutions. He had little patience for slow, process-oriented bureaucracies. While accused of micromanagement and overcentralization by those who did not know him well, Pagonis was, in reality, a minimalist. He was capable of absorbing and retaining huge amounts of data and applying a concept of "building-block" logistics. His approach was, in effect, a military adaptation of the "just-in-time" theory of management that demanded very careful monitoring to ensure that exactly the right support, tailored for the mission at hand, would be provided at exactly the time it was required.

Yeosock told Pagonis to have a logistics plan ready to brief to King Fahd once they landed in Saudi Arabia. He needed an outline for all major logistics requirements, including the use of ports and roads and the degree to which indigenous Saudi transportation supplies and labor would be put to best use. Pagonis developed the three primary logistical tasks that would shape the buildup: the reception of forces in the theater, the onward movement of those forces to forward areas within the theater, and the sustainment of forces as they prepared for combat. He briefed Yeosock at about 0700 on August 5, just before Yeosock boarded the aircraft for Saudi Arabia with Schwarzkopf and Secretary of Defense Dick Cheney. The next day, King Fahd issued the invitation for American troops to assist in the defense of Saudi Arabia. On August 8 the President announced the commitment of American forces.

While INTERNAL LOOK 90 provided a conceptual blueprint for Desert Storm, the CENTCOM leadership was obliged to hammer out most of the details of the operation through a process of ad hoc decision making and eleventh-hour improvisation. The American Army had never projected such a large force so quickly over so great a distance. The operation could not progress without capitalizing efficiently on indigenous Saudi support. Here, Pagonis' experience would be the essential planning link between Saudi support and American requirements.

Once in Riyadh, Yeosock outlined his command's missions and tasks. Only a few American forces were permanently stationed in Saudi Arabia to help him. A United States military mission of 38 officers and enlisted men who were training Saudi Arabian land forces and a handful of other soldiers from his old outfit provided some additional help to get things started. Initially, Yeosock relied heavily on the PM-SANG office, appointing the project manager, Brigadier General James Taylor, as his interim chief of staff. Yeosock's small group had little time to prepare as the division ready brigade (DRB) of the 82d Airborne was soon to arrive.

Actually, the first paratroopers on the ground in Saudi Arabia were not the infantry battalions, but 76 soldiers and staff officers of the XVIII Airborne Corps assault command post who arrived midmorning on August 9. Brigadier General Edison Scholes, corps chief of staff, led the soldiers down the ramp into the oppressive heat and humidity of

Dhahran Airport. His C-141 was the only military aircraft in sight. Scholes ordered his soldiers to quickly gather their equipment and prepare to leave because he knew that the gargantuan aerial convoy assembling behind him would soon make sleepy Dhahran the busiest airport in the world. No one was happier to see him than a sweat-soaked but smiling Yeosock and his meager staff. Yeosock pointed to a motley assortment of trucks and buses waiting to take them to a Saudi air defense site 5 kilometers southwest of the air base. Scholes optimistically christened the place "Dragon City" in honor of the symbol on the XVIII Airborne Corps patch.[2]

During the early days, as soldiers and equipment poured into Dhahran under the mounting threat of a preemptive Iraqi strike, Scholes and his staff constantly updated their plan of defense, which changed and grew more bold with each arriving aircraft. Eventually, as the situation on the ground stabilized, this hourly process solidified into three distinct "Desert Dragon" plans, each of which would represent a milestone in the ability of the corps to defend against Iraqi incursion.

THE 82D AIRBORNE DIVISION DEPLOYS

Major General James Johnson's 82d Airborne Division's deployment began in the early evening of August 6 as a typical North Carolina thunderstorm rolled over Fort Bragg. At 2100 sharp, Sergeant First Class Elijah Payne, the corps watch NCO, ended four days of mounting tension with a brief phone call to Staff Sergeant John Ferguson, the division watch NCO. Few words were exchanged. Both sergeants had been through the "sequence" many times, both in training and for real. With further phone calls, the familiar alert began to cascade down Ardennes Street. Within two hours the side streets and parking lots surrounding Ardennes began to crowd with soldiers carrying rucksacks and duffle bags. Cars were parked everywhere, some to stay, others with engines running occupied by tearful wives and girlfriends saying goodbye. When the call came, the division's three brigades stood in varying degrees of readiness. The 2d Brigade, commanded by Colonel Ronald Rokosz and designated DRB 1, was fully prepared to deploy without notice, with one battalion packed aboard the aircraft within 18 hours. Assembly and preparation of the force proceeded rapidly throughout the night in torrential rain. The 1st and 3d Brigades were training in locations scattered from Fort Bragg, North Carolina, to Fort Chaffee, Arkansas. Soldiers not training were on leave or in schools. FORSCOM had anticipated that the deployment would require the entire division in Saudi Arabia as soon as possible, so the call went from division down the chain of command to bring everyone back to Fort Bragg immediately. [3]

The division staff briefed every brigade and battalion commander at midnight. Tension in the room rose markedly when Lieutenant Colonel

Steven Epkins, the intelligence officer, recounted the Iraqis' armored strength. To logical military minds, Saddam's best option seemed to be to continue the attack into Saudi Arabia to seize the airfields, ports, and oil fields. The corps commander, Lieutenant General Gary Luck, told the division to be prepared to fight for the ports if necessary. Presuming that they might arrive unopposed, Luck intended to defend key facilities and to launch long-range preemptive counterattacks with attack helicopters. As a result, deviating from the established sequence, the division's aviation brigade would go in early. For added killing power, Luck gave the division a multiple-launch rocket system (MLRS) battery from 3-27th Field Artillery. [4]

Aircraft scheduling was a problem from the start. An airborne brigade, including the normal contingent from corps and division necessary to support it, required at least 250 C-141 loads. But US Transportation Command (USTRANSCOM), the Defense Department's headquarters for military transportation operations, could initially guarantee only 90 aircraft. While this figure would eventually increase as Schwarzkopf's insistence on greater lift priority began to take hold, the number was still frighteningly low. The airborne soldiers were involved in a deadly race to get to Saudi Arabia first with the most tank-killing power. With Saddam's Republican Guard already on the Saudi border, the Americans had to build a survivable force from bases 8,000 miles away. Every lost movement or unavailable aircraft increased the inherent risk of the venture. With fewer aircraft than expected, the division had to make last-minute compromises. To accommodate more tank killers, thousands of soldiers and hundreds of tons of equipment from the division support command, engineer, and air defense battalions would follow on later aircraft and ships.

While leaders planned, the first units moved into the corps marshalling area, a fenced-off area of barracks and parking lots adjacent to Pope Air Force Base, next door to Fort Bragg. The first troopers of the lead brigade departed at 1000 on August 8, 36 hours after being alerted. The last of the first deploying brigade left four days later. The 82d's load-out and departure process had to be adjusted daily. To make essential departure times from Pope, both Air Force and Army planners worked day and night reconfiguring loads to fit tactical exigencies at the other end of the operation. The initial pulse of combat power needed in the theater immediately required an enormous surge in aircraft. USTRANSCOM dispatched C-141 and giant C-5 aircraft to Pope from bases all over the world. For the first time the President activated the Civilian Reserve Air Fleet. Overnight, crewmen accustomed to relatively simple palletized loading for Air Force aircraft found themselves pondering weight, balance, and cubic-foot requirements for Boeing 747s, which only the day before had been carrying parcels for UPS. The corps ground liaison officer, Major Drew Young, assisted by paratroopers from each deploying unit, compensated for uncertainty by simply reallocating aircraft and reconfiguring loads on a moment's notice. In one 12-hour period on the third day, eight C-5s arrived unannounced at Pope, and the division scrambled to push combat soldiers and equipment to the loading areas to keep ahead of the Air Force. In seven days an entire division ready brigade—4,575 paratroopers and their equipment—arrived on the ground ready to fight in Saudi Arabia. The remaining two brigades and their equipment flew out between August 13 and September 8 using 582 C-141 sorties. By August 24 more than 12,000 soldiers from all three brigades, including all nine infantry battalions, were on the ground.

THREE VECTORS

On August 8, 1990, at the conclusion of the first of a long series of briefings on the Gulf, General Vuono swiveled around in his chair to address the crammed balcony of the Army Operations Center (AOC) in the basement of the Pentagon. Warning the audience that it was going to be a long haul, Vuono urged them to "coordinate, anticipate, and verify—make sure of your information; make sure you have the complete picture, and keep the forces in the field informed."

After the adjustments under the Goldwater-Nichols Act to increase the authority of unified commanders and the Joint Staff, the Services retained significant responsibilities under Title 10 of the US Code. The Department of the Army is responsible for manning, equipping, training, and sustaining the forces provided to the unified commands through FORSCOM, the specified command responsible for mustering forces for the Joint Chiefs of Staff. FORSCOM is also the largest command in the Department of the Army. One of FORSCOM's major components is the US Third Army. In fact, many of the personnel assigned to FORSCOM were dual-hatted as members of Third Army so that, with the deployment of Third Army headquarters as ARCENT, the Department of the Army had to assume many of FORSCOM's functions.

To do so, the Army Staff (ARSTAF) organized for emergency operations as it had done under numerous crises ranging from the *Exxon Valdez* oil spill to Operation Just Cause. The difference in this case was that the Gulf crisis appeared to be a long, drawn-out affair with the very real prospect for major combat. The main conduit into the ARSTAF was the Crisis Action Team (CAT), established in the operations center under Major General Glynn Mallory, the director for operations and mobilization. Newly arrived from commanding the 2d Armored Division, Mallory took over the Army operations center at a critical time. With subordinate intelligence, logistics, personnel, and mobilization cells, the CAT operated 24 hours a day handling immediate requirements. For longer-range planning, a strategic planning group concentrated on staying two to three moves ahead of Saddam. On top of these specially organized cells, the remainder of the ARSTAF continued to function normally.

Vuono was determined that the Army would emerge from the Gulf in as good or better shape than before. Early on, he established three vectors to serve as guideposts for the ARSTAF in dealing with the crisis: the Army forces deployed in the Gulf had to win the war; at the same time, world-wide readiness had to be maintained; and finally, the Army had to proceed with the ongoing reshaping and restructuring brought about by the end of the Cold War. Vuono reserved for himself the responsibility of adjudicating among those often conflicting priorities. To aid in his decisions, he used "executive board" meetings of staff principals and selected special staff to consider and recommend options. Vice Chief of Staff General Gordon Sullivan served as the director of the board. Members included Lieutenant General Dennis Reimer, the deputy chief of staff for operations, who coordinated with the Joint Staff and accompanied Vuono on his trips to the theater; Lieutenant General Charles Eichelberger, the deputy chief of staff for intelligence, who represented the Army in National Foreign Intelligence Board meetings; Lieutenant General William Reno, the deputy chief of staff for personnel; and Lieutenant General Jimmy Ross, the deputy chief of staff for logistics.

First, and of prime importance, was assuring overwhelming success in Desert Shield and later Desert Storm. Vuono's guidance was straightforward: "Maintain a trained and ready force"—an imperative that had enormous ramifications for mobilization and training of Reserves as well as for modernization of the Active components. Sending the 24th Infantry Division as part of the XVIII Airborne Corps raised the issue concerning the deployability of the 48th Infantry Brigade, Georgia National Guard. Under existing war plans the 48th was the roundout brigade for the 24th. The Army leadership wanted to deploy the brigade because, at the time, the shortage of combat power available to confront Saddam was so acute that Schwarzkopf needed every unit the Army could provide. However, the Army was reluctant to deploy the brigade immediately as part of the 24th's deployment to Saudi Arabia for several reasons. Under US Title 10, the President could call up a Reserve unit for 90 days and, if required, extend it an additional 90 days. Peacetime planning called for the brigade to be a late-deploying unit in order to allow time for postmobilization training to prepare for combat. Defense guidance to the Army on August 24 reflected General Schwarzkopf's priorities and authorized call-up of only combat service and combat service support Guard and Reserve units. Combat units were specifically excluded since the length of the operation was unknown and postmobilization training, deployment, and redeployment would leave the roundout brigade fewer than three months in theater. After the President's decision to reinforce the theater for offensive operations, Congress granted authority for the combat units to be called up for one year on November 30, and the Army activated the 48th Brigade and later the 155th from Mississippi and the 256th from Louisiana.

In order to meet the immediate need for additional combat power to augment the 24th Infantry Division, the Army decided to send the 197th Infantry Brigade from Fort Benning, Georgia. If the Iraqis did launch a preemptive attack in the early fall, the 48th Brigade, even if activated in August, would still be tied up in postmobilization training. The mobilization plan called for crew and small-unit training to begin immediately after call-up, but collective training had to be delayed until individual soldier skills were brought up to standard. The brigade also had difficulty with maintenance of equipment due to a general lack of operator knowledge, mechanic diagnostic skills, and knowledge of the Army maintenance system. While officers and NCOs understood the tenets of AirLand Battle, they were not sufficently practiced in the intricacies of combined arms operations that required the continuous synchronization and integration of many very complex battlefield systems and functions. Vuono pledged that no soldier would deploy who was not trained and ready for combat. He was determined that the Army would not repeat the Korean War experience where hastily mobilized Reserves were thrown into combat unprepared, suffering terrible casualties.

Vuono had promised Yeosock that he would support him with all that he could muster from the Department of the Army. Vuono would offer options, issue guidance, set priorities, and force actions through the system in order to ensure their implementation. In short, the Department of the Army would centrally control the movement, training, equipping, and sustaining of forces deployed to the Gulf.

At the same time, Vuono would not let the Gulf crisis drain the Army dry and prevent a response to another crisis that might arise in some other part of the world. In his second vector, worldwide readiness, Vuono promised to avoid repeating the hollow European Army of the Vietnam era. While stability in Europe was promising, other hot spots were always ready to demand Army intervention. Vuono relied on a base of Active forces and trained Reserves to meet these contingencies. During Desert Shield, General Mallory and the AOC monitored crises in Liberia and Somalia that led to eventual Navy and Marine evacuation operations that might have required Army forces. In any case, the Philippines, Korea, and Latin America required close attention, and Army missions at home, ranging from fire fighting to emergency relief, might require rapid response by forces not involved in the Gulf.

As units were identified to deploy to Desert Shield, Vuono's intent was to shift missions to nondeploying units and, where possible, to backfill essential functions with Reservists called to active duty. Once XVIII Airborne Corps all but emptied Forts Bragg, Stewart, Campbell, and parts of Hood and Bliss, the Army had to reconstitute its contingency forces. Without knowing how long the deployment to the Gulf would last or that it would grow to its eventual one-half million soldiers, the ARSTAF earmarked I Corps at Fort Lewis, Washington, to become the new contingency corps centered on the 7th Infantry Division at Fort Ord, California, and on the remainder of the inactivating 9th Infantry Division at Fort Lewis.

The third vector involved reshaping the Army. Regardless of what happened in the Gulf, the Army was well down the road to restructuring into a smaller force. Every move and every disbanded unit had an effect on every other unit. Responding to budget pressures and the negotiation of the Conventional Forces in Europe (CFE) Treaty then in progress, Army planners anticipated removing one United States corps from Europe, including two divisions, an armored cavalry regiment, and most of the corps' support structure. The remaining corps would have to develop a new way of operating to cover the old two-corps sector. By August 1990 the communities and soldiers involved anxiously awaited news of base closures. Many measures could be taken to lessen the impact of closures and unit movements on the Gulf crisis, but nothing would stop or reverse the reshaping. The challenge was to reshape the Army and to sustain the deployment of forces in Saudi Arabia at the same time.[5]

FAMILY SUPPORT

The demographics of the Army that deployed to the Gulf differed significantly from earlier mass-conscripted formations that had fought in World War II, Korea, and Vietnam. Fifty-three percent of the Army was married, and 52,000 soldiers were married to other soldiers. Nine thousand military couples deployed to the Gulf, 2,500 of whom had children. Sixteen thousand of the 45,000 single parents deployed. In sum, the Army of the 1990s went to war with enormous family responsibilities. Having no extra soldiers, the Army could leave few behind. Its readiness, in keeping with Vuono's vectors, absolutely depended upon each soldier's meeting his or her military responsibilities.

Meeting these conflicting demands depended on community support, both within the Army and in surrounding civilian communities. Each unit had ready community support plans to maintain soldiers' ties with families left behind, ensuring that they had access to financial, medical, and social assistance. Single and dual military parents had to establish care arrangements in the event they were deployed. The plans included powers of attorney, appointments of short- and long-term guardians, applications for identity cards, and other requirements that ensured the supported family member had access to military benefits. Commanders reviewed the plans and could separate soldiers from the Service whose plans failed to provide adequate support. The overwhelming majority proved adequate when tested by the Gulf War.

As each unit deployed overseas, a functioning chain of command and headquarters staff remained in place until that unit returned. Aside from duties like maintaining property and accounting for personnel, the rear detachment command structure also provided dependents with official services, particularly the essential link with the Red Cross in emergencies. More than 150 Family Assistance Centers were established to serve as focal points for that support. A unit "chain of concern" that the families themselves established to help one another often tied directly into the Family Assistance Center. Families of more senior personnel ensured that younger families were not overwhelmed by problems stemming from the deployment of a family member. A noteworthy off-shoot of the chain of concern was an informal telephonic notification system that matched official unit alert rosters and speeded up the sharing of information.

The tremendous outpouring of community support for soldiers and their families also eased the burden of deployment. Communities surrounding military facilities, often economically hard hit by the deployments, organized relief efforts for the needy and special events such as parades and picnics to demonstrate their support for the military. Merchants donated goods for both children and their parents. Toys went to the local military kids, while footballs and frisbees went to their parents in the Gulf.

By its very nature, XVIII Airborne Corps was well prepared to meet the demands of long-term, out-of-area deployments. Each unit participated in several off-post exercises each year that required a rear detachment chain of command and informal family care system to take care of dependents. Having just experienced Operation Just Cause, many of the 82d Airborne Division troopers and their families were old hands at dealing with problems arising from deployment. Not surprisingly, those most practiced had fewer problems.

THE SAUDI ARABIAN THEATER

Saudi Arabia is a vast, mostly empty country about the size of the United States east of the Mississippi. Roughly 1,300 miles north to south and 1,400 miles east to west, the country is mostly desert except for a thinly populated band along the coastal plain. The population lives in small, widely separated towns and villages in the vicinity of the Persian Gulf oil fields and at sources of water along ancient pilgrimage routes.

Populated areas are connected by a system of two-lane asphalt roads. Hard-surface roads also link Saudi Arabia to Kuwait, Iraq, Jordan, Qatar, the United Arab Emirates, Bahrain, and Yemen. A series of secondary

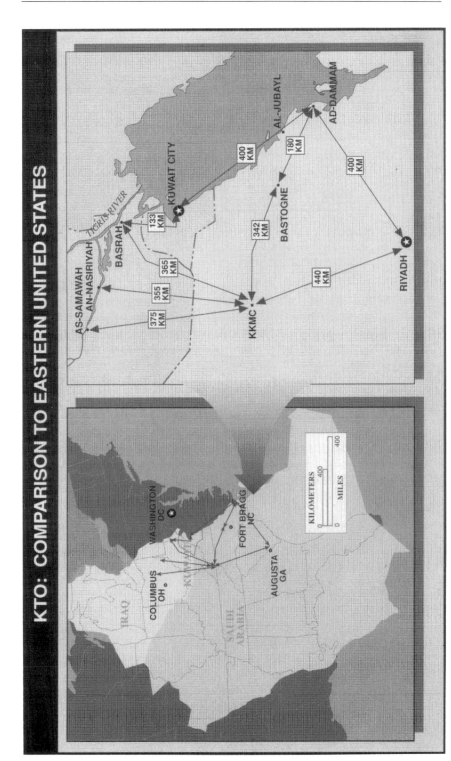

KTO: COMPARISON TO EASTERN UNITED STATES

roads tie the major cities and towns to minor towns and villages, with a series of dirt tracks between the smaller villages. Paralleling the trans-Arabian pipeline just south of the Iraqi border is Tapline Road, a major east-west roadway. The major north-south artery is the 500-kilometer-long coastal highway that runs from Kuwait, through the length of Saudi Arabia, to Qatar.

Rail facilities are limited, with only one active, standard-gauge, single-track line that runs from the port of ad-Dammam to Riyadh. Seaports are more extensive with seven major ports capable of handling more than 10,000 metric tons of materiel per day. Five secondary ports can handle 5,000 to 10,000 metric tons, and seven others, up to 5,000 metric tons per day. Four serve as outlets to the Persian Gulf and another three are located in the west along the Red Sea coast. Most military supplies and equipment would come into the ports of ad-Dammam and al-Jubayl. These two modern, high-capacity ports, when operated by ARCENT, would provide a reception and transshipment capacity equaled only by ports in Europe, Japan, and North America.

Airfields in Saudi Arabia are modern and well-equipped. Two of the largest, Dhahran and Riyadh, are fully capable of accommodating, day and night in all weather, 149 C-141 cargo aircraft and 3,600 short tons of cargo per day. Additional small but well-equipped airfields are scattered throughout the country.[6]

YEOSOCK'S THREE HATS

In analyzing the upcoming campaign, Yeosock viewed his command in terms of three functions, each serving a distinct and essential purpose. First, as commander of a numbered field army, he was responsible for dividing scarce resources among war-fighting units in accordance with the CINC's campaign plan. Because no combat commander ever receives all the firepower, supplies, and transport he thinks necessary, Yeosock personally assumed the apportionment task—one made even more difficult because the corps commanders were peers. Second, as CENTCOM's Army commander, Yeosock was expected to coordinate with the other US Services and allied ground forces. ARCENT headquarters planned for ground operations and operated the theater communications zone (COMMZ), which coordinated joint, combined, and Coalition operations, including host-nation support. Yeosock was responsible for providing all common supplies and services, such as food, fuel, ammunition, and transportation, to all Services within the theater. Third, as a Service intermediary between Schwarzkopf and various other Army four-star commands that provided soldiers, equipment, and Army-specific training and doctrinal guidance, Yeosock took his unique position very seriously. From his study of past wars, Yeosock recognized that all too often the attentions of combat commanders were needlessly diverted, even in the heat of combat, to noncombat tasks. Therefore, in his theater army commander role, he was determined to unburden the corps commanders from housekeeping and diplomatic chores by assuming them himself.

Yeosock would have to build the field army in Saudi Arabia incrementally. The building process required a sense of balance and timing and a finely honed instinct to judge and manage risk. Balance was important to ensure that while priority in deployment went to combat soldiers, enough logistics support and command overhead—just enough—followed along to sustain and control combat units in the field. Nevertheless, every seat on an airplane that went to a typist or a cook meant one less for a combat soldier.[7] Realizing that he might impede the efficiency of the later buildup by having so few support troops and activities in place to meet the combat units and move them forward, Schwarzkopf nevertheless put fighting soldiers at the head of the deployment line. His commitment to maintain a small logistical overhead was derived both from the practical necessity to get a viable fighting presence into theater as quickly as possible and the more emotional imperative inherited from his experience in Vietnam. Both Schwarzkopf and Yeosock were determined to avoid another massive, inefficient logistical depot like Long Binh or Qui Nhon where the Army had created enormous permanent bases at great expense.

Yeosock knew that he had to set a personal example by building his own Army headquarters and support organization on a shoestring. Yet he had to supply American forces with all the goods and services that they could not provide for themselves. This support ran the gamut from housekeeping functions such as transportation, administration, and security, to more combat-oriented functions such as air defense, intelligence gathering, and ammunition resupply. Schwarzkopf gave Yeosock the difficult mission of building a very austere theater support structure while keeping peace among the combat commanders of all Services. Thus Yeosock became both the traffic cop and the chief judge of Desert Shield.

Yeosock set to work building his support team using INTERNAL LOOK 90 and the troop list that had been drafted for that exercise as his game plan. According to procedures little changed since World War II, the theater should have developed progressively following detailed, computerized Time-Phased Force Deployment Data. Unfortunately, the shift in mission and region from Iran to Iraq forced CENTCOM to generate this data manually. Planners had to put in place large command and control structures to handle transportation, construction, administration, medical requirements, supply, maintenance, and military police, among others. These logistics units would bring their own headquarters staff and the additional supplies, housing, and administration to support themselves as well as the combat soldiers. Based on INTERNAL LOOK figures, the ARCENT logistics overhead eventually should have grown to 120,000,

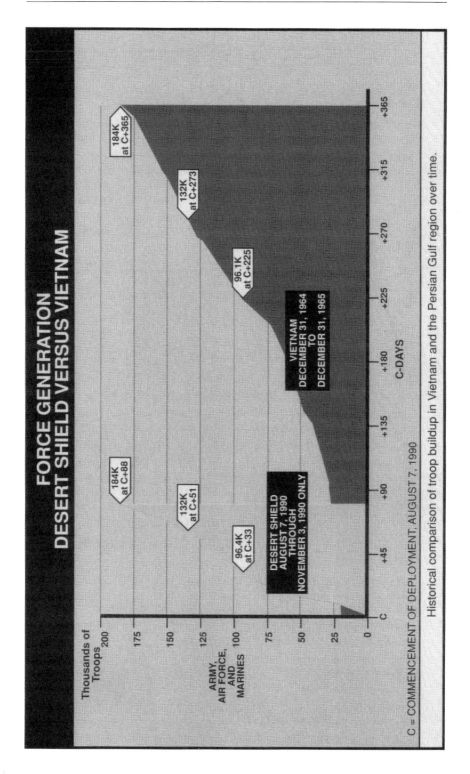

FORCE GENERATION
DESERT SHIELD VERSUS VIETNAM

Thousands of
Troops

184K at C+88

132K at C+51

96.4K at C+33

184K at C+365

132K at C+273

96.1K at C+225

DESERT SHIELD
AUGUST 7, 1990
THROUGH
NOVEMBER 3, 1990 ONLY

VIETNAM
DECEMBER 31, 1964
TO
DECEMBER 31, 1965

ARMY,
AIR FORCE,
AND
MARINES

C-DAYS

C = COMMENCEMENT OF DEPLOYMENT, AUGUST 7, 1990

Historical comparison of troop buildup in Vietnam and the Persian Gulf region over time.

including at least 15 generals. Most of the structure would come from activated Army National Guard and Army Reserve units. Two years were required to create such an enormous infrastructure during World War II, six months in Korea, and one year in Vietnam. Needless to say, Yeosock would not have that much time in Southwest Asia.

Schwarzkopf's demand for a buildup of unprecedented speed and austerity compelled Yeosock to devise an incremental method for building the theater in which he would call forward only enough support to do a job and only at the moment the job needed to be done. He allowed ARCENT headquarters to grow from about 300 soldiers during the buildup to about 1,000 during Desert Storm. His total support structure at echelons above corps remained below 38,000, a mere third of the projected requirement for this campaign. Such a high "tooth-to-tail" proportion was unprecedented for a fighting force so large and so far from home. In developing his headquarters, Yeosock combined the functional support organization with his own staff. Pagonis would serve as commander of 22d Support Command as well as Yeosock's ARCENT deputy commanding general for logistics. Yeosock formed subordinate command headquarters only when the functional requirements grew to the point that the appropriate ARCENT section could not handle them. For example, he called forward the Army Reserve's 416th Engineer Command under Major General Terrence Mulcahy only when the construction program became so complex that his own staff could no longer deal with it.

This building-block approach to theater support was not without risk or controversy. Most of the support above corps level is located in the National Guard and Army Reserve. Taking only what was needed most affected the Reserve component structure. To keep overhead down, Schwarzkopf was willing to accept political criticism for not accepting some Reserve units. By not introducing additional commands and organizations into the theater, the Army did not activate many well-trained, well-prepared units that could have provided substantial logistical support.

AD HOC LOGISTICS AND WORLDWIDE SUPPORT

In his own unique style, Pagonis adapted and refined logistics doctrine as he went about building a theater of war. He arrived in Saudi Arabia with 21 officers in trail and set about creating the structure necessary to support a modern contingency force. A firm believer in leading from the front, Pagonis spent much of his time traveling from one problem area to another in his Toyota 4x4, usually using a cellular telephone to pass requests over commercial satellite lines directly to logistics centers and staff sections in the United States.

Pagonis relied heavily on trusted agents—soldiers whom he personally knew and in whom he had total confidence. He used his team as an extension of himself. Although they were not necessarily high-ranking—many were sergeants—each was skilled in a particular logistical function and was empowered to act alone in order to cut through red tape and fix a problem on the spot. One of the earliest members of Pagonis' team, Lieutenant Colonel Mike Velten, formed an ad hoc transportation organization to move troops using Saudi contract buses. This infant organization, consisting of a captain from the 7th Transportation Group and about a dozen soldiers, set up shop in a tent, contracted for buses and materials-handling equipment, and began moving soldiers and their baggage through the airport at Dhahran.

Pagonis centralized all logistics functions in a huge tent about one-fourth the size of a football field. By congregating all functional experts in one place, he could immediately detect a problem from their chatter and, if necessary, track it from port to foxhole. At times the tent resembled the New York Stock Exchange on a heavy trading day. In the age of computers and satellite communications, however, Pagonis still relied on the old, proven 3x5 card to ensure that he kept his hand on the pulse of his command. Any soldier at any level could originate a card detailing a

General Pagonis addressed 22d Support Command soldiers on the eve of the war.

problem, with full authority to send it, by any means available, directly to the boss.

That the size and speed of the buildup in Saudi Arabia would overwhelm the small logistics operations center, requiring a more structured support command of some sort, became apparent early in August. During the first month of Desert Shield, CENTCOM planners worried about whether the President would allow the call-up of enough Reservists to permit full staffing of a theater army area command (TAACOM). First priority for Reserve activations necessarily went to units providing essential services not readily available in the Active force, such as stevedores, communications specialists, and medical technicians. Thus by default, Pagonis' select team became essentially an ad hoc TAACOM staff, completely assuming the function of troop movement and support. On August 19 Yeosock appointed Pagonis commander of the 22d Provisional Support Command. By August 22 when President Bush authorized the limited activation of the Reserves, an improvised 22d Support Command was already in operation and functioning well. [8]

The urgency to build the theater quickly resulted in a streamlined system for getting the necessary supplies to the region. Both Yeosock and Pagonis used the telephone extensively to pass requirements directly back to the United States and often energized support organizations for a quick response. Help came directly from the Army Chief and Vice Chief of Staff, assisted by the entire ARSTAF as well as the Army Materiel Command (AMC) and the Defense Logistics Agency. Often the Chief or the Vice took the most urgent requests directly from Army leaders in the theater and passed them to the required source for action. CINCs from other theaters provided soldiers and equipment. In the United States, major commanders and school commandants responded to calls for specially skilled technicians and soldiers by sending their best on a moment's notice, a response completely contrary to traditional peacetime practice. Similarly, American industry and business went to extraordinary lengths to provide products immediately and to put aside, for the moment, concerns about contracts and payment. A generation of senior soldiers, all of whom had lived through the long years of Vietnam, pledged that whatever the cost to their own particular establishment, this conflict would be supported properly.

When heavy equipment transporters (HETs), used primarily to haul heavy armor, ran critically short of tires, Yeosock turned to General Ross, the Army's chief logistician in the Pentagon, to find 3,000 tires and rush them to the theater. Ross in turn relayed the requirement through the AMC commander, General William G.T. Tuttle, to Major General Leo Pigaty, commander of the Army's Tank-Automotive Command in Warren, Michigan. Pigaty's contracting officer could locate only 800 tires worldwide, and just one manufacturer, Firestone Tire and Rubber in Des

Tanks loaded on heavy equipment transporters in Saudi Arabia.

Moines, Iowa, was producing them at a glacial rate of 40 per month. Pigaty discovered, however, that General Tire and Rubber Company produced a civilian version of the tire for logging, construction, and oil-drilling vehicles. Pigaty personally called General Tire and Rubber's CEO, who offered to direct his retailers and distributors across the country to ship whatever they had in stock from the nearest airport. Ken Oliver, the local General Tire dealer in Waco, Texas, had 74 tires. Immediately after receiving the call for help, he rented a cargo trailer at his own expense, hooked it to his pickup truck, loaded the tires, and made an overnight trip with his precious 1,400-pound load to Tinker Air Force Base, Oklahoma. When the energetic Oliver returned to Waco, he called Pigaty's office in Warren saying that he figured the troops needed those tires as quickly as possible and did not want to wait for commercial transportation.[9]

HOST-NATION SUPPORT

With the arrival of additional personnel in late August, Pagonis expanded the functions of the 22d Support Command's host-nation support operation. After many decades of importing technology and labor to build up their own infrastructure, the Saudis were comfortable dealing with foreign contractors for support. Therefore, when a military unit needed supplies or equipment, a contracting officer would simply pay cash on the spot and send the bill to the Saudis. In the early days of the buildup, the Support Command had to go to extraordinary lengths to purchase goods and services fast enough to keep up with the accelerating arrival of troops. In one case Lieutenant Colonel Jim Ireland, desperate for additional soldier living space, heard of a vacant civilian apartment

Host-nation support at work. Above, Saudi heavy-equipment transporters carried newly arrived self-propelled artillery to tactical assembly areas. Below, both military and commercial fuel trucks used fuel supply point distribution centers.

complex in Dhahran. He looked over the site, decided the price was right, and paid the landlord with cash. In another case, Velten, the transportation officer, had several hundred newly arrived XVIII Airborne Corps troops stranded at the airport. Looking for transportation for these troops, Velten cruised the streets of Dhahran in his pickup truck. Whenever he saw a truck or a bus parked on the street, he pulled over to the side of the road and, in proper Middle Eastern form, negotiated a deal with the usually nonplussed driver. The vehicles arrived as promised. That kind of initiative and ability to perform under enormous pressure with little supervision kept soldiers moving forward through the ports during those early days at a rate of nearly 4,000 per day. [10]

While the Saudis provided support during the first two months without any formal agreement with the United States, a buildup of the dimensions expected soon made some written agreement necessary. Verbal agreements were codified by the Department of Defense negotiating team dispatched on October 17, 1990, with the Saudi government agreeing to pay the costs of all contracts with American forces.[11] In time, ARCENT would contract for food, fuel, long-haul trucks and drivers, water, and other key items necessary for comfort and sustainment. In addition to port facilities and telecommunications, the Saudi government provided 4,800 tents, 1,073,500 gallons of packaged petroleum products, 333 HETs, 20 million meals, and 20.5 million gallons of fuel per day, as well as bottled water for the entire theater and supplies for Iraqi prisoners of war. Saudi contributions substantially shortened the time needed to prepare for combat and undoubtedly shortened the length of the conflict once hostilities commenced.[12] Nonetheless, the pressure of building and organizing the host-nation support effort was tremendous as combat units poured into Saudi Arabia at a pace that even Pagonis and his team found difficult to manage.

SADDAM PAUSES

The Iraqis' rapid seizure of Kuwait raised fears among regional states that it might be just the first step in a broader program of expansion. Those fears were heightened as the Republican Guard's logistical tail closed on al-Jahra west of Kuwait City, and units deployed along the Saudi border showed no sign of downloading their supplies and digging in to defend. American military intelligence analysts concluded that the Iraqi units in Kuwait and southeastern Iraq—soon dubbed the Kuwaiti theater of operations (KTO)—were capable of continuing the attack into Saudi Arabia. Moreover, within days of the Kuwaiti operation, the Iraqi 3d Corps, garrisoned in Basrah, moved its armored units into assembly areas along the Iraqi border. Their presence there suggested that they might form a second echelon should the Guard move into Saudi Arabia.

Sometime between August 3 and 15, Saddam paused to analyze the situation. At the time, American intelligence believed the Iraqi leader was surprised by the international reaction to the Kuwaiti operation and that he had three options. He could withdraw in the face of international pressure, perhaps under the terms of an Arab-engineered compromise. He could simply hunker down and attempt to deter the United States and its growing Coalition by establishing a "fortress Kuwait." Not only had his willingness to stand up to the West already won him great acclaim in the Arab world, but his control of Kuwait upset regional balance and constituted a constant danger to the Saudis. Or he could preempt the West by taking the Saudi oil fields and perhaps several thousand Westerners in Saudi Arabia.

An Iraqi push into Saudi Arabia would have been the most significant offensive operation ever undertaken by Saddam's military. His commanders offered two options: a full-scale offensive against the key cities of al-Jubayl, Dhahran, and perhaps Riyadh, or a limited attack on a local objective such as Hafar al-Batin or King Khalid Military City (KKMC), 80 kilometers inside Saudi Arabia. The full-scale offensive option, requiring some eight to nine heavy divisions, would have involved deep operations to destroy forward Arab forces, inflict heavy Coalition casualties, and secure northeastern Saudi Arabia. American analysts believed that once all of the Iraqi 3d Corps was deployed into the KTO, the Iraqis would be postured for such an offensive. If Saddam used the 3d Corps as the lead echelon, he could employ the Republican Guard as his follow-on force to secure Dhahran. Such an offensive might have threatened Riyadh and the stability of the Saudi monarchy. An operation of this magnitude, however, would have faced significant difficulties. The Iraqi military's deepest operation to date had been the Kuwaiti invasion, and already indications were surfacing that the Iraqi logistical system was feeling the strain. A deep operation into Saudi Arabia would have entailed an advance in excess of 300 kilometers, twice the distance covered in conquering Kuwait. In any case, preparations for such an offensive would have required a minimum of two days, allowing the allies at least 12 to 24 hours' warning.

The second option, a limited attack, was much more likely. With a requirement for only two or three heavy divisions, the Iraqis could mount an attack at almost any time with perhaps only six to eight hours' warning. A limited attack offered a particularly attractive goal: if successful, it might divide the Coalition's Arab forces and destroy their will to fight. Like a full-blown invasion, it would also threaten the stability of the Saudi regime, which had invited Western forces to protect the kingdom from just such an event. American commanders knew that the sooner Coalition forces arrived in theater, the less likely further Iraqi offensive actions would become.[13]

The rapid and unequivocal commitment of Coalition ground forces on August 8 probably caused Saddam to back away from escalation. On the diplomatic front, he opened negotiations with his old nemesis, Iran, generously offering to recognize the 1975 Iran-Iraq border, to withdraw Iraqi troops from Iranian territory, and to release Iranian prisoners of war. His offer was tantamount to a surrender of all gains made in the eight-year war with Tehran. Ominously, the deal also allowed him to withdraw his forces along the Iranian border and send them to Kuwait. Saddam also announced the recall of 14 reserve divisions deactivated since the end of that war. Meanwhile in Kuwait, Iraqi 3d Corps regular divisions began the relief of the Republican Guard along the border with Saudi Arabia. As the Guard units returned to preinvasion laager areas in southeastern Iraq, the first Iraqi regular infantry divisions deployed along the Saudi border to begin building Saddam's "fortress Kuwait."

In transitioning to the defense, Iraqi dispositions reflected Saddam's emerging strategy of deterrence. His forces soon established an echeloned defense of Kuwait and a strategic defense of Iraq, both designed to make an attacker pay dearly. By late September, the Iraqi defenses in the KTO had 22 divisions—13 light and 9 heavy. Fourteen were in the forward defenses. Ten infantry divisions defended the Saudi border and the coastline, backed by four heavy divisions immediately available as corps reserve. In addition, the Iraqis retained six Guard and two regular army divisions in the theater reserve, of which five were heavy divisions. Evidence of mobilization and training throughout Iraq suggested that more military forces would be dispatched to the KTO as soon as they were nominally ready.

Central to this defense was an increasingly elaborate obstacle system among the forward infantry divisions. The 16th Infantry Division was typical. Within 15 kilometers of the Saudi border astride a key line of communication, the division defended a frontage of almost 45 kilometers with two brigades forward and a third brigade 15 kilometers to the rear. Like most infantry divisions in Kuwait, the unit had an attached armor-heavy brigade. The armored brigade was split with a mechanized battalion forward on the division's western flank along the main road into Kuwait and the balance on the forward eastern flank wrapped around and behind the infantry. This key brigade thus anchored both flanks while providing a strong tactical counterattack force. Supporting forward was a formidable fire-support system consisting of six full battalions of artillery capable of ranging the entire division sector.

To further strengthen its defenses, the division established an integrated system of obstacles and fortifications that could be supported directly by fire and maneuver. Elaborate artillery fire plans supported by large ammunition stocks created multiple kill zones throughout the depth of the defense. Dug-in wire communications ensured that command and control would remain intact. A double line of earthen berms marked the forward line of defense. Forward armored units used the earthworks to screen movement and to provide cover from direct fire. Antitank ditches protected the flanks of these forward armored units and channeled the enemy into killing zones. Next was the main line of defense, a system of concertina wire and antitank ditches in front of the infantry. Forward infantry positions, laid out in the classic two-up/one-back pattern, covered the complex with direct fire. As more engineering equipment became available, the division would add fire trenches and minefields to this impressive defensive array.

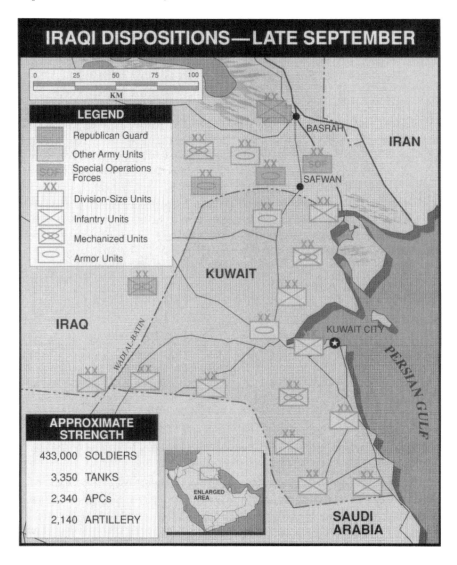

Behind these forward static defenses, the Iraqis maintained a heavy division in operational reserve as a counterattack or blocking force. Hunkered down far to the north, the Republican Guard and several regular heavy divisions waited to conduct a multidivision counterattack. Iraqi forces west of Kuwait, acting in an economy-of-force role, screened the theater's western flank far into the featureless desert.

As Fortress Kuwait took shape in aerial photographs, Army planners became increasingly convinced that Saddam had shifted to a strategy of defensive deterrence based on the threat of attrition warfare. Although such a strategy made an Iraqi offensive increasingly unlikely, it also suggested that Saddam would not evacuate Kuwait without a fight. Nevertheless, the threat of an Iraqi invasion of Saudi Arabia continued to haunt analysts and commanders well into October.

SPACE AGE IMPROVISATION AND BRUTE-FORCE LOGISTICS

On August 22, 1990, the first Army pre-positioned ship, the *USS Green Harbor*, completed its 2,700-mile trip from Diego Garcia to discharge its cargo at ad-Dammam. During the mid-eighties, the Army had stocked the *Green Harbor* and three similar vessels with enough tentage, food, ammunition, and water purification and refrigeration equipment to provide a logistical jump-start to any Gulf operation until seaborne transport arrived from the United States. After the *Green Harbor* arrived, the logistics race was well under way and the theater in Saudi Arabia continued to build at an extraordinary rate. As Pagonis continued to develop the initial support network for the theater, he also established the basic systems that would sustain the rapidly expanding theater for many months to come. By August 29, the 22d Support Command headquarters had 58 soldiers in country. More than 300 of the 7th Transportation Group's 400 soldiers and civilians were employed as long-haul truck drivers and stevedores who were fully occupied with off-loading supplies from the pre-positioned ships and receiving 18,215 troops and more than 2,000 vehicles through both airports and seaports of debarkation.

The limited time available and the CINC's stringent limitations on rear-area manpower forced Pagonis to create a logistics infrastructure to sustain forces in a distant theater by relying primarily on bases of supply in the United States. Pagonis would rely heavily on host-nation support to reduce the need for supplies and equipment from the States. Technology and the management skills of General Pagonis and his Support Command logisticians made the system work, but often just barely. Thanks to lessening tensions in Europe and other regions of the world, supplies, parts, and equipment were available. Commodity managers throughout the world were poised to provide practically anything CENTCOM needed on a moment's notice. The major breakdown in the system occurred in the communications link between the requesting forward unit in the theater and the requisite source of supply. The 22d Support Command improvised techniques to improve communications between the theater and the United States. Pagonis worked the system most effectively with his ever-present cellular telephone. His staff relied on a direct, single-channel tactical satellite linkage to Fort McPherson, Georgia.

Colonel Chuck Sutten's 11th Signal Brigade, ARCENT's organization responsible for communications support, was a sort of phone company for the developing theater. Like the Support Command, the Signal Brigade's ability to provide essential services was impeded substantially by severe restrictions imposed on the number of soldiers and the amount of signal equipment allowed into theater during the early days of the buildup. Sutten's problem was made particularly difficult because the CINC's deployment restrictions meant that other essential functions such as supply, maintenance, and administration remained split between major Stateside facilities and forward deployed detachments in theater. Just to survive in such an awkward environment required far more intertheater telephone hookups than any signal planner could ever have foreseen. Sutten initially had only two tactical satellite task forces consisting of 139 soldiers who operated mainly tactical satellite multichannel radios, a virtual godsend. The radios allowed Sutten to keep telephone communications open between ARCENT headquarters in Riyadh and the 22d Support Command at Dhahran Air Base, as well as to other more forward bases as they began to develop. As the theater expanded, the 11th Signal Brigade received more of their organic tactical communications equipment, and by September Sutten had established a continuous telephone network between ARCENT, 22d Support Command, and XVIII Airborne Corps. By the time the ground war started, Sutten had built the largest and most complex communications network ever installed in an active overseas theater. Until this system was mature, however, satellite communications filled the void and allowed Sutten to keep information flowing.[14]

The difficulties forward units faced in transmitting logistics requests electronically to other units inside Saudi Arabia exacerbated communications problems. Most of the Army's automated internal logistics reporting and supply-requisitioning procedures worked well in peacetime as long as units and supporting logisticians were linked by commercial telephone. However, the lack of telephone linkages was not the only problem in the KTO. Desert Shield occurred right in the midst of an enormously complex changeover within the Army to a more modern automated requisition system. Units not yet converted were still obliged to fill out punch cards manually and to deliver them by hand. Some units had computer terminals down to company level that permitted them to transmit requests electronically. These terminals queried and interacted with every level of supply within the theater in attempting to locate and fill a requisition. Yet occasional differences in equipment and software among fully automated units prevented even the best equipped from exchanging data. In one very serious case, the entire 1st COSCOM, XVIII Airborne Corps' main logistics unit, was in the process of converting to a more modern version of an automated supply system when alerted for deployment. 1st COSCOM and the 82d Airborne Division were on the new system while the rest of the corps had yet to convert. The 1st COSCOM managed to resolve the problem only by operating both systems throughout the campaign. [15]

Adaptability, innovation, and ingenuity worked to fill holes in the logistics system. When one logistics node broke contact with another, soldiers resorted to the so-called "sneaker net" in which soldiers transported floppy disks and computer tapes from one node to the next by any means available. The logisticians forced the system to work, and had well-stocked depots been present in theater, it might have worked as designed. But with depots nearly half a world away, just a few days' delay imposed by an occasional requirement to carry supply transactions over long distances by hand caused very serious interruptions in service.[16]

AMERICAN INDUSTRY RESPONDS

For the most part, the American industrial base was not well prepared to surge or begin accelerated production of many urgently required items at the onset of Desert Shield. Of greatest concern were critical "war stoppers" such as Hellfire and Patriot missiles. First fielded in 1983 as a counterair system, the Patriot missile represented an evolutionary leap forward. The heart—and brain—of the missile was its computer software, allowing it to serve in other roles by modifying its programming. With the proliferation of tactical ballistic missiles like Saddam Hussein's modified Scuds, engineers converted the Patriot to an antitactical missile system. They programmed it to look higher on the horizon for incoming missiles than it did for aircraft and to calculate the higher velocities achieved by such weapons. The resultant PAC-1 radar and software changes went to the field in 1988, followed by the PAC-2 warhead and fuse changes in 1990. When Desert Shield began, only three PAC-2 missiles were available, all three marked "experimental."

Patriot missile production in August 1990 was geared to deliver about 80 of the PAC-1 model each month. However, production of the PAC-2 version had barely started. On his own initiative, Colonel Bruce Garnett, the US Army project manager for the Patriot, began to explore acceleration of the PAC-2 program as early as August. He found a ready ally in General Sullivan, who intervened personally to step up the process.

Even if speeded up, the warhead assembly line in the United States would not be fully operational until the end of December. Fortunately, Raytheon Corporation was already producing the new warhead in Germany on contract with the Deutsch Aerospace division of Messerschmidtt-Boelkow-Blohm (MBB), a German industrial giant. Garnett knew that warheads were one of the most critical and time-consuming components of the missile to produce, but getting the warheads to the assembly line in Orlando, Florida, from Germany was not easy. With most military airlift committed to Desert Shield, Raytheon had to lease airplanes to fly them from Europe to Dover, Delaware, and then on to Camden, Arkansas, where the final explosive material was poured and X-rayed. Getting the warheads to Orlando for final assembly presented a similar dilemma, which Raytheon solved by contracting with air carriers who were certified to fly hazardous materials.

In Orlando, the Martin-Marietta Company completed the assembly and began to ship the missiles from Patrick Air Force Base near Cape Canaveral, Florida. This circuitous process would eventually increase the production rate of the new missile from 9 in August to 86 in September, 95 in October, and 117 in November and December when MBB began to produce the missile in Germany. By January 1991 Raytheon reached a peak of 146 missiles, effectively doubling their output to meet the Army's demand for 600 missiles before Desert Storm.[17]

While the contractors deserve great credit for their extraordinary efforts, which included producing on a 24-hour, three-shift-per-day, seven-day-a-week schedule, the collective effort involved hundreds of vendors, the transportation industry, and Garnett's office staff. Every weapons manufacturer responded to the Desert Storm crisis, with everyone competing for the same scarce resources.

Mr. Dick Slaughter, the senior engineer for missile production, along with the 185-person staff in the program manager's office, coordinated with the Army, other government offices, and Raytheon to meet this accelerated procurement schedule. Slaughter faced innumerable challenges. By November, for example, the ARC Company in Camden, Arkansas, which performed the warhead X-ray inspections, was inundated with Patriots and other types of warheads stacking up for inspection. Slaughter found an excess X-ray machine at the Lonestar Plant near Texarkana, Texas, which he was able to procure and send to Camden to break the logjam. When US production of the new warhead finally came on line in late December, obtaining warheads from Germany was no longer necessary. By then, MBB was building complete missiles in their plant in Trobenhausen and sending them directly to Saudi Arabia.

Slaughter credits the fact that the production line was at least lukewarm in August 1990 with meeting the eventual demand. According to him, six months earlier no amount of heroics could have gotten the PAC-2 in the hands of the soldiers on time.[18]

Though less important, desert uniforms provide another example of industry's response. Enough desert battle dress uniforms (DBDUs) were available in war reserve stocks to outfit an entire corps with two uniforms per soldier. In September, Yeosock directed that all soldiers be outfitted with four sets of DBDUs, exceeding the supply 10 times. In November the VII Corps deployment would add another 145,000 soldiers to the list. Only enough desert camouflage material existed in war reserve stocks to produce an additional 200,000 uniforms. While new material was manufactured, the Defense Personnel Support Center (DPSC) used existing stocks to begin production in their Philadelphia factory. Meanwhile, the Defense Logistics Agency negotiated contracts with Wrangler Jeans Company, American Apparel, and 13 other contractors throughout the United States. By February contractors were producing 300,000 DBDUs a month. Despite such laudable efforts, the industry simply could not catch up and most VII Corps soldiers would go into battle clad in dark green BDUs.

The problem of ration supply was another example of the difficulties inherent in supporting an active theater of war from a near-cold industrial start. In January 1991 the Army, the DOD executive agent for food and water, had to provide 39.2 million meals per month to feed 435,000 troops from all Services in theater. Additionally, the CINC directed the Army to keep a 60-day supply of rations—78.4 million meals above the daily requirement—as a contingency reserve. In August 1990 industry was providing 3.9 million rations per month to the Army and could, if necessary, surge to 45.1 million by January. With the requirement for the additional 60-day supply, the theater food service manager, Chief Warrant Officer Wesley Wolf, would not be able to achieve his 60-day reserve before May 1992. To fix the problem, DPSC simply went on a nationwide shopping expedition. Thanks to the microwave, commercial food preservation technology had come a long way in the decade preceding the war. Individually packaged food items such as "Lunch Bucket" and "Dinty Moore" were tasty, were already popular with younger soldiers, and could remain on the shelf for a relatively long period without spoiling. Commercial products, at least initially, added variety to mealtimes and were preferred by many to the MRE. Before the war ended, the Army purchased almost 24 million individual commercial meals and managed to get theater stockages up to the required 60 days by the end of January.[19]

BUILDUP CLOGS PORTS AND ROADS

Once the sea lines of communications were opened in late September, the seaborne materiel pipeline began dropping millions of repair parts, equipment, and other supplies on the docks of ad-Dammam and

Port operations at ad-Dammam, Saudi Arabia.

al-Jubayl. By September stevedores had discharged 17,540 tracked and wheeled vehicles, 450 aircraft, and 1,521 sea-land containers, each stuffed with ammunition, repair parts, or other supplies. Practically every loose item shipped to Saudi Arabia was packaged in commercial shipping containers. Unfortunately, the thin forward logistics structure in theater soon fell behind in its effort to track and account for the materiel and move it off the docks to soldiers in the desert. [20]

Faced with increased requirements and time pressures, shippers often provided only the minimum documentation that transportation regulations allowed. Consequently, the contents of most containers could not be accurately determined until they were unloaded. Because the personnel needed to document the receipt of materiel were not among the early arriving units, stacks of containers sat in ports unprocessed, their exact contents unknown. Locating a specific high-priority item that may have been in any one of several hundred containers became almost impossible. The problem was not one of availability—the success soldiers had in scrounging almost anything they needed attests to that—but simply one of asset visibility and in-theater distribution. The problem could only be fixed by opening each container, sorting out the contents, and repackaging them for shipment forward.[21] This process wasted both time and manpower. The problem with containers arriving by aircraft was mitigated somewhat since shipments were usually high-priority, critically needed items that could be tracked by aircraft tail number. Still, shipments by air got lost. At intermediate stops in Spain or Germany, Air

Containers were off-loaded at the Port of ad-Dammam, Saudi Arabia.

Force ground crews frequently unloaded containers with high-priority designations and replaced them with even higher-priority materiel.

Soldiers and leaders' individual initiative and determination to get the job done made the logistical system work. Often logisticians up and down the chain, from combat battalions through division to corps support commands, established direct-request networks with supply centers in the States rather than rely on "the system." While this often solved immediate problems for individual units, multiple requests for the same item created further confusion and delays. Space age scrounging by satellite became a common high-tech method for tracing missing items or for finding new sources for items in short supply. XVIII Airborne Corps used its own organic tactical satellite communication system to establish a callback network between the 1st COSCOM in an-Nuayriyah and supply points at Fort Bragg.

According to doctrine, at least two transportation networks should have been in Saudi Arabia, one to receive and transload ship and airborne materiel at the airports and seaports and another to move materiel by road to forward units. But neither the time nor the soldiers were available to build a traditional transportation structure. Therefore, Pagonis appointed another trusted subordinate, Colonel David Whaley, as his transportation tsar and gave him responsibility for establishing an efficient system to move materiel from port to deployed units. Whaley began humbly enough with contract buses and eventually expanded to a theaterwide transportation fleet of 3,500 vehicles moving across a road network of 2,746 miles.

Main supply routes, or MSRs, were the arteries of Whaley's system. Among the two major northern arteries, MSR Audi was a very good multi-lane road that ran from Dhahran along the coast to just north of al-Jubayl. Tapline Road, named MSR Dodge, ran generally northwest from MSR Audi to Hafar al-Batin and then onward through Rafha across the rest of Saudi Arabia. The two southern routes were MSR Toyota and MSR Nash. Toyota, an excellent multi-lane road, ran between Dhahran and Riyadh. Nash ran north from Riyadh to Hafar al-Batin, where it intersected with Dodge. Nash was a multi-lane road for about one-third its length where it narrowed to two lanes. Some of these roads were well surfaced and in good repair, but none could stand up to the high volume of heavy military traffic about to be inflicted on them. Distances were enormous from ports and airfields to forward logistics bases and combat units within the theater. Troops and materiel moving from Dhahran to the logistics base at King Khalid Military City had to travel 334 miles along the northern MSRs. Because roadways were relatively straight and generally flat, traffic could move quickly, and vehicle operators easily bypassed accidents and obstacles by driving on the shoulders. When large traffic jams occurred, the sight of heavily laden trucks striking out on the flanks

MSRs were constantly jammed, often with several convoys abreast.

to carve out five or six additional lanes of traffic in the open desert was not uncommon.

Whaley established a series of convoy support centers to increase road network efficiency. These centers resembled huge truck stops in the desert, and like all truck stops, operated 24 hours a day, providing fuel, latrines, food, sleeping tents, and limited vehicle repair facilities. The convoy support centers quickly became welcome oases for overworked and exhausted long-haul drivers.

While the MSR arteries allowed supplies to flow efficiently from port to major stockage areas, the capillaries of the system were practically nonexistent. Engineer construction units like the 212th cut roads off the MSRs. Most travel from corps and division depots forward was done off-road across rock-strewn or sandy desert terrain that destroyed precious tires at a frightfully high rate. Forward units were equipped with commercial utility cargo vehicles (CUCVs) and 2½-ton and 5-ton trucks with trailers, many of which were older than their drivers. With such relentless and rugged use, trucks continually broke down en route to forward areas. The only practical solution was to exchange older trucks for the newer heavy expanded mobility tactical truck (HEMTT). The HEMTT was a state-of-the-art cross-country vehicle designed by the Oshkosh Company of Wisconsin—a company long respected for producing rugged, reliable off-road machinery. While Abrams, Bradleys, and Apaches might capture the limelight during the war, the superbly reliable

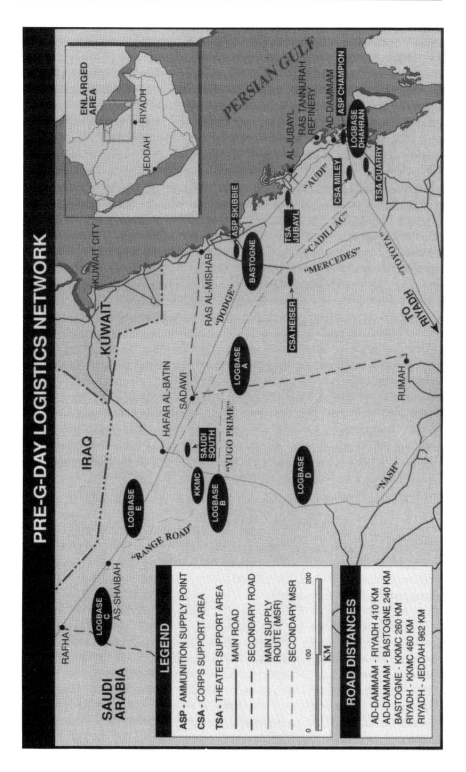

HEMTT would keep its more glamorous cousins in fuel, ammunition, and repair parts. To help HEMTT drivers get around in the desert, the corps and division support staffs scoured United States depots to find extra radios, global positioning systems, night vision goggles, and recovery vehicles to act as escorts for trucks traveling off-road. By February, forward units had replaced more than 400 older tactical trucks with 926 HEMTTs, and some units had turned in the less reliable CUCVs for high-mobility, multipurpose wheeled vehicles (HMMWVs).[22] Despite the millions of miles driven, military drivers compiled remarkable safety records in the desert and on such thoroughfares as Tapline Road, known as "suicide alley."

MODERNIZING ON THE RUN

General Vuono was determined to give the force the best possible combat edge. He focused his effort on fielding the M1A1 with its 120mm gun and on-board chemical defense systems to ensure an overmatch against the Iraqi T-72M1 tank. A secondary effort was to upgrade the Bradley to the A2 model, which included a Kevlar spall liner that significantly improved crew protection. Vuono called on US Army Europe to contribute 783 M1A1s from its war stocks to replace the older M1s of the XVIII Airborne Corps and, later, elements of VII Corps. In early estimates, the M1A1 nearly doubled the combat power of the M1s to meet the Iraqi armored threat. The concept of in-theater modernization was not received with unanimous enthusiasm. Both the ARSTAF and Schwarzkopf were concerned that tank crews might be called on to fight while transitioning to an unfamiliar tank. However, the transition to an improved Abrams was much simpler than the change from the M-60 Patton-series tank to the Abrams. The same held true for the upgraded Bradleys, which were functionally identical to the older "vanilla" Bradleys they replaced. Rather than work the issue through the maze of supporting to supported CINCs—the tanks and Bradleys in question would come from European war stocks—Vuono talked the tank modernization plan through with Schwarzkopf. Vuono carefully matched it to the campaign plan to guarantee that the effects of tank modernization on the readiness of the CINC's forces would be minimal. Schwarzkopf agreed to the plan and the program began. From November 6, 1990, through January 15, 1991, AMC successfully accomplished what came to be known as the M1A1 rollover program in the theater. AMC received the M1A1s from Europe, applied several upgrades, and returned them to fully operational standards for issue to units in theater. The rollover was made possible by 84 tons of tools and equipment shipped from Anniston Army Depot and by more than 300 civilians deployed from six different depots with augmentation from contractors. The tanks were handed off under the Total Package Fielding concept to the Abrams tank project manager and issued to deployed units in record time, allowing the units in theater time to train on the new tanks before the ground war started. Morale and confidence soared. Soldiers received these tanks and other new equipment with great enthusiasm and appreciation for the edge their Army was giving them.

Throughout Desert Shield and Desert Storm, AMC upgraded a total of 1,032 Abrams tanks. The most significant improvement ensured that nearly every armor battalion went into the ground war equipped with the far more powerful 120mm gun. AMC also applied reactive armor plates to the older Marine M60-series tanks in an effort to reduce their vulnerability. AMC issued the armored combat earthmover (ACE) vehicle and new mineplows to engineer units in combat divisions. To meet the CINC's demand for any means to haul tanks over great distances, AMC gathered 1,059 heavy-equipment transporters from war reserve stocks, nondeploying Active Army units, and training centers. Pagonis' staff contracted for an additional 333 through host-nation support. In an ironic epilogue to the end of the Cold War, AMC managed to locate and lease more than 270 HETs from former Warsaw Pact countries, including Czechoslovakia, the former East Germany, and Poland. Vehicles intended originally to carry Soviet tanks into combat against Americans would now transport American tanks into battle against Soviet-equipped Iraqis.[23] The German army also provided key support. When Saddam's chemical threat caught the Army short of adequate chemical defense equipment, the German army donated its excellent "Fuchs" armored chemical-detection vehicles. These vehicles would allow soldiers under mobile cover to sniff out and warn unprotected soldiers of a chemical attack.

SEEKING BALANCE IN LOGISTICS SUPPORT

Anticipated high casualties and the pervasive fear of Saddam's chemical weapons led planners to bring what would turn out to be too much medical infrastructure into the theater. By February, four hospitals with more than 13,530 beds and 24,000 medical soldiers comprised almost 5 percent of the total deployed force. Not only did medical facilities have very few patients during Desert Shield, but such a huge organization was not needed to handle combat casualties. Better-quality, better-disciplined soldiers tend to be in better shape, have fewer health problems, and take better care of themselves, even under such harsh climatic conditions. In one of the hottest climates on earth, not one soldier died of heat stroke, and the rate of heat injury was substantially less than in any Stateside Army post in the south.[24] Gastrointestinal diseases such as dysentery never became the factor they were in earlier wars, largely due to bottled water and the healthy—albeit unpopular—MRE. As a result, theater nonbattle hospital admission rates in Desert Shield were one-sixth those of World War II and about one-third those of Vietnam for similar periods of time. Nevertheless, the medical mobilization caused a significant reduction in support to military families in the United States and drained a number of trained medical specialists in American civilian hospitals as well. To fill the gap, the Surgeon General implemented a plan to backfill vacancies in United States civilian and military hospitals with selected Army Reserve medical professionals.[25] Fortunately, the medical system was not stressed fully during the war in large measure because Saddam chose not to employ weapons of mass destruction. Had such weapons been used, a greater proportion of the medical infrastructure in theater would have been necessary.

Having too much ammunition can be as much a vice as a virtue, particularly in a contingency operation where shipping space is always constrained. During Desert Shield, more than 350,000 tons of ammunition were shipped into theater. Faced with the prospect of the Army's first large-scale tank-on-tank fight since World War II, ARCENT planners turned in part to combat experience in that earlier conflict to estimate ammunition consumption rates. However, those rates did not take into account the enormously greater lethality of modern precision munitions with the result that daily expenditure rates were far less than anticipated. Unlike first battles in earlier wars, the superior fire discipline of combat soldiers and highly accurate weapons in Desert Storm greatly reduced the number of rounds fired in direct combat engagements. While available figures are inexact, estimates indicate that the Abrams main gun required less than 1.2 rounds for each enemy tank destroyed, contrasted with World War II tank engagements where each main gun averaged 17 rounds per kill.

Nevertheless, perceived shortages were alarming at the time. Armor-piercing 25mm ammunition for the M2 Bradley fighting vehicle caused particular concern. AMC conducted an intensive worldwide search for tungsten rounds and managed to locate and ship more than 3 million before the war began, representing almost 80 percent of the estimated requirement. When Desert Shield began, a newer, more lethal depleted uranium penetrator was in the process of replacing the older tungsten penetrator round. Tactical commanders went to great pains to ensure that Bradley crews would use the precious penetrator rounds only against armored targets. Yet a check of total expenditures after the war indicated that Bradley crews had used far fewer penetrator rounds than expected, averaging only six 25mm rounds for each Iraqi armored carrier destroyed. Superior firing discipline again made the difference. One 1st Armored Division company commander instructed his Bradley crews to engage light armor by firing a single ranging round and then to follow with no more than three rounds for killing effect. Later, during a night engagement, he recalled with great satisfaction being surrounded by the distinctive "crack, pause, crack-crack-crack" sound of his unseen Bradley crewmen firing exactly as they were told.

In spite of some unforeseen problems and occasional delays, the American Army had succeeded in establishing a logistics infrastructure capable of supporting half a million troops from all Services, the same number sustained in Vietnam at the peak of deployment. By November, just 90 days into the campaign, ships were unloaded smoothly and the trucking network extended the sinews of the coming war efficiently toward the tent cities and camps already sprouting in the desert. The logistics system strained to the breaking point to keep up, but bad as it was in November, Yeosock, Pagonis, and the Support Command had come a long way from that lonesome morning back in August. When the two generals stood alone on the sweltering tarmac at the Dhahran airport to greet the first paratroopers from the 82d Airborne, they had nothing more in hand than some Bedouin tents, a colorful caravan of Saudi buses, and a pocketful of unanswered questions.

DESERT DRAGON I

After arriving in Saudi Arabia, the three infantry battalions of the 82d Airborne's 2d Brigade formed the nucleus of Desert Dragon I. An Apache battalion, a Sheridan light tank company, a battalion of 105mm howitzers, and a platoon of MLRS supported the lightly armed paratroopers.[26] The brigade's first mission was to form an enclave to secure Dhahran air base and the port of ad-Dammam far enough outside the city to keep the port and air base beyond Iraqi artillery range. From inside this secure perimeter, American forces would gradually expand, first up the coastline and later into the interior. Although the 82d can deploy quickly, it is a very lean force that can only reasonably be expected to sustain itself and delay an enemy advance for 72 hours. General Scholes, the senior XVIII Airborne Corps officer on the ground with the lead elements, expected an attack by six heavy Iraqi divisions, some of them Republican Guard, preceded by commando air assaults and supported by air and missile strikes with chemical weapons. He had a limited armor capability in the division's Sheridan armored reconnaissance vehicle—a very light "tank" in the mind of its most ardent supporters, the crews of the 3-73d Armor. Although its main armament, the Shillelagh missile, was an effective tank killer out to 3,000 meters, the Sheridan is not designed to fight head-to-head against tanks. Like the M113 troop carrier, the Sheridan is an aluminum vehicle, vulnerable to heavy machine-gun fire and a certain kill for even the most obsolete Iraqi tank. To thicken the antiarmor defenses, Scholes would rely on TOW missiles. The brigade's TOW antitank missile systems also outranged Iraqi armor by more than 2,000 meters, and both Sheridans and TOWs had full night capability.

The conditions necessary for dismounted "light" soldiers to defend against mobile armored formations have not changed appreciably since

M551 Sheridan light tanks of 3-73d Armor, 82d Airborne Division, flown into Dhahran in early August, provided the only armored fighting vehicle for first-arriving American forces.

82d Airborne troopers, mounted in TOW-equipped HMMWVs, occupied deploying positions along coastal sabkhas.

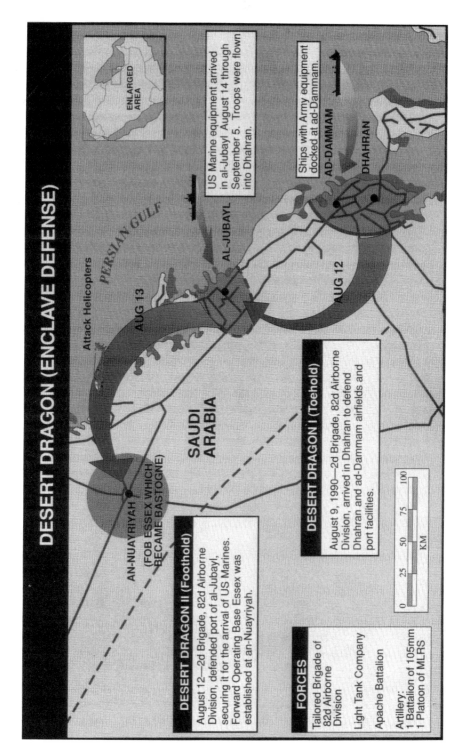

DESERT DRAGON (ENCLAVE DEFENSE)

ENLARGED AREA

PERSIAN GULF

Attack Helicopters

US Marine equipment arrived in al-Jubayl August 14 through September 5. Troops were flown into Dhahran.

Ships with Army equipment docked at ad-Dammam.

AL-JUBAYL

AUG 13

AD-DAMMAM

DHAHRAN

AUG 12

AN-NUAYRIYAH
(FOB ESSEX WHICH BECAME BASTOGNE)

SAUDI ARABIA

DESERT DRAGON II (Foothold)

August 12—2d Brigade, 82d Airborne Division, defended port of al-Jubayl, securing it for the arrival of US Marines. Forward Operating Base Essex was established at an-Nuayriyah.

DESERT DRAGON I (Toehold)

August 9, 1990—2d Brigade, 82d Airborne Division, arrived in Dhahran to defend Dhahran and ad-Dammam airfields and port facilities.

0	25	50	75	100

KM

FORCES

Tailored Brigade of 82d Airborne Division

Light Tank Company

Apache Battalion

Artillery:
1 Battalion of 105mm
1 Platoon of MLRS

the Hundred Years War. Whether longbowmen of Henry V at Agincourt or the paratroopers of the 101st at Bastogne, the light infantry defender must accomplish three essential tasks to withstand an armored attack. First, he must break the charge of the heavier force. Henry V took advantage of a plowed hillside knee-deep in mud. The 82d sought to engage the Iraqis at points along the coast road closely bordered by sabkhas, or coastal salt flats, which could easily be traversed by the 82d's light vehicles but would bog down much heavier Iraqi tanks. Second, the light force must be able to engage at long range before the heavy force can use its superior weight to slam into and bowl over the defender. Henry V's technological edge rested with the longbow and cloth yard arrow, which could dismount an armored knight at 300 yards. The 82d planned to cover the sabkhas at ten times that distance with the concentrated fires of TOWs, Sheridans, and artillery, and at a hundred times that distance with attack helicopters and Air Force close air support. Third, the light force must develop enough confidence in their weapons and leaders that they will not be intimidated by the psychological shock of advancing armor. Henry V had his yeomen; General Luck had paratroopers who had spent nearly two decades concentrating principally on the task of equipping and training to defend against a mechanized enemy.

In accordance with doctrine, the 82d fights jointly. By the end of August, the United States Air Force had in place a substantial force of more than 200 ground attack aircraft, including the A-10.[27] The corps air liaison officer, Lieutenant Colonel Terry Buettner, planned to direct close air support using rectangular "kill boxes" drawn around the existing Saudi air defense and control grid. Once cleared by the Saudi forces, an open kill box would permit unhindered air attack without further control from the ground.[28]

Although the tactical situation was tenuous in the extreme, the forces of Desert Dragon I had already accomplished two critical missions. First, the line drawn in the sand by the paratroopers deterred an Iraqi incursion into Saudi Arabia. Although Saddam and his military council must have known that the paratroopers could not defeat a sustained effort to take Dhahran, they also knew that the force blocking their path was no mere speed bump. With open terrain and clear weather, American air superiority would have badly mauled any armored force, particularly if it were tied to the main coastal road. More important was what the thin line of paratroopers represented. Should he harm them, Saddam would find himself embroiled in a larger war against forces en route, a war he had no hope of winning. Second, the presence of the paratroopers eased the panic and mass exodus that ensued after the invasion. Soon after Kuwait fell, rumors spread among Saudis, foreign workers, and American civilians alike that the Iraqis were headed south, intent on treating them as horribly as they had treated the Kuwaitis. Civilians fled from the Iraqis in panic, jamming the roads. Cities and refineries emptied as frightened citizens and foreigners sought refuge.[29] Most serious, however, was the potential damage to the Saudi defenses. Virtually all of the country's air defenses and maintenance operations for its high-tech F-15 and Tornado fighters were in the hands of foreign technicians. If the technicians fled, Saudi Arabian skies would be open to Saddam's air force. Already, families of Saudi air force officers had fled to the west coast, fearing Iraqi chemical air strikes. After the Americans arrived, confidence returned, panic abated, and the oil market stabilized.

DESERT DRAGON II

On August 12 Desert Dragon II expanded the defensive enclave to accommodate the arrival of an additional brigade. The 4-325th Airborne Infantry moved north 110 miles to occupy the port of al-Jubayl in order to protect the arrival of the 7th Marine Expeditionary Brigade, which began to download its equipment at Dhahran on August 14. Additional forces allowed General Scholes to create a forward operating base at an-Nuayriyah, which he named FOB Essex. Five roads converged on Essex, including the main coast road. If held long enough, FOB Essex would back Iraqi armored columns well into Kuwait. Moreover, the move to Essex allowed attack helicopters to engage the enemy earlier and provided additional space and time for maneuver. On the negative side, the exposed position of Essex astride Tapline Road risked bypass and encirclement. Even if Essex or al-Jubayl were surrounded, the 82d would retain absolute air and sea control and could use either medium to evacuate the bases if necessary.

Ten days into the deployment, 4,185 troops of the 82d were on the ground. With 15 Apaches and 23 other helicopters, the division was able to establish a strong defensive screen on the northern approaches. It also had on the ground 19 of 51 M551 Sheridans, 56 of 180 TOW systems, 20 Stinger teams, 3 Vulcans, 20 105mm howitzers, and 3 MLRS launchers with 10 missile pods.[30] Its August 24 situation report declared that ARCENT had a "potent combat force" with almost a full airborne division and two battalions of attack helicopters, and it concluded: "As of today, we are confident in our ability to detect and punish a major armored attack."[31] Even with that optimistic note and in spite of large numbers of combat aircraft arriving in the theater daily, available bombs and other aerial munitions were inadequate to exploit the air power. The airlift had put enough combat power on the ground in Saudi Arabia to make the Iraqis hesitate at the line in the sand, but if they had attacked, the expected air power advantage would have been seriously diminished by the lack of antitank munitions. Fortunately, fast sealift ships were about to arrive, carrying with them the heavy forces necessary to build a credible defense.

When asked in postwar testimony before the House Armed Services Committee whether he could have stopped an immediate invasion by Saddam, General Schwarzkopf replied, "I think we would have had to rely on tactical fighter squadrons to interdict his supply lines as he came across. It would not have been easy. I think we would have found ourselves in an enclave type of defense, the very toughest thing.... But I think we could have stopped him." [32]

THE 24TH INFANTRY DIVISION (MECH) DEPLOYS

At the same time that the 82d received its order to load out on August 6, FORSCOM instructed the 24th Infantry Division to move one armored brigade to the port at Savannah within 18 hours. The threat was so severe that General Luck likewise ordered the division to be prepared to fight immediately on arrival at Dhahran.[33] For almost a decade, the Southwest Asia mission had formed a centerpiece for planning and training within the 24th. Whether the regional enemy would be Soviet, Iranian, or Iraqi did not particularly matter; all threatening regional states possessed a respectable array of heavy armor. The "Victory" Division would perform the classic mission of linkup with an airhead that airborne forces had previously established. The airborne troops would seize a preemptory lodgement and hold it against a superior enemy until the heavy armor of the 24th arrived to make the lodgement secure. In an era of global strategic warfare, however, the 24th would be expected to reinforce from more than 8,000 miles of ocean rather than from a 100-mile stretch of European highway. Luck was convinced that the period of greatest danger in the campaign would end with the closure of the 24th into Dhahran. The challenge, therefore, was to get the division loaded and across the ocean before Saddam reached the vulnerable airhead. The division's sense of urgency was palpable. Just as the first of the 82d's aircraft took off for Saudi Arabia, the vehicles of the 2d Brigade of the 24th arrived fully stocked with fuel and ammunition ready to load aboard Navy fast sealift ships.[34]

The sealift of the 24th proceeded rapidly, with the first of 10 ships departing on August 13. But the load-out was not without problems. Essentially, the 24th had the same difficulty with ships that the 82d had with aircraft. Because of difficulties activating reserve shipping, planners were unable at any one time to predict which ships would be available to load. Ships closed on the port between August 11 and 19. On August 12, without knowing specific ships or arrival times, the 2d Brigade moved by rail and highway to Savannah, 40 miles away. On that day, the first fast sealift ship, the *Capella*, began loading. The Navy was troubled by the Army's insistence on combat-loading its vehicles with ammunition and fuel. Not since World War II had they outloaded a heavy Army division

24th Infantry Division vehicles were loaded aboard fast sealift ships at Savannah, Georgia.

configured for immediate combat. Despite the Navy's objection, the Defense Department waived its peacetime prohibition on combat loading. The division placed 100 additional chemical, medical, fire support, and communications specialists aboard each ship. The air defenders placed Vulcan antiaircraft guns and Stinger missiles on the decks of every ship to protect the ships from a preemptive Iraqi aerial attack during the vulnerable unloading operations at ad-Dammam.

The requirement to close on the airhead as quickly as possible convinced the Navy to dispatch one of the fast sealift ships, the *Antares*, before scheduled boiler repairs were completed. It was a calculated risk and, carrying elements of both the 24th Division's aviation brigade and division support command, the *Antares* broke down and drifted disabled for two days in the mid-Atlantic. Brigadier General Joe Frazar, the assistant division commander for support of the 24th, headed a 50-soldier detail sent back from Saudi Arabia to Rota, Spain, to assist in transloading the equipment to another ship, the *Altair*, which finally arrived in Saudi Arabia on September 23. For three weeks the division was obliged to defend without benefit of its maintenance and supply system and without the protection of its own organic aviation brigade. Gradually, the 24th's tail caught up with its teeth. Eventually the 24th Division deployed 1,600 armored and 3,500 wheeled vehicles and 90 helicopters on 10 ships. Most of the division's soldiers flew on 57 military and chartered civilian aircraft. Thirty-one days into the operation, two heavy brigades were in field assembly areas en route to their defensive sectors.[35] The division's third brigade, the 197th Infantry (Mech) from Fort Benning, Georgia, was also inbound and would complete the move into the desert on September 14.

THE 101ST AIRBORNE DIVISION
(AIR ASSAULT) DEPLOYS

Helicopters were essential to the combat power necessary to sustain airborne forces in the Dammam-Jubayl airhead. To strengthen the aerial covering force, Luck ordered Major General Peay, commander of the 101st Airborne Division (Air Assault), to send his aviation brigade and 2d Brigade by Air Force C-5 and C-141 aircraft beginning on August 17.[36] During the next 13 days, in one of the largest global combat deployments by air, the 101st filled 56 C-141s and 49 C-5s to move 117 helicopters, 487 vehicles, 123 equipment pallets, and 2,742 troops to the theater. The equipment from the other two brigades of the 101st went by sea from Jacksonville, Florida. Problems with shipping continued to plague the operation. The 101st had to load aboard old ready-reserve fleet ships that had been pulled hastily out of fleet storage and rushed to Jacksonville. The 10 ships dedicated to the division were in poor repair and required an average of 23 days to make the voyage to ad-Dammam.[37] Ironically, some

Lieutenant General Gary Luck, commander, XVIII Airborne Corps, and Major General J. H. Binford Peay III, commander, 101st Airborne Division, just before Desert Storm began, February 1991.

More than 350,000 tons of ammunition were delivered to Southwest Asia. Highly lethal MLRS rockets, shown here, reduced the tonnages necessary to support a campaign.

of these ships were the same ones that had taken the division to Vietnam. Fear of an imminent Iraqi attack against the airhead led the 101st, like the 24th, to deploy its initial brigade with its full basic load of ammunition. The 24th and the 82d had depleted the corps' ammunition reserve to such an extent that the last two brigades of the 101st arrived in theater without adequate stocks of Dragon, TOW, Hellfire, and Stinger missiles and other critical ammunition.

Even with the 101st en route, Luck did not have enough combat helicopters to screen the vast expanses of desert between his vulnerable airhead and the Iraqis. The 2-229th Attack Helicopter Battalion from Fort Rucker, Alabama, and the 12th Aviation Brigade from Wiesbaden, Germany, both equipped with Apaches, were soon deployed. Collectively, Luck would be able to put into the air more than 1,000 helicopters to cover a sector 215 by 130 miles, an area roughly the size of South Carolina.

DESERT DRAGON III

The door on Saddam's offensive option closed a little more on August 27 when the first fast sealift ship carrying armor from the 24th Infantry docked at ad-Dammam. Instead of only air power and long-range defensive fires, the Coalition now had the tanks and Bradleys of the 24th, enabling them to maneuver against the Iraqi armored formations on better terms. The presence of an armored force also freed attack helicopters to range farther north in order to begin killing the enemy earlier.

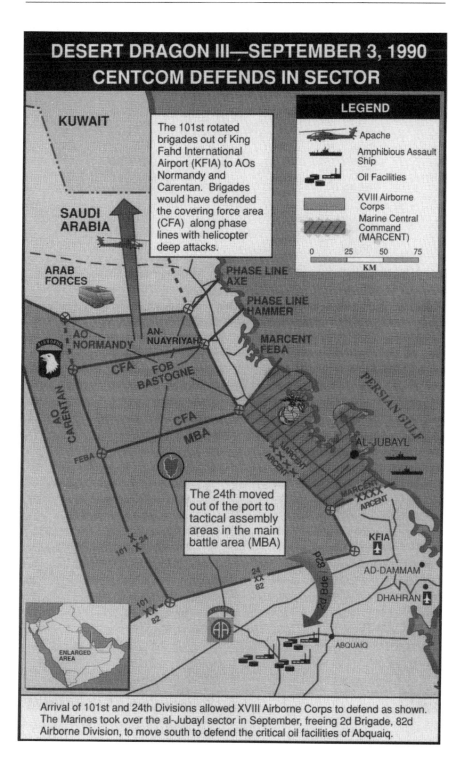

DESERT DRAGON III—SEPTEMBER 3, 1990
CENTCOM DEFENDS IN SECTOR

KUWAIT

The 101st rotated brigades out of King Fahd International Airport (KFIA) to AOs Normandy and Carentan. Brigades would have defended the covering force area (CFA) along phase lines with helicopter deep attacks.

SAUDI ARABIA

LEGEND

Apache

Amphibious Assault Ship

Oil Facilities

XVIII Airborne Corps

Marine Central Command (MARCENT)

0   25   50   75
KM

ARAB FORCES

PHASE LINE AXE

PHASE LINE HAMMER

AO NORMANDY

AN-NUAYRIYAH

MARCENT FEBA

CFA

FOB BASTOGNE

AO CARENTAN

CFA

MBA

FEBA

PERSIAN GULF

AL-JUBAYL

XXXX MARCENT ARCENT

XXXX MARCENT ARCENT

The 24th moved out of the port to tactical assembly areas in the main battle area (MBA)

KFIA

X 101 X 24

24 XX 82

101 XX 82

2d Bde 82d

AD-DAMMAM

DHAHRAN

ABQUAIQ

ENLARGED AREA

Arrival of 101st and 24th Divisions allowed XVIII Airborne Corps to defend as shown. The Marines took over the al-Jubayl sector in September, freeing 2d Brigade, 82d Airborne Division, to move south to defend the critical oil facilities of Abquaiq.

On September 1 the corps ordered the 101st Airborne Division to relieve the 82d at FOB Essex. Besides serving as an important forward attack helicopter base, Essex had become the key site for the corps' signal intelligence systems. Eventually it would grow into a major logistical base. Soldiers of the 101st noted an interesting comparison between the position of Essex in Saudi Arabia and the Belgium city of Bastogne during the Battle of the Bulge. Both sat astride five key intersecting roads leading to the heart of the allied defenses. The analogy was too striking to ignore. When the 101st took over Essex, they renamed it FOB Bastogne.

Desert Dragon III called for the 101st to establish AO Normandy north of FOB Bastogne to allow five battalions of Cobras and Apaches to operate at will. In the battle zone or covering force area, the 101st could mass fires from 93 attack helicopters, 180 TOW antitank systems, 10 artillery battalions, and Air Force close air support to delay, disrupt, and wear down the Iraqi armor. The plan called for the division's long-range aerial killers to

Major General James Johnson discussed artillery fire planning for Desert Dragon III, October 1990.

blind the enemy by knocking out his lightly armored reconnaissance vehicles and then stripping away equally thin-skinned air defense and artillery vehicles on the road. Should the enemy persist in its advance, the 101st would continue to engage at maximum range, withdraw slowly to preserve most of its force, and eventually hand off the battle to the 24th.

As the enemy reached the main battle area, the 24th would destroy it. Massed fires on engagement areas and counterattacks by Abrams tanks would halt and contain the enemy penetration and set up conditions for further corps counterattacks. Subsequent attacks by armor and Bradleys supported by close air and attack helicopters would break up the enemy's following divisions. The 82d would defend the critical facilities of Dhahran, ad-Dammam, and Abquaiq and eliminate commando raids on rear areas.

COALITION OPERATIONS

Although Army forces provided the vast preponderance of combat power for the Desert Dragon plans, the Iraqi threat was so great that General Luck needed every available ounce of combat power he could conjure. A provisional Arab mechanized division, designated the Eastern Area Command under Saudi Major General Saleh Bin Ali Almohayya, was positioned closest to the border and would be the first to fight. This force was well-equipped with 267 M60A3 and AMX-10 tanks,

Camp Eagle II, base camp for 101st Airborne Division (Air Assault). Tents were provided by the Saudi government and erected by members of the 101st near King Fahd International Airport in November 1990.

accompanied by 800 fighting vehicles and 140 pieces of artillery. The problems Scholes, and later Luck, faced in integrating the Arabs into the XVIII Airborne Corps scheme of defense were essentially cultural and organizational. Neither the Saudis nor the Americans had any formal cooperative agreements for combined warfare, nor had they much experience working together during exercises. The Saudis had great potential, however, because they were absolutely committed to defending their homeland and were willing to accept the advice of their more experienced partners on the battlefield. Many of their officers spoke English and had been trained in the US and other Western military schools. On the other hand, the Saudis had never operated formations larger than a battalion and had no provisions for a division headquarters. Nor had they much experience with integrating the wealth of artillery, helicopter, and fighter-bomber firepower the Americans were about to provide to them. Scholes began the Army's frontline relationship with the Saudis by assigning a trusted agent, Major John Turner, as liaison officer to General Saleh.

The Saudi fighting concept called for a static position defense. The American officers began to persuade and train them to execute a mobile covering force battle in which they would engage the Iraqis at long range and fall back behind American forces before becoming decisively engaged. A mobile defense is very difficult to execute even by an experienced force, and language and cultural differences, not to mention the Coalition's radically dissimilar equipment that could easily be mistaken for Iraqi, heightened problems significantly. To lessen these difficulties, in September CENTCOM formed the Joint Liaison Organization headed by corps plans officer Colonel John Marcello. The JLO's charter was to devise methods for recognizing forces and for controlling fires among this increasingly polyglot assortment of armies and nationalities. The JLO was the first to standardize the use of orange recognition panels on the rear decks of armored vehicles to assist in spotting Coalition forces from the air.

Aircraft recognition presented a similar challenge. By September more than 1,000 helicopters crowded into a coastal enclave that had rarely seen more than a few dozen. These aircraft included French Gazelle and Puma helicopters identical to the French-supplied Iraqi versions of the same aircraft. Scholes dispatched another liaison team to the Saudi air base at Dhahran, which controlled all airspace in the eastern provinces. The Eastern Sector Control Center was a state-of-the-art facility equipped with air traffic control radars, computers, and a down-link station for the Airborne Warning and Control System (AWACS). Working with the Saudis, Major Robert Brown developed low-level flight routes and procedures. The Saudis returned the favor by turning over a large network of unused desert landing strips, controlled by ARAMCO, for use by Army

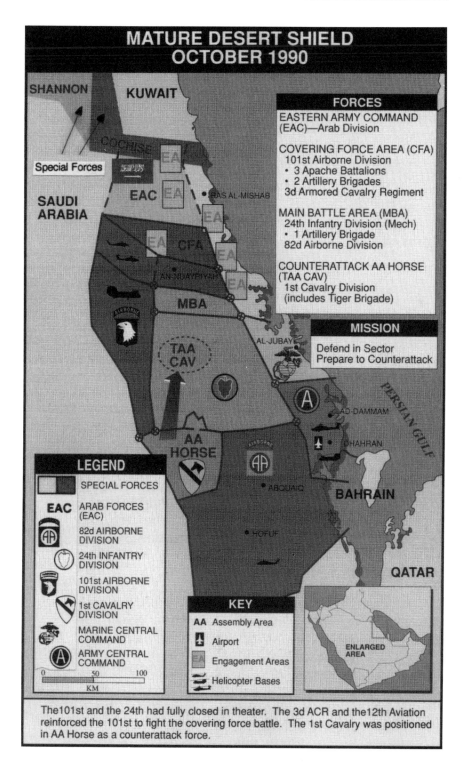

MATURE DESERT SHIELD
OCTOBER 1990

SHANNON

KUWAIT

COCHISE

Special Forces

SAUDI
ARABIA

EAC

EA

RAS AL-MISHAB

EA

CFA

EA

AN-NUAYRIYAH

EA

MBA

AL-JUBAYL

TAA
CAV

AA
HORSE

AD-DAMMAM

DHAHRAN

PERSIAN GULF

ABQAIQ

BAHRAIN

HOFUF

QATAR

FORCES

EASTERN ARMY COMMAND
(EAC)—Arab Division

COVERING FORCE AREA (CFA)
101st Airborne Division
• 3 Apache Battalions
• 2 Artillery Brigades
3d Armored Cavalry Regiment

MAIN BATTLE AREA (MBA)
24th Infantry Division (Mech)
• 1 Artillery Brigade
82d Airborne Division

COUNTERATTACK AA HORSE
(TAA CAV)
1st Cavalry Division
(includes Tiger Brigade)

MISSION

Defend in Sector
Prepare to Counterattack

LEGEND

	SPECIAL FORCES
EAC	ARAB FORCES (EAC)
	82d AIRBORNE DIVISION
	24th INFANTRY DIVISION
	101st AIRBORNE DIVISION
	1st CAVALRY DIVISION
	MARINE CENTRAL COMMAND
Ⓐ	ARMY CENTRAL COMMAND

0   50   100
KM

KEY

AA	Assembly Area
	Airport
EA	Engagement Areas
	Helicopter Bases

ENLARGED
AREA

The101st and the 24th had fully closed in theater. The 3d ACR and the12th Aviation reinforced the 101st to fight the covering force battle. The 1st Cavalry was positioned in AA Horse as a counterattack force.

helicopter units. As new Services or allies arrived, they joined the system by sending liaison representatives to the Eastern Sector Control Center.

Once the Marines established their own enclave at al-Jubayl, Schwarzkopf charged XVIII Airborne Corps with securing their left flank. Luck regarded his boundary with the Marines as critical since it paralleled the key coastal highways. The combination of a high-speed avenue of approach with a boundary between two Services made this region the most vulnerable point in CENTCOM's defenses. A skillful enemy would most certainly choose to attack along a boundary because fire support, surveillance, and movement are always much more difficult to execute near the confluence of two dissimilar units. In fact, during INTERNAL LOOK, "enemy" controllers chose to attack along precisely the same boundary and, on paper at least, nearly reached al-Jubayl before being stopped.

Luck was also concerned about essential differences in doctrine between the two forward forces. The Marines preferred to keep ground forces farther back and nearer to the coasts than Army forces and to control the vacated ground using fires from their Harrier ground support aircraft and naval gunfire. The Marines did not have the armored staying power necessary to fight well forward. They had only 123 tanks—all older M60s—that were overmatched by the Iraqi T-72s. With only two other battalions of extremely thin-skinned and vulnerable light-armor vehicles, the Marines were capable of limited maneuvering against the Iraqis outside their narrow coastal enclave. Luck insisted on keeping as much ground force forward as possible, so he assigned Colonel Doug Starr's 3d Armored Cavalry Regiment to bolster the covering force. The regiment had just recently arrived from Fort Bliss, Texas, and was equipped with 123 of the latest 120mm version of the Abrams tank. To bolster the coastal forces, Schwarzkopf attached the British 7th Armoured Brigade to the Marines, and for Desert Storm he replaced the British "Desert Rats" with the Army's "Tiger" Brigade, also equipped with the latest Abrams tanks.

The XVIII Airborne Corps gained the combat power necessary to take the battle to the Iraqis with the arrival of Brigadier General John Tilelli's 1st Cavalry Division from Fort Hood, Texas. The "Cav" would be the last major maneuver unit to join Desert Shield before the arrival of VII Corps from Germany in January 1991. Luck placed the 1st Cav in Tactical Assembly Area Horse located in the southwestern portion of his area of operation, 150 kilometers from the proposed site of the covering force battles. It would be the corps' counterattack force, the key "defeat mechanism" to destroy the Republican Guard in a massive armored clash once the Guard became stalled in front of the 24th.

DESERT SHIELD COMBAT POWER XVIII AIRBORNE CORPS SUMMARY, NOVEMBER 5 (C+90)	
• Tanks	763
• Artillery	
-Howitzers	444
-MLRS	63
-ATACMS Launchers	18
• Armored Fighting Vehicles	1,494
• Air Defense	
-Patriot Launchers	24
-Hawk Launchers	24
-Vulcans	117
-Stinger Teams	320
• Attack Helicopters	227
• Support Helicopters	741
• Infantry Battalions	18
• TOW Vehicles	368

Just three months after its call-out order on a thundering night in August, the corps had in place almost 800 tanks, 525 artillery pieces, and 227 attack helicopters, manned, maintained, and supported by 107,300 soldiers. Most of this force had reached the theater aboard 600 C-141s, 375 C-5s, and 300 commercial aircraft. [38]

THE SUPPORT STRUCTURE MATURES

As equipment began to pour off the docks in ad-Dammam, the enormous tent that housed the logistics operations center began to fill with logistical support agencies to keep up with the constant demand for service. One such operation was AMC's United States Army Support Group (USASG). To project the wholesale logistics system into the theater, the USASG was established almost exclusively with civilian volunteers from Depot Systems Command. Another was AMC-Southwest Asia, which included the logistics assistance representatives (LARs)—civilians who served directly in the field with troop units, providing technical advice and a means of contact with AMC.

The USASG officially began operations at Dhahran on November 17, 1990, but had civilians on the ground conducting special maintenance missions as early as August. Its purpose was to reduce the amount of materiel in the supply pipeline, shorten the time required to move it, and manage the movement of defective items back to the United States.[39] It was also charged with providing the highest level of maintenance practical in the forward areas. The goal was an in-theater return rate of 70 percent, which would reduce the turnaround time for repair and minimize the evacuation of critical materiel from the theater to repair facilities in the United States. The support group's primary maintenance mission was "component repair." The thrust was to provide a flexible, rapid turnaround capability to enhance readiness, ease pressures on the supply pipeline, and cover the entire spectrum of combat and tactical vehicles, ground support and troop support equipment, weapons systems, and missile electronic and communications equipment. [40]

Defense pundits, long critical of the Army's overreliance on high-tech weaponry and equipment, predicted that long supply lines and the brutal desert climate would impede the Army's ability to keep an effective force in the field. Yet Herculean efforts by maintenance logisticians, including the USASG and LARs, achieved readiness rates unprecedented in Desert Shield or any other modern military campaign. Fleet readiness averages for the M1A1 tank, the Bradley, and the HMMWV exceeded 90 percent. The most complex war machine the Army had ever fielded, the Apache helicopter, maintained an 86 percent readiness rate in spite of the fact that soldiers maintained most of their aircraft in the open desert without benefit of hangars or machine shops.[41]

While the forces in theater continued their preparations and training, the whole of United States Army Europe transitioned to a new and unprecedented mission, a REFORGER in reverse. This transition was not accomplished in a vacuum. Units in Germany had followed the buildup during Desert Shield with considerable interest and effort. No one knew precisely which units would be tapped to reinforce those in Southwest Asia, but everyone clearly recognized that German-based combat units were candidates to strengthen the shield.

Early in August, United States Army Europe ordered the 421st Medical Evacuation Battalion to fly 12 UH-60 helicopters from their base in Wiesbaden, Germany, to Dhahran. Simultaneously, units from the 11th and 12th Aviation Brigades were alerted for deployment. Staffs in these units began intensive planning to deploy by any means necessary, including flying the distance with their own twin-engine aircraft. The V Corps' entire 12th Aviation Brigade deployed to ports in Livorno, Italy, for upload on ships. The brigade reinforced XVIII Airborne Corps with two attack helicopter battalions, a command aviation battalion, and a task force of 16 CH-47D Chinooks and 12 UH-60 Blackhawks.

CENTCOM was particularly keen to receive the additional medical helicopters. Should the Iraqis attack XVIII Airborne Corps with chemical weapons, ARCENT expected high casualties, and the ability to move them to hospital ships or to other evacuation points as quickly as possible was critical. The 421st began its long transit from Germany on August 22 with a flight of six MEDEVAC Blackhawks. Helicopters from an 11th Aviation Brigade special detachment based on Cyprus met them in Italy and escorted them across the Mediterranean. At the end of August, six more helicopters completed the transit and proceeded to Saudi Arabia.

By the time the President dispatched VII Corps from Germany to reinforce XVIII Corps already in Saudi Arabia, the logistics infrastructure was already firmly in place. Problems would arise, of course, particularly once VII Corps ships began to close on Saudi ports at the end of the year. But by then a complete, if somewhat fragile, supply, communications, and transportation network awaited the inevitable stresses and strains that further theater expansion would bring.

NEW LOGISTICS CONCEPT EMERGES

From the experience of Desert Shield and later Desert Storm, a new method emerged for projecting and sustaining a large military force far from home. The concept was forced out of the traditional logistical structure by the imperative to move forces at unprecedented speed with the narrowest margin of tail to tooth. The new concept demanded a constriction of logistics bureaucracies in favor of functional building blocks assembled and transported to the theater to provide just enough support and management oversight to get the job done—and no more. The combination of rapid movement and thin overhead could only have been possible because of the efforts of quality soldiers who harnessed modern data processing, rapid transcontinental mobility, and global communications to meet constantly changing demands.

Any system created ad hoc in the crucible of battle will be imperfect. At times, only the initiative and flexibility of leaders at all levels kept the engine driving Desert Shield from running out of gas. Perfection is not the standard, and obvious imperfections diminish neither the remarkable managerial skill of those who modified the system to make it work nor the value of the system as a model for how a future contingency force should be projected and sustained.

Notes

1. 22d Support Command After-Action Report, December 31, 1991, Vol I, Tab B, p. 1-1.

2. Lieutenant Colonel C. Lane Toomey, XVIII Airborne Corps G3 Plans, April 15, 1992.

3. CINCFOR message dated 070246Z August 1990, "Deployment, Southwest Asia."

4. HQ XVIII Airborne Corps 82d N+2 briefing slides, "OPLAN 14-90," August 6, 1990.

5. Interview with General (Retired) Carl E. Vuono, June 1, 1992.

6. ODCSLOG Operation Desert Storm Sustainment Brochure (Washington, DC: December 1991), pp. 19-20.

7. Lieutenant General John J. Yeosock, "H+100 An Army Comes of Age in the Persian Gulf," *AUSA Green Book* (Glendale, MD: Holliday, Tyler Corporation, October 1991), pp. 44-58.

8. Frank N. Schubert and Theresa L. Kraus, eds., *The Whirlwind War: The United States Army in Operations Desert Shield and Desert Storm* (Draft) (Washington, DC: US Army Center of Military History, January 1992), p. 102.

9. Interview with Major Ronald Dade, contracting officer, US Army Tank Automotive Command, May 7, 1992.

10. Interview with Lieutenant Colonel Michael Velten, February 13, 1992.

11. Schubert and Kraus, p. 109.

12. Yeosock, p. 50.

13. Assessment derived from numerous information papers produced from August to October 1990 by Dr. Norman Cigar, HQDA, DAMI-FI, on "Iraqi Likely Courses of Action."

14. ARCENT Theater Signal Command Desert Shield/Storm After-Action Report, April 25, 1991, p. I-A-1.

15. 1st COSCOM After-Action Report, p. 11-1.

16. ODCSLOG Brochure, p. 94.

17. Interview with Mr. Dick Manning, Raytheon Corporation production manager for the Patriot missile, September 24, 1992.

18. Interview with Mr. Dick Slaughter, senior engineer for Patriot missile production, Patriot Project Manager's Office, September 23, 1992.

19. ODCSLOG Brochure, p. 31.

20. *Ibid*. p. 28.

21. *Ibid*. p. 59.

22. *Ibid*. p. 79.

23. *Ibid*. pp. 78-81.

24. Office of the Surgeon General, Department of the Army, briefing slides entitled "Non-Battle Injury Rates from Desert Shield and Desert Storm, September 1, 1990 to June 3, 1991."

25. Schubert and Kraus, p. 146.

26. 82d Airborne Division Command Report Narrative, "Operation Desert Shield and Desert Storm," p. B-1, and interview with Lieutenant Colonel William Harrison, XVIII Airborne Corps FSE, May 19, 1992.

27. Lieutenant Colonel Terry Buettner, XVIII Airborne Corps ALO, March 25, 1992.

28. *Ibid*.

29. Interview with Brigadier General Richard F. Timmons, assistant division commander for operations, 82d Airborne Division, June 6, 1991.

30. ARCENT Situation Report, August 17, 1990.

31. Colonel Richard Swain, *ARCENT History* (Draft)(Washington, DC: US Army Center of Military History, undated), p. 70.

32. General Schwarzkopf's testimony before Congress, June 12, 1991.

33. CINCFOR message and XVIII Airborne Corps message dated 070900Z August 1990, "Deployment."

34. 24th Infantry Division (Mech) Frag Order Laser Victory, August 7, 1990.

35. 24th Infantry Division (Mech), "A History of the 24th Infantry Division (Mech) Combat Team During Operation Desert Storm: The Attack to Free Kuwait (January-March 1991)," p. 1, hereafter cited as *24th Infantry Division History*.

36. 101st Airborne Division (Air Assault), "History of Operations Desert Shield/Desert Storm: Command Report," July 1, 1991, p. 3.

37. *Ibid*. p. 5.

38. XVIII Airborne Corps CG Update briefing slides, November 5, 1990.

39. ODCSLOG Brochure, pp. 10-11.

40. *Ibid*. pp. 11-12.

41. *Ibid*. p. 68.

Chapter 3

PLOTTING THE CAMPAIGN

Even for Master Sergeant Joseph Lloyd, a Special Forces soldier used to such things, the meeting was very strange indeed. Lloyd, who commanded Special Forces team 595, had been bouncing around the Saudi desert in search of the Kuwaiti 35th Armored Brigade for more than six hours. He knew the brigade was camped somewhere near Hafar al-Batin about 50 miles from the Kuwaiti border. Lloyd doggedly sought out his charge, Colonel Salam al-Masoud, a figure whose reputation among the Kuwaitis had already begun to escalate from respect to veneration. By late afternoon, Lloyd found the cluster of eight white Bedouin tents that formed Salam's encampment. When Salam emerged, Lloyd was struck that the soldier he sought was a huge, muscular, black man. Accustomed to such reaction, Salam extended his massive hand and greeted Lloyd with an unassuming grace that belied his reputation as an exceptional warrior. The Sandhurst graduate had served with the 35th Brigade his entire career, earning his reputation in combat at a key intersection northeast of Kuwait City near the town of al-Jahra. Unlike most of the Kuwaiti army, the brigade had tried to withstand the onslaught of the advancing Iraqi armored columns until faced with encirclement. At that point, Salam had reluctantly withdrawn what remained of the brigade across the Saudi border.

During the first few months of Desert Shield, the Saudi command had gradually moved the 35th farther back from the border, fearing that the Kuwaitis might react recklessly to the news of atrocities in their homeland. Further retreat had done nothing for Kuwaiti morale. Salam hoped that the Americans' presence would convince his disheartened soldiers that they would soon have the opportunity to take back their lost country.

As he approached the 35th Brigade command post with Salam, Lloyd noticed the homemade Shaheed Brigade pennant flying outside the tent that served as the brigade's tactical operations center. Inside, colorful carpets covered the ground, and furniture, as usual, was conspicuously absent. Sitting on the carpeted floor, Salam offered Lloyd sweet, hot tea and introduced his operations officer, Major Suleiman, a graduate of the Jordanian Staff College. Suleiman, in turn, introduced the brigade's battalion commanders. Lieutenant Colonel Hamid, a nervously aggressive officer who at one time had run the Kuwaiti armor school, commanded the newly formed 2d Mechanized Battalion. Lieutenant Colonel Ahmed from the 7th Armored Battalion was a graduate of the armor advanced course at Fort Knox. His battalion had carried the lion's share of the fighting the previous August. Lieutenant Colonel Ali was a colorful, yet reflective and quiet national soccer hero who commanded the 8th Armored Battalion. Also a US armor advanced course graduate, Ali spoke fluent English.

Lloyd explained to the Kuwaitis that his team would live with them and assist them with training. When Salam took the floor, he offered his gratitude to both his Arab brothers and the Americans for their help. But in a solemn tone he emphasized that his army would lead any attack back into Kuwait and that Kuwaiti blood, preferably that of an officer, would be the first blood spilled in any ground war. Lloyd was pleased with his reception. The Kuwaitis seemed far more proficient in military operations than the other units he had advised during his 17 years in Special Forces.

Lloyd's detachment joined the 35th Brigade at the end of October. In the following three months, his teams trained the Kuwaitis on mine-clearing, Iraqi defensive tactics, aircraft and armored vehicle identification, and tank-killing techniques. At the same time, the Americans learned a great deal from the Kuwaitis about the nature of their mutual enemy. Satellites might count Iraqi tanks with great precision, but Salam's officers provided a perspective on personalities and tactical techniques, both good and bad, that they had observed from years of professional elbow rubbing with their neighbors to the north. These insights, passed assiduously by Lloyd up the chain to CENTCOM, formed an essential chapter to a very small book of knowledge concerning the personality and fighting ability of the Iraqis.

Lloyd, undeterred by his very limited Arabic, spent almost every evening after dinner with Salam discussing the day's training and upcoming plans. Lloyd's respect for his giant companion increased in proportion to the rapport that grew between them. Several times Salam invited Lloyd to be his guest at supper. Although by then no stranger to Arab cuisine, Lloyd still blanched a little when offered the "delicacies" *of the meal: the tongue and less identifiable organs of a grilled goat. Despite his macho Special Forces "snake-eater" image, Lloyd had his limits. He became adept at surreptitiously tucking the offensive portions back into his pile of rice.*

The ultimate test of Lloyd's effectiveness came in December when the 35th Brigade received new Yugoslavian M-84 main battle tanks, derivatives of the T-72 tanks used by the Soviets. Concerned about secrecy, the Yugoslavian training team that accompanied the tanks wanted the Americans kept away from them. To his credit, Salam refused, a gesture that demonstrated just how much he had accepted Lloyd and his team. Ironically, Salam, the tanker, put his trust in Lloyd, the light infantryman, to teach his men how to operate and maintain the M-84s. Lloyd knew little about tanks, but he did know how to train and he was not about to violate the Kuwaitis' trust by saying no. Late every night, Lloyd and his team studied manuals about Soviet tanks. During the day, the Special Forces soldiers instructed their charges with the self-assurance and skill learned from many years of similar experiences with other armies in Africa, South America, and Asia.

Tension mounted considerably in the 35th Brigade as the air war started. Salam, distressed at not having orders, worried that the Saudis

The close relationship between Special Forces soldiers and their Arab counterparts helped hold the Coalition together.

might attack without him. Only 10 days before the ground war began, the 35th received its mission from the Muthannah Task Force.[1] Salam's brigade would spearhead the entire Joint Forces Command-North's attack and lead the force into Kuwait City. The brigade was going home and Lloyd and his team were going with them.

Just how much Lloyd's team and teams like his affected the fighting proficiency of those they advised is difficult to measure. Perhaps their most important contribution was simply that they symbolized America's commitment to restoring Kuwait's freedom. Lloyd's team helped shore up the 35th Brigade's flagging morale and in the process became part of the glue that held the Coalition together as part of the overall CENTCOM effort.

TRANSITION TO THE OFFENSE

The challenges that faced Master Sergeant Lloyd in October also faced leaders throughout the US Army in the early uncertain months of Desert Shield. While the hurried buildup of forces continued through August and September 1990, the US and its Coalition partners sought a strategy to confront Iraqi intransigence and Saddam Hussein's outrageous behavior. By late September the Coalition high command was resigned to the fact that economic sanctions and the deployment of a single American corps were not sufficient to drive Saddam out of Kuwait. They resolved to look seriously at offensive options.

Based on political guidance issued by Washington, the Desert Storm Campaign plan that General Schwarzkopf crafted consisted of four phases, which had been roughed out conceptually by September. The first three were reserved primarily for Coalition air operations. The Coalition would strike strategic targets first, then assure air supremacy by crippling the Iraqi air defenses. The air forces would then prepare the battlefield by striking tactical targets on the ground. The fourth phase would be a ground offensive. The first three phases were initially developed by Air Force planners in Washington and the fourth by Army planners under Schwarzkopf's personal supervision at CENTCOM headquarters in Riyadh. Planning began in late September and continued without interruption until the ground war commenced in February. Schwarzkopf, given the score by Washington, composed the symphony he would eventually conduct. How he set the notes to paper is the subject of this chapter.

AIRLAND BATTLE FORMS THE
CAMPAIGN GAME PLAN

History all too often reinforces the familiar maxim that armies tend to fight the next war as they did the last. However, the Gulf War proved to be a dramatic exception. AirLand Battle, the war-fighting doctrine applied by the American Army in Desert Storm, not only survived the initial clash of arms but, in fact, continues as a viable foundation for the development of future war-fighting doctrine. The durability of the Air-Land Battle concept is owed to three factors. First, unlike past instructions for the conduct of war, the 1986 version of AirLand Battle was a vision of what was possible rather than an owner's manual for the equipment and force structures available at the time. In fact, if the 1986 edition of FM 100-5 possessed a fault, it was that some concepts were so far ahead of capabilities that many balked at their full implementation with the tools then at hand. Second, the conditions of combat and the dynamics of the Desert Storm battlefield proved to be modeled with remarkable fidelity to FM 100-5. Third, and perhaps most notable, is that AirLand Battle represented a way of thinking about war and a mental conditioning rather than a rigid set of rules and lists of things to be done in lock-step fashion. Its four tenets, *initiative, agility, depth,* and *synchronization*, are timeless, immutable precepts for present and future wars.

Initiative implies offensive spirit, boldness, audacity, and the propensity to take risks in the heat of battle. In the attack, it means never allowing the enemy to recover from the shock of initial contact. To exploit initiative, a plan must emphasize speed and the ability to shift the main effort quickly. The goal is to create a situation so fluid that the enemy loses track of events and becomes psychologically detached to the point of incoherence.

Agility is reacting, both physically and mentally, more quickly to change than the enemy. Rapid adjustment must be built into plans and training in order that they not be uncoordinated reactions to the enemy's initiative. Battle drills and playbooks enhance agility at the tactical level, and contingency plans at all levels enable the coordinated shifting of forces or fires with minimum delay. Both leaders and units must be agile enough to overcome the routine frictions and confusion of battle. To overcome friction, leaders must continuously "read the battlefield," decide quickly, and act without hesitation.

In Desert Storm, *depth* was the tenet in which the concept was clearly ahead of the capabilities. Depth requires accurate intelligence, means of attack, and the momentum of around-the-clock operations that extend space and time deep into an enemy's rear. By attacking the enemy throughout the depth of his dispositions, commanders rob him of his freedom to act with flexibility. To achieve this capability, commanders must see current and projected enemy dispositions and then attack them with Air Force, Navy, and Army air power, long-range fires, and Special Forces action. By the time of Desert Storm the Army had long-range attack means only in the newly deployed Army Tactical Missile System (ATACMS) and attack helicopters. It would still rely heavily on Coalition air forces to achieve true depth for both intelligence collection and attack.

Conceptually, *synchronization* is similar to blending the different instruments of an orchestra to produce the desired harmony and timing of a musical piece. Commanders, like musical directors, must trust the various sections to play their parts without direction according to the musical score. Like directors, commanders serve to set the tempo and vary the emphasis of the various instrumental sections. As an orchestra needs a good score, an army must have detailed plans that all units can understand and execute with minimal direction. The product—synchronization—is a maximum economy of force, with every resource used where and when it will make the greatest contribution to success so that nothing is wasted or overlooked.

Doctrine only works if a quorum masters it. The Army was fortunate to be given two decades to grow a generation of leaders taught, trained, and selected based on this new way of thinking about war. The Army was equally fortunate to be given time by Saddam to create from the tenets of AirLand Battle a plan for a sweeping end-around maneuver that soldiers would nickname "the Great Wheel." Taking on an enemy perceived to be significantly superior in numbers and ruthless in the use of chemical weapons could only be approached with care. Offensive options in August and September were limited. In September Schwarzkopf believed that 8 to 12 months would be needed to assemble forces necessary for a credible offense. In those uncertain days, Schwarzkopf's planners were more concerned with obtaining a foothold and surviving than with offensive action. [2]

FORMING THE PLANNING TEAM

In first-rate armies, planning for war is continuous. The march to war is too rapid for a commander to begin his own planning only after receiving a plan from above. Even if his plan later proves to be off the mark, the process of deriving a plan has its own intrinsic merit. Just as physical exercise fosters agility and strength, aggressive planning hones the mental abilities and agility essential to deal with the intellectual stresses of war. Parallel planning is the process of several interrelated planning efforts running concurrently without one depending entirely on another. In August and September, offensive objectives were only faint concepts of a ground war that no one at the time wanted to fight. Schwarzkopf's job was to mold the planning effort to produce the score for the symphony that would become the Desert Storm campaign plan.

The role of military planners at all levels, regardless of the operation, is to reduce risk and guesswork and to devise a simple scheme that can be clearly understood and violently and relentlessly executed by all levels of command. Though a good plan reduces luck to a science, imaginative planners capable of transforming luck to certainty are difficult to assemble even in the best of armies.

Almost a half-century before Desert Storm, General George C. Marshall said:

> *Warfare today is a thing of swift movement—of rapid concentration. It requires the building up of enormous firepower against successive objectives with breathtaking speed. It is not a game for the unimaginative plodder.*[3]

Marshall's words lost nothing of their import in the years separating the two wars. Schwarzkopf's commitment to find exactly the right balance of human chemistry to coalesce his vision of the pending campaign into a realistic, achievable plan was derived from this realization. To be sure, CENTCOM possessed its share of officers who were anything but "plodders," but very early in Desert Shield, CENTCOM and ARCENT staffs were very thin and just able to keep up with the immediate practical problems of moving soldiers and equipment into the theater. They had little opportunity to shift from the practical present to the theoretical future. In any event, day-to-day operators tend to flex a set of intellectual muscles different than those suited to future planning. General Vuono, recognizing the need in Saudi Arabia for a more conceptually grounded group of planners able to separate themselves from day-to-day operations, offered up a group of SAMS graduates for that purpose. Schwarzkopf readily accepted the offer.[4] He intended to use the group principally to focus on the planning process and to ensure secrecy at a time when leaks might inadvertently induce a preemptive Iraqi move or disrupt the fragile Coalition.[5] He would focus this new body entirely on the fourth phase of the campaign, the ground offensive.

This special planning group would achieve considerable notoriety after the war. Lieutenant Colonel Joe Purvis, the senior member, came from the Joint Staff of Pacific Command in Hawaii. Major Greg Eckert arrived from the 4th Infantry Division at Fort Carson, Colorado, where he had been the division's training officer. Major Dan Roh had been the executive officer of the 708th Main Support Battalion, 8th Infantry Division, in Germany, and Major Bill Pennypacker, the executive officer of the 1st Brigade, 1st Infantry Division, at Fort Riley, Kansas. The four officers arrived at CENTCOM headquarters in Riyadh between September 16 and 18, 1990.[6] Purvis later asked for Navy Petty Officer First Class Michael Archer from the CENTCOM staff to serve as an administrative and security assistant. Archer was bright and articulate, and his specialty in intelligence could be used to the group's advantage.[7] Other specialists would join the group periodically to lend expertise in other areas.

Although the Purvis group forms the nexus of the story of Desert Storm planning, it was, in reality, only one layer of a larger parallel effort comprising all levels of command. Nevertheless, a careful recounting of the group's role demonstrates how the course of the campaign evolved.

The "Bear" with three of his planners after Desert Storm. Left to right: Lieutenant Colonel Greg Eckert, Major Dan Roh, and Colonel Joe Purvis. Lieutenant Colonel Bill Pennypacker is missing from the photo.

Military planning in the American Army is not the exclusive purview of SAMS, the Command and General Staff College, or any other single institution. The Army has traditionally prided itself on its ability to "grow" officers in the school of experience as much as in formal courses. The Purvis group represents a larger body of officers imbued with equal skills and experiences. Certainly others could have done as well, but Purvis and his three majors were the ones who were on the hot seat in September 1990.

GUIDANCE, PROCESS, AND ANALYSIS

The planning group worked directly for General Schwarzkopf and soon became his sounding board and intellectual alter ego. Very tight security measures, as well as Schwarzkopf's personality, fostered this unique relationship. In addition to the five members, Schwarzkopf would initially allow no more than five additional key people access to the group's efforts: himself and his aide-de-camp; his chief of staff, Marine Major General Robert Johnston; Rear Admiral Grant Sharp, the operations and plans officer; and Colonel John Buckley, the chief of the CENTCOM plans division.[8] The group faced a demanding taskmaster in a pressure-cooker environment. On September 18, Schwarzkopf presented his initial guidance for the offensive plan: "Assume a ground attack will follow an air campaign... study the enemy dispositions and the terrain and tell me the best way to drive Iraq out of Kuwait given the forces we have available."[9] From the beginning, everyone understood that a frontal assault into the teeth of the Iraqi defenses was to be avoided at all costs.

Purvis' first challenge was to develop a plan for the planning process itself. He directed his group to collect specific background information on subjects that each member knew well. Pennypacker took enemy, Eckert, friendly forces; Roh would analyze logistics on both sides. Although the demand for secrecy made data collection difficult, the common network and shared cultural bias that existed among the SAMS graduates in the theater provided a remarkably effective shadow network for exchanging information and discussing concepts. The group came to rely heavily on this essential peer exchange that continued to expand throughout the planning phase.

The group spent nearly a week gathering data for their analysis, applying the factors of METT-T that each had learned and practiced since they had been lieutenants. *Mission, enemy, terrain and weather, troops and transport available, and time,* with some occasionally more sophisticated extrapolation, provided virtually every category of data necessary to formulate a plan.

Mission

Purvis assumed the task of refining a mission statement by analyzing the explicit planning imperatives as well as those implied by the situation. He began with the President's stated objectives: unconditional withdrawal of Iraqi forces from Kuwait, restoration of Kuwait's sovereignty, destruction of Iraqi capability to produce and employ weapons of mass destruction, and destruction of Iraq's offensive capability. Some longer-ranging political objectives implied at the time were to restore regional stability, to hold the Iraqi government accountable for war crimes, to restore Free World access to Middle East energy sources, and to strengthen cooperation between the US and Arab states in the region.[10]

The military aspects of Schwarzkopf's mission were clear. To liberate Kuwait, CENTCOM would have to attack dug-in Iraqi forces in the Kuwaiti theater of operations with air and ground forces. Some believed a ground offensive could be shortened or made unnecessary with aggressive air operations. An intensive air attack combined with psychological warfare and the pinch of international sanctions might erode Iraqi support for the war enough to convince Saddam to withdraw his forces from Kuwait. The concept appealed to many concerned with the high cost in casualties likely to result from a ground offensive. Nevertheless, achieving the objective would be very difficult given the limited forces available in September.

One of the critical lessons of the Vietnam war was that no military intervention should be contemplated without a clearly defined objective, a clearly understood strategy, and adequate means to achieve the objective. The end-state for an attack against Saddam's military had to be defined precisely in order to know when to proclaim victory and call a halt to the operation. In September and early October, the only reasonably achievable end-state was simply to eject Iraq from Kuwait and to restore the legitimate government. Destroying Saddam's war-fighting capabilities and holding him accountable were, at that time, not achievable with available forces.

Schwarzkopf's instructions to avoid an attack into the Iraqi's strongest defenses called for an indirect approach to reach and destroy Saddam's operational center of gravity. The concept of center of gravity suggests that a nation's ability to fight can most readily be unhinged by seeking out the one pivotal element of its force that, if destroyed, would cause all of its force to collapse. In addition to military power, a center of gravity might include political leadership, the economy, a critical industry, or the will of the population. Only by identifying an assailable center of gravity can an attacking force assure decisive results without wasting resources on secondary efforts. Schwarzkopf identified Iraq's first military center of gravity as the Republican Guard.

Enemy

The planning group began their analysis of the enemy with very little firsthand knowledge. In September, information revealed a well-equipped, battle-hardened foe who would have the advantage of secure internal lines of communication. He had an impressive array of modern equipment, mostly of Soviet design, including weapons of mass destruction. An unknown factor was the will of the Iraqi armed forces to fight. For nearly 40 years the intelligence telescope had been focused almost exclusively on the Warsaw Pact. Now, painfully little time was available to shift focus to the KTO. While the intelligence focus shifted from Europe to the Middle East, the group concentrated on what little they could glean from Iraq's performance in the eight-year war with Iran and in the short two-day operation to seize Kuwait.

The historical insights available from the Iran-Iraq War were meager to say the least. Shortly after its September 1980 attack into Iran sputtered to a halt, the Iraqi military went into a strategic defense, seeking to wear down the numerically superior Iranian army. The initial battles had been too bloody even for Saddam, so he used less costly local attacks to secure more defensible terrain or to blunt Iranian aggression. The resulting stalemate continued until 1985 when the Iraqis experimented briefly with limited offensives supported by heavy doses of artillery and air support.

Gradually, the Iraqis became more active and began to exploit the superior strategic and operational mobility of their reserves.

The Iranian offensive which captured the al-Faw peninsula in 1986 effectively ended the stalemate. In April 1988, the Iraqis launched a series of corps-level counterattacks to regain territory lost to Iran. The operations were carefully rehearsed and meticulously orchestrated. The Iraqis preceded each division- and corps-level attack with an extensive heavy artillery preparation, accompanied by liberal use of chemical weapons and air strikes. Preparation, planning, and brutal application of firepower paid off. By July, the war was essentially over. Throughout eight years of war, the Iraqi army had engaged in offensive operations for fewer than eight months.

As a result of the Iran-Iraq War, the Iraqi army expanded from 12 divisions of 350,000 men in 1982 to 56 divisions of 1,100,000 men by late 1989, making it the fourth largest military power in the world. It was organized and trained along British lines and was largely equipped with the best tanks and armored vehicles Moscow and other foreign arms bazaars had to offer.

The Iraqi army consisted of three distinct levels of competence. Infantry divisions were on the bottom. In the Iran-Iraq War, they proved capable at best of maintaining a static defense. Since the end of the Iran-Iraq War, Saddam had allowed his infantry divisions to atrophy so that even a respectable static defense in Kuwait would be beyond the proficiency of most without significantly more equipment and training. One notch up in competence were the regular army heavy divisions, manned by long-service professional soldiers trained well enough to keep tanks and armored vehicles operating. At the top was the Republican Guard.

If the regular army provided the bulk of the Iraqi military muscle, the Republican Guard was its heart. Created originally as a palace guard of two brigades, by July 1990 the Guard had grown to a separate corps with 28 combat brigades arrayed within eight divisions, including armor, mechanized infantry, infantry, and special forces. The Guard possessed the best equipment Baghdad could provide. While a regular army armored division might field 250 tanks, usually a motley mix of older T-54s, T-55s, and T-62s, a Guard armored division had 312 of the more modern T-72s. Some Guard armored brigades had the T-72M1, the best Soviet tank then available on the world market. Similar disparities existed between regular and Guard mechanized infantry divisions. The artillery brigades within the Guard were equipped with Austrian, French, and South African artillery systems, many of which were superior in range to any in the US inventory. Guard air defense units had the proven SA-6 mobile surface-to-air missile, normally used to protect high-value strategic targets.

Because the Republican Guard was Saddam's strategic reserve, he kept them carefully separated from the regular army. The Guard operated directly under General Headquarters (GHQ) control. Many of its officers and soldiers, selected from the very best of Iraq's available manpower, came from Saddam's hometown of Tikrit, and the overwhelming majority were, like Saddam, Sunni Moslems. A notable exception was the Guard commander, Lieutenant General al-Rawi, who, although a Shia, was a Saddam Hussein devotee of unquestionable loyalty and respectable reputation.

Not only was the Guard better equipped, it was better paid. During its expansion in the mid-eighties, the Guard offered enlistees cash bonuses, new cars, and subsidized apartments. As it deployed into the KTO, the Guard continued to maintain a separate and exclusive existence. Guard bunkers in Kuwait were appointed with the best furniture, carpets, and appliances, largely stolen from the Kuwaitis. Closer to the center of the Iraqi logistical system at Basrah, the Guard never ran short of food, water, or military supplies, while regular units often suffered shameful neglect. Officers from regular units were known to cultivate and bribe the Guard for spare parts, supplies, and luxury items.

The Guard's special status came at a high price. Baghdad expected the Guard to fight even if other units folded and positioned them in the KTO to backstop the regular units. Eighteenth century European armies kept unreliable conscripts aligned and moving forward in combat by placing professional NCOs at the end of each file. Armed with short swords and lances, they were to kill any soldier who showed signs of flight. The Guard provided Saddam's file closers. He positioned them at the theater rear boundary, not only for counterattack, but to block retreat and to punish those foolish enough to run. Nevertheless, counterattack was the Guard's specialty, and several years of successful practice against the Iranians had made them fairly proficient at it.

When the Iraqi army returned to the attack against the Iranians in 1988, the Guard was in the vanguard, translating the lessons of mobile defense into offensive operations. Acting either as an independent force or in concert with regular army formations like the 3d Corps, the Guard conducted the main attack in at least five operations, demonstrating its superior planning, training, equipment, and, most importantly, its esprit de corps. As it became more practiced in the offense, the Guard used amphibious and airmobile forces to cut off retreating Iranian units. To those familiar with past Iraqi operations, the Guard's dominant role in the invasion of Kuwait came as no surprise.

The KTO was so vast that if it was to perform as a theaterwide operational fire brigade, the Guard needed theaterwide mobility. To this end Saddam purchased more than 2,000 heavy equipment transporters, each capable of carrying a T-72 tank great distances over improved roads. He had enough HETs to carry all three Guard heavy divisions in Kuwait simultaneously. Thus the Guard could either reinforce anywhere in Kuwait in fewer than 24 hours or, should the war not develop as planned, be recalled to Baghdad in a matter of days.

Although Saddam treated the Iraqi air force as an elite group, it was not, unlike the Republican Guard, capable of bold offensive action. Its greatest contribution was to preserve its aircraft strength to pose a continuous over-the-horizon threat. To maintain its intimidation value, Saddam made sure his air force remained the largest in the Middle East with a total strength of more than 750 aircraft. However, the quality of the aircraft and crews was very uneven.

The elite of the Iraqi air force was its complement of 64 French Mirage F-1s and their French-trained pilots. The F-1 squadrons executed most of the successful strikes against the Iranians in the Iran-Iraq War. Occasionally they did engage in air-to-air combat, but only when they had numerical superiority. An Iraqi F-1 was responsible for the Exocet strike on the *USS Stark* in 1987, which caused the death of 37 sailors.

Despite its numbers, the Iraqi air force was no match for the Coalition, nor could it offer credible support to Baghdad's ground forces. Close air support, as practiced by the US and other Western air forces, was unknown to them. Iraqi fighter-bombers might attempt independent air interdiction against point targets, but they were incapable of working under the control of forward ground units. Even the Iraqi attack helicopter fleet of Soviet Hinds and French Alouettes and Gazelles was incapable of much beyond rudimentary support as flying artillery.

A large, complex hodgepodge of Soviet, French, and other systems, Iraq's air defense was glossy on the surface but functionally flawed underneath. Baghdad relied heavily on its French-designed KARI command and control network to coordinate air defenses from an underground air defense operations center in Baghdad. The country had been subdivided into five air defense sectors, each under a sector operations center (SOC). Each SOC in turn controlled a number of warning and control regiments and interceptor operations centers. These centers coordinated the flights of air interceptors and the fires of an overlapping system of surface-to-air missiles and antiaircraft artillery (AAA). Should the Coalition destroy the central air defense operations center, the KARI network would be beheaded and each SOC would have to operate independently. Once control of the system was isolated, each segment was vulnerable to being overwhelmed and destroyed in detail. Should a SOC or subordinate center be taken out completely, an aerial breach would result through which an attacker could strike deep into Iraq.

Iraq protected its forward troops in the KTO from air attack with a mixture of missiles and guns. The most serious threats to army aviation were short-range systems like the SA-9 and SA-13 missiles, along with the shoulder-fired SA-14s and SA-16s. The density of antiaircraft artillery in theater was of particular concern to US Army planners. More than 3,700 AAA systems larger than 14.5mm were spread throughout the KTO. The deployed army supplemented the AAA with the fires of more than 10,000 machine guns, 12.7mm or larger.

Iraq possessed both Scud missiles and weapons of mass destruction. Iraq's Scud-B was originally designed by the Soviets to deliver a one-ton payload to a maximum range of 300 kilometers. The Iraqis modified it during the war with Iran to deliver a half-ton warhead to 475 kilometers. A newer version, the al-Abbas, could range 600 kilometers with the same payload. The modified Scuds were notoriously inaccurate. The al-Abbas at maximum range had an error of about 4 kilometers. Baghdad possessed both fixed and mobile launchers. Intelligence had detected a total of 64 fixed sites in western Iraq, all aimed at Israel. Twenty-eight of those fixed sites were complete, and the remainder were nearing completion. No one knew exactly how many mobile launchers the Iraqis had, but the best guess before the war was 48 of various design. Some analysts suspected the Iraqis were producing more, perhaps many more. The hunt for mobile launchers would be the thorniest problem of the war.

The Coalition most feared Saddam's weapons of mass destruction. He not only possessed them in great quantities, but he had used them on his own people in the past. Saddam had built a large arsenal of mustard and nerve agents and had provided artillery, aircraft, and missiles capable of delivering them. The same systems could deliver Saddam's anthrax and botulinum biological weapons.

The Iraqi military machine was a significant opponent. It was a huge force, larger in total size than the German field army in France during the Normandy landings in World War II and twice as large as the North Korean army that invaded South Korea in June 1950. It was also well-equipped. The more advanced armor on the T-72 and T-72M1 could sustain direct hits from older 105mm rounds fired by the US M-1 Abrams at 2,000 meters. Iraqi T-72M1s and T-72Ms had laser range finders, and the 125mm gun, standard on all T-72s, could penetrate the Abrams at 1,000 meters. The BMP-1, the world's first operational infantry fighting vehicle, was equipped with a 73mm smooth-bore cannon. Their French-made self-propelled 155mm artillery systems had automatic loaders that allowed for high rates of fire.

Stocked with more than 320,000 tons of ammunition openly bunkered in vast depots inside the KTO, the Iraqi army could fight for two weeks without resupply. An additional two million tons of ammunition were dispersed inside Iraq, allowing the army to absorb a great deal of punishment and continue to fight. The Iraqis were experienced in combat, although with the exception of the Republican Guard, "battle-hardened" would prove to mean "battle-weary." The senior army leadership of committed professionals had learned a great deal about fighting during eight years of war. Most officers possessed university degrees from local or foreign institutions and the more senior staff officers had trained at the best Soviet, Chinese, and European staff colleges. Senior staffs had demonstrated respectable skill in planning and executing the invasion of Kuwait. In two weeks, the Iraqis had been able to deploy eight divisions, 140,000 troops, 1,100 tanks, 610 artillery pieces, and 610 armored vehicles, accompanied by engineers, air defense, and all required logistical support. Some units had traveled as far as 700 kilometers to reach the Kuwaiti front. Finally, to support their military operations, the Iraqis had established a redundant command, control, and communications network unequaled even by some first-rate Western armies. The network reached from each of the multiple command centers in and around Baghdad, through intermediate headquarters in the KTO, to the lowest Iraqi unit along the Saudi border.

Like any army, Iraq's also had weaknesses. The most striking was Saddam Hussein. Never trained as a military man, Saddam had a reputation for exercising strict personal command over his armed forces in the field. Overcentralization by an incompetent leader stifled Iraq's ability to put together a credible offensive operation for most of the eight-year war with Iran. Only after the disastrous al-Faw campaign in 1986 did Iraqi general headquarters gain some degree of planning and operational leverage, and only then did the army perform well enough to beat the Iranians. Even with such a significant concession, however, Saddam reserved major decisions for himself, and he rewarded failure harshly. On one occasion he executed a unit commander merely for getting lost in the mountains. After seeing the price of failure so dramatically demonstrated after the Iranian seizure of al-Faw, senior Iraqi commanders, particularly those in the Guard units, sacrificed themselves and their men slavishly to avoid disgrace in the eyes of their leader. No commander would consider independent action, particularly if failure was likely. Thus CENTCOM planners realized from the beginning that should they be able to sever the linkages between Saddam and his commanders in the field, the army would probably be incapable of large-scale maneuver.

Another vulnerability was the quality of manpower available to Iraqi general headquarters. Challenging missions like attack, passage of lines, and counterattack could only be accomplished effectively by certain units, principally the Guard and 3d Corps. Even within the best units, tactical and technical proficiency was not always apparent. Complex artillery skills—particularly those requiring extensive training, such as counterfire and rapid adjustment of observed fire—as well as flexibility and mental quickness, were simply beyond the limited competence of most Iraqi artillerymen. Iraqi artillery commanders were capable only of executing planned, massed fire missions. Even with reasonably proficient crews, good tanks and armored vehicles were nothing without proficient, flexible commanders. Iraqi maneuver units had repeated problems in coordinating boundaries during the Iran-Iraq War. Most significantly, other than during the short attack into Kuwait, the Iraqis had never demonstrated much ability to fight at night.

Not all Iraqi equipment was first-rate. Although the T-72 and its improved versions, the T-72M and T-72M1, were excellent, they made up less than 20 percent of the Iraqi tank inventory. Only the improved T-72s had laser range finders, and even they had to close inside 2,000 meters to have any hope of killing an Abrams. As for the BMP-1, the American Bradley was a quantum leap ahead in lethality, mobility, and crew surviv-ability. The Iraqi artillery had a long range to be sure, but without precise target-finding devices or equipment to increase accuracy, such as meteorological stations, computerized fire control, and precision posi-tion-locating and ranging devices, the total artillery system was grossly inaccurate. Most of the artillery was towed, leaving it at the mercy of counterbattery fires, especially when prime movers had been destroyed.

Finally, the Iraqi army would be on its own in the KTO. Neither the air force nor the air defense command was capable of protecting ground forces from air attack. Soldiers could rely only on camouflage, deception, and entrenchment to survive prolonged aerial bombardment. The Iraqi logistics system was hard-pressed just to supply the army in peacetime. Even a moderate interruption would effectively deny units along the Saudi border access to such essentials as food and water.

While planners could count tanks and artillery pieces, they were less successful in measuring the will of the Iraqi military to fight, an intangi-ble that would potentially have enormous impact on the war. The Iran-Iraq War seemed to show that the frontline infantry were as badly motivated as they were equipped and trained. If subjected to any pres-sure whatsoever, they would break and run. The regular army heavy divisions would fight, probably with some tenacity, surrendering only if retreat were impossible. The Guard, however, was expected to fight to the death and to maintain its cohesion and ability to fire and maneuver even if badly mauled.

Terrain and Weather

Planners expected both terrain and weather to influence operations in the KTO significantly. The US Army had learned to fight in the desert during years of experience at the National Training Center and in numerous BRIGHT STAR exercises in Egypt and Sudan. However, not all deserts are the same. The planners were particularly concerned about trafficability of the desert terrain in the western end of the KTO. On the coast, where Desert Shield forces were initially concentrated, the ground is generally flat with a well-developed network of roads connecting the big ports and coastal cities. Just off the roads, however, large sand dunes and sabkhas impede movement. Some dunes rise 20 or more feet presenting serious hazards to low-level flight, particularly at night. Sabkhas are like thin ice when it rains. Soldiers can traverse them on foot, but vehicles often break through and wallow up to their bellies in mud.

Following the Saudi-Iraqi border from about 10 miles inland west to the Wadi al-Batin, the land becomes flatter, with fewer dunes and numerous small rocks. Approximately 125 miles inland, the Wadi al-Batin offers both opportunity and threat. The wadi is little more than a pronounced dry streambed that runs the length of the Kuwait-Iraq western border and continues well south into Saudi Arabia to form a natural attack route from Saudi Arabia northeast into Iraq. Conversely, the wadi also points like an arrow toward King Khalid Military City or Riyahd farther to the south. The wadi would prove useful mainly as an aid to ground and low-level air navigation. Its gentle, wide, sloping sides would not hinder crossing or movement unless flooded by winter rains.

The area between the wadi and Rafha, 170 miles farther to the west, becomes progressively more rocky. The Saudis knew that this large plateau was at least trafficable by vehicle inside Saudi Arabia because Bedouins routinely crisscrossed the area in their trucks following herds of sheep, goats, and camels. Rocks were hard on tires and would play havoc with the rubber track pads of armored vehicles, but the region was generally passable. No one knew, however, how hospitable this same region would be farther north inside Iraq. This unknown was significant because any offensive thrust into Iraq that swung west to avoid the main Iraqi defenses would have to transit this desert. Purvis' concern and curiosity were both heightened when the Iraqis appeared to have neglected defending the area. They would only have done so, the group surmised, if they knew it to be impassable.

In September, all the group had to work with were maps, data provided by employees of ARAMCO, and what little they could glean from Saudis familiar with the area. Maps for the whole region were in short supply, some were outdated, and even the most current offered very little information on trafficability. Major Pennypacker would later undertake a

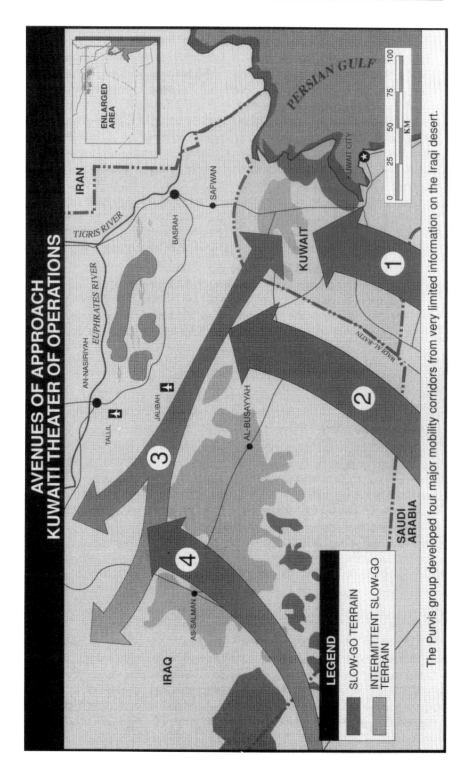

**AVENUES OF APPROACH
KUWAITI THEATER OF OPERATIONS**

The Purvis group developed four major mobility corridors from very limited information on the Iraqi desert.

LEGEND

SLOW-GO TERRAIN

INTERMITTENT SLOW-GO TERRAIN

reconnaissance by vehicle and helicopter to sample the terrain firsthand. However, in the early stage the mission was so closely held that the group could not ask too many questions about the region west of the Wadi al-Batin for fear of exposing their offensive planning options.

Saudi weather is among the most inhospitable in the world, the temperatures in August and September sometimes reaching 140 degrees Fahrenheit. American soldiers simply could not function efficiently in such heat. The planning group seriously questioned the ability of soldiers to function at all clad in heavy chemical protective overgarments. Units could not be expected to go into action without at least three weeks of conditioning and acclimatization. Heat would also affect engine coolants and seals and could actually warp metal and plastic parts. Dust, sand, and heat are deadly enemies to electronic equipment like radios, computers, and the "black boxes" on aircraft and other combat vehicles.

Between November and March, temperatures moderate considerably. Nighttime lows sometimes dip below freezing. Sandstorms are common during the winter months, whipping clouds of fine dust miles into the air and limiting observation to less than 100 meters. The region receives most of its limited rainfall during this period, often in deluges that turn dry wadis into raging torrents. When wet, the clay-based sand turns into thick, viscous mud. Analysis of the weather alone favored an offensive operation between November and March to avoid the worst heat of the region.

Troops and Transport Available

The troops available to Schwarzkopf were a mix of US and Coalition army, navy, air, and marine forces. In September the Coalition was clearly outnumbered. XVIII Airborne Corps was still in the process of deploying, although by early October it would field the 82d Airborne Division, the 101st Airborne Division, the 24th Infantry Division, the 3d Armored Cavalry Regiment, and the 12th Aviation Brigade. The 1st Cavalry Division was still en route. The Marine amphibious force had most of one division ashore with its accompanying air wing. Coalition forces in September included the initial elements of a British armored brigade and a French light armored division, the Royal Saudi Land Forces, two Saudi Army National Guard brigades, the Kuwaiti brigade, and a mix of smaller Arab forces from Egypt and several other countries.

The Coalition air forces were formidable, and though the Army planners were focusing on a ground offensive, the role of air power would be a key part of the overall campaign. As its name implies, AirLand Battle doctrine relies on exploitation of the third dimension to a degree unequaled by any other doctrine in history. To be successful, every combat function of the coming campaign, including fire support, reconnaissance, liaison, communications, and maneuver, would bring an essential and indivisible aerial component to the battlefield. Army aviation would contribute to the effort, but the AirLand Battle tenet of depth, which seeks to engage the enemy ground forces at the earliest stages of battle, remained largely the preserve of the air forces. For that reason, the planning group sought from the beginning to synchronize air and land components into a single joint force capable of striking the enemy from the depths of his territory to within immediate contact with frontline soldiers. The guidance by September 25 stipulated that the third phase of the air offensive, battlefield preparation, would have to reduce the Iraqi armored forces by at least 50 percent in order to achieve desired force ratios for the ground attack. This figure was originally derived during INTERNAL LOOK planning for the counterattack phase of OPLAN 1002-90. An old doctrinal rule of thumb calls for at least a three-to-one force advantage over an opponent before launching an offense. Ideally, a six-to-one or better ratio at the point of penetration is desirable to ensure success. Favorable ratios can be achieved in two ways. An attacking force can concentrate an overwhelming mass in front of a weak spot in the enemy's defenses, or the force can wear down the enemy's defenses with fires before close combat begins. The campaign plan sought to do both.

Major Eckert struggled with the assessment of some of the Coalition partners in his analysis of friendly troops available. Two parallel efforts begun early in the deployment were directed at this problem. The first was General Yeosock's formation of the Coalition Coordination and Communications Integration Center (C³IC). The second was the employment of Special Operations forces, like Master Sergeant Lloyd's team, to train with and assess the fighting qualities of Coalition forces.

Schwarzkopf considered the Coalition's center of gravity to be the Coalition itself. If the frail bonds of the Arab-Islamic commitment to the US-led Coalition could be broken, perhaps by drawing Israel into the war, the Coalition would quite likely be fragmented and torn apart. He knew that forging some unusual instrument at the scene would be necessary to hold the Coalition together. Yeosock used the C³IC at the beginning of Desert Shield to gain entrance to the Saudi power base and to obtain host-nation support. Later, along with a network of mobile liaison teams, the center would provide another avenue for information and clarifying orders. The C³IC helped to hold up a fragile Coalition that did not benefit from any long-term agreements like those of NATO. Without status-of-forces agreements and other established standards like those in Europe, the C³IC provided one avenue to solidify the Coalition. Yeosock, and later Schwarzkopf, turned the C³IC into an ad hoc "directed telescope" that they could focus on specific issues for resolution in an informal, collegial manner. Collocated at the Saudi Ministry of Defense building with Schwarzkopf's CENTCOM and the Saudi commander's headquarters, the C³IC was jointly manned by American and Saudi officers.

Special Operations forces included a special aviation battalion, a psychological operations group, civil affairs units, and a variety of other uniquely organized and trained elements. For the most part the control of these units would remain under the Special Operations Command Central, or SOCCENT, commanded by Colonel Jesse Johnson. On August 31, the Special Forces Group from Fort Campbell, Kentucky, was first to arrive in country, and its initial mission was to support the Saudi Arabian land forces and the Saudi Army National Guard. In this case, foreign internal defense, or FID in Special Forces jargon, included assistance in organizing, training, and advising the Arabs in both conventional and unconventional warfare.[11] What Schwarzkopf needed most from Special Forces was some semblance of "ground truth" concerning the Coalition forces' ability to fight—a delicate problem. The SOF became another "directed telescope" with enough experience to draw frank, objective conclusions and pass them in confidence to CENTCOM.

Because logistics could become an Achilles heel for the Coalition, whatever plan was developed would have to undergo the litmus test of supportability. General Pagonis' work in establishing the sustainment base for Desert Shield was an important first step, but it centered on supporting a defensive enclave restricted to the coastal region. The enormous distances covered by any offensive maneuver would place a

Special Forces NCOs taught essential combat skills to newly enlisted Kuwaiti volunteers.

particular strain on available transportation. The American Army was organized and equipped for defense in Europe and was therefore critically short of long-haul transportation. Trucks of all sorts, particularly fuel tankers and heavy-equipment transporters, were continually in demand. Throughout the campaign, available transportation would be an annoying tether on Purvis' planning concepts, continually reining him back toward logistics bases each time he stretched too far too fast with too large a force.

Time Available

Assessing time available consists of determining when to start, how long actions will take, and how to synchronize the actions of each segment of an operation so that all work in synergy. No one could tell if or when the Coalition would go on the offensive. When to start a one-corps offensive depended on the maturity of the logistics buildup and how long it would take XVIII Airborne Corps to be fully combat-ready. Estimates indicated that full readiness would require between 45 and 90 days. Thus, mid-October was the earliest any attack with available forces could be attempted.

Determining the length of the operation was a matter of predicting the time necessary for each of the four phases. The US Air Force estimated that the first three phases of the campaign would require about two weeks. The length of the fourth phase, the ground offensive, depended on the success of the previous phases and other subjective factors difficult to estimate. With known rates of movement and estimates from the intelligence preparation of the battlefield, planners could anticipate Iraqi actions and reactions to the Coalition attack with some measure of confidence. Yet the only assertion that could be made about the length of the fourth phase was that it would take longer with a smaller force than with a larger one. It would also cost more in casualties.

What distinguishes a great plan from a good one is the timing necessary to synchronize a large number of concurrent and interdependent events. Schwarzkopf's task would be to orchestrate the movements and actions of many disparate parts to bring them harmoniously to exactly the right place in time to achieve a single aim. Since the factors of METT-T change with time, any analysis of an impending operation must be continuous. The group's initial five-day study of METT-T, completed on September 25, was only the first iteration of an assessment that would be revisited over and over again. In those first five days of collecting information, Pennypacker and Archer had only scratched the surface of Iraqi capabilities and limitations. Of all the factors of METT-T, the enemy was a true moving target. Other than the enemy, much of the detailed early analysis would change very little over time. The assumptions built upon that information would prove remarkably prescient once real war began.

THE FIRST OFFENSIVE PLAN

The group began the formal development of a one-corps plan with a briefing to Admiral Sharp, the CENTCOM J5, on September 25. Sharp was a personable but demanding officer willing to listen and learn more about ground warfare. Purvis first wanted to ensure that his planning imperatives were on track. He told Sharp that the long distances throughout the theater and the limited transport made a sweeping end-around move infeasible. Therefore, the plan intended to concentrate as much combat power in the smallest space possible against the weakest Iraqi point he could find to lessen the cost of a penetration. Once through, the force would bypass centers of concentration en route to the Republican Guard. Second, he verified the need to destroy 50 percent of the enemy's combat power during the third phase of the air operation. He planned to measure combat power in terms of destroyed enemy vehicles and equipment. The group also highlighted the imperative to keep an unblinking intelligence eye constantly on the enemy in order to react immediately to Iraqi countermoves.

Armed with Sharp's approval, the group developed several options for a single-corps attack. On October 2, Lieutenant Colonel John Carr from the 21st Support Command joined the group for a week to inject a dose of logistical feasibility into any concept they might devise. In developing courses of action, the group resolved to retain enough combat power in the rear to secure CENTCOM ports and reception airfields against terrorists. They would also need Patriots to protect the force from air or Scud missile attack. Until the eve of the armistice, CENTCOM believed that the Iraqis would employ chemical weapons, probably at the point of penetration but potentially anywhere in the theater. The Purvis group's mission statement for the one-corps offensive plan was simple: "On order, friendly forces conduct offensive operations to eject Iraqi forces from Kuwait; be prepared to secure and defend Kuwait." [12]

On October 4, Schwarzkopf held a map exercise at the Oasis Club on Dhahran Air Base for XVIII Airborne Corps and division commanders to review the defense plans. Convinced that Saudi Arabia could be defended successfully, he told his commanders to start thinking about the offense.[13] Not knowing exactly what the CINC had in mind, General Luck instructed his subordinates to concentrate on developing lower-level plans that would apply regardless of the grand design. He knew, for example, that any plan would have to take out the enemy's artillery and destroy reconnaissance and forward defensive positions, so he ordered the development of a counterbattery program and a plan to carry the corps on a limited offensive through the two Iraqi defensive belts.

Equally important was the "shot in the arm" that this opportunity would give to soldiers not accustomed to waiting for the enemy to act first. As far back as August, before deploying to Saudi Arabia, the commander of the 101st Airborne Division's 1st Brigade required each of his three infantry battalion commanders to plan for potential attacks into Kuwait. The first battalion planned an air assault defense against an armored counterattack, while the second developed plans for an air assault into Kuwait City to seize and defend key installations. The third planned an air assault onto the high ground north of Kuwait City near al-Jahra.[14] Now their planning could take on a new and more immediate dimension.

Purvis presented the one-corps concept and three courses of action to Schwarzkopf on October 6. Schwarzkopf selected the first course of action for further study, but he was troubled by the considerable risk that every option presented. Even if the Air Force succeeded in isolating the KTO and destroying 50 percent of the Iraqi ground combat power, the Coalition would still attack greatly outnumbered against a relatively unbroken enemy. The concept he chose called for an extensive two-week air attack, followed by an advance into southern Kuwait between the "elbow" and the tri-border area. Coalition ground forces would drive northeast into Kuwait through the defensive line and then turn east to sit astride the main north-south highway to Basrah out of Kuwait City. When ordered to proceed, the attack would continue to secure the northern Iraqi-Kuwaiti border and cut off the Republican Guard in the KTO before the Guard realized what the corps was doing. With the border secured, the Guard could either attack or give up and walk out of the KTO while air attacks and artillery struck their abandoned equipment. The 24th Infantry Division would make the main attack with the 1st Cavalry Division and the 3d Armored Cavalry Regiment, while the Marines and the 101st protected the rear and the 82d protected the lines of communication. Coalition forces would protect the left flank. Schwarzkopf was not terribly comfortable with the one-corps option, but he recognized that the plan was as good as could be expected with the forces available. His greatest concern was not whether the operation would succeed; if air power did all that was expected, the attack would be able to move through the Iraqis fairly quickly. The real issue was the prospective human cost of the operation. Even with all the advantages of technology, initiative, and air superiority in his favor, the one-corps option would mean that too many soldiers would die. Should things go badly, the friendly force could stop and protect itself at any time, so it was not in jeopardy of complete destruction, but the mission might fail if such a stop became necessary.[15]

Schwarzkopf may not have liked the concept any more than his planners, but under considerable pressure from Washington to present some offensive option, he sent his chief of staff, General Johnston; Air Force Brigadier General C. Buster Glosson; and Purvis to Washington. Air Force

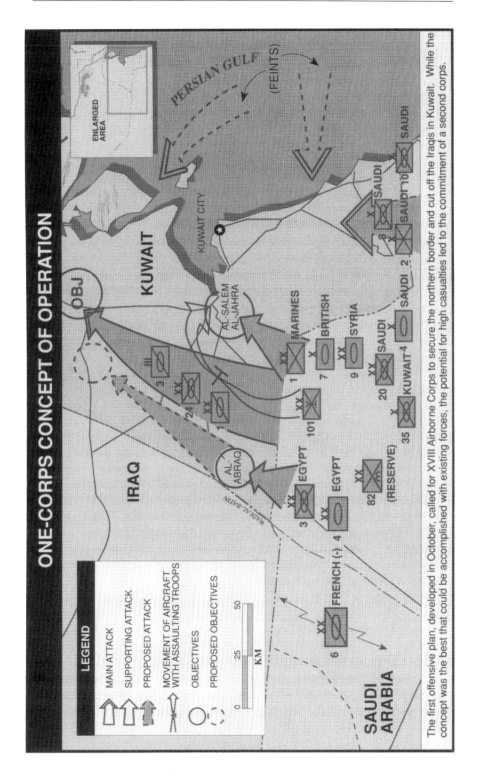

ONE-CORPS CONCEPT OF OPERATION

The first offensive plan, developed in October, called for XVIII Airborne Corps to secure the northern border and cut off the Iraqis in Kuwait. While the concept was the best that could be accomplished with existing forces, the potential for high casualties led to the commitment of a second corps.

Major Rick Francona, on loan to CENTCOM from the Defense Intelligence Agency (DIA), also attended. On October 10 each of the attendees briefed Cheney and Powell at the Pentagon. The next day the group went to the White House to brief the President. The air portion of the plan was accepted without much argument, but the ground attack stirred up some controversy. Johnston's wrap-up of the briefings stated that success could not be guaranteed without an additional corps and he indicated that at least 90 days were necessary to accomplish such a reinforcement. Purvis recalls that some of the civilian members present did ask about an Inchon-like amphibious option, which the military leaders were quick to oppose. The need for a second corps had surfaced.[16]

TWO-CORPS OPTION

After Purvis returned to Riyadh on October 15, Schwarzkopf wasted no time ordering him to begin planning for a two-corps attack. Now the planners had the forces to develop a feasible option, although Schwarzkopf ruled out both amphibious and airborne operations. While they both held promise, both would put American lives at greater risk. An amphibious assault on the heavily fortified Kuwaiti coast was impossible unless the sophisticated mines guarding the approaches could be cleared, a task that the Navy claimed could require as long as a month. CENTCOM's early assessment of the Iraqi air defense network suggested that an airborne insertion would be equally costly. Isolated and relatively immobile once on the ground, the 82d would be difficult to support and sustain from the air alone. Airborne forces were ill-suited for warfare in open desert, particularly against mobile armored forces, and the Guard would be no more than a day's march from any prospective airhead. Schwarzkopf believed airborne forces would be better suited to attack airfields or built-up areas less likely to contain tanks. He did see real value in using the airborne and Marine forces to tie down the Iraqis by making them believe that both options would be exercised. In fact, with their high media profile and fearsome reputation, airborne and Marine amphibious forces would distract Iraqi planners until the war's end. The amphibious threat alone forced Saddam to keep seven divisions focused on the coast to crush a landing that never came.

On October 16 the Purvis group began to develop a plan for a two-corps attack deep inside the great Iraqi desert west of the Wadi al-Batin. They had to identify how a second corps should be configured. Although it had not yet been identified, VII Corps was the most likely candidate. Clearly, the corps would need to be armor-heavy to match the Iraqi predominance in armor. It made sense to give the prospective heavy corps responsibility for the main effort. Unquestionably, the Guard would be the center of gravity and the main objective. To match such a powerful mass of first-rate armor would require at least three heavy divisions. Even if the air attack destroyed up to half of the Iraqi ground forces, the Coalition would only outnumber the enemy about two to one at the point of the attack. The prospects offered by a swing several hundred kilometers to the west might give logisticians heart failure, but the maneuver conjured up images of great end runs like Rommel's sweep around the British 8th Army at Gazala in May 1942 or Guderian's XIX Panzer Corps' brilliant slip through the Ardennes and dash to the English Channel in May 1940. Logisticians might dampen the ardor of the planners, but the prospect of a second corps opened up limitless opportunities to exploit the unmatched agility of American armored forces.

On October 17 Schwarzkopf momentarily lifted the veil of secrecy that surrounded the planning effort so that the British forces commander, Lieutenant General Sir Peter de La Billiere, and Yeosock could be briefed separately on the one- and two-corps planning options. Both generals believed the as yet sketchy two-corps plan was feasible and supportable so long as both corps swung far enough west of the Wadi al-Batin to envelop all of the static Iraqi forces and avoid the dense Iraqi defensive belt. They pointed out that psychological operations and strategic deception, especially in the case of the one-corps plan, would help to even the odds by causing desertions and fooling the Iraqis about the actual location of the attack. Both also zeroed in on the importance of establishing logistical bases deep in the western desert to support a wide swing for the two-corps attack.

In giving the heavy corps responsibility for the main attack west of the Wadi al-Batin, the planners had to determine how other forces would be employed in secondary and supporting attacks. The group considered putting XVIII Airborne Corps either east or west of the main attack or even passing the main attack through XVIII Corps. By October 21 the different options were complete and had been approved by Admiral Sharp and Brigadier General James Monroe, the ARCENT G4, for presentation to the CINC.

When Schwarzkopf saw the concept for a two-corps attack, he suddenly became very animated and enthusiastic about the course of action that placed XVIII Airborne Corps wide to the west of the main attack. Standing at the map and pointing at the two corps arrows, one aimed at the Euphrates River and the other to the east of the northern border of Kuwait, he said in a booming voice, "I sit on Highway 8... I've threatened his Republican Guard; now I'll destroy it."[17] Although no one knew it at the time, at that moment the concept of the Great Wheel became fixed in the CINC's mind. The XVIII Airborne Corps was now committed to cutting Highway 8 south of the Euphrates River in what would prove to be one of the longest single envelopments in history. The as yet unnamed heavy corps would conduct the main attack between the wadi and XVIII Corps and sweep northeast to secure the Kuwaiti northern border with

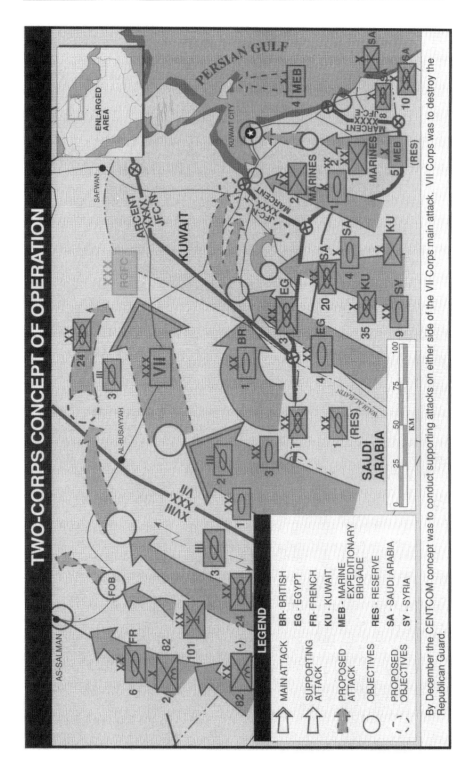

TWO-CORPS CONCEPT OF OPERATION

By December the CENTCOM concept was to conduct supporting attacks on either side of the VII Corps main attack. VII Corps was to destroy the Republican Guard.

LEGEND

MAIN ATTACK	BR - BRITISH
SUPPORTING ATTACK	EG - EGYPT
	FR - FRENCH
PROPOSED ATTACK	KU - KUWAIT
	MEB - MARINE EXPEDITIONARY BRIGADE
OBJECTIVES	RES - RESERVE
	SA - SAUDI ARABIA
PROPOSED OBJECTIVES	SY - SYRIA

Iraq. The Marines were originally plotted adjacent to the main attacking corps just east of the wadi and assigned a very limited attack objective that would secure the ARCENT lines of communication. Coalition Arab-Islamic forces would have similarly limited attack objectives along the Kuwaiti southern border to tie down frontline Iraqi units. Amphibious forces would remain embarked to threaten the Kuwaiti coastline. Schwarzkopf's only change to this concept was to insist on engaging the Republican Guard force before going on to secure the Kuwaiti northern border. He emphasized that the Guard was the *main operational objective* and that it must be completely destroyed.

SELECTING A CORPS

In October, at the same time that rotation of divisional-size units and additional Reserve call-ups were being considered, the ARSTAF began to look more intensely at reinforcement options. Though the two-corps plan would not get aired outside of Schwarzkopf's tight inner circle until after the decision to send a second corps had been made, it was evident that any reinforcement would have to be in the form of one of the Army's heavy corps. The three candidates were III Corps at Fort Hood, Texas, and V and VII Corps in Germany.

III Corps had already supported the Desert Shield deployment with the 1st "Tiger" Brigade of the 2d Armored Division, the 3d Armored Cavalry Regiment, and the 1st Cavalry Division. The corps still had a brigade of the 2d Armored Division, the 1st, 4th, and 5th Infantry Divisions (Mech), and the large 6th Cavalry Brigade (Air Combat) equipped with Apache helicopters. With some of its heavy forces already in the Gulf, sending the rest of the corps made sense. However, three concerns argued against using III Corps. First, deploying the rest of the corps would deplete the Army of its Stateside heavy forces, and to take such a risk flew in the face of Vuono's readiness vector should another crisis arise. Second, each of the corps' heavy divisions had a roundout brigade in the Reserve components. Earlier concerns with mobilizing and deploying the 48th Infantry Brigade for more than 180 days remained, and the Army knew the other roundout brigades would take some time to become combat ready. The other roundout units faced similar difficulties. Third, the distance from the United States to the Gulf argued against III Corps. If the reinforcement was to be expeditious, the Army could not afford to have three heavy divisions bobbing about at sea for more than four weeks. The state of some of III Corps' equipment also caused concern. The divisions had not all been modernized to the M1A1 Abrams, for example, and the 6th Cavalry Brigade (Air Combat) had not fully recovered from extensive wind damage to many of its aircraft caused by a storm that devastated Fort Hood in 1989. Collectively, the Army planners concluded they would get more combat power more quickly by turning to Europe.

Ordinarily, deploying one of the Germany-based corps would be out of the question. First, it had never been done in more than 45 years of standing watch in Europe, and second, getting NATO approval for an out-of-theater deployment seemed unlikely. Fortunately, times had changed from the earlier tensions of the Cold War. The two Germanies were reuniting, the Berlin Wall was down, and American cavalry no longer patrolled along the Warsaw Pact border. Furthermore, the Army had already broken the mold in a small way on the out-of-theater deployment with V Corps' 12th Aviation Brigade which had joined XVIII Airborne Corps in the Gulf. This was more than a symbolic breaking of tradition. The way was open to an even larger effort if the political hurdles could be overcome. Perhaps the deciding factor in selecting a European-based corps over a US-based one was the existing plan to inactivate VII Corps. In any event, both European corps were fully modernized and the distance from Germany to the Gulf could be covered in only two weeks' sailing versus four to five for III Corps.

Some negotiation over the units to be sent was still necessary with Commander-in-Chief, US Army Europe and Seventh Army, General Crosbie Saint. General Saint wanted to carefully select which units to send in order to keep a viable force in Germany and to stay on track with as much of the scheduled force reduction program as possible. The two corps in Germany were essentially equal. Sending VII Corps to the Gulf would serve as a stopover before inactivation in the United States. The eventual decision was a compromise. VII Corps would deploy with its headquarters, support structure, and 1st Armored Division, along with V Corps' 3d Armored Division and 1st Infantry Division (Mech). Notably, only the Army of the eighties could have built a corps for combat in this manner. The Army shared a common doctrine under AirLand Battle that was understood and followed. Soldiers trained to the same standard proven on the "battlefields" of the NTC and at Grafenwohr and Hohenfels. Officers shared a common doctrinal background. Elimination of regional proclivities between major commands had fused the Army into a single fighting machine with interchangeable parts—a machine that would be tested in February when the last arriving combat brigades would go directly from the docks in ad-Dammam into attack positions as the ground war started.

THE CHAIRMAN ENDORSES THE TWO-CORPS PLAN

General Powell met with Schwarzkopf in Riyadh on October 22 and 23. After being briefed on both the one- and two-corps options, Powell assured Schwarzkopf that he would get whatever he felt he needed to succeed. Upon his return to Washington, Powell endorsed the two-corps plan and recommended reinforcing CENTCOM with VII Corps as soon as possible. Meanwhile, Purvis' planning group had to sort out many issues that Powell raised during his visit. For one thing, the logistics buildup and force positioning had to be delayed until the last possible moment in order to convince the Iraqis that the attack would come directly at them through Kuwait rather than around their right flank well to the west. Should US forces reposition themselves for the attack too soon, Saddam might react by moving the Republican Guard into the western desert to oppose them.

Schwarzkopf wanted Yeosock to flesh out the details of the theater ground plan for CENTCOM at the same time that he worked on the ARCENT offensive plans. He temporarily transferred Purvis and his planning group to ARCENT on October 24 to work under the operational control of Brigadier General Steve Arnold, the ARCENT G3. It was an unusual arrangement, to be sure. The group remained in the CENTCOM building for security reasons, but now, at least mentally, moved down one level of command to work on time sequencing and phasing for both the one- and two-corps options. Even though on October 25 Secretary Cheney announced the reinforcement of the theater on all national networks, this dual effort would continue for the next five days until Schwarzkopf told the planners to focus exclusively on the two-corps plan.

While the CINC's planning group was still playing with the "big pieces" of the entire Coalition ground force, Arnold was able to get permission from Schwarzkopf to bring a few more planners into the game. On October 26, the group briefed selected XVIII Airborne Corps personnel and two days later picked up a small group from the corps and ARCENT to aid in the effort.

VII CORPS PREPARES TO DEPLOY

By the time the President announced the deployment of VII Corps on November 8, 1990, the situation in the Gulf had reached a point where offensive action seemed inevitable. The VII Corps commander, Lieutenant General Frederick Franks, Jr., had received enough warning to alert a few of his staff and commanders to prepare for deployment from garrisons in Germany. In fact, as early as August, Franks had had the foresight to keep planning efforts warm for eventual deployment. The 4-229th Attack Helicopter Battalion of the corps' 11th Aviation Brigade had been alerted in August to deploy with its 18 AH-64 Apaches to join the 12th Aviation Brigade already en route to the desert. The warning order set the corps staff in motion and obliged them to focus on a non-European battlefield for the first time in two generations. Even after the 4-229th was dropped from deployment consideration, Franks had wisely kept a select group of planners together. Franks anticipated the prospect of rotating other units with those already in Saudi Arabia should the deployment last many more months. While the group was small, the effort they initially put forward would prove to be a valuable warm-up for the corps' eventual deployment in November.

Early VII Corps planning efforts were strapped by the same shortage of maps that the Purvis group had encountered. By the time the corps was alerted for deployment, the increased demand severely strained the Defense Mapping Agency. Satellite collection was tasked to provide the data for 1:50,000-scale maps of the operational area. ARCENT had chosen that scale in November and the DMA had suspended all other projects to fill the order. The DMA was then unable to shift production to the 1:100,000-scale maps requested by VII Corps. In total, the DMA produced 13.5 million maps, 10 million in 1:50,000. Getting the maps into the theater and moved forward further strained the already stretched logistical system. The Theater Map Depot moved more than 800 pallets of maps to Dhahran, Riyadh, and KKMC. Units using the "plenty squared" formula added to the problem by requesting blanket coverage of the area. Faced with the logjam on distribution and the lack of 1:100,000 maps, both corps used their organic topographic units to create 1:100,000 maps from the 1:50,000 versions.[18]

VII Corps, nicknamed the Jayhawk Corps, was in a significant state of flux in the fall of 1990. Army force reduction plans called for closure or realignment of many corps units and caserns. The entire 1st Infantry Division (Forward), a reinforced brigade located at Goeppingen, was already in the process of furling its flag. At the same time the corps would receive another Apache unit, the 6-6th Cavalry, fresh from training at Fort Hood. Franks found himself in the bizarre position of having to reduce and realign some units while planning possible deployment for others, all the while continuing to train the rest of the corps as best he could. He wanted to push training harder, but the already tight schedule for major training areas and ranges could not be disrupted on the odd chance that the corps might deploy to Desert Shield.[19] While the announcement on November 8 did not totally surprise the corps, it definitely put many of the reduction efforts on hold for the duration of the war. Two battalions from the 1st Infantry Division (Forward) were among the first units to deploy even though the brigade was in the process of closing down. Franks decided to use these soldiers to assist in running support activities for the corps at the ports.

FAMILY SUPPORT CHALLENGE IN GERMANY

The massive deployment of VII Corps and other units from Germany presented unique family support challenges. USAREUR units deploying in August and September laid the initial groundwork, but the order of magnitude rose tenfold with November's reinforcement announcement. Thirteen major military communities, each comprising three or more subcommunities on more than 40 different installations, gave up large numbers if not nearly all of their military members to the deployment.

Fortunately, every married soldier had prepared a Noncombatant Evacuation Operations (NEO) packet containing much of the same information required for the deployment. Powers of attorney, wills, and other critical documents had only to be updated. Military couples and single parents' NEO packets included family support plans that covered arrangements for dependents in such emergencies. Specified guardians, however, were often back in the United States and few soldiers had time to escort family members home. Arranging for those dependents to travel required close cooperation between their guardians and the Army.

With much of VII Corps already scheduled for inactivation, many family members wondered if it would be better to await the return of their loved ones in the US. Should large numbers of dependents disperse to the United States, however, community support would be seriously degraded and the concept of the chain of concern would suffer equally. Encouraged to remain in place, most of the 300,000 family members affected by the deployment chose to do so.

Units remaining in Germany, the deploying units, and their rear detachment chains of command, working with the informal chain of concern network of spouses, ensured adequate care and meticulous and continuous command attention to family support. Locally, many Germans—often German army partnership units—volunteered to assist American family members left behind. In many cases, German commanders attached sergeants to assist American rear detachment commanders in working out problems with the local German community. This unprecedented effort was a source of great comfort to the deploying soldiers as well as to those left behind.

VUONO CREATES A REPLACEMENT SYSTEM

Once the decision to reinforce Desert Shield had been made, General Vuono was faced with the probability that the Army would soon engage in large-scale combat. If combat losses were too great, Vuono's limited pool of trained replacement manpower might not be enough to support his first two vectors. Therefore, he made four key personnel decisions to ensure that a pool of soldiers would be available should casualties decrease the existing pool. His "stop loss" policy essentially canceled routine reassignments, delayed some scheduled retirements for soldiers with critical skills, and postponed discharges. He retained in command for the duration brigade and battalion commanders who had more than three months remaining on their command tours. Commanders within three months could be released if a replacement was available and the incumbent was en route to a critical assignment or career school such as the War College. He also dispatched a number of unassigned lieutenant colonels and colonels to the theater to be ready to take over battalions, brigades, and other key positions should casualties claim the incumbents.

Vuono would not permit the draining of nondeployed Stateside units. Whenever replacements were absolutely necessary, he insisted that intact crews be sent rather than individual soldiers. The largest slice of available military manpower was the Individual Ready Reserve (IRR) consisting of recently released soldiers who had completed active duty but remained committed to the Reserves. The opportunity to activate the IRR came on January 18 when the President authorized the call-up to active duty for 24 months of a million Reservists. Within the ARSTAF, some trepidation existed about the wisdom of calling back ex-soldiers. Some estimated that fewer than 50 percent would respond to the call, and those who did respond would take a great deal of time and effort to retrain. The IRR's response exceeded even the most optimistic expectations, however. Almost 90 percent of the 20,000 soldiers who received a mailgram notice reported to mobilization stations by February 1, 1991. Soldiers who were expected to need weeks of training were able to revalidate individual and crew proficiency in just a few days. Some IRR Abrams and Bradley crews who had served with units in Germany assembled at stations there and qualified after a single live-fire battle run on the demanding training tables at Grafenwohr. As the air operation progressed, the Army placed more than 13,000 IRRs on active duty in critical combat and support skills. More than half of these soldiers served overseas in Europe or Southwest Asia.

CENTCOM RECEIVES VII CORPS

As Jayhawk units scrambled to deploy from Germany, the ARSTAF tabbed the 1st Infantry Division at Fort Riley, Kansas, to join VII Corps in Saudi Arabia. The deployment came as no surprise to the "Big Red One" commander, Major General Thomas Rhame. He had been exercising the division for some months on breaching operations and desert combat during several rotations at the National Training Center. Rhame was not privy to the Purvis plan, but he involved his division in operations he knew would be required in the future. It was like a theatrical production in which the costumes and scenery were known, the stage was identified, and the cast was selected. All that remained was to complete the script and assign specific roles to the players. Much could be done without knowing the script, and some of what was practiced ahead of time would influence the eventual roles that each player would be assigned.

November was a chaotic month for all concerned. The Purvis group finally scrapped the one-corps plan and turned full attention to the two-corps option. On November 10 they briefed Schwarzkopf on a plan for the initial positioning of VII Corps and subsequent movement of both corps into attack positions west of the Wadi al-Batin. Schwarzkopf's guidance was to keep everything in place east of the wadi to maintain the deception of an attack into Kuwait for as long as possible. At that point he accepted placing VII Corps immediately west of XVIII Airborne Corps. Depending on XVIII Airborne Corps' eventual mission, they would have to devise a crossover plan to pass the corps around or through VII Corps at the right moment to get both corps into attack positions before launching the ground offensive.

The main thrust of the planning effort during the remainder of November was to bring VII Corps on board in a manner that would facilitate reception, movement to initial assembly areas, and subsequent combat. Naturally, the plan was logistics-intensive. The movement from port to logistics areas would have to be made quickly in spite of limited road space with even more limited transportation. Operationally, General Arnold's expanded planning staff was hard-pressed to sort out the crossover plan between the two corps as well to assign missions that would take advantage of the unique capabilities of the various Coalition forces.

On November 13, Franks brought his division, corps artillery, armored cavalry regiment, separate brigade, corps support commanders, and primary staff officers to Saudi Arabia for a leaders' reconnaissance. The next day at Dhahran, Schwarzkopf gave an overview of the concept to all US Army commanders down to division level at what may have been the most important meeting of the entire war. As Schwarzkopf defined his concept of the operation in general terms, he specified destruction of the Guard as the objective of the overall campaign, assigned VII Corps the main attack mission, and set mid-January as the time to be ready to execute the Great Wheel.

Planning in VII Corps at the time was focused on getting to the theater, but time was too tight for mistakes. Every decision made in Germany would directly affect the ability of units to form up and fight in the KTO. Commanders on the leaders' reconnaissance made dozens of calls back to Germany to energize the already busy staffs and to redirect attention to specific needs. XVIII Airborne Corps soldiers with extensive experience in the austere Desert Shield environment reminded VII Corps officers time and again to bring everything that might be needed and not to count on getting anything in theater.

SECRECY AND REFINEMENT

Security surrounding the planning process continued to be very tight. The concept was classified "Top Secret, Special Category," one of the highest levels of classification used by the military. General Arnold and the ARCENT planning staff could brief only commanders and a few planners from each division, cavalry regiment, corps artillery, and separate brigade.

Such a level of security created friction with the media. Perhaps at no time since the Inchon Landing during the Korean War had it become so essential to cloak from the enemy such a major operational maneuver. In a region of the world in which secrets are not well preserved, Schwarzkopf faced the very difficult task of moving 255,000 soldiers into attack positions over a three-week period without tipping off Saddam. Had Saddam gotten wind of the movement, he could easily have shifted the Republican Guard southwestward and reoriented them toward VII Corps. Given time, he could also have extended the defensive barrier farther westward across VII Corps' path. The planning group was well aware that either action could cost the lives of thousands of soldiers.

Unlike Inchon, which was planned and prepared under a news black-out in Japan, the Great Wheel was being planned in Riyadh, which was literally crawling with reporters. In Japan, communications had been deliberate enough to ensure that inadvertent slips to the media were intercepted before damage could be done. In the era of instant global communications where raw, unfiltered information is routinely broadcast, any similar leak would have found its way to Baghdad within minutes. The CINC's legitimate concern with operational security greatly limited access to the plan even within his own headquarters. Restrictions on media access to sensitive areas that might jeopardize the plan were even more severe.

November and December were devoted to refinement of the plan. ARCENT approved several major decisions that shaped the positioning of units for the attack. The XVIII Airborne Corps would attack along the line from Rafha to as-Salman to an-Nasiriyah in the Euphrates Valley. Schwarzkopf scotched an earlier idea to go farther to the northwest to as-Samawah. He ordered a shorter envelopment to ensure that the corps would cut off Highway 8 and eliminate any opportunity for the Guard to escape destruction by VII Corps. Schwarzkopf was concerned that a wider envelopment of as-Samawah farther to the west would spread XVIII Airborne Corps too thinly, thereby opening a large gap with VII Corps. Should the Guard turn on Luck's forces by thrusting up Highway 8, VII Corps would be too far to the east to provide timely reinforcement.

Franks was uncomfortable with placing the initial VII Corps tactical assembly areas immediately adjacent to XVIII Airborne Corps. He wanted to move as far west as possible to reduce the distance and number of moves necessary to get to his attack position. Schwarzkopf approved moving the corps west up to the Wadi al-Batin, but no farther.

CENTCOM also needed to decide how to utilize the military capabilities of other Coalition forces. The British 1st Armoured Division had been aligned with the US Marines from the start. The British wanted a more important role in the main attack to make the best use of their capabilities, so they asked to become part of the VII Corps main effort and in December won Schwarzkopf's approval for attachment. The British division had been aligned originally with the Marines to provide the armored punch necessary to protect the lightly armored and relatively immobile Marines from Iraqi armor. Schwarzkopf replaced them with the "Tiger" Brigade then attached to the 1st Cavalry Division.

Schwarzkopf intended for the Marines and the Arab-Islamic forces to form an anvil against which VII Corps would crush the Guard. He placed the Marines between two Arab forces, each about a corps in strength. The Egyptian corps and a Syrian division were to the left of the Marines, and a smaller formation of Saudis, Moroccans, Qatari, and other units were tucked into an enclave to the east along the coast. By moving farther east, the Marines would also be closer to their sea line of communication.

The French 6th Light Armored Division also needed to be integrated into the plan. Assembled from units from all over France and named "Daquet" in honor of a small, feisty, antlered deer, the French force was roughly equivalent to an armored cavalry regiment. As such, it was ideally suited to a screening and security mission. The French could have gone with either US corps in December, but the decision to place them with XVIII Airborne Corps was based on common sense. Daquet was deployed into the theater and supported from the port of Yanbu on the Red Sea. Pushing them farther west with XVIII Airborne Corps shortened their lines of communication.

Schwarzkopf decided in late November to make the 1st Cavalry Division the theater reserve. He was concerned about a potential Iraqi preemptive attack down the Wadi al-Batin, and he wanted to place the division in a position to defend Hafar al-Batin or KKMC, located just west of the wadi. The Cavalry began movement on December 27, the same day the French were placed under the tactical control of XVIII Airborne Corps and the "Tiger" Brigade went under the operational control of the Marines.

Once they had received Schwarzkopf's November 14 concept briefing, each corps began to develop and analyze new courses of action. Yeosock then received individual brief-backs from each corps commander. Luck, who briefed on November 30, was most concerned about fuel. Precious few tankers were available in the theater, and if XVIII Airborne Corps was expected to attack all the way to the Euphrates, Luck would need many, if not most of them. Fuel tankers were just one commodity that Yeosock and his staff would have to broker between the two corps.

Franks, who briefed Yeosock during a short visit the week before his main headquarters deployed to Dhahran, suggested two variations to the draft concept plan. He wanted either to place XVIII Airborne Corps on his eastern flank or to pass through XVIII Airborne Corps after it had established a breach. With XVIII Airborne Corps on his right, Franks could swing VII Corps farther to the west without having to worry about an assailable open flank. The second alternative preserved VII Corps combat power by having XVIII Airborne Corps open and secure the breach. Franks reasoned that both options committed the most combat power to smashing the Guard without the need to conduct a time-and-resource-consuming breaching operation. Franks' alternatives were feasible variations of earlier plans that the Purvis group had considered, but again, concern over casualties prevailed. Neither Schwarzkopf nor Yeosock was receptive to the thought of pitting the lighter XVIII Airborne Corps against such a heavily defended zone.

After briefing Yeosock, the corps commanders continued to work on their individual plans. Luck used the BCTP team from Fort Leavenworth, which had helped with defensive plans in October, to war-game several iterations of his plans and train the staff. A larger contingent from BCTP had arrived on November 30 to assist ARCENT in offensive planning. Franks would use them in January but in December could only do a limited amount of war-gaming. Yeosock recognized his need to synchronize the plans of both corps, so he convened a map exercise on December 27 that proved useful in identifying and resolving the ever-increasing logistical challenges.

THE LAND COMPONENT COMMANDER (LCC) ISSUE

Schwarzkopf's span of control could easily become overextended. The two US corps were contending with the US Marines, the French, the British, and the Arab-Islamic forces for many of the same resources. The Coalition had already grown to a multinational, multi-Service force under the shared control of CENTCOM and the Saudi prince, Lieutenant General Khalid bin Sultan. The Saudis had insisted on commanding all Arab forces. Yet the need to maintain unity of command called for establishing a land component commander in charge of all ground forces. Schwarzkopf recognized this dilemma and discussed it at length with his deputy commander, Lieutenant General Calvin Waller. If General Powell was analogous to George C. Marshall during World War II and Schwarzkopf occupied Eisenhower's role as Supreme Allied Commander, Schwarzkopf wondered who should have command of all ground forces.[20] There was no easy answer during World War II and none was forthcoming in November and December 1990 either. Political sensitivities argued against placing Arab forces under an American land commander. Technically, CENTCOM did not control Arab-Islamic forces, and Khalid was Schwarzkopf's political equal.

British and French forces posed fewer problems for integration. Years of NATO exercises and numerous standard agreements dealing with doctrine and training had created a common cultural bias essential for armies to operate together efficiently in the field. All three armies went to extraordinary lengths to create formal bonds through exchange of liaison teams and close association among commanders through personal and unit partnerships. In addition, the US, France, and Britain established strong, instantaneous communications among all major fighting units, in some cases down to regimental level.

Schwarzkopf's practical and philosophical obsession with trading tail for teeth presented another argument against creating a separate LCC. If he approved another headquarters to control both ARCENT and the Marines, and perhaps the Arab forces, he would create another staff layer complete with a four-star general and all the staff accoutrements that go along with it. In retrospect, a few hundred more soldiers might seem insignificant, but at the time resources were stretched so thin that another major headquarters in Saudi Arabia was out of the question.

Schwarzkopf made the tough decision to retain the land component commander responsibility for himself, with Waller serving as his primary assistant for ground combat issues. The decision created numerous challenges and difficulties. Though Yeosock was clearly charged with commanding the two US corps, Schwarzkopf was within his rights as the LCC in going directly to the corps commanders with instructions. From the other direction, the two corps commanders dealt directly with Yeosock. Lieutenant General Charles Horner, as the joint forces air component commander (JFACC), could go directly to the CINC, whereas Yeosock competed with the Arab command and the Marines for Schwarzkopf's attention. This rather convoluted arrangement certainly went against the principles of simplicity and unity of command. That it was made to work as smoothly as it did was attributable to the powerful personalities and professionalism of the senior commanders.

THE PLAN EXPANDS

Consumed initially with the need to clear the ports and move forward into the desert, the VII Corps planning effort for the offensive did not get off the ground until relatively late. Franks had very little time to tie together the complicated wheeling movement his corps was about to execute. It was conceivable, in fact, that some of his subordinate divisions might have just enough time to dock, unload, acclimate, and go into battle. Like any good coach, he recognized the need for a pregame "chalk talk" session to clearly set his intent and to embed the game plan in the players' minds at the earliest possible moment. On New Year's Day, he huddled with his regimental, separate brigade, and division commanders at KKMC, even while most of VII Corps was still loading out in

Germany or was at sea. As the first step in embedding the plan, Franks and his G3, Colonel Stan Cherrie, gave a short briefing. Three days later came the main event when the BCTP staff, recently imported in its entirety from Fort Leavenworth, conducted an elaborate and thorough computer exercise.

The war-gaming facility at KKMC looked at first glance as if a movie crew had mistakenly dumped Star Wars paraphernalia into the middle of a set intended for *The Thief of Baghdad*. KKMC was originally built in 1974 to house a Saudi National Guard brigade. Two magnificent pools, topped by cascading falls and sparkling fountains flowing over beautiful mosaic tiles, formed the centerpiece of the KKMC complex of buildings. On the right, an olympic-sized pool occupied one side of a glassed-in gymnasium. The central building surrounded the fountains in a quadrangle of three- and four-storied glass and concrete offices and barracks. Multicolored, onion-shaped minarets marked the mosque towering over the complex, which soldiers called "Emerald City." With French, British, Saudi, and other soldiers of indeterminate origin wandering about, it had the air of an international bazaar.

On January 4 Franks and the VII Corps senior leadership gathered around a horseshoe of tables in a huge room in the midst of this incongruous setting. In three days the group would play out each phase of the corps' draft plan. The BCTP threat team carefully constructed a computer model of Iraqi forces the corps would face. The normal BCTP process was streamlined and tailored for the war game. A group of about 20 BCTP operators worked behind dividers, entering corps and division orders directly into the mainframe. As an event or operation developed, these operators passed the computer results to corps leaders. Periodically the corps group would break down into unit huddles to work out any planning wrinkles brought to light during each computer run. Considerable cross talk and coordination with other unit groups during the war game solidified the plan and cut down on later confusion as each commander clarified his actions to his boss and those around him. While the computer simulation in this exercise had some utility, more valuable to Franks was the interchange and team "chatter" among his commanders. In those three days he was able to implant his intent and operational concept firmly in the consciousness of his commanders and staff.

IRAQI DISPOSITIONS IN NOVEMBER

By the end of November, Saddam had deployed 28 divisions to the KTO, representing 60 percent of his available combat power and 40 percent of his divisional strength. Another six infantry divisions entered the KTO as he reactivated reserves or fleshed out understrength infantry brigades, which he pulled off the Iranian border and sent south to thicken forward defenses. As these new infantry units deployed to the KTO, they plugged gaps in the first line of defense and began to create a second defensive line, notably along high-speed avenues of approach into Kuwait. The Iraqi engineers lived up to their reputation as prodigious builders. As soon as a first defensive belt of wire, trenches, and mines was completed, they began the construction of a second, this time complete with a menacing system of fire trenches filled with crude oil. By November, the Iraqis had arrayed nearly 150 battalions of tube and rocket artillery throughout the KTO. The system of defensive firepower they developed called for the massing of several battalions of artillery into carefully planned box-like concentrations plotted principally around each defensive belt. The object of the artillery plan was to saturate American forces stalled in front of these belts with tons of projectiles.

Command and control of these forces ultimately rested with Iraqi general headquarters in Baghdad. The headquarters forward element was located at Basrah. As always, the high command divided tactical control between the Republican Guard and the regular army. Al-Rawi's Guard divisions served as a theater reserve for the KTO and Saddam's strategic reserve. In addition to the Republican Guard, three regular army heavy divisions also performed the role of theater reserve, albeit through separate command channels. Command of the forward defenses and their operational reserves rested with four corps headquarters.

Special Forces teams patrolled the Kuwait-Iraq border area to provide early warning.

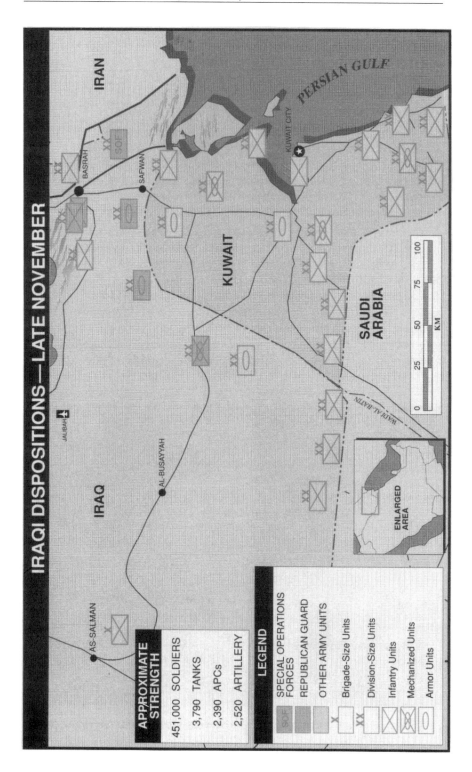

IRAQI DISPOSITIONS—LATE NOVEMBER

IRAN

PERSIAN GULF

KUWAIT CITY

BASRAH

SAFWAN

KUWAIT

SAUDI ARABIA

KM

0   25   50   75   100

ENLARGED AREA

WADI AL-BATIN

JALIBAH

AL-BUSAYYAH

IRAQ

AS-SALMAN

APPROXIMATE STRENGTH

451,000 SOLDIERS

3,790 TANKS

2,390 APCs

2,520 ARTILLERY

LEGEND

SOF — SPECIAL OPERATIONS FORCES

REPUBLICAN GUARD

OTHER ARMY UNITS

X — Brigade-Size Units

XX — Division-Size Units

Infantry Units

Mechanized Units

Armor Units

During the Purvis group's planning efforts in September and October, Iraqi defenses west of Kuwait remained relatively stable. Five Iraqi divisions had occupied the western desert opposite the two American corps. Two infantry divisions—one in place since mid-August—were tied into the Iraqi frontal defenses in Kuwait across the Wadi al-Batin. A 45-kilometer gap existed between these two divisions and the 26th Infantry Division, the next major combat formation arrayed westward along the border. The gap was covered to some extent by two second-echelon heavy divisions, the 52d Armored Division and the Republican Guard's Tawakalna Mechanized Division. These formations were centered some 65 kilometers behind the forward infantry division and were positioned to strike any Coalition force that sought to exploit the 45-kilometer gap by attacking up the Wadi al-Batin toward Basrah. The Iraqis had used this armored ambush technique against the Iranians. The objective was simply to lure a large armored formation far enough up the wadi that it could not withdraw and then destroy it by a mobile flank attack from two directions. Some 20 battalions of artillery out of the 150 in theater were available to support these units. By November and December the picture had not changed significantly, and it was expected to stay about the same through January.

SCHWARZKOPF'S SYMPHONY

Schwarzkopf anticipated that two weeks would be needed to execute the Great Wheel. The air operation was planned for about the same amount of time but could be continued or shortened depending on weather and the ability of the Air Force to destroy Iraqi equipment.

In order to maintain the deception, the two corps would not begin to move into final attack positions west of Wadi al-Batin until air power had blinded Saddam. The crossover of the two corps would have to be completed entirely during the air operation, not before. Franks and Luck would have just two weeks to conduct one of the most complex movements of major ground forces in history. More than 64,000 wheeled and tracked vehicles and 255,000 soldiers from the two corps would have to be shifted laterally as much as 300 miles. Concurrently, the 22d Support Command would have to construct and stock two enormous logistics bases with 60 days' supplies to support each corps.

During the weeks of the air operation, some details of the plan would change, but the essential concept was solid enough to remain intact. The ground offensive would commence on Schwarzkopf's orders with the two supporting attacks on the flanks of VII Corps' main attack. On the right of VII Corps, the Arab forces and the Marines would begin with artillery and naval gunfire preparations, while the 4th Marine Expeditionary Brigade feinted an amphibious landing off the Kuwaiti coast. To the west of VII Corps, XVIII Airborne Corps would commence their attack at

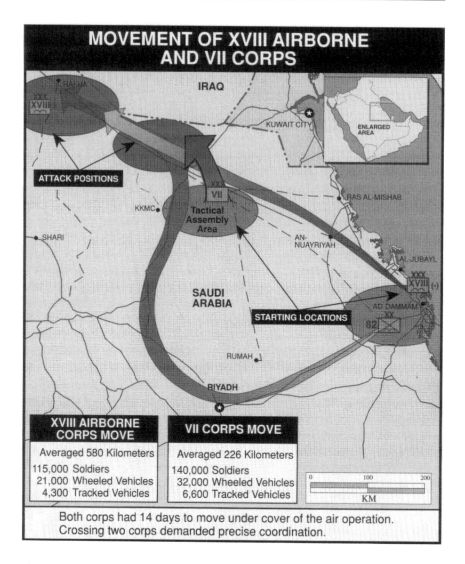

MOVEMENT OF XVIII AIRBORNE AND VII CORPS

XVIII AIRBORNE CORPS MOVE	VII CORPS MOVE
Averaged 580 Kilometers	Averaged 226 Kilometers
115,000 Soldiers 21,000 Wheeled Vehicles 4,300 Tracked Vehicles	140,000 Soldiers 32,000 Wheeled Vehicles 6,600 Tracked Vehicles

Both corps had 14 days to move under cover of the air operation. Crossing two corps demanded precise coordination.

the same time as the Coalition forces and Marines, with simultaneous ground and air assault thrusts. These two attacks would continue for 24 hours before VII Corps began the main attack.

Schwarzkopf wanted to do two things with the supporting attacks as preconditions for the success of the main effort. First, Arab and Marine attacks into Kuwait and the amphibious feint would reinforce the deception plan and keep the Iraqis focused to the south and east. Second, the distraction caused by the Arab and Marine thrust would give XVIII Airborne Corps time to push largely unopposed into Iraq to close off any chance that the Republican Guard might escape. The plan for the main attack called for five armored divisions to form a spoke of the Great Wheel. If these divisions were to maintain alignment along the spoke, those near the hub would have to advance relatively slowly while those near the rim would have to charge very far, very fast. Alignment was important to avoid piecemeal engagement once contact with the Republican Guard was made. If the rotation went according to plan, all five divisions would turn shoulder to shoulder and slam into the Guard simultaneously in a collision of unprecedented violence and shock effect. Audacious, ambitious, and complex, the Great Wheel would be ready to start turning by mid-February.

ARCENT used the time remaining before Desert Storm to continue planning, to build up logistics bases, and to train for anticipated operations. Once the air attacks began, all of the planners who had had a hand in the eventual campaign plan would be able to see their efforts put into practice. Purvis and his group were returned to the CENTCOM chief of staff's control on January 27, 1991. Their main mission while the air operation continued was to assist Schwarzkopf in his decisions for each 72-hour cycle.

CONTINGENCY PLANS BECOME "AUDIBLES"

Once the big picture was approved, the ARCENT planners were left with two essential missions. The first was to impress the CINC's vision for the Great Wheel firmly in the psyche of those who were to execute it so that they, in turn, could refine the broad concept into simple orders. The second was to work closely with both corps planning staffs to develop a series of contingency plans. Contingency planning is based on the premise that no operation will develop exactly as intended. Unforeseen impediments, which Clauswitz termed "the frictions of war," invariably deflect a plan from its intended course. To accommodate the unexpected, the planners identified four critical stages or decision points when changes in the Great Wheel's direction, speed, mission, and committed forces might be needed. The first could come immediately after the breach when commanders would assess damage, make necessary adjustments to the time schedule, and turn against the operational reserve with ground and air attacks. The second, and most critical, would occur at Phase Line Smash where Franks would form his armored fist and swing it toward the Republican Guard. The third was when, after smashing through the Guard, Franks would redirect the corps against the remaining Iraqi units and, if possible, block their withdrawal into Iraq. The fourth and last would place the force in the optimum position to end the conflict on the most favorable terms.

The contingency plans were essentially option plays or "audibles" that corps commanders would call on the move to accommodate the enemy's reactions. Thus, precise intelligence on enemy movements was absolutely vital to making the right call. CENTCOM and ARCENT intelligence would have to watch all enemy armored reserves much as a football coaching staff high in the stadium might observe a defensive team lineup for each play. Armed with these "key intelligence reads," the quarterbacks would be able to call exactly the right audible to capitalize on successes or to exploit weaknesses in the enemy's defensive formation. All planning staffs developed elaborate decision matrices to assist in determining the right audible. Subordinate units studied their portions of the plans and ran practice sessions on makeshift sand tables to set the game plan more firmly in all of the players' minds. Each of the corps commanders expressed distinct concepts in his operational plans.

XVIII AIRBORNE COMMANDER'S CONCEPT

General Luck intended to strike with helicopter-borne air assault forces from the 101st deep into the Euphrates River Valley, then follow with heavy armor to sever Highway 8 nearly 200 kilometers deep into Iraq. The corps faced relatively weak forces consisting primarily of infantry units scattered over hundreds of miles of open desert. Luck would accept risk with a bold thrust of the 101st northward to grasp Highway 8 as quickly as possible. Once astride the highway, the division would have to hold on long enough for the 24th Division to link up and completely shut off any possibility of escape. [21]

Each of Luck's divisions had its own separate mission and independent axis of attack. The French 6th Light Armored Division, reinforced with a brigade of the 82d Airborne, was the corps' initial main effort. The 6th would launch a lightning-fast attack up the hard-surfaced road that ran from the border to the town of as-Salman. After securing the town and a nearby fighter base, the French would screen to the west while the rest of the corps advanced. The 101st was to launch the largest air assault attack in history deep into Iraq to get astride Highway 8. The 24th Infantry Division would follow the 101st on the ground, with the 3d ACR on their right screening the boundary with VII Corps, and would become the corps' main effort when it broke into the Euphrates River Valley. With the bulk of his combat forces blocking Highway 8, Luck could then turn the 24th eastward and move along the highway to join VII Corps in the destruction of the Republican Guard. After nearly six months in the desert, Luck felt confident that XVIII Airborne Corps, joined by the 212th Field Artillery Brigade in November, was ready to accomplish its mission. His Active and Reserve combat support and combat service support units brought the corps' total strength on the eve of the war to 117,844 soldiers, 28,000 vehicles, and 980 aircraft.

VII CORPS COMMANDER'S CONCEPT

Franks' plan was for the 1st Infantry Division to conduct the breach of Iraqi defenses in a deliberate, carefully rehearsed, and heavily supported attack. Originally, the entire corps was supposed to pass through the lanes opened by the "Big Red One," but by the start of air operations the Iraqis had failed to extend their defenses to the west, leaving that area relatively undefended. Franks, in a move that showed great adaptability, flexibility, and confidence in his subordinate leaders, decided to modify the plan by slipping the 2d ACR and the 1st and 3d Armored Divisions around the west of the breach. He kept the brunt of his initial attack on his right with the 1st Infantry Division's breach against the Iraqi 26th and 48th Infantry Divisions. Once the breach was complete, the British 1st Armoured Division would thrust through the opening and turn sharply east to destroy the waiting second-echelon forces and spoil any Iraqi plan to spring a two-division armored ambush against the right flank of VII Corps.

The movement of the two US armored divisions forward into the battle area would be controlled, deliberate, and cloaked from enemy view by the advance of the 2d ACR. While the breach and the move on the west were independent actions, the attack on the Republican Guard depended on the success of both operations. The breach was necessary to provide a secure conduit for the heavy logistical forces required to support the advance of the corps. If the Iraqis were able to oppose and delay the advance on the west of the breach, the whole main attack could be jeopardized. Momentum was key. Once the breach site was secure, Franks would form his corps into a tightly clenched fist to shatter the Guard in a massive blow. More than any single factor, the momentum of the armored advance depended on logistics. An armored corps in the attack has a voracious appetite for fuel and ammunition. Franks insisted on no operational pauses until the Republican Guard was destroyed. Any operational pause would take away this key timing edge and allow the Guard to set its defenses. A stable, unbroken enemy would only cause more delay and more casualties. VII Corps units could halt briefly to realign themselves or refuel on the move, but the momentum of the corps would continue unrelentingly until soldiers, supplies, and fuel were exhausted.

Despite the Iraqi border units' continued poor performance in early skirmishes, uncertainty remained. Franks went everywhere in the corps, seeing commanders, checking signals, and talking to soldiers. Franks had one of the most powerful corps the American Army had ever fielded. With three modern armored divisions—the 1st, the 3d, and the British 1st; the 1st Infantry Division (Mech); the 2d ACR; the 11th Aviation Brigade; the 42d, 142d, 75th, and 210th Field Artillery Brigades; the 7th Engineer Brigade; and a host of Active and Reserve component combat support and combat service support units, the corps boasted almost 145,000 men, more than 45,000 vehicles, and more than 600 aircraft.

THE THEATER RESERVE

To counter a possible Iraqi preemptive attack through Hafar al-Batin toward Riyadh, the 1st Cavalry Division had been placed west of the Wadi al-Batin on the ARCENT boundary with the JFC-North. While technically under Schwarzkopf's direct control, Tilelli's division also performed a vital task for VII Corps in persuading the Iraqi high command that American armored forces would indeed attack up the Wadi al-Batin. Once ARCENT did attack, the 1st Cavalry Division would fix the attention of the enemy by striking defensive positions along the wadi with Apaches and artillery and conducting a feint with a one-brigade ground attack.[22] These actions were scheduled to continue until the division was released from its theater reserve role. Although both US corps commanders wanted the 1st Cavalry released to their control at the first opportunity, Schwarzkopf intended to delay that decision to the last possible minute in order to reinforce the Egyptians if necessary and to keep his options open for as long as possible.

TRAINING AND REHEARSALS

Unlike previous wars, the soldiers dispatched to Saudi Arabia arrived in theater thoroughly trained. Instead of green crews only recently introduced to their equipment, most tankers, Bradley crewmen, pilots, and artillerymen had developed an almost instinctual familiarity with modern, high-tech war machinery that could only have been accrued through years of constant training. While personnel turbulence remained a problem in some units, most crewmen had worked and lived together for a considerable time and had bonded well in the tough training environments of the National Training Center and live-fire ranges in Germany, Fort Hood, Texas, and elsewhere. Once on the ground in Saudi Arabia, time, space, and ammunition were available in varying degrees to hone combat skills to an even sharper edge. Units trained most intently on nuclear, biological, and chemical (NBC) individual protective measures and re-zeroed individual and crew-served weapons. Commanders conducted classes on a wide array of topics such as the Iraqi army, Arab customs and culture, and standards of acceptable conduct in Saudi Arabia. Some Iraqi equipment was available and leaders and soldiers studied it firsthand. Acclimatization was particularly important to XVIII Airborne Corps soldiers who arrived in brutal August heat. Learning that the desert environment could be unforgiving, soldiers were instructed in forced drinking of water and gradual physical toughening through exercises and road marches. Pilots discovered that night flying in the desert was extremely difficult. It was all too easy for even the most experienced aviator to lose all sensation of height when flying close to the ground, particularly using night vision goggles in flat, featureless desert terrain. A few unwary pilots, unable to accurately judge their altitude, flew into the ground. Others, when flying low level at night, struck sand dunes. General Luck soon established training areas and firing ranges to further exercise and prepare his corps for combat. Until November, Luck's training guidance emphasized the defense, concentrating on moving long distances, navigating, and coordinating maneuver up through division level. Luck described it as "... actually the best training we've probably ever had in this Army because of the resources and space put at our disposal."[23]

Luck shared his hard-won experiences with later-arriving units. As soon as notification arrived of VII Corps' planned deployment, XVIII Airborne Corps soldiers began a helpful, long-distance, lessons-learned dialogue with Stateside and European-based units. The ARSTAF and TRADOC published handbooks and pamphlets to pass this knowledge through official channels. VII Corps began collecting lessons when elements of its 11th Aviation Brigade were alerted in August, and Franks continued when VII Corps was alerted. One of his first stops in early November was Luck's headquarters. XVIII Airborne Corps agreed to "sponsor" VII Corps to save time getting the European-based corps on its feet in the desert. After 40 years in Bavaria, VII Corps had the most to learn about fighting in the desert and the least time to learn it. The huge amount of new equipment thrust on them once in theater compounded the training problem. Such items as the Global Positioning System, unmanned aerial vehicles, mine plows, and mine rakes all required a period of familiarization and subsequent crash courses on maintenance and employment. As ammunition became available, VII Corps began live firing of individual and crew-served weapons such as the AT-4 antitank missile, new to many soldiers in the corps. Apache attack helicopter crews discovered ways to avoid losing control of the Hellfire caused by laser backscatter from the fine sand suspended in the air. Overall, corps units fired every major weapon from the Abrams to the MLRS.

Both corps constructed elaborate models of Iraqi defenses. XVIII Airborne Corps dug a complete triangular Iraqi battalion battle position and used it to run a series of exhaustive rehearsals and battle drills by all units expecting to participate in the breach or to assault prepared positions during the advance. The 1st Infantry Division continued the excellent training in breaching operations it had begun at Fort Riley and the NTC. Using aerial photographs and templates as a guide, they constructed a 5-kilometer-wide replica of the forward Iraqi trench system complete with fighting positions, command and control bunkers, and mortar, tank, and artillery revetments. Units started training in the ports and carried it over into the movement to the assembly areas where they expanded from individual vehicles and aircraft to multi-unit operations.

VII Corps conducted a grand dress rehearsal. General Franks intended to exploit the opportunity offered by the westward shift of his corps into

The operation was rehearsed down to the lowest levels. Above, the 1st Infantry Division conducted a sand-table exercise just before beginning the breaching operation. Below, 24th Infantry soldiers practiced dismounting from a Bradley.

attack positions. He would use the 250-kilometer move to rehearse his own Great Wheel maneuver, including the formation of the armored fist he intended to thrust at the Republican Guard. His staff was not too sure the idea was a good one. Without other distractions, the movement west threatened to be a very confusing affair. The corps would have to cross the rear of XVIII Airborne Corps and two of Franks' divisions would in turn cross each other's paths. At any one time at least 30,000 vehicles would be moving, often in converging directions, across four or five roads. The rehearsal would add to this confusion by requiring both the 2d ACR and the 1st Armored Division to cross Tapline Road twice—once to get to the staging areas and again in the rehearsal movement north. Nevertheless, Franks believed strongly that the benefits of this dress rehearsal far outweighed the risks.

Franks first moved Colonel Don Holder's 2d ACR to staging areas north of KKMC. On February 14 Major General Ron Griffith's 1st Armored Division moved from its position northeast of Hafar al-Batin south across the Tapline Road to a staging area south of the 2d ACR. Shortly thereafter, Major General Paul Funk's 3d Armored Division crossed MSR Sultan, the highway between KKMC and Hafar al-Batin, from its tactical assembly area south of Tapline Road and took up a position just west of the 1st Armored Division. The three combat units were now lined up in a stance ready to conduct the rehearsal on February 16 and 17. While the moves into the staging area were in progress on the 14th, the Iraqis hit Hafar al-Batin with a Scud missile, an ineffectual attack that nevertheless raised the tension level in the corps considerably.

Once the three units were in place, the plan was for the massive formation to approach and cross Tapline Road from the south using the road to represent the berm along the Iraqi-Saudi border. The 2d ACR would identify the crossing sites and coordinate with the military police to stop traffic for the move. The regiment would continue north in battle formation, practicing movement-to-contact and drills along the way. Both divisions would follow the cavalry across the road in their own combat formations led by divisional cavalry squadrons.

The rehearsal started early on February 16 and was completed by February 18. Only combat itself could have been more impressive. The lessons learned from corps to squad were used to refine techniques and the overall movement plan. In just six short days VII Corps would repeat the same maneuver against the Iraqis.

Prior to Desert Storm, no American Army had ever planned, prepared, rehearsed, or trained so thoroughly for a first campaign. In prior conflicts, the pressing need to get on with the war, coupled with an inexact picture of the enemy and poorly prepared soldiers, meant that first battles proved to be bloody schools in which green staffs and units were obliged to refine their skills on the battlefield. In Desert Storm the Purvis group, along with hundreds of similar staffs, had enough time to think through the campaign carefully and to devise and revise a method of attack that best suited the time-honored factors of METT-T. In addition, the campaign planners possessed a doctrine, AirLand Battle, that proved remarkably suitable to the unique circumstances of the theater. Commanders at all levels were determined to leave nothing to chance. Young soldiers could pay no higher compliment to those who planned and prepared the campaign than to profess, as most of them did, that the sweat and energy expended in preparation made the real thing seem almost anticlimactic.

Notes

1. Force Muthannah, under a Saudi commander, consisted of the Royal Saudi Land Forces 20th Mechanized Brigade and the Kuwaiti 35th Armored Brigade .

2. Schubert and Kraus, p. 174.

3. Army Chief of Staff George C. Marshall in 1941 address to OCS graduates, as quoted in Paul F. Gorman's *The Secret of Future Victories* (Alexandria, VA: Institute for Defense Analyses, October 1991), p. 45.

4. Vuono interview.

5. Schubert and Kraus, p. 174.

6. Swain, pp. 99-100.

7. Colonel Joe Purvis, interview and manuscript review, June 10, 1992.

8. *Ibid*.

9. General H. Norman Schwarzkopf with Peter Petre. *It Doesn't Take a Hero* (New York: Bantam Books, October 1992), p. 354.

10. Slide entitled "Strategic Objectives" from Purvis briefing on Course-of-Action Development, undated.

11. Army FM 31-20, *Doctrine for Special Forces Operations*, April 1, 1990, p. 3-1.

12. Slide entitled "Mission" from Purvis briefing.

13. Interview with Lieutenant General Gary Luck, February 21, 1992.

14. Phone conversation with Colonel James T. Hill, commander, 1st Brigade, 101st Airborne Division (Air Assault), May 12, 1992.

15. Purvis Diary.

16. Purvis review of draft chapter manuscript, June 10, 1992.

17. Swain, p. 114.

18. *US Army Central Command Military Intelligence History*, Colonel Donald Kerrick, committee chairman, approximate date April 1991, pp. 68-72, hereafter referred to as *ARCENT MI History*.

19. Provided by Lieutenant Colonel Terry Johnson, then deputy commander, VII Corps 11th Aviation Brigade, November 1991.

20. Brigadier General Timothy Grogan's interview with Lieutenant General Calvin Waller, May 1991.

21. XVIII Airborne Corps OPLAN Desert Storm, January 13, 1991, p. 4.

22. VII Corps After-Action Command Report, Operation Desert Storm, Vol 15, Part 1A, "The Executive Summary," and Part 1B, a narrative summary that describes, by phase, 1st Cavalry Division operations.

23. Luck interview.

Chapter 4

SHAPING THE BATTLEFIELD

At precisely 0200 on the morning of January 17, 1991, a group of Iraqi soldiers standing watch just beyond the border berm was startled by the scream of turbines and the beat of helicopter rotors passing just a few feet above them. Seconds later, trailing rotor wash buffeted the terrified Iraqis and covered them with stinging particles of flying sand. The thundering sound of the invisible armada faded quickly as the Apaches rushed northward deep into the Iraqi soldiers' homeland. Inside the aluminum and titanium cocoon of White Three, the lead Apache in the six-helicopter formation, both pilots could sense little else but the narrow, red-lit world defined by their instruments. Chief Warrant Officer Dave Jones was totally focused on an inch-square lens at the end of a tube attached to his helmet and positioned just in front of his right eye. Although the Army named this the Pilot's Night Vision Sensor, pilots simply called it "the system." The outboard part of the system, an infrared sensor, was slaved to follow Jones' head movements, and as he looked through the eyepiece he could see a surreal photonegative image of a giant Air Force MH-53J Pave Low helicopter just 50 feet to his left front. Digital altitude and airspeed numbers flashed along the rim of his eyepiece to enable Jones to fly without having to look back inside the cockpit. In the front seat Chief Warrant Officer Tom "Tip" O'Neal strained to catch visual cues through the narrow tubes of the ANVIS-6 night vision goggles. The goggles' twisted fiber-optic bundles amplified the limited light of the moonless night enough to allow O'Neal to continue flying should anything knock out or degrade the system. Just south of the border, O'Neal picked up flashes from Iraqi machine-gun fire and the bright streak of a heat-seeking missile launched by some nervous Iraqi at unseen objects above him.

The Pave Low helicopters, their Air Force partners, were along to assist the Apaches in navigating to the release point using their sophisticated inertial and satellite navigation system and terrain-following radar. The Pave Lows—White One and Two—would also be ready to rescue Apache crewmen should anyone get shot down. In addition to the two Pave Lows, four Apaches flew in an echelon right formation. In the back seat of White Six was Lieutenant Colonel Dick Cody, 1-101st Aviation, the commander of Task Force Normandy.

Jones and O'Neal had been together since their unit had first received Apaches at Fort Hood, Texas, more than two years earlier. Jones was a square-jawed Indiana native with sandy blond hair, a ready smile, and a self-effacing modesty that belied his extraordinary skill and confidence. Sixteen years in the Army, 10 of them in the cockpit, and experience as an AH-1 Cobra instructor pilot made him the "old pro" in a company comprising mostly younger men. Cody referred to Jones as his "recruiting poster for warrant officers."[1] His co-pilot had less than six years in the Army. Dark-haired, with a mustache and wide-set eyes, O'Neal was a true product of the eighties. His battalion handle, "Gadget Man," aptly described his knack with computers and his wizardry with Apache electronics.

The six White Team helicopters, flying in total radio silence, crossed the border at 120 knots at an altitude of 75 feet. Although the Apache's environmental control unit blew a steady stream of fresh air into their faces, the crewmen felt some discomfort in their bulky chemical overgarments. From 40 kilometers out, O'Neal could make out a glimmer of light near the target. Oblivious to the threat of war, the Iraqis had left the lights on. The team slowed to 80 knots and descended to 50 feet as they approached the release point. Two minutes later Jones saw the Pave Lows slow to a hover. Through his goggles O'Neal could see intense points of light drop to the ground as the MH-53J crews dispensed chemical light sticks to precisely mark the location of the release point.

Jones hovered carefully over the chem lights to allow O'Neal to update his navigation system. After selecting the prestored coordinates on the keyboard of the Doppler navigation control head, O'Neal pressed the "enter" button to reinitialize his fire-control computer. The remaining White Team Apaches completed the update and followed Jones as he edged up to his first firing position 5.5 kilometers from the Iraqi radar complex. Twenty kilometers to the west, the Red Team of two more Pave Lows and four Apaches completed the same maneuver south of a second radar complex.

In clipped, mechanical tones, Jones and O'Neal methodically worked their way through the prefire checklist to set up for the first target. Jones maintained a steady hover while, in the front seat, O'Neal flipped the night vision goggles up off his face and looked down at the video screen of his primary target-acquisition system. With the right handgrip manual tracker switch, he slewed the laser onto his first target, a square, box-like object on his screen that defined a dug-in electric power generator just a few meters to the left of the main Iraqi command and control van. By hitting power sources first, the pilots would silence the radar site before it could alert the Iraqi central control headquarters in Baghdad. The laser spot was centered on the target approximately 4 miles away. O'Neal punched in the lower left outboard missile and spun it up so that the missile would recognize the coded laser energy reflected from the target once he squeezed the launch trigger.

While O'Neal was engrossed in his work, the rest of White Team fanned out on line, settling into position at 0237, exactly 57 seconds early. For the longest minute of the war, four Apaches hung suspended in total darkness 50 feet off the deck. Lieutenant Tom Drew in White Five broke radio silence just long enough to broadcast "Party in ten," the code to fire in 10 seconds.

At precisely 0238, O'Neal launched the first shot of Desert Storm. Jones faintly heard the muffled swoosh and the familiar sparks thrown aside by the Hellfire's booster motor. In a second the missile disappeared into the darkness. Jones calmly whispered into the intercom, "This one's for you, Saddam," as he kept the target box in his small screen aligned with the pipper indicating O'Neal's line of sight. O'Neal's right thumb was on the manual tracker switch holding the laser spot on the generator and sending digital information to Jones on where the target-acquisition system was focused. Seconds later the missile streaked in from the upper left of O'Neal's video screen. The explosion momentarily "whited out" on O'Neal's screen as 17 pounds of Hellfire explosive vaporized the generator.

O'Neal immediately "squirted" the laser on the second target, a nearby command and control van, and took it out with a second missile. On the periphery of his screen he could see the methodical destruction of the site as other team members, moving steadily forward at an even 20 knots, hit antennas, radar dishes, and buildings. Within minutes Jones could see nothing through his infrared sight but burning dots of light.

Jones guided the Apache forward in line with the other aircraft and broke off the attack just 1,500 meters from the target. In four minutes White Three had scored seven for seven. O'Neal had hit the westernmost end of the site, while the other White Team Apaches struck the buildings *and radar dishes in the middle and eastern end. Completely destroyed, the site would not reactivate during the war. White and Red Teams collectively created a 40-kilometer gap in the line of early warning sites that ran the length of the Iraqi-Saudi Arabian border. Leaving the radar site in flames, the Apaches slipped smoothly into formation with the Pave Lows and turned south, 50 feet above the desert floor.*

FINAL REINFORCEMENTS

Even as Task Force Normandy opened up the Iraqis' extreme western flank to Coalition air, Saddam continued to improve his defenses in Kuwait. Forty-one Iraqi divisional headquarters were in the theater, an increase of 13 since November.[2] Five of the new units were infantry divisions that joined the coastal and forward defenses. Three additional regular army armored divisions completed the formation of two regular army corps, which would serve as operational reserve for the KTO. The first, the Jihad Corps, consisted of the 10th and the 12th Armored Divisions and was oriented on the defense of the Wadi al-Batin. The second, the 2d Armored Corps, made up of the 17th Armored and 51st Mechanized Divisions, was fixed on the defense of mainland Kuwait from amphibious assault. The creation of these two corps-sized operational reserves freed up the Republican Guard to act in its traditional role of strategic reserve.

The rest of the new divisions—all infantry—deployed west of Kuwait, thickening and adding depth to the defenses in that area. Two went into the line just west of the Wadi al-Batin. The other three deployed along key lines of communication as far west as as-Salman and as far north as an-Nasiriyah and an-Najaf. The Iraqis, however, had failed to close off the western approach to the KTO with an obstacle belt as extensive as the elaborate one inside Kuwait. Analysts examining the defenses believed that Saddam had decided to accept risk in the west, probably assuming that a western attack would be too difficult and the route too long for the Coalition to consider. Saddam had a residual force of 24 divisions in Iraq, largely the dregs of recently mobilized infantry units that possessed little military value. Therefore, further reinforcement of the theater was unlikely. Obviously, Saddam had left the back door to the KTO open, and from all appearances he had neither the capability nor the inclination to close it.

SEEING THE BATTLEFIELD

Developing a comprehensive intelligence picture of the Gulf had not been easy. The US intelligence community had spied on the Warsaw Pact for decades using signals intelligence (SIGINT), human intelligence (HUMINT), and imagery intelligence (IMINT). The rapid development of the

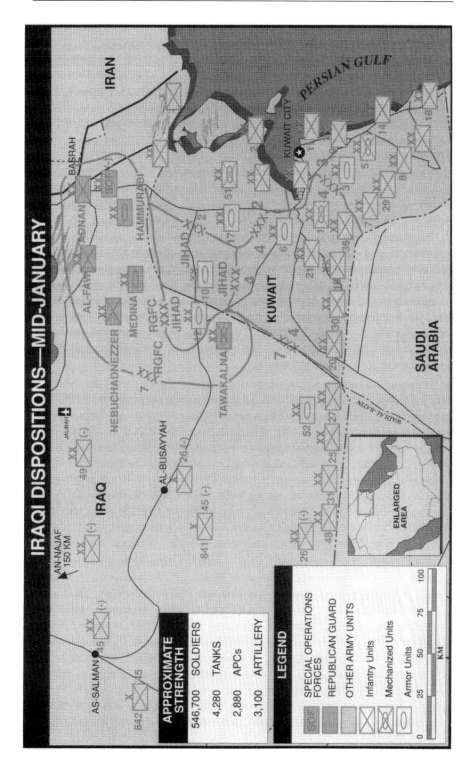

IRAQI DISPOSITIONS—MID-JANUARY

APPROXIMATE STRENGTH

546,700	SOLDIERS
4,280	TANKS
2,880	APCs
3,100	ARTILLERY

LEGEND

SOF	SPECIAL OPERATIONS FORCES
	REPUBLICAN GUARD
	OTHER ARMY UNITS
	Infantry Units
	Mechanized Units
	Armor Units

0 25 50 75 100
KM

Gulf crisis in mid-1990 meant that the intelligence system had to be turned quickly against an unexpected foe. Problems were inevitable.

An enemy's intentions can be most effectively determined from high-level intelligence sources. Saddam's occupation of Kuwait presented the US with its first major post-Cold War intelligence dilemma. The 45-year standoff in Central Europe permitted the US to do sophisticated collection from a variety of means—strategic, operational, and tactical—and to fuse that intelligence for use at every level. Warsaw Pact intentions were known, and most importantly from the tactical level, detailed knowledge of Warsaw Pact commanders and capabilities was the basis for planning. In Europe, intelligence battalions down to division level provided continuous coverage and updates on the "enemy" situation.

Baghdad's concept of a defensive war of attrition, coupled with an appreciation of American skill in electronic eavesdropping, caused the Iraqis to harden much of their command and control system and impose severe limits on radio and radar transmissions. The US effort was further hampered by the need for Arabic linguists, particularly those skilled in the Iraqi dialect, to exploit what little data could be gathered. Once the air war began, however, signals intercepts became more profitable as hardened communications were damaged or destroyed and the Iraqis were driven to use less secure communications.

Human intelligence was particularly difficult. Because the brutally efficient Iraqi internal security regime was extremely paranoid of foreign intelligence penetration, clandestine HUMINT—spying in the classic sense—was almost impossible. Nevertheless, HUMINT did play a key role in assessing Iraqi capabilities and targeting the Iraqi military. Years of data collection on Soviet equipment elsewhere in the world provided comprehensive information on much of Iraq's arsenal. While the lack of Arabic linguists hampered many units, the 101st Airborne Division deployed with 132 trained linguists who were put to great use in debriefing Kuwaiti refugees prior to Desert Storm. US Army intelligence played a large part in this effort, debriefing more than 400 sources.

The decline of Soviet military power freed the intelligence community to shift focus to the Iraqis. However, even without Soviet distractions, demands on the available intelligence systems were enormous. They were expected to support enforcement of the blockade by monitoring land, sea, and air traffic into Iraq. Early in the crisis, national systems searched for Western hostages. Later, targeteers required thousands of photographs to provide the detail necessary to prepare target folders to support the bombing operation.[3] With its generally clear skies and sparse ground cover, the KTO was an ideal region for overhead observation. However, the KTO was poorly mapped and overhead systems were needed to support the development of 1:50,000-scale maps for an area the size of the eastern United States. The same systems were then used to monitor Iraqi military deployments inside both the KTO and Iraq. This heavy load created periodic gaps that could result in losing track of entire Iraqi divisions.

Reconnaissance aircraft could have bridged the gap in coverage. With its MACH III+ speed, the SR-71 Blackbird was capable of flying over Kuwait at will as it had done in the 1973 Arab-Israeli War, photographing a 30-mile swath at 2,000 miles per hour. The SR-71, however, had been mothballed only the year before. Reconnaissance aircraft available in theater—RF-4C, U-2, TR-1, and Tornado—could produce wide-angle imagery but were not survivable enough to fly over the KTO until a coordinated air operation began. [4]

In addition to problems in seeing the battlefield, getting the information to the users proved difficult. Doctrine calls for units in contact with the enemy to use their tactical intelligence or reconnaissance means to collect information against him. Forward units are responsible for developing information on the disposition and composition of enemy forces to their direct front. The higher headquarters then combines that information with additional data to form a picture of the enemy at a specific level, normally two echelons below their own. For example, battalions are concerned with platoons, and brigades with companies. The higher the unit, the wider and deeper the focus. The tactical intelligence structure was designed to draw intelligence from the bottom up, building on it gradually as it proceeds upward. The corps is the upward limit of the tactical intelligence system.

In contrast, strategic intelligence, intended to support a host of users at the national level, has only limited application to tactical theaters. It is generally suitable for longer-term planning, usually at theater or national level. While strategic intelligence organizations are capable of producing tactical intelligence, it is not their primary mission. That is not to say that extremely detailed information was unavailable from very high levels. In some cases strategic sources in the US or Riyahd had imagery on individual emplacements and weapons. Intelligence units above corps, like ARCENT's 513th MI Brigade, are intended to bring strategic and tactical intelligence together. They fuse national products with those of the corps and below, giving the theater commander a comprehensive picture of the enemy.

In the desert, commanders' expectations, especially below corps, remained unmet. They required much more specific intelligence than ever before, driven in part by the burgeoning information required to fully apply precision weapon systems in an offensive operation. Finished intelligence produced at the national level was not necessarily suitable for tactical planning. At the same time, Schwarzkopf's decision to bring in ground combat units first delayed arrival of higher-level intelligence battalions. The first such unit could become only partially operational by September 7 since all of its personnel and equipment did not arrive until November. The only Army aerial collection capability—III Corps' 15th MI Battalion which replaced the XVIII Airborne Corps' organic 224th MI Battalion still in the US on counterdrug operations—did not arrive until mid-October. The critically needed Joint Imagery Processing Center—the only facility that could produce annotated, hard-copy photographs—did not arrive until December. ARCENT's organic intelligence structure was not complete until C+160, the day the air operation began.[5] Moreover, in order to mask intentions, CENTCOM directed that intelligence collection units remain well back from the border, severely hampering their effectiveness. Thus XVIII Airborne Corps' MI battalions arrived between September and October but were unable to develop a good picture of the battlefield until they moved into forward positions on January 19. The same proved true for VII Corps. Not configured for contingencies and embedded in the NATO intelligence structure, VII Corps had to rely on higher echelons for most intelligence information.[6] The intelligence structure, designed largely for the defense of Europe, was inadequate for the grand offensive maneuver envisioned for Desert Storm.

CREATING AN UNBLINKING EYE

The initial task of national strategic intelligence was to maintain an accurate picture in the KTO at a level sufficient to satisfy tactical planners. The Defense Intelligence Agency, the intelligence arm of the Joint Staff, needed outside assistance to meet the increased tactical demands. The DIA responds to a host of users including the National Command Authorities, the unified commands, and other departments. Neither it nor the CENTCOM J2 was staffed to produce sufficient tactical intelligence. While the DIA had some analysts well-versed in tactical intelligence, the agency's requirements pulled them in many directions. Obtaining the level of detail required by each Service requires a fundamental understanding of that Service's needs. Knowledge of Army tactics, weapons, and operational methods enables trained analysts to cull very specific information of value to tactical commanders. An Army officer reviewing satellite photos of ICBM sites could count the individual silos, but he would not be able to pick out other details to know if the installations were operational. Each Service carries its own cultural values and technical expertise developed from many years of military experience. Making tactical intelligence assessments without the benefit of such a background is difficult, if not impossible. In the case of the Iraqi invasion of Kuwait, an inexperienced analyst looking at the Iraqis shifting forces to the border on August 1 believed that they were merely training. Only an Army officer familiar with the last-minute starts and stops of tactical maneuver saw the moves as a final shift to attack positions.

The individual Services were capable of developing Service-specific tactical intelligence at the national level and, in an unprecedented move, agreed in late August to man a DOD-level Joint Intelligence Center in Washington to produce tactical intelligence for the KTO. One of the most successful examples of their extraordinary effort was the series of tactical "templates" produced by the Army's Intelligence and Threat Analysis Center (ITAC). First produced in hard copy and later transmitted digitally, the templates depicted every Iraqi division in the KTO on 1:50,000-scale maps. Accurate to 400 meters, the templates showed individual tanks, armored vehicles, artillery positions, trucks, command posts, and supply facilities and provided commanders with a blueprint of the Iraqi obstacle system. To ensure that the templates remained accurate as the ground war drew close, ITAC provided a daily update on the Iraqi defenses west of the Wadi al-Batin.[7]

Washington's efforts, however, did little to make field commanders happy, particularly after VII Corps arrived from Europe and began offensive planning. Dissemination remained a problem and even though satellites were producing thousands of miles of coverage per week, the appetite for tactical information was almost limitless. Unit commanders wanted target-quality photographs annotated with locations of specific objects down to the nearest hundred meters. Of course variations existed among units, especially between the corps. XVIII Airborne Corps, as the Army's contingency corps, was better structured to deal with strategic intelligence agencies. The corps received fully processed satellite imagery via the Tactical Exploitation of National Capabilities (TENCAP) Imagery Exploitation System located at Fort Bragg. ARCENT and VII Corps lacked such a capability. As for battlefield surveillance, the need to maintain an "unblinking eye" on the enemy, particularly once the war began, made the sporadic and sometimes spasmodic imagery coverage of the KTO unacceptable.

The lack of terrain intelligence, particularly in the western Iraqi desert, compelled XVIII Airborne Corps to take extraordinary measures to gather terrain information. Luck made it his highest intelligence priority, and made frequent requests for imagery on the region with little success. After he was given permission to conduct cross-border operations, he was forced to rely on long-range surveillance patrols and the use of Apaches to videotape the terrain at night with their on-board cameras. Selecting supply routes and determining trafficability were critical calls that had to be delayed until the last minute.

Part of the answer to the dissemination and surveillance problems would come from the Army intelligence team in the United States. This

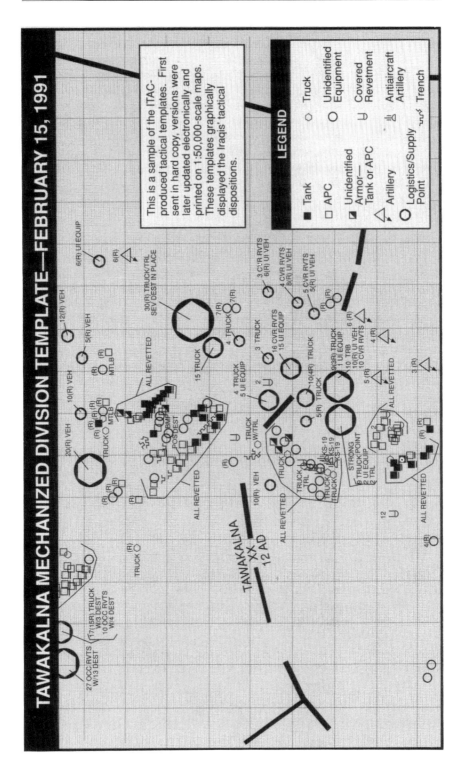

TAWAKALNA MECHANIZED DIVISION TEMPLATE—FEBRUARY 15, 1991

This is a sample of the ITAC-produced tactical templates. First sent in hard copy, versions were later updated electronically and printed on 1:50,000-scale maps. These templates graphically displayed the Iraqis' tactical dispositions.

LEGEND

■ Tank

○ Truck

□ APC

○ Unidentified Equipment

▪ Unidentified Armor— Tank or APC

Ṵ Covered Revetment

◁ Artillery

⚫ Antiaircraft Artillery

○ Logistics/Supply Point

ᴗ Trench

team fielded 12 major systems with more than 100 major end items between early January and February 24. In battlefield surveillance, two systems proved invaluable: the Joint Surveillance Target Attack Radar System (JSTARS) and the unmanned aerial vehicle (UAV).[8]

Before Desert Shield, the Army and the Air Force had been developing JSTARS, principally as a means to help the ground commander determine which deep targets to attack and when. JSTARS is a highly modified Boeing 707 aircraft equipped with a synthetic aperture radar. In the targeting mode, the radar can search a 4x5-kilometer area and provide locations of assembly areas and individual vehicles to an accuracy sufficient for attack by air or artillery. As a surveillance system, JSTARS can range several hundred kilometers to paint a 25x20-kilometer sector. It would be able to watch all of Kuwait and major portions of southern Iraq. The system was designed to operate in both modes simultaneously. In either mode, JSTARS can detect all moving targets and many stationary features such as the Iraqi obstacle system. Information produced by the radar could be passed to ground stations and AWACS in near real time.

Prompted by Brigadier General John Leide, CENTCOM J2, Schwarzkopf requested on August 10 that the two existing JSTARS prototypes be released to participate in the surveillance war.[9] The suggestion ran into resistance in Air Staff systems-development circles at the Pentagon and at the Tactical Air Command at Langley Air Force Base. The Air Staff did not want to risk the prototypes and possibly the entire program should they be lost. Tactical Air Command and, by extension, General Horner, the JFACC, did not want the headaches that JSTARS and its ground support components would impose on a theater support system already stretched to the limit. Air Force pressures against deployment prompted Schwarzkopf to reverse course in September, saying that "Desert Shield is not suitable in time or place for the introduction of JSTARS."[10]

The issue was not dead, however. Battlefield coverage by overhead systems remained a serious problem that would probably worsen in the winter. December, January, and February, normally cloudy months, could reduce photographic coverage by 40 to 60 percent. Meanwhile, VII Corps' European JSTARS tests proved so successful in September that General Vuono pressed for deployment of the system, as did General Franks upon his arrival in theater in November. The Air Staff acquiesced after Congress questioned why the system had not been deployed.[11] The CINC requested that JSTARS arrive in theater no later than January 15.

The JSTARS package that was deployed consisted of two E-8A aircraft and six ground stations that would be able to maintain almost continuous coverage over the KTO in nightly 11-hour flights inside Saudi air space. The system complemented side-looking airborne radar missions mounted by XVIII and VII Corps' own organic Mohawk aircraft. Ground stations were deployed at CENTAF Tactical Air Command Center, ARCENT Main, ARCENT Forward, and with the Marines, VII Corps, and XVIII Airborne Corps. As ARCENT's main effort, VII Corps had priority for JSTARS coverage.[12] Much of the time XVIII Airborne Corps was unable to receive JSTARS data because its ground station module was so far to the west at Rafha.

The system first flew January 14, less than 72 hours before the air operation began. The flight crew was joint Army-Air Force with the Army manning JSTARS ground stations with a sergeant and two soldiers—an action that raised Air Force eyebrows. Horner and his staff already regarded the system with some suspicion; the level of rank the Army assigned to it further colored their view of its utility.

Soon after the shooting started, cloud cover over the KTO seriously restricted target detection. Aircraft arrived on station ready to bomb, however, and Horner's staff found themselves with B-52s inbound to the KTO with no suitable targets. When someone suggested JSTARS, Horner said, "Fine, get the officer in here." Shortly afterward, Private First Class Timothy Reagan was ushered in. He explained that his sergeant was in the latrine. Horner asked if he had any targets. Reagan led the skeptical general out to his JSTARS ground station and showed him a convoy of some 40 Iraqi vehicles that he had tracked for the previous half-hour. Convinced by the evidence—and impressed by the young soldier's expertise—Horner directed the bombers against the convoy and watched on

Boeing 707 configured as JSTARS.

Reagan's monitor as the B-52s destroyed it. Private Reagan had "made" JSTARS in the eyes of the air component commander. [13]

Although JSTARS guaranteed all-weather coverage to a depth of 150 kilometers, tactical commanders still needed a close-in system to see over the next hill. XVIII Airborne Corps capitalized on the Horus radar possessed by the French 6th Light Division. Horus is a prototype moving-target indicator mounted on a Puma helicopter that functions much like the JSTARS. In its first use, the all-weather Horus cued Apaches and MLRSs for night deep operations. Another technical solution was to employ drones—UAVs in military parlance—equipped with television cameras and other sensors. The Navy and Marines possessed the Israeli-designed Pioneer drones. When the air attacks started, the Army had only an experimental platoon of five Pioneer UAVs at Fort Huachuca, Arizona. With a 100-mile range, day-and-night capability, multiple-hour endurance, and near-real-time data link, the Pioneer could have served both as a scout and as a means of precise, instantaneous targeting. However, the Army's single platoon did not arrive in theater until January 26 and did not fly its first mission until February 1. As the main attack force, only VII Corps would have access to Pioneer. [14]

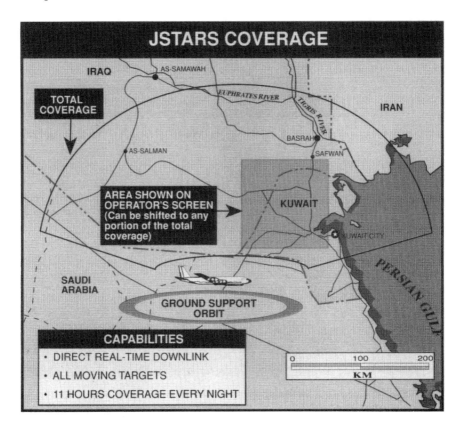

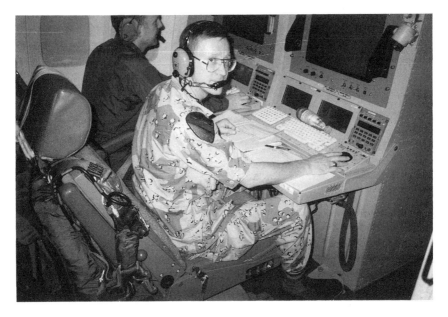

Colonel David Schulte, chief of the BCE, manned an operator's station during a JSTARS orientation mission.

JSTARS operators followed the ground war from 10 stations, two of which were manned by Army personnel.

Military Intelligence soldiers preparing a UAV for a VII Corps targeting mission.

The other half of the intelligence problem was dissemination, with imagery the biggest challenge. The intelligence system before Desert Storm was not designed to push all the required intelligence down to the tactical level. During the previous 20 years, the Army and the other Services had dismantled their capability to produce tactical imagery at lower levels. Instead, the Army chose to capitalize on electronically generated imagery products from corps to divisions. Called secondary dissemination, this method replaced the familiar aerial exploitation units in divisions and corps. Rather than tactical units developing their own negatives for study on a light table, photographs would be analyzed at a higher level, converted to digital data, and transmitted to the using units for reassembly at special terminals. Much like a closed-circuit video relay of the pictures, such links were still largely incomplete. Now, on the eve of war, off-the-shelf purchases and prototypes had to be fielded because transmission of digital data required bandwidths well beyond those of the standard communications net allocated to intelligence.

Four separate satellites were used to transmit imagery. An AIA-to-ARCENT satellite link transmitted imagery directly to ARCENT. Starting on August 14, an Army Space Programs Office satellite and a borrowed Navy navigation satellite transmitted more than 30,000 images to XVIII Airborne Corps. XVIII Airborne Corps linked its organic satellite capability—the TENCAP Imagery Exploitation System at Fort Bragg—with its forward units using prototype terminals equipped with TENCAP-compatible radios. Prior to deployment from Europe and throughout Desert Shield and Storm, VII Corps received imagery transmitted by XVIII Airborne Corps via tactical terminals. Once deployed, another secondary imagery dissemination was developed and fielded in three weeks to pass imagery to VII Corps and subordinate divisions. To provide a redundant imagery transmission capability to all forward units, a team under Major John Healy from the Intelligence Center and School forged the fourth satellite link to the forward corps and divisions using the TROJAN satellite for secure voice and digital imagery transmission. [15]

Getting new equipment fielded in time was a close-run race, one that in some cases was completed too late. TROJAN, while proposed for deployment on November 7, did not get to the theater until February. A G2 team designed, built, and readied 12 trailer-mounted TROJAN terminals, and on February 8, the ARCENT G2 laid out a program to field TROJAN. Units about to receive TROJAN terminals still had to be trained on a system that functioned much like electronic mail, facsimile machine, and telephone all in one. Once in place, TROJAN was the principal channel for transmitting templates. Civilian contractors did not complete the 1st Infantry Division's 72 hours of training until the day before the ground war began.[16]

Even with the best efforts of those dedicated to solving the dissemination problem electronically, moving imagery and other intelligence products forward required enormous manpower. Tactical commanders, faced with a looming ground war, needed the intelligence immediately, not when TROJAN was in place. Meanwhile the Joint Imagery Processing Center began operation in mid-January—just in time to handle the increased load of U-2 and RF-4C imagery that began to flood in once the air war began. The answer to getting the material forward was manual courier. Throughout January and February, daily couriers carried 200 pounds of annotated photos, maps overprinted with Iraqi templates, and other intelligence documents, moving 27 tons of material from one end of the theater to the other. Despite their efforts, the system was less than ideal and division commanders remained frustrated. The information was available, but tactical commanders had enormous difficulties getting their hands on it. Generals Rhame and Griffith dispatched their intelligence officers daily to the rear to collect the most recent templates, imagery, or other appropriate documents. Once their units began to move, the problem was compounded as units tried to get updates en route. Frustrations crossed corps boundaries as collection efforts gave priority to the main attack by VII Corps, leaving fewer systems available to support XVIII Airborne Corps. Generals Peay and McCaffrey grew especially concerned with the continued lack of surveillance of the western KTO. Their fears were understandable, but they remained unresolved.

Intelligence fixes were not restricted to machines. One of the most important was an Army intelligence initiative to recruit, train, and deploy Kuwaitis to the theater as linguists in intelligence units. At the initiative of General Eichelberger, nearly 300 Kuwaiti volunteers—mainly college students in the United States—came into theater under this program as sergeants in the Kuwaiti Army. National military intelligence support teams from the DIA provided a direct link from each corps and ARCENT to the national intelligence community, complete with their own data and imagery transmission capabilities.[17] Additionally, intelligence information was shared liberally among the Coalition allies. Access to sensitive material, particularly US overhead imagery, impressed French and other allied leaders for its quality and accuracy.

The mastermind behind this effort was the ARCENT G2, Brigadier General John Stewart, Jr. Dual-hatted when the crisis began as the ARSTAF assistant deputy chief of staff for intelligence and the AIA commander, Stewart was totally immersed in the intelligence effort supporting the theater, personally supervising the intelligence picture presented to the Army's leadership. Stewart demanded excellence from his subordinates; his daily staff calls were an intense and sometimes painful experience for the ill-prepared. Once the decision was made to augment the DIA with Service intelligence to form a DOD Joint Intelligence Center, Stewart manned the JIC with Army intelligence professionals from the Intelligence and Threat Analysis Center. Meanwhile in the theater, XVIII Airborne Corps pushed ARCENT and CENTCOM planners to war-game and provide predictive intelligence and to focus on how to disseminate intelligence to ground units.

In late December, General Vuono personally ordered Stewart's transfer to the theater as ARCENT G2 to develop an intelligence operation capable of supporting Army-level offensive operations. Stewart was clearly the right man for the job. He was dedicated to supporting the tactical commander, and he took over a staff that was doubling in size even as it shifted to offensive planning. As Stewart would later recount, "The leadership challenge during this period was to instill a sense of immediate urgency in the entire G2 staff. We did that, but not without concern and a little pain."[18]

Stewart's other mission was to build confidence and trust within the corps and divisions that ARCENT G2 would deliver the needed intelligence on time. The operations order kicking off the ground attack would be enough to move the units into Iraq. From that point forward, the corps commanders, especially General Franks, would call "audibles" based on Iraqi reactions. Anticipating that requirement, ARCENT planners worked up a series of concept plans based on probable Iraqi moves. Stewart promised the commanders that as they reached these major decision points in the ground battle, he would provide the intelligence assessments necessary to select the right concept plan. To achieve that end, Stewart planned intelligence collection, production, and dissemination to mesh with the needs of the corps commanders. Early on, Franks and Stewart met to synchronize the critical decision points in the fight, particularly the read on RGFC actions that would enable Franks to decide whether to continue northeast or turn to the right. The result was an intelligence and electronic warfare synchronization matrix that, with the commanders' decision points as its foundation, would produce useful, predictive tactical intelligence. Those "key reads" would be the ultimate proof of the ability of Army intelligence to support the commander fighting the ground battle.

THE AIR OPERATION: A CLASH OF CULTURES

Preparing for the ground battle brought to the forefront longstanding cultural differences between the Air Force and the Army, differences that had begun to emerge as early as August. The two Services' operating environments are fundamentally different. Air Force doctrine rests on the principles of centralized control and flexible execution. Air Force planners regard anything more specific than that as the "bag of tricks" necessary to accomplish the mission—what the Army refers to as tactics, techniques, and procedures. The Air Force therefore is able to change its tactics, techniques, and procedures very rapidly without any effect on its doctrine. This general view of doctrine allows the Air Force to accommodate last-minute proclivities in a campaign by capitalizing on the flexibility of its principal operational element—the aircraft. While an Air Force operation might consist of, at most, several hundred distinct combat elements, all of which are relatively easy to schedule, observe, and direct, the Army's operational elements consist of hundreds of thousands of individual soldiers and units, widely scattered and tucked within terrain folds and foliage. The essence of joint operations is full synchronization and integration of combat power. This means that all Services must approach the battlefield from the same perspective, with each complementing the other in achieving the commander's goal. When Army commanders select specific tactics, techniques, and procedures to accomplish a mission, they do so guided by doctrinal principles. Joint doctrine allows for joint control while maintaining appropriate flexibility in execution.

The 31 initiatives dialogue of 1984 led the Army to expect the Air Force to comply with the mutually accepted agreements on battlefield air interdiction. The difference between air interdiction and BAI is critical. Whereas AI reaches deep to strike strategic targets approved by the CINC, BAI attacks targets nominated by corps commanders that are closer to ground tactical units. BAI provides one of the most powerful means for the corps commander to shape the deep battlefield. AirLand Battle doctrine relies on the premise that some discrete portion of ground attack air power would be directed to kill or at least to hold distant enemy formations in place long enough for ground forces to maneuver against them. The process of deep attack involves much more than just indiscriminate strikes by tactical aircraft at any lucrative object located in front of friendly forces. Instead, the commander carefully focuses his limited air power on the targets most critical to the maneuver. In the offense, the corps commander chooses his axes of advance and then carefully calculates time and distance to determine which enemy forces arrayed deep against him threaten his advancing columns.

The integration and synchronization of combat power to strike deep, high-value targets creates synergism. For example, the culminating ground operation of Desert Storm required that Iraqi chemical delivery systems, especially artillery, be destroyed. Equally essential, the Republican Guard would be battered, cut off from higher headquarters, and fixed in place until VII Corps could smash through its defenses. Early attacks on forward command and control systems would prevent alerting the RGFC to the direction and size of the main attack. By targeting just those threats, Franks sought to "shape" the battlefield to facilitate the movement of his own forces. Hitting those targets simultaneously as ground forces destroyed frontline divisions might collapse the Iraqi defense of the KTO.

The function of BAI, therefore, is not only to attrit the enemy but, more importantly, to take away his freedom of maneuver, his capability to sustain himself, and his will to resist in order to shape the battlefield for the decisive maneuver. Since BAI was most essential to Generals Luck and Franks for shaping the battlefield for the coming ground operation, its availability was crucial, and they trusted that it would be available. To support their schemes of maneuver, the corps commanders wanted to be able to direct air attacks against the most important targets beyond the reach of their organic attack systems. The issue was not how much of the total air effort was devoted to shaping the battlefield; the Army recognized competing priorities such as air-to-air and air interdiction of deep theater targets. The issue was that corps commanders needed to control the effects and timing of BAI targeted within their zone. Placing BAI under an overall category of interdiction reduced the corps commander's influence on the process.

THE INTERDEPENDENCE OF
AIR-GROUND OPERATIONS

Air planners have long sought to vindicate the view that the ever-increasing accuracy of air-delivered munitions has made it possible to win wars the "clean" way—through strategic targeting. In this view, the application of air power then becomes a campaign—if not a separate war—distinct from ground combat. The Army, on the other hand, does not recognize the distinction. Instead, ground commanders see air power as the means to weaken the enemy and shape the battlefield. Desert Storm once again surfaced this fundamental difference.

In early August, Checkmate, a special Air cell under the Air Force Chief of Staff, asked Colonel Thomas Leavitt, chief of the Operations and Contingency Plans Division with Department of the Army's Directorate of Operations and Mobilization in the Pentagon, for an informal Army review of a contingency plan for offensive air operations against Iraq. Leavitt pulled in two members from the Crisis Action Team—Major Dan Farley, one of his Middle East planners, and Major Tom Odom, the Middle East current intelligence officer for the ARSTAF. Leavitt told the two, "There's an Air Force organization called Checkmate working a compartmented air operations plan against targets in Iraq. They've asked for low-level Army assistance. Go down, find out what they want, and give them what you can. Keep this close hold."[19] In Checkmate, Farley and Odom joined a small planning cell of colonels headed by a brigadier general. The planners briefed the concept—a strategic "takedown" of Iraq to be completed in a week that would force Saddam to withdraw his forces from Kuwait. The Checkmate plan had no provision to target the Iraqi forces poised on the Saudi border. Dubbed "Instant Thunder," it became the basic plan for air operations in Desert Storm. Although, at the direction of the Chairman, JCS, and the Secretary of Defense, the air planners soon modified it to include targets in the KTO, some Air Force planners continued to believe that victory was achievable through air power alone. The Army, in contrast, remained convinced that ground and air power applied in synergy would be necessary to eject Saddam from Kuwait.

THE CINC'S VISION

On January 15 Schwarzkopf visited his air planners at the Tactical Air Command Center for final discussions before the war. It was not a pleasant experience. General Horner laid out his plans for a phased, sequential operation beginning with strategic air attacks, followed by the establishment of air supremacy, attacks on the Republican Guard, and finally, attacks on the forward defenses of the KTO.

Schwarzkopf grew increasingly angry as Horner briefed the *sequential* nature of the air plan. Fearing that the shooting war might end prematurely, the CINC wanted a *simultaneous* campaign. He wanted to hurt Saddam's military power across the board so that should Saddam withdraw from Kuwait, at least a portion of his Army would be crippled by air power. Schwarzkopf wanted the KTO and the Republican Guard to be hit from the beginning of the operation—a major change just two days before the operation was to begin. It was only the first of a series of last-minute changes.

Horner held daily targeting meetings with Schulte and other component representatives.

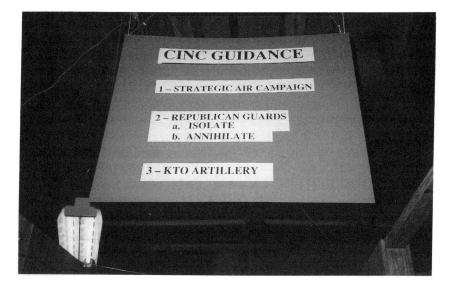

Schwarzkopf's guidance to Horner was posted in CENTAF's "black hole," the restricted access targeting center.

As JFACC, Horner faced an enormous challenge in mounting the air operation against Saddam. Once the operation began, he would juggle three days of events simultaneously: the air attacks that day, the creation of an air tasking order (ATO) for operations the next day, and the formulation of a 48-hour advance military attack plan. The most visible symbol of that challenge was the daily ATO, a 300-page document that directed the planning and packaging for strikes of more than 1,200 land-based fighters, fighter-bombers, and bombers in addition to sea-based aircraft, support aircraft, and rotary-wing aircraft. Dissemination of this huge daily document proved enormously difficult. When division air liaison officers did not receive the ATO, they had no idea whether targets nominated by their division were attacked or what aircraft were scheduled to operate in their area. The air power assembled in Saudi Arabia was comparable to the largest airline in the world, flying in a fraction of the globe's airspace, with Horner as its president in charge of scheduling. Managing the flow of the air armada would be tricky, so early on Horner decided to keep it as simple as possible. Targeteers would have only two categories of offensive air available: air interdiction and close air support. BAI went by the wayside.

THE TARGETING CONTROVERSY

Meanwhile, ARCENT and the subordinate corps also prepared for the beginning of the war, concentrating on the targeting issue. Under Yeosock's broad guidance, Generals Arnold and Stewart worked out the targeting procedures to shape the battlefield. Their goal was an expansion on the early planning imperative to destroy 50 percent of the Iraqi artillery, armor, and mechanized systems in the KTO and at least 90 percent of the artillery capable of reaching the breach areas. Targeting priorities were command and control facilities like headquarters and communications sites; artillery; tanks and armored vehicles; and logistics, including supply dumps, maintenance locations, and refueling points.

Target development and validation took four days. On day one, Stewart focused intelligence collection on Arnold's designated priority target areas. Using these priorities, Stewart's collection management team tasked specific systems to target designated areas. Nationally controlled systems or theater reconnaissance aircraft like the U-2 and the RF-4C Phantom II would overfly the chosen site to look for suitable targets. Electronic intelligence (ELINT) disclosed unit locations that could be further refined through airborne direction-finding using ARCENT and the corps aerial exploitation battalions.

The same battalions tracked enemy radars, revealing air defense locations and target-acquisition batteries to support Saddam's formidable artillery. Airborne radars like those in the TR-1, the Mohawk, and JSTARS also folded into the collection effort. The Mohawk's side-looking radar gave moving target indications that were used to tip off other systems like JSTARS. Human intelligence sources also played a growing role. As more enemy deserters came across the lines, their debriefings were used in targeting.

On day two of the targeting cycle, Stewart's people reviewed the input from the collection effort, then developed potential targets and loaded them into the data base for use in the ATO. To make the cut, targets had to be located to within 100 meters. Stewart used the list on day three to identify high-value targets. He and Arnold then prioritized those targets in accordance with the commander's guidance. Meanwhile, Stewart again tasked the collection system to confirm that the targets were still there. Day four continued the validation and refinement process until the targets were struck.

Target validation and revalidation were enormously important. The Air Force required that targets be revalidated eight and then again four hours prior to attack. Given an average of 110 ARCENT-submitted targets per day and the size of the area, managing the effort to revisit each target was an almost impossible task. The accuracy requirement only increased the difficulty. Targeteers joked that they had to supply target folders with a picture clearly marked "Place bomb here!"[20] Only satellites, RF-4Cs, U-2s, TR-1s, Tornados, and UAVs were capable of meeting the required 100-meter accuracy. Only 24 RF-4Cs, 5 TR-1s, and 6 U-2s were in theater, and only VII Corps had access to UAVs. With the Iraqis observing strict radio silence and remaining static in XVIII Airborne Corps' sector, Luck's only recourse to verify targets was long-range surveillance which he was precluded from inserting until one week prior to the ground offensive. Six of the RF-4Cs were in Turkey and were largely unavailable for Stewart's needs. The same systems were already heavily tasked for other collection requirements. To make matters worse, the Air Force shaved its own reconnaissance requirements off the top to support the strategic bombing effort. RF-4C missions so diverted were not offered up to the Army as part of the available pie at the theater reconnaissance meeting. This practice continued until it was brought to the attention of General Waller, the deputy CINC, on February 7.[21]

Despite the best efforts of Stewart's target team, ARCENT could not reconfirm the nominated targets within the prescribed time. To ease this difficulty, ARCENT liaison teams at CENTAF received target lists that could be piggybacked against CENTCOM-directed TR-1 missions providing real-time intelligence data to Air Force hunter-killer teams of F-16s, A-10s, and F-15Es. Similar measures were established for JSTARS. Ultimately, Stewart's targeteers arrived at an 18-hour window for target validation, processing 70 percent of the targets within that time.

Even as Arnold and Stewart solved the timing problem, a more critical issue arose in the air operation. After intensively managing the targeting process, Stewart and Arnold found that less than half of their requested targets made it to the ATO. The result was an immediate outcry from the corps commanders who, having lost their ability to designate BAI targets, still expected to influence the general interdiction effort to conform with corps plans to shape the battlefield. The number of corps-nominated targets actually flown quickly became the litmus test for air support. As far as Luck and Franks were concerned, the issue was critical. [22]

The view of commanders at ARCENT and below did not match that of the CINC. Luck and Franks timed their plan to shape the battlefield in relation to G-Day, the first day of ground operations. Both commanders wanted seven days of sustained air attacks directed at Iraqi units in their path of advance, but they were in the dark as to exactly when G-Day would occur. Consequently, in January, at the very beginning of the air operation, the corps commanders began submitting target nominations that would allow them to shape the battlefield from south to north. When the Air Force did not immediately strike those targets, the outcry equaled that over the loss of BAI. Attempting to close the communications gap, Arnold briefed the CINC on ARCENT targeting concerns on January 26. Schwarzkopf rejected the brief as a purely ARCENT view.

As for the Air Force, General Horner was reacting to the CINC's demands. As the JFACC, Horner saw the CINC daily—and Schwarzkopf was definitely talking to him. Once the air operation began, Schwarzkopf put his personal stamp on the ATO by redirecting the targeting at the eleventh hour. On occasion he would wait until after the ATO for the next day was ready to pick a specific Republican Guard division at the 1900-hour meeting. Such late changes could adversely affect targeting, and as a minimum caused delays.

THE ROLE OF THE LAND COMPONENT COMMANDER

The next effort to ease the conflict over targeting came 10 days into the air operation with the first meeting of the CENTCOM Joint Targeting Board. The meeting resulted largely from the efforts of Colonel David Schulte, chief of ARCENT's battlefield coordination element. By doctrine the LCC's representative, the BCE served instead as the ARCENT's interface with Horner's staff, making it one of several competing voices in the daily targeting meetings. As the BCE chief, Schulte did not have daily access to the CINC's briefings where Schwarzkopf would often issue guidance directly to Horner.

General Waller was aware of the friction between the Air Force and the Army but was uncertain of the cause or the significance. Schulte had served with Waller on two previous assignments, and because Waller trusted his judgment, he told Schulte to evaluate the situation. In behind-the-scenes talks, Schulte explained ARCENT's frustrations with the process, convincing Waller to take up the issue with the CINC. As a result, Waller convinced Schwarzkopf to appoint him head of the Joint Targeting Board with full authority to review the daily ATO. The change was at best a partial solution, for while it did allow the Army more say in the process, the CINC continued to make last-minute changes to targeting.

ARCENT was ill-equipped to handle those changes. Schwarzkopf's decision cycle was often inside that of the targeting effort. The result at ARCENT and below was frustration, particularly among targeteers forced to scramble to come up with new targets based on old data that often proved wrong. Ultimately, Stewart built a target data base on all the Iraqi units, regardless of their priority in the eyes of the corps commanders, to ensure that targets were available when such last-minute changes were made.

The eleventh-hour changes also affected the air operation, particularly in its earlier stages when dumb bombs were the main weapon being used against ground forces. Horner's F-16 pilots used Stewart's six-digit locations to set their inertial guidance systems to fly to the targets, only to find nothing and then divert to secondary targets less important to corps commanders' desires. Even if the target was only 1,000 meters away, the pilots could not see it from 25,000 feet and would often complain about poor targeting during debriefs. Horner, chastened by Schwarzkopf about poor results, reacted by changing his techniques in managing the operation. Already fundamentally flawed, the targeting effort soon faced additional challenges. The first came from Iraq.

THE SCUD WAR

In a typical act of defiance in December, Saddam test-fired three of his Scuds at targets inside Iraq. While the launches did not threaten the Coalition or Israel, they did heighten tension. Fortunately the firings also allowed US Space Command to tweak its detection systems and to improve warning times to the theater. Nevertheless, the firings were a clear warning that Saddam would use the weapons if attacked. On January 18, in retaliation for Coalition air attacks, he launched the first of 86 modified Scuds against Israel and Saudi Arabia. The next day eight missiles fell on Israel, injuring 47 people and causing extensive damage to civilian property.

Patriot Defense

The 11th ADA Brigade was responsible for air defense of Saudi ports and airfields. Each corps had its own organic air defense units. Colonel Joseph Garrett, the 11th ADA commander, coordinated all of these forces and integrated them with the Coalition air and air defense forces. Garrett

Patriot firing batteries were positioned to defend Dhahran.

established a network of command and control centers to link the deployed battalions, allowing them instantaneous access to the latest operational and intelligence picture.

On the night of January 20, A and B Batteries, 2-7th Patriot, were on alert for more of Saddam's Scud attacks. Space Command's missile warning satellites and radars had broadcast an alert over the CENTCOM warning net just minutes before, prompting the B Battery tactical control officer to blow a warning siren and place his launchers under computer control. The battery crew immediately donned chemical gear and took shelter as the computer announced it was engaging an incoming missile. Next door, the adjacent battery was similarly engaged as the battalion computer coordinated the action between the two batteries. Far above, Iraqi Scuds began their dive into the atmosphere at more than 5,000 miles per hour, and as the air thickened, they began to buffet. Slowed to 4,400 miles per hour by the increasingly dense air, the missiles began to break apart. Below, Patriot launchers boomed, spitting two missiles out of the canisters for every Scud. In moments, the sound of the missiles breaking the sound barrier announced that they had achieved their maximum speed of 3,700 miles per hour. Scuds and Patriots now closed at more than 8,000 miles per hour. In a climactic vision of flame and sound, the engagements ended in seconds as three of four Scuds launched at Dhahran were intercepted. The fourth missed the city completely. Later, crews would dub this evening "the night of a thousand Scuds." The Dhahran batteries had fired 8 Patriots and those at Riyadh had fired more than 30. The high expenditure rate soon raised concerns that the supply of Patriots might run short despite the best efforts of Raytheon and the Patriot program manager's office.

The very crudeness of Saddam's modified Scuds increased the Patriot's challenge. The PAC-2 version was designed to counter a more advanced tactical ballistic missile whose performance parameters could be predicted. Instead, the Patriot had to intercept an incoming missile that often was in the process of breaking up. Hitting the incoming missiles as they wobbled and weaved was complicated by the debris from disintegrating missiles. Because the missiles in effect created their own decoys, tactical control officers at each firing battery had to learn the art of picking out the heavier warheads as they fell away from the missile debris. Eleven software improvements had been necessary to give the Patriot an antitactical ballistic missile capability. Contractors who accompanied the first Patriot batteries that arrived in Saudi Arabia in mid-August and stayed with them throughout the crisis refined the software so that the computer could better distinguish warheads from debris. The teamwork paid off as these units continued to engage Saddam's Scuds.

The success that American Patriot batteries had defending Saudi Arabia raised eyebrows in Israel. Although Israel had bought its own Patriots, the crews were still in training at the US Army Air Defense School in Fort Bliss, Texas, when the war began.[23] The Israeli government had rejected an offer of American-manned Patriots to fill the void. However, with Saddam's missiles landing in his country, Israeli Defense Minister Moshe Arens called Secretary of Defense Cheney and accepted the offer. Following Cheney's conversation with Arens, President Bush phoned Prime Minister Shamir and promised to do all he could to prevent further attacks on Israel, persuading the Israeli leader to wait rather than retaliate.[24] Fewer than 27 hours later, Colonel David Heebner's 10th Air Defense Brigade from Darmstadt, Germany, was positioning two of its batteries in Israel. The brigade had not trained for a deployment outside Europe but reacted quickly, assisted by the 32d Air Defense Command. Using a combination of US Air Force and El Al aircraft, the units began arriving on January 19. They were fully operational in three days, just in time to take on Saddam's next volley.[25] The Patriot tactical missile had served as a key political tool to keep Israel out of the war. But Patriots were purely defensive and the United States had to do more than just parry Saddam's blows.

The Hunt for Saddam's Scuds

The key to ending the Scud threat was to destroy the launchers. The fixed launch sites—all in western Iraq—were easy to target and relatively easy to put out of action. But Scuds were also launched from Soviet-made MAZ tractors or locally produced trucks and trailers. Loading a missile on its launcher and prepping it for firing could be done in hidden positions, allowing the crew to drive to a surveyed launch position, set up, and fire with minimum exposure. Intelligence looked hard for such sites, but the bottom line was that the Iraqis could launch the missiles from almost anywhere. They further complicated the problem by using decoy trucks with large pipes mounted to resemble missiles. Finding a Scud launcher under such circumstances was difficult at best.

Scuds quickly became CENTCOM's priority target and Horner redirected air sorties accordingly. By January 24 CENTCOM had diverted 40 percent of all air sorties to Scud hunting at a considerable cost to ARCENT's efforts to prepare the battlefield. General Leide used JSTARS to find Scuds on the road. National intelligence agencies focused on suspected launch areas and targeted Iraqi strategic communications with available jammers.

One of the units targeting Saddam's Scuds was a newly formed platoon in the 201st MI Battalion, the 513th MI Brigade's electronic warfare component. Captain Eric Kennedy, A Company commander, had formed the platoon by pulling soldiers from other duties to man the TLQ-17, a high-frequency jammer, known as the "Sandcrab." First Lieutenant Brian O'Neil, Kennedy's former executive officer and now Sandcrab platoon leader, selected volunteers with previous experience on earlier versions of the TLQ-17, a system normally used against tactical VHF communications. With an antenna 320 feet long, 300 feet wide, and 60 feet high, the Sandcrab was anything but mobile. The antenna boosted the jammer's power to almost 5,000 watts, making it ideal for detecting long-range, high-frequency communications used to control Scud launches. Operating from three remote bases named Tombstone, Broken Axle, and Mesa, O'Neil's "Sandcrabbers" were especially effective in driving the Iraqis into less secure communications that were vulnerable to interception.[26] Chief Warrant Officer James Roberts, assigned to the 525th MI Brigade, combined the data from the Sandcrab with other signals intelligence—including TENCAP and tactical systems—to develop a comprehensive scheme for targeting Scuds. This scheme proved to be more accurate than existing theater or national methods, and was subsequently adopted by ARCENT as the primary means for verifying Scud targets.

To find and kill Scuds, US Special Operations Command created a special 877-man Joint Special Operations Task Force (JSOTF) of aviation

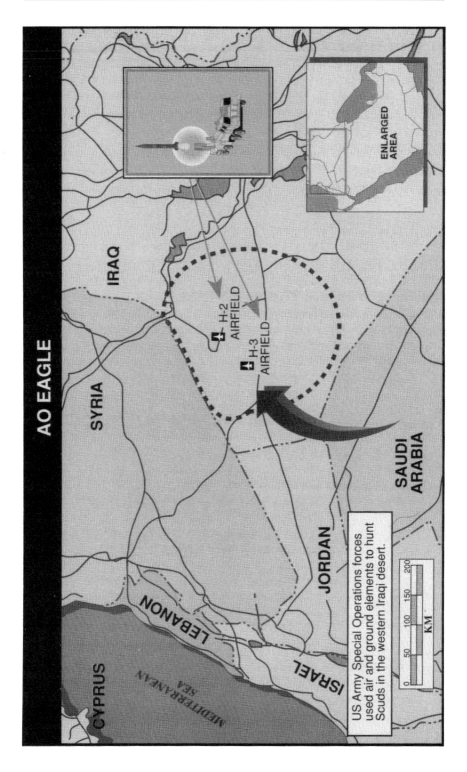

US Army Special Operations forces used air and ground elements to hunt Scuds in the western Iraqi desert.

and ground forces and placed them directly under CENTCOM control working with British special forces. JSOTF planners focused their search for the launchers near Scud support facilities around the fixed launcher complexes at H2 and H3 airfields in western Iraq, some 75 kilometers from the Jordanian border, and in the vicinity of al Qa'im on the Syrian border. Saddam had scattered his Scud support over a huge area to hide and secure it, so the JSOTF area of operations, AO Eagle, was likewise extended over several hundred square miles.

Beginning on February 7, Special Operations forces infiltrated deep into Iraq to destroy communication sites, ambush mobile launchers, and direct armed helicopter strikes against fixed facilities associated with Scud launchings. In one instance, a reinforced Ranger platoon carried in Special Operations helicopters raided a strategic communications facility near the Jordanian border. The Rangers toppled the 350-foot microwave tower, destroyed the communications site, and returned safely to base.

Combining the eyes of Special Forces soldiers on the ground with Air Force firepower proved most effective. In the early morning hours of February 21, a Special Forces reconnaissance team deep in Iraq spotted an Iraqi convoy almost a mile from their hide position using night vision devices. The team verified their own position using a Global Positioning System and determined the exact map spot of the target with a hand-held laser range finder. The team's powerful lightweight transmitter broadcast the air support request more than 200 miles. Within minutes, an F-15E Strike Eagle was on the way, vectored into the target area by AWACS. Effective antiaircraft fire disrupted the first pilot's attack, however, and he missed the target. Still determined, the SF team called in a second F-15E to destroy the target. This Strike Eagle did not miss and the team observed the convoy disappear in a huge fireball followed by several secondary explosions. Meanwhile, the first F-15E pilot used his on-board radar to locate more Scud support vehicles, and AWACS continued to shuttle in additional F-15Es until all the Iraqi vehicles were destroyed. To be safe, the ground SF team moved to a new hide site to radio each battle damage assessment (BDA) to al Jauf. Even after the raids were completed, the enemy apparently never realized that they were being watched from the ground.

Faced with such an absolute effort, the Scud attacks dropped dramatically in frequency and accuracy. Of the 86 Scuds launched, Baghdad fired almost half from western Iraq. During the 20 days from January 18 to February 6, the Iraqis launched 29 Scuds from the western desert. As key support facilities were destroyed, the Iraqis were forced to hip-shoot their missiles. In the next 22 days, Iraq launched only 11 missiles and 2 of those fell harmlessly in the open desert.

The effort to blunt Saddam's Scud threat succeeded, but at a price. The diversion of air power to fly Scud combat air patrols and the intelligence to support counter-Scud operations directly impeded the effort against Iraqi ground forces in the KTO. Scud busting extended the air effort by more than a week. Ultimately, the Scud hunt meant that ARCENT targeting goals would not be reached before the beginning of the ground war.

MEASURING PROGRESS AND MAKING ADJUSTMENTS

Battle damage assessment provided the daily measure of progress toward the ARCENT goals and had become a hot issue, only slightly less contentious than Scud hunting. ARCENT was the theater authority for the enemy ground situation, responsible for assessing damage done by allied bombing. The reasoning was simple: if the opening of the ground operation was contingent upon reaching a 50-percent attrition of Iraqi armor and artillery, the ground commander responsible for the main effort—General Yeosock—should make that call. [27]

Given that targeting was already a sensitive issue between ARCENT and CENTAF, BDA would inevitably become equally controversial. Assessing battle damage was much more art than science. Ideally, after every strike an imaging system, either RF-4C, U-2, or Tornado, would overfly the scene to determine effects. But with so many competing demands on the theater imagery system, BDA imagery ranked low in priority. Even imaged targets were hard to analyze because unless a tank or armored vehicle exploded catastrophically, determining if it had been hit at all was difficult. [28]

General Stewart developed a formula for estimating BDA: using armored vehicles and artillery as the baseline, he at first counted only 50 percent of A-10 pilot claims and all imagery-reported kills as confirmed. As the campaign progressed, the BDA cell in the ARCENT G2 modified the process to reduce the weight of A-10 claims from one-half to one-third and to accept only 50 percent of all F-111 and F-15E kills supported by gun video. [29]

Naturally, this procedure caused some concern, particularly with the tension between the Services over Army targeting. Air commanders felt that their pilots' successes were being discounted, perhaps in an attempt to force them to restrike targets in the KTO. Washington's concerns were just the opposite. Both the Defense Intelligence Agency and the Central Intelligence Agency were producing BDA reports based solely on their analyses. Lacking theater reconnaissance reports, the national BDA figures suggested that ARCENT was exaggerating Air Force successes. Later events would prove that Stewart was more correct than any of his critics.

The system remained controversial, but Stewart continued to broker the process, operating on the theory that if he angered both sides in the debate equally, perhaps the BDA was close to the mark. In any case, he was determined to give the ground commanders his best estimate on the damage to Iraqis regardless of its emotional impact. In one of his more contentious but correct calls, Stewart reassessed the attrition of the Republican Guard Tawakalna Division, adding to its strength after high-quality U-2 imagery showed many of its combat systems to be untouched.[30]

Meanwhile, the air operation and the targeting effort went on. Faced with disappointing results from less precise F-16 and B-52 strikes, especially against dug-in armor, Horner changed tactics on February 6 and turned to precision strikes with FB-111 and F-15E bombers. Frustrated by poor-quality target information, he pulled out of retirement the technique of fast forward air controller (fast FAC) used in Vietnam. At the height of that conflict, pilots with forward air controller experience in slower propeller-driven aircraft performed similar roles flying jets in the more lethal air defense environment over North Vietnam. Horner assigned each fast FAC a 30x30-mile kill box, easing the ARCENT targeting problem since target boxes were not tied to the ATO. The Air Force defined the kill boxes by latitude and longitude. Army planners further subdivided them and used the kill boxes instead of engagement areas, normally defined by geographic features. Targeteers helped select and orient kill boxes so that they included the most important Republican Guard and regular army heavy divisions. Using their Pave Tack sensors, FB-111s picked out the warmer vehicles inside each kill box, "plinking" them with laser-guided bombs. Later as U-2 H-camera imagery became available from the Joint Imagery Processing Center, Stewart's targeteers provided annotated imagery that gave six-digit coordinates for each target in the kill box. These kill arrays allowed FB-111 weapons officers to program in each target before takeoff, and results continued to improve.[31]

The kill box technique was not an unqualified success in the eyes of ground commanders. Although the technique generated lots of sorties, three problems emerged. First, the kill boxes were an Air Force control measure, meaning that selection of the target was the prerogative of squadron and aircraft commanders flying the missions rather than the supported ground commander. This situation in turn decentralized the targeting, making it difficult, if not impossible, for the ground commanders to find out which targets had been hit. Finally, the Air Force selected kill boxes based more on geometrical convenience than on the corps commander's scheme of maneuver. The boxes were not necessarily centered over the most menacing Iraqi defenses. The kill box concept worked as well as it did in practice because during the air operation the battlefield was almost completely static and there was plenty of time to be methodical and deliberate.[32]

On February 9, Secretary Cheney and General Powell were briefed on the progress of the air effort. Using ARCENT's BDA, the commanders told both men that 50 percent of Iraqi armor and artillery would be destroyed by February 21. With the goal of a February 21 G-Day, Horner's targeting of the KTO intensified, but friction continued. At the same time the Air Force increased the number of ARCENT targets flown on the ATO, it decreased the number of sorties flown against each target. This allowed the Air Force to meet the CINC's last-minute demand to maintain the number of air interdiction targets attacked without impinging on the strategic effort. Apprised by Colonel Schulte, General Waller intervened as he had in the matter of available RF-4 sorties.[33] During the war, ARCENT ultimately submitted 3,067 targets for the ATO; 1,241 were flown. Another 1,582 targets were submitted directly to Air Force target-eers or to the flying wings. These were flown as non-ATO targets, notably kill boxes and kill arrays.[34]

In contrast to the concern over BAI, Army ground commanders were pleased by Horner's plan for close air support for the ground operation. His innovative technique called for preplanned CAS, nicknamed "flow CAS" by CENTAF. With the number of aircraft at his disposal, Horner saw that the most efficient method of employing sorties to support the ground forces in contact with the enemy would be to push them forward at regular intervals. Under the control of the airborne command and control center (ABCCC)—the equivalent of a flying "tactical CP" for the Air Force—the sorties would check in with the air liaison officers (ALOs) at each corps to see if units on the ground had targets. If they had none, the CAS missions would divert to interdiction missions under ABCCC control. Horner's decision made sense and ground commanders saw that it would be inherently more responsive than keeping aircraft and crews on standby. Meanwhile, the air battle continued as the Coalition and the Iraqis took their first steps toward ground battle. The first came with the Iraqis' seizure of the Saudi border town of Khafji.

THE IRAQI ATTACK ON KHAFJI

Blinded by the Coalition's complete seizure of the air, Saddam's forces nervously awaited the beginning of the ground campaign. As early as January 22, ARCENT noted increased Iraqi patrolling along the front lines, particularly in the area north of Khafji.[35] This low-key activity continued until January 28 when the Marines reported the possibility of Iraqi remotely piloted vehicles flying over the border area.[36]

An alert analyst 7,000 miles away almost prevented the Iraqi effort at Khafji. On January 26, Chief Warrant Officer Donna Smith got a call on the Army side of the Joint Intelligence Center, buried in the bowels of the Pentagon. National intelligence had intercepted an Iraqi transmission that proposed a commanders' conference be held in the Iraqi 3d Corps sector two hours after the intercept. Smith recognized a jewel when she saw one, and she quickly consulted an imagery technician to find a likely location for the conference. They frantically culled the imagery file on hand and found one very promising photo that showed a large building most likely to house a meeting of senior officers in the intercept area.

Smith, who quickly had the ARCENT shift leader in Riyadh on the phone, talked him through the circumstances of the hit while the imagery tech digitally transmitted the pictures. With just minutes to spare, Air Force targeteers found two FB-111s suitably armed and flying near the target area. The pilots punched in the new coordinates and were on the target in minutes. They overflew it once at higher altitude and confirmed the building was lighted at one end with a conspicuous number of military and civilian vehicles outside. Rolling in hot, the bombers plastered the target with 2,000-pound bombs. The next day reconnaissance systems confirmed that the building and the surrounding vehicles had been obliterated. Intelligence later learned that the 3d Corps commander was not at the meeting. Next to the ruins, however, the overhead picture showed an Iraqi helicopter on the ground, a strong indication that it was not a good day for someone important to Baghdad.

During the evening of January 29, the Iraqi 5th Mechanized Division, supported by elements of the Iraqi 1st Mechanized and 3d Armored Divisions, launched brigade- to battalion-size probes across the border into Saudi Arabia. Coalition forces quickly beat back an attack southwest of al-Wafrah by a brigade of armor. Confused and apparently lost, the brigade attempted to reenter Iraqi lines at the wrong point and was at least temporarily hung up in the obstacle belt. The second attack by an armored battalion, hit by Coalition missile and air attack as it cleared the lanes through the obstacles, quickly turned back as well. The third, a mechanized brigade, pushed south to the now abandoned Khafji, holding it briefly before being driven out by Coalition ground and air attacks. While the limited attacks occurred, elements from 1st Mechanized and the 3d Armored shifted forward to screen their withdrawal, acting as a covering force against any Coalition counterattack.[37] The action was a division-level reconnaissance-in-force. Possibly lured into the attack by an elaborate deception effort mounted by the XVIII Airborne Corps, Saddam, blinded and battered by the air operation, had hoped to preempt the Coalition ground operation, inflicting as many casualties as possible to embarrass the allies before withdrawing. While the XVIII Airborne Corps was actually in the process of moving to the west, corps and divisional deception teams had established an elaborate electronic and visual signature south of al-Wafrah about 30 kilometers from the border. Intended to mask the corps' movement and deceive the Iraqis into thinking its forward headquarters and units were moving into attack positions, the deception effort may have caused Saddam to jump the gun.

Khafji highlighted the difference in quality between Saddam's infantry and his regular heavy forces. The operation was complicated, involving heavy units from two corps and at least three divisions in a night passage-of-lines and subsequent attack. Coordination problems were evident as the units missed their passage points in returning. Movement times were slow and often delayed, allowing the Coalition to react more quickly. Khafji showed them incapable at this stage of the war of mounting an operational maneuver involving multiple divisions. On the other hand, it demonstrated that at least in the regular heavy forces the will to fight remained substantial. As an example of a coordinated military operation, Khafji was not pretty, but the Iraqis did execute the basic mission—under almost constant pounding by air, artillery, and occasional naval gunfire.

Taking that lesson to heart, General Franks keyed on the heavy units that formed the tactical reserve of the Iraqi 7th Corps, especially those that could threaten his open right flank as his units cleared the breach and drove north. The more quickly these Iraqi units could be destroyed— either by air or by the British 1st Armoured Division—the more quickly the remainder of VII Corps would be able to charge through on its way to the Republican Guard. Speaking to his targeteers, Franks slapped the map where armor was closest to the breach and said, "I want you to make that unit go away!"

With a single gesture Franks doomed the Iraqi 52d Armored Brigade, part of the 52d Armored Division, which soon became known among Air Force and Army targeteers as the "go-away brigade." The division's mission was to act as the tactical reserve to the Iraqi 7th Corps. The 52d Armored Division was to shift from its positions in support of the 26th Infantry to an area near al-Ethami.

The move was ill-timed. The 52d Brigade did not close on its new positions until January 12. With hand shovels and one backhoe, the brigade commander began the task of digging his tracks into the rocky soil. Two of the armored battalions were fully exposed when the air operation began; the third was dug in to an average depth of only one meter.

For the 52d, the shooting war began with the appearance of an A-10 at 1000 on January 17 and continued throughout the day, leaving 13 vehicles destroyed and 15 men dead. Already operating on a marginal supply system, the loss of transport—especially fuel tankers—would immobilize the unit's tracked vehicles for later destruction.

Coalition air attacks then turned on the brigade's armored vehicles. The unit lost an average of three to four tanks every day and the crews soon learned to stay away from their vehicles to stay alive. The BMPs were the last category of vehicles to be struck in the final five days before the ground war. Attempts at decoying the attackers with burning tires proved marginally effective, at best delaying the destruction of the remaining tracks. After the hapless brigade commander reported his unit as 10 percent effective on February 21, a division inspector visited the unit to verify the report. Just as the inspection began, another A-10 arrived and proceeded to work over the remaining vehicles, leaving no doubt that the reports had been accurate. The brigade commander thought himself to be the unluckiest soldier in the Iraqi army. As he watched his unit crumble under an unrelenting aerial assault, he couldn't help but notice that the other two brigades of his division were sitting in the desert equally exposed but relatively untouched.

The division inspection led to a last-minute attempt to reconstitute the brigade. Drivers sent back to division to pick replacement vehicles on February 15 returned with 20 BMPs and one T-55. Despite the brigade commander's attempts to hide them alongside burning vehicles, at least three were smoking hulks by the end of the day. On G-Day none of the battalions had more than seven tanks left. The 75th fared the worst, with only 3 remaining of its original 22.

The brigade's personnel situation was no less disastrous. Another 300 troops deserted or failed to return from leave once the air attacks began. Some 35 soldiers were killed in the attacks and another 45 were wounded. With less than 10 percent of its tracked vehicles and some 500 beaten troops to begin the ground war, the 52d Armored had become the "go-away brigade" in fact as well as in name.

The destruction of the 52d Armored illustrates the synergy that can be achieved by targeting air power according to the corps commander's intent using BAI as discussed above. In this case, air power was used effectively to destroy a threat to the ground commander's plan of maneuver. The 52d was no longer capable of reinforcing the Iraqi forward defenses once the breaching operation began. Nor was the battered unit able to threaten Franks' right flank as VII Corps pushed through the breach toward the Republican Guard. A key element of Franks' operational design—shaping the battlefield with air power—had been achieved.

ARMY SUPPORT OF THE AIR OPERATION

Staff Sergeant Ronnie Wint and his two crew mates from A Battery, 1-27th Field Artillery, had spent the last six hours in their MLRS launcher fighting traffic along Tapline Road when their battery commander, Captain Jeff Lieb, radioed the mission to strike an Iraqi surface-to-air missile site farther than 100 kilometers away. Wint's driver, Private First Class Russell Sullivan, quickly pulled out of the congested road and roared off cross-country to find the firing point and to exchange his two "six-pack" rocket pod containers for two pods each containing a new, as yet untried, tactical missile system. Five kilometers down the road, Wint's launcher pulled into the A Battery assembly area where the gunner, Sergeant Steve Hannah, quickly loaded the two missile pods. Wint then paused briefly at the survey control point pegged into the ground to update his on-board position-locating device and continued a short distance to the firing point. Once in position, Hannah punched target data into his fire control panel and completed the prelaunch sequence. It was now 1830 on January 17, the first day of the air operation.

The first ATACMS mission was to take down the al-Abraq SA-2 surface-to-air missile site located 30 kilometers inside Kuwait astride one of the key Air Force transit routes into the KTO. Once the mission was sent to Sergeant Wint's crew, both the ARCENT deep battle cell and the Air Force began the painful process of clearing a path for the missile. The Air Force had never had to contend with an Army missile that would climb so high to reach a target more than 100 kilometers distant. A corridor was

Staff Sergeant Wint, 1-27th Field Artillery, fired the first long-range precision tactical missile strike in history, January 18, 1991.

finally opened after midnight. At 0042 on January 18, the first shot that VII Corps had fired in anger since World War II also became the first precision strike by an Army missile in history. Two minutes after launch, the missile disgorged a thousand baseball-size bomblets directly over the Iraqi missile site with catastrophic effect.

COMBAT SEARCH AND RESCUE (CSAR)

As epitomized by Task Force Normandy and the ATACMS strike, Army elements were in the fight from the opening of the air operation. Conventional operations like the Apache raid on the Nukhayb radar site and Patriot Scud busting were spectacular and drew immediate attention. Others, like search and rescue, psychological operations, and the JSOTF Scud-hunting effort, operated in the shadows.

When an American aircraft went down over Iraqi-controlled territory, rescuing a surviving pilot before capture required fast action. Thanks to the CSAR effort mounted under the direction of Colonel Jesse Johnson at SOCCENT, some downed pilots were rescued. An example was the Army's rescue of an F-16 pilot on February 17. Engine failure caused his aircraft to crash 40 miles inside Iraq. The call came from the AWACs at 1815, and within minutes modified MH-60 Blackhawks from the 3-160th Aviation were in the air. By 2000 Chief Warrant Officer Thomas Montgomery located and picked up the pilot as enemy vehicles closed in on him. Seeing the enemy, Montgomery contacted the AWACS and requested support. Within minutes an F-16 was on station to destroy the enemy vehicles.

As in Montgomery's case, secretly infiltrating enemy territory, finding a downed pilot, and then racing back to friendly airspace was risky business. In the high-threat, Iraqi-controlled territory, Schwarzkopf firmly believed that he needed special crews to rescue downed pilots. Colonel Johnson got the mission more or less by default. With the consolidation of the Air Force's search-and-rescue helicopters under the control of US Special Operations Command, the Air Force was not resourced for the mission. Without dedicated, specially equipped helicopters, the Air Force had limited CSAR capability. The Navy faced similar limitations. Its rescue helicopters were fine for over-water missions, but Desert One proved that they were less well-suited for land operations. The Army had an organic capability to pick up its downed aviators, but it lacked the range for deep pickups unless it used Special Operations aircraft that had already been assigned to SOCOM. That left Johnson at SOCCENT to manage the missions under his centralized control. By default, Johnson assumed responsibility for CSAR in all of Iraq and Kuwait and for 12 nautical miles into the Gulf.

His was not a light responsibility. In deciding to launch a CSAR mission, Johnson had to judge whether to risk the lives of two crews to save those of one or two men. He also had to determine if special aircraft were available. When such calls came, they usually went to Lieutenant Colonel Dell Dailey's 3-160th Aviation, whose aircraft were equipped for deep insertions and could serve in the CSAR role. During Desert Shield, Dailey had used volunteer pilots from the Air Force, Marines, and Navy to train his crews. Taking the "downed pilots" out into the Saudi desert, he would leave them for night recovery by his CSAR crews. This program not only proved valuable to his pilots, but served as a confidence builder for pilots involved in the air war.

Sometimes, however, conflicting missions prevented SOF aviators from accepting a CSAR mission. In one case, an Air Force F-16 pilot was shot down near Basrah. Although he suffered a broken leg, he managed to hide long enough to come up on the radio. When the CSAR request came into SOCCENT, Johnson had nothing available so he asked the other Services if they could pick up the pilot. The Army said yes.

Late on the afternoon of February 27, the 2-229th Attack from Fort Rucker, Alabama, serving with the 101st, received word that the F-16 pilot from the 363d Tactical Fighter Wing had been shot down near the causeway west of Basrah. The 2-229th was already operating in that area and had a UH-60L standing strip alert as a rescue aircraft for the unit's Apaches. Agreeing to take the CSAR mission, the battalion launched the UH-60 with two AH-64 escorts. A pathfinder team and a medical team led by Major Rhonda Cornum were on board the Blackhawk. General Luck tried to abort the mission from his tactical command post, knowing that whatever shot down the F-16 was equally capable of downing a Blackhawk, but he was unable to reach the unit in time. As it launched, an Air Force AWACs took over its control and directed it on a straight vector to the downed pilot's last known position. That vector put the low-flying Blackhawk directly over a concentration of armor and infantry, probably belonging to the Republican Guard al-Faw Infantry Division. The Iraqis shot down the Blackhawk, which crashed almost directly into their position at about 130 knots and disintegrated. Having been damaged by friendly fire, both AH-64s returned to base. Dust storms precluded another attempt to locate the Blackhawk until March 1 when the recovery team found five soldiers' remains at the crash site. Cornum, Staff Sergeant Daniel Stamaris, and Specialist Troy Dunlap had been taken prisoner.

The results of CSAR were mixed. Although initial estimates had predicted that 40 aircraft would be lost on the opening night of the air war, only three losses occurred. During the entire air and ground war the Coalition lost only 52 aircraft. Twenty-two pilots and crew survived: 14 were captured immediately and 8 evaded capture—2 for more than 24 hours. Of seven CSAR missions launched, three were successful. Each of the Service's special operations aviation units was credited with one recovery.

WINNING THE PSYCHOLOGICAL BATTLE

The psychological operations campaign was another Special Operations success, one of the most important of the Gulf War. As part of an overall campaign plan, PSYOP, or propaganda, can be a combat multiplier if the circumstances surrounding its employment are favorable. Saddam began waging his own PSYOP campaign early in the Gulf War as Baghdad Betty's broadcasts entertained American soldiers along the border each night. Some broadcasts were more amusing than others: one warned the troops that Robert Redford, Sean Penn, and Bart Simpson were seducing their wives back home. With such inept input, Saddam's propaganda created more support than disruption for the Coalition.

Managing CENTCOM's PSYOP campaign fell to the US Army 4th Psychological Operations Group (POG), especially the 8th Psychological Operations Battalion. By late August, 10 people under Colonel Anthony Normand, commander of 4th POG, were in Saudi Arabia working out a comprehensive plan to use 117 themes to target Iraqi soldiers and civilians. Submitted to the JCS on September 20, the plan got lost in the swirl of competing actions. Although it was too late to execute the original time-phased plan, the Office of the Secretary of Defense approved most of the broad themes of the plan on December 14, 1990. A strong message from Schwarzkopf to the JCS questioning the continuous delays was the catalyst that broke the plan loose. [38]

To offset the delay in Washington, Normand worked on a Coalition plan using a cell of Saudis, Egyptians, Kuwaitis, and British. On November 28, the Voice of the Gulf began daily radio broadcasts and the 8th PSYOP Battalion worked up leaflets highlighting the world stance against Saddam. The 8th Psychological Operations Task Force and Normand's cell also produced a video, "Nations of the World Take A Stand," which was distributed worldwide and also smuggled into Iraq.

The expanding demands for PSYOP and the pull of planners to fill vacancies at ARCENT and elsewhere quickly overwhelmed 8th POTF. To fill the void, Colonel Layton Dunbar, Normand's successor, deployed his full headquarters to the theater. Under the operational control of CENTCOM, Dunbar used the OSD-approved themes to develop programs which stressed the superiority of Coalition forces over those of Iraq and the inequality between Republican Guard forces and regular Iraqi units. Headlining world support for offensive actions, it emphasized that Saddam was the cause of the crisis and sought to allay regional fears about the Coalition's respect for Arab culture and private property.[39] The Voice of the Gulf broadcast in Arabic hammered home these messages to Saddam's troops 18 hours per day.

While the Voice of the Gulf filled the airwaves with its message, the Air Force filled the skies with leaflets, derisively called "bullshit bombs."

During the course of the war, the Air Force dropped 28 million leaflets over Kuwait and Iraq. The CINC himself recommended one of the most successful techniques employed in the campaign. MC-130 Combat Talons dropped leaflets on Iraqi units that identified the units by name and warned that they would soon be bombed. The leaflets suggested that the soldiers desert rather than risk their lives. That same night the B-52s would deliver on the promise. On many occasions, the MC-130s returned again to release more pamphlets saying "We told you to leave." The leaflets heightened the psychological effect of the B-52 bombings, especially among Iraqi troops along the Kuwait border. They lived in deplorable conditions and once the ground war started these pitiful soldiers surrendered quickly. Ninety-eight percent of captured prisoners had the leaflets in their possession. One Iraqi frontline commander reported the PSYOP campaign was "second only to allied bombing" in demoralizing his division. [40]

As the 8th POTF liaison officer to CENTAF, Army Major Jack Summe coordinated the leaflet drops with Air Force Brigadier General Buster Glosson's targeting cell. Summe was often received with disdain in the cell. Targeteers were always quick to chide him about his infamous leaflets. However, when reports filtered into CENTAF of thousands of Iraqis surrendering, opinion changed. When Jack Summe walked into the targeting cell on February 25, he received a standing ovation.

FINAL PREPARATIONS: THE G-DAY COUNTDOWN

Grimly, ARCENT and the subordinate corps along with the rest of the Coalition ground forces began a series of cross-border operations designed to further confuse the already dazed Iraqis. General Yeosock intended to reinforce the deception effort to further convince the Iraqis that the main effort would come directly from the south into Kuwait. CENTCOM dropped leaflets with Marine Corps emblems on Iraqi coastal units and pamphlets with VII Corps and XVIII Airborne Corps logos in Kuwait, far from the real location of these forces. Loudspeaker teams moved up to the border berm and played recordings of tracked vehicles before quickly retreating. On occasion the Iraqis fired at the sound with artillery. Fire-finder counterbattery radars immediately picked up the Iraqi rounds, allowing American artillery units to return fire and destroy Iraqi artillery positions.

SPECIAL RECONNAISSANCE

Special Forces continued to actively support the campaign plan by inserting reconnaissance patrols hundreds of kilometers deep into Iraq. The teams were emplaced principally near Highway 8 to detect any attempt by Republican Guard reserves to counterattack or retreat. The insertion of the teams went smoothly enough. Dailey's pilots in the

3-160th were old hands at special operations flying. They came in 20 feet off the desert floor at 140 knots in the dead of night and dropped their charges into isolated landing zones. Problems arose at daylight when the teams attempted to hide in terrain absolutely void of folds or vegetation. Not a hill, not a bush, not even a small depression was visible for miles. The ground was hard, usually with only a surface covering of sand. Although the ground is softer along the Euphrates River Valley, water in the valley meant crops and people. Good hiding places were nearly impossible to find.

Still, ARCENT needed the intelligence and on February 23 eight Special Forces teams flew into Iraq. Several, unable to find hide sites in the barren terrain, were extracted; the Iraqis discovered others. Teams that chose softer cultivated areas to dig in soon found themselves surrounded by inquisitive farmers. Even so, such missions were not wasted efforts. Even in their often too brief stay, the teams confirmed for the ARCENT commander that no major reinforcements were headed into the KTO.

XVIII AIRBORNE CORPS: CLEARING THE WEST

XVIII Airborne Corps opened its pre-G-Day operations on February 15 with a series of cross-border reconnaissance missions. The 101st was one of the first to make contact with the enemy. That evening two teams of two AH-64s from the 1-101st Aviation crossed the border into Iraq on a route reconnaissance. Other Apaches screened the mission along the corps line of departure supported by EH-60 Quickfix and EF-111 Raven electronic warfare aircraft. Meanwhile, C Battery, 2-320th Field Artillery, displaced forward to provide fire support. The Apaches did not encounter the enemy, but later analysis of their mission videotapes showed an Iraqi position overlooking what would become MSR Newmarket.

On the 17th another team of Apaches, this one from the 2-229th Attack with Cobras from 2-17th Cavalry, flew north to engage the bunker complex. After hitting the position with 30mm cannon fire, the pilots were surprised to see 10 Iraqi soldiers emerge from the position to surrender. Calling forward the aviation brigade Pathfinder detachment, the Apaches covered the Iraqis until the ground troops arrived. Elsewhere, a similar engagement between another 2-229th team supported by C Company, 3-502d Infantry, resulted in the capture of 30 more Iraqis. All were from the 2d Battalion, 843d Brigade, 45th Infantry Division at as-Salman.

Documents captured in this unique operation revealed the 45th Division's subordinate headquarters locations. Prisoner debriefings confirmed the poor state of morale within the Iraqi infantry on the front lines and sparked an even larger raid on another Iraqi position nearby. The attack began at 0810 on February 20 as Apaches from 2-229th Attack and Cobras from 3-101st Aviation struck the target. A and B Companies of the 1-187th Infantry were on standby to secure the area. They did not

PSYOP loudspeakers were mounted on helicopters to support 101st pre-G-Day raids.

have long to wait before the Iraqis hoisted several white flags. Capitalizing on the first surrenders, a PSYOP team from the 311th MI Battalion dropped leaflets and used loudspeakers to persuade more Iraqis to give up. Shortly afterward, the 1-187th Infantry landed, swept the site, and captured 406 prisoners. The 101st raided the position again the next day, capturing another 13 Iraqi soldiers and eliminating an entire battalion without casualties. Moreover, the raid allowed the 101st to secure its MSR before the ground war began.[41] ARCENT soon encouraged other units to try the same technique.

Meanwhile, the 82d Airborne Division began armed reconnaissance missions along MSR Texas. At 0130 on February 18, the 82d and the Air Force teamed up to pound the 45th Infantry Division. A joint air attack involving four A-10s teamed with two attack helicopter battalions hit Objectives Rochambeau and White. Eleven AH-64s, three UH-60s, and one OH-58 from the 1-82d Aviation attacked Rochambeau, destroying bunkers, armored vehicles, and 18 of the enemy. Twelve AH-64s and three UH-60s from the 12th Aviation Brigade's 5-6th Cavalry pummeled White, destroying hangars, supply dumps, bunkers, and antiaircraft positions. The raids continued over the next several days. The 1-82d Aviation and the 5-6th Cavalry repeated the two-battalion-deep attack on the 20th, this time supported by the 1-17th Cavalry in a zone reconnaissance. The

1-201st Field Artillery, a West Virginia National Guard battalion, supported these raids. In one attack, the Guardsmen fired 227 rocket-assisted projectiles in support of a French action to clear passage points along the border.[42] On February 23 the 2d Brigade of the 82d, under the operational control of the French 6th Light Armored Division, seized an escarpment that dominated MSR Texas 30 kilometers north of the Saudi border.[43] Combined deep operations between the French and the 82d made the most of both units' strengths. While the 6th Light Division had limited helicopter night capability, they had a formidable daylight force in two combat aviation regiments. The 82d, augmented by the 12th Aviation Brigade, provided a potent night capability with up to three Apache battalions, enabling round-the-clock deep operations that crippled the Iraqi forces along MSR Texas.

Similar cross-border raids occurred in the 24th Infantry Division sector. The 24th's aviation brigade mounted deep attacks against the scattered Iraqi positions across the border. During the evening of the 19th, B Battery, 4-41st Field Artillery, attacked an Iraqi border post using a single Copperhead round. Guided by two lasers from a specially modified armored personnel carrier called a FIST-V, the shell completely destroyed the post and killed four enemy. Another Copperhead attack destroyed a second border post on the 21st. By the 22d, the 24th Infantry had virtually completed its preparation of the battlefield, and by the next day the same was true for all of XVIII Airborne Corps. Luck's divisions were poised to cut Highway 8 some 250 kilometers to the north.[44]

VII CORPS: DECEPTION AND PREPARATION OF THE BREACH

On Luck's right flank, VII Corps engaged in similar preparations. Yeosock placed the 1st Cavalry Division and the 2d Brigade, 101st Airborne Division, under the operational control of VII Corps to protect Tapline Road during XVIII Airborne Corps' move to the west. Franks seized that opportunity to move the 1st Cavalry Division well forward along the Wadi al-Batin just west of the Egyptian Corps. This move not only secured the line of communication, it also freed the 3d Armored Division from its counterattack mission enabling it to move west with the rest of VII Corps. Furthermore, it allowed Franks to conduct raids and feints to reinforce the deception effort and destroy Iraqi artillery.

Beginning on February 7, VII Corps Artillery and the 1st Cavalry Division began a series of artillery raids near the Wadi al-Batin. The raids served three essential purposes. First, Franks believed they would give the Iraqis another reason to think that the main Coalition attack would come up the wadi. Second, just as he insisted on a pre-G-Day rehearsal for maneuver, Franks knew the raids would provide the opportunity to shake out fire support, including strategic and tactical air power as well as rockets and artillery. Third, Franks intended the raids to take down completely all Iraqi guns within range of the wadi. He remained most concerned about the danger posed by Iraqi artillery. The Air Force had done a good job so far in killing some artillery, but revetted guns were the hardest target for air power to kill and many batteries remained intact.

The most efficient way to kill artillery is with other artillery. Franks wanted to learn a bit more about the enemy's most enigmatic arm. So far he had a good idea from Khafji how well the Iraqi maneuver units would perform, but Iraqi guns were strangely silent there. Of all the Iraqi branches, the engineers and artillery came into the conflict with the best reputation for professionalism, and the overall quality of the artillery weapons was second to none. Of the artillery capable of reaching the breach, most were towed howitzers arrayed in a roughly continuous belt of guns 14 to 20 kilometers north of the berm. The majority of self-propelled artillery remained farther to the rear with the operational and theater reserves. Brigadier General Creighton Abrams, Jr., the VII Corps artillery commander, kept his shorter-ranged tubes well back in assembly areas. To reach the Iraqis during the raids, they were obliged to march to the southern edge of the berm, fire, and then withdraw.

General Tilelli's 1st Cavalry Division fired the opening round of the pre-G-Day firepower battle on February 7. At 1400, an artillery forward observer FIST-V eased up just behind the berm, raised its "hammerhead" sight, and lased an Iraqi observation tower 5 kilometers to the north. These 40-foot-high towers were a particular nuisance because in the flat

Franks and Abrams planned pre-G-Day artillery raids with their staff.

Brigadier General John Tilelli (third from the left) discusses a pre-G-Day raid with his commanders and staff.

1st Cavalry guns fired at maximum range to engage distant Iraqi batteries. Superior precision and lethality gave US artillery a distinct edge; however, Iraqi guns could shoot farther.

terrain they could see as far as 30 kilometers into the American sector. They were so small that neither "dumb" artillery projectiles nor bombs could hit them. A 155mm howitzer located 10 kilometers to the rear fired a single laser-guided Copperhead projectile. Thirty seconds later the first of seven towers disappeared in a flash of light and black smoke. An adjacent battery followed the Copperhead shot by dropping 400 bomblets on the target, killing anyone near the tower.

On February 13, artillery action accelerated with a carefully choreographed raid conducted by three MLRS batteries, two from the 42d Field Artillery Brigade and one from the 1st Cavalry. At dusk, the three batteries—27 launchers in all—crept up to the berm. The crews in 18 launchers punched previously located targets into their fire-control computers and the huge box-like launch pod containers, each holding 12 rockets, automatically slewed toward the targets. At precisely 1815, soldiers standing at the berm watched as 216 rockets rippled away with successive roars, leaving behind white smoky fingers pointing toward Iraq. A few seconds later, a succession of white puffs appeared just above the horizon as warheads popped open to disgorge 140,000 bomblets on top of the hapless Iraqi batteries. Launcher crewmen nicknamed the MLRS "the grid square removal system" for good reason. The third MLRS battery was linked directly to the Q37 counterbattery radar. Should the Iraqi artillery shoot back, only a few seconds would be needed for the radar to pinpoint the target and the rocket battery to smother it with another 70,000 bomblets. In this engagement and in all subsequent artillery ambushes executed before G-Day, the Iraqis never took the bait. Relief among VII Corps artillerymen was mixed with curiosity. What had happened to Saddam's most fearsome arm?

In a word, Saddam's artillerymen had simply failed to make technological improvements in their over-the-hill gunnery that had been available for 20 years. Surprising their Israeli opponents, the Egyptians dramatically demonstrated the precision-guided munitions revolution in the opening tank and antitank missile engagement in the October '73 War. The precision revolution progressed more slowly to indirect fire because to hit an unseen target with the first round required refinements in the ability to locate both the target and the firing position, as well as the ability to predict very accurately the ballistic course of a projectile. Ballistic refinement arrived with the development of digital fire-control computers, precise weather-measuring devices, and devices to measure the velocity of a projectile in flight. Target-acquisition radars, laser range finders, and the now indispensable GPS allowed a similar precision in locating targets and firing positions. If all of the parts are assembled and employed properly, the radius of error for a "dumb" artillery projectile is easily cut in half. DPICM or bomblet artillery munitions, in turn, have almost tripled the kill radius for artillery. This quantum jump in precision and lethality meant that for the first time in history the artillery kill radius was greater than its radius of error. In other words, if American artillery shot at an Iraqi position, it died. Iraqi artillery, on the other hand, possessed long range but little else. The Iraqis avoided activating what few artillery radars they did have for fear of immediate detection and destruction. They had failed to invest in the technology necessary to achieve a first-round kill, learning the hard way that range without precision is no advantage at all.

The biggest pre-G-Day firepower raid occurred on the night of February 16 and early morning of February 17 with a combined artillery and attack helicopter feint by VII Corps artillery and the Apaches of 2-6th Cavalry from the 11th Aviation Brigade. Five battalions opened a 2-kilometer-square corridor by saturating the Iraqi air defenses with artillery fire. Five kilometers into Iraq, Lieutenant Colonel Terry Branham's squadron fanned out into a line about 15 kilometers wide. Artillery continued to pound targets on the sides of the formation and beyond the objective area.

Branham's Apache crews selected their targets 10 kilometers from the objective and then waited to reach a prearranged firing line 2 kilometers farther north. The squadron moved forward at just under 30 knots and fired continuously for nearly five minutes. Each troop and crew worked its sector of the target area, a line of towers and communications buildings. After five minutes, the Apaches broke for the border, reaching it within seconds of the planned recrossing time. Franks and Abrams observed the feint from the 1st Cavalry Division Artillery command post. Linked to the corps deep battle cell and the 11th Brigade command and control aircraft by TACSAT, the entire operation was a carefully rehearsed drill for later deep attacks. Just before the attack began, an orbiting electronic warfare aircraft hit on an active Iraqi antiaircraft radar directly in the planned path of the Apaches. A quick adjustment to the fire plan sent 12 MLRS rockets to turn off the radar permanently.

As the pre-G-Day raids progressed, problems began to appear. The first was with targeting. Wide-area satellite imagery could only locate Iraqi artillery to within about 400 meters. To hit the target reliably with artillery required a precision of at least 100 meters. Therefore, while imagery might provide a wealth of information, each prospective target identified on available satellite photos had to be confirmed by a second, more precise locating source before it could be hit. The preferred method was to overfly an area with one of the UAVs assigned to VII Corps. To keep up with the demand for target-quality intelligence, Franks decided to use his drones for targeting first and intelligence collection second. Battle damage assessment, however, remained a nagging problem; not enough UAVs were available both to target the enemy and to reassess previous strikes. If the target was moving, JSTARS also gave great

"Steel rain" from an MLRS battery filled the night sky during a 1st Cavalry Division counterbattery raid February 21, 1991.

The MLRS effects were devastating. Iraqi artillery was never able to return fire effectively.

precision, but the firing unit had to be readily available to engage the target quickly. Should the enemy artillery open fire, counterbattery radars provided the most precise and immediate locations.

The many layers of bureaucracy charged with integrating the indirect fire support function frustrated early attempts to establish a responsive indirect fire program. Too often, important targets such as FROG rocket battalions moved before they could be targeted. Once struck, BDA was still a problem and VII Corps was never able to determine accurately how many tanks and artillery pieces remained in its path. To improve indirect fire support, Abrams and his deputy commander, Colonel Raymond Smith, who served as the corps fire support coordinator, empowered junior staff officers to order indirect fire strikes themselves by comparing detected targets with a current target priority list. If the target met the engagement criteria, the officers could attack it.

The last major deception effort occurred on February 20 and involved Colonel Randolph House's 2d Brigade, 1st Cavalry Division, in a reconnaissance-in-force maneuver directly into the Wadi al-Batin. On the evening of the 19th, Lieutenant Colonel Michael Parker's 1-5th Cavalry sent a company across the berm to check out crossing points and to look for mines. The rest of the 2d Brigade jumped off at noon. Ten kilometers into the wadi, 1-5th Cavalry engaged an Iraqi infantry battalion supported by tanks, BMPs, and artillery. A Company led the 1-5th Cavalry's diamond formation with its Bradleys and made first contact. The trailing tank companies pulled up alongside and supported the infantry fighting vehicles, hammering the position with main-gun fire. Finishing the action soon appeared to be just a matter of rounding up prisoners from a nearby bunker complex. [45]

The combat was not one-sided. Since February 7 when Tilelli's division began probing the wadi, the Iraqis had reinforced the area. Under cover of darkness, they brought in additional artillery and antitank guns. They dug an AT-12 battery of 100mm antitank guns in along the shallow walls of the wadi. The Iraqi gunners allowed the 1-5th Cavalry's point element to pass and waited for the initial action to wind down before they engaged the middle of the formation from the flanks. The 100mm guns hit three of the brigade's vehicles, a Vulcan carrier and two Bradleys, and an M-1A1 tank struck a mine. Three American soldiers were killed and another nine wounded. House extracted the brigade after destroying the AT-12s with a combination of A-10 aerial attacks and indirect fire. [46]

Despite its cost, the action guaranteed that the Iraqis would continue to look for the main attack through the Wadi al-Batin. It also proved conclusively that at least some Iraqis were still willing to fight after 33 days of air attack. This was a valuable lesson that Franks discussed with his commanders. If the Iraqis were given time to organize a defense and if friendly attacking formations drove into that defensive zone, losses could still be high. This reinforced the need for speed and a massed fist to attack the Republican Guard before they could react and reorient their defenses against the main attack.

A FINAL ASSESSMENT

With the closing moments of the pre-G-Day air operation drawing near, General Stewart used a combat effectiveness model as a safety check on his assessment of damage inflicted by Coalition air attacks. Stewart's analysts had developed the technique to provide greater understanding of the state of Iraqi combat forces. Using the BDA figures as a start point, the model incorporated data on leadership, command and control, discipline, and morale. Most importantly, it emphasized the differences in the will to fight among the three distinct levels of Iraqi units.[47]

Baghdad's frontline infantry units had been the hardest hit. The 4th Corps in southwest Kuwait and 7th Corps west of the Wadi al-Batin made up the Iraqi forward defenses in ARCENT's sector. Largely composed of recalled reservists, the two corps were at the low end of the Iraqi military pecking order even before the war began. Now Stewart judged 4th Corps to be about 58 percent combat-effective. The 7th Corps, made up of the bottom of the Iraqi manpower pool, was at 42 percent.[48] Both might put up a limited defense in place.

Behind the forward defenses were the reserves, made up of the regular army heavy divisions. Some, like the Iraqi 7th Corps' 52d Armored Division, were only 50 percent combat-effective. Others, like the 1st Mechanized and 6th Armored Divisions, retained substantial combat power as 4th Corps' operational reserve. The 1st Mechanized was the strongest, estimated at 90 percent combat-effective. It might—as it had in the Khafji operation—move forward in a true counterattack.[49] More regular heavy divisions remained intact as part of the theater reserves. The Jihad Corps—the 10th and 12th Armored Divisions—retained an average combat effectiveness of 59 percent. Stewart believed both would attempt to fulfill their role as a GHQ reserve counterattack force but predicted significant problems in command and control.[50]

Colonel Mohammed Ashad, commander of the 50th Armored Brigade, 12th Armored Division, was, in the words of one observer, "a cocky bastard" totally dedicated to his brigade of T-55s. Based on remarks that during the war with Iran he had "lived in [his] tank and loved [his] tank," he appeared to care more for his tank than he did his family. Originally part of the 6th Corps, the 50th had deployed into the KTO in September as part of the 12th.

Even with a hard-nosed commander like Mohammed, morale in the 50th was not good. No one felt the call of battle as some had in the war

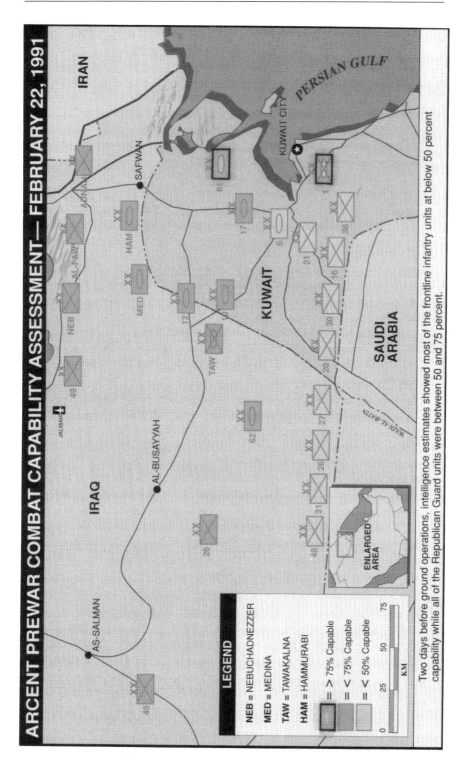

against Tehran. Rather, they approached deployment to the KTO with trepidation. Keeping up the men's spirits was difficult as they sat in the same revetments since September; 20 percent had deserted by late February. The best Mohammed could do was to keep his men busy working on their tanks—a challenge in itself.

The 50th's tanks—like 90 percent of the regular army heavy units—were tired horses. Track wear was heavy and batteries were in short supply. Engines designed for the plains of Europe ran hot, and the addition of side skirts and exhaust deflectors only increased that tendency. Only a man "with the army in his blood" could love such a stable of doubtful mounts. Nevertheless, Mohammed was determined that when the order to move came, his unit would be ready.

The air operation tested but did not break that resolve. Although worried by the continual flights of aircraft headed north toward Iraq, the 50th was not hit until January 19 when an A-10 made an ineffectual attack from high altitude. Soon the attacks grew in intensity, especially against soft-skinned vehicles like trucks and tankers. APCs and tanks, protected by revetments and carefully camouflaged under Mohammed's intense supervision, fared much better. As a result, the 50th lost only eight tanks and a handful of other armored vehicles to the air attacks. Thanks to its commander's resolve, the brigade had survived when its sister unit, the 46th, had not.

At the top of the Iraqi military hierarchy, the Republican Guard remained the greatest threat with a composite strength of 66 percent. Stewart knew that the Guard retained the will to fight. Even the Tawakalna, the most heavily battered of the three Guard heavy divisions, stood at 57 percent of its prewar combat effectiveness. Unable to mount a classic divisional counterattack, the Tawakalna would fight by brigades. Although the Medina Armored Division had lost a brigade's worth of tracks, it still had 65 percent of its fighting strength and the requisite command and control to mount division-level attacks. Its sister, the Hammurabi Armored Division, could muster 72 percent of its combat power. Like the Medina, the Hammurabi remained capable of division-level counterattacks. If such an attack proved impossible, Stewart believed the Hammurabi might be used to defend Basrah. As for the Guard infantry divisions, they were all above 60 percent combat-effective but would probably serve as a blocking force or assist in defense of Basrah.[51]

The Tawakalna was a newly formed Republican Guard division comprised of brigades bloodied in the war against Khomeini. Two brigades were mechanized infantry equipped with BMPs. The 9th Brigade, the only armored brigade, had T-72M1 tanks equipped with infrared sights and in some cases laser range finders.

The men of the Tawakalna's 55th Battalion, 9th Tank Brigade, sat out the air attacks comfortably in their bunkers. Inside Iraq, closest to the nexus of the KTO supply line, they were well fed and cared for, especially when compared with the less fortunate infantry farther south. To protect their tanks, the crews built several revetments for each and placed wooden dummies as decoys in empty ones. Whenever fighter aircraft appeared, they lit tires and oil drums beside undamaged tanks to make the pilots believe the tanks were burning hulks.

The mission of the 55th Battalion of the Tawakalna was to defend in place and counterattack if possible. Lieutenant Saif ad-Din, commander of 3d Platoon, 1st Company, had all three of his tanks fueled and loaded. His eight soldiers were well-trained, unbowed, confident, and anxious to fight.

Stewart's final pre-G-Day assessment was that 41 days of the air operation had indeed battered and fixed the Iraqi army, but its central corps of heavy units—especially those in the Republican Guard—had not been defeated, much less destroyed. Much of the Iraqi second echelon, to include the "go-away brigade," had been beaten down successfully by air strikes and artillery. General Franks would be able to ride roughshod over the frontline infantry units, but he still had a significant fight waiting for him deep in Iraq. Five divisions of the Republican Guard formed an unbroken barrier in his path. The war would not be won until the Guard was destroyed.

Notes

1. Interview with Lieutenant Colonel Dick Cody, March 17, 1992.

2. *ARCENT MI History*, pp. 7-13. The figure of 41 divisions is due to General Stewart's postwar assessment of the Iraqi forces in the ARCENT sector. Prewar assessments determined that 43 divisions were in the KTO and placed the Iraqi 31st and 47th Infantry Divisions in the forward defenses facing VII Corps. Neither division was encountered in that area and the 24th Infantry Division captured only a small number of 47th Infantry soldiers in the area near an-Nasariyah. Hence, the strength in divisional units was readjusted to 41.

3. Department of Defense, *Conduct of the Persian Gulf War: Final Report to Congress Pursuant to Title V of the Persian Gulf Conflict Supplemental Authorization and Personnel Benefits Act of 1991 (Public Law 102-25)*(Washington, DC: April 1992), pp. 122-125, hereafter cited as *Title V*. (*Title V* is available in classified and unclassified versions.)

4. *Ibid.* p. 6.

5. *Ibid.* p. 6-99.

6. *Ibid.* pp. 6-98 thru 6-100.

7. Brigadier General John Stewart, Jr., "Operation Desert Storm, The Military Intelligence Story: A View From the G2, Third US Army," April 1991, pp. 12-13.

8. Ibid. p. 15, and *ARCENT MI History*, pp. 6-2 and 6-3.

9. USCINCCENT message dated 100043Z August 1990, "Joint Stars Deployment To Saudi Arabia."

10. USCINCCENT message dated 031713Z September 1990, "JSTARS Deployment."

11. DAMO-FDI Executive Summary, "JSTARS Status Inquiry," August 22, 1990; DA ODCSOPS memorandum for Mr. Lawrence Prior, HPSCI, "HASC Marks and Desert Shield," September 6, 1990; DAMO-FDI memorandum, "HQUSAF Position on Deploying JSTARS," September 20, 1990; DAMO-FDI Executive Summary, "Joint Surveillance Target Attack Radar System (JSTARS) Deployment," October 2, 1990.

12. *ARCENT MI History*, pp. 6-94 and 6-95.

13. Interview with Colonel Robert Noonan, April 14, 1992.

14. *ARCENT MI History*, pp. 6-86 and 6-97.

15. *Ibid.* pp. 6-95 thru 6-97.

16. *Ibid.* pp. 6-87 through 6-90, and Lieutenant Colonel William Doyle's memorandum, "Deployment of TROJAN in Desert Storm," May 8, 1992.

17. *ARCENT MI History*, pp. 6-86 thru 6-101.

18. Stewart, p. 4.

19. As quoted by Colonel Thomas Leavitt and Major Thomas Odom.

20. *ARCENT MI History*, Vol 6, p. 131, "Imagery Support for Point Targets," JULLS Input No. 13355-39800(00003).

21. Colonel David Schulte, "Notes as Chief, BCE, Desert Storm," p. 37.

22. Interview with General Frederick Franks, Jr., April 30, 1992.

23. Robert M. Stein, "Patriot ATBM Experience in the Gulf War" (Draft), February 28, 1992, pp. 19-20.

24. *US News and World Report* Staff, *Triumph Without Victory: The Unreported History of the Persian Gulf War* (New York: Random House, 1991), pp. 246-247.

25. Schubert and Kraus, pp. 21-23.

26. Captain Eric Kennedy, memorandum, "Deployment of Sandcrab in Desert Storm," May 8, 1992; *ARCENT MI History*, Chapter 10, p. 10-17; and ARCENT Lessons Learned Report, p. 56.

27. Stewart, p. 19.

28. *Ibid.* pp. 19-20, and Major General John Stewart, Jr., DCSINT USAREUR, memorandum for HQ TRADOC ADCSCDD, "Desert Storm," March 18, 1992.

29. *Ibid.*

30. *ARCENT MI History*, pp. 21-23.

31. *Ibid.* p. 6-72, and Schulte, p. 37.

32. Brigadier General Creighton W. Abrams, Jr., "VII Corps Artillery Commander's Report, Operation Desert Storm," March 1991.

33. Schulte, pp. 43-44.

34. *ARCENT MI History*, p. 6-74.

35. *Ibid.* Chapter 8, Annex E, and ARCENT INTREP/O2/222100Z January 1991.

36. *Ibid.* and ARCENT INTREP/29/091000Z February 1991.

37. Defense Special Assessments, January 29-30, 1991; CIA spot commentaries, January 29-30, 1991; ARCENT INSUMS, January 29-30, 1991.

38. USA John F. Kennedy Special Warfare Center and School, "USA Special Operations Lessons Learned, Desert Shield/Storm," undated, pp. 3-10.

39. HQ USCENTCOM OPLAN Desert Storm 001, January 5, 1991, pp. B-1, B-2, and C-3.

40. USAJFKSWC, pp. 3-10.

41. 101st Airborne Division (Air Assault), "History of Operation Desert Shield/Operation Desert Storm," signed Colonel William J. Bolt, chief of staff, undated, pp. 35-43.

42. 1-201st Field Artillery, "196th Field Artillery Brigade After-Action Report, Operation Desert Shield," April 29, 1991.

43. 82d Airborne Division Command Report Narrative, "Operation Desert Shield and Desert Storm," pp. 8-10.

44. XVIII Airborne Corps Operation Desert Shield Chronology (from August 7 through redeployment).

45. *US News & World Report* Staff, pp. 285-287.

46. *Ibid.*

47. *ARCENT MI History*, Chapter 8, Annex A, Appendix 2, and ARCENT INTREP/40/171500Z February 1991, "Combat Effectiveness Assessment Methodology."

48. ARCENT INTREP/40/171500Z February 1991; ARCENT INTREP/44-91/220700Z February 1991; ARCENT INTREP/45-91/220900C February 1991; ARCENT INTREP/46-91/220901C February 1991; ARCENT INTREP/47-91/210902C February 1991.

49. *Ibid.*

50. *Ibid.*

51. *Ibid.*

Chapter 5

THE GREAT WHEEL

The tanks of Task Force 1-37th Armor charged forward to lead the 3d Brigade, 1st Armored Division, against the Tawakalna. Sergeant First Class Anthony Steede, a platoon sergeant in Delta Company, was riding high. His crew had already killed two enemy tanks as his tank, Delta 24, began rolling forward from the firing line. In the few minutes it took to reach the ridge to its front, Delta 24 had fired six more main-gun rounds, striking T-72s or BMPs with each shot. As Steede crested the ridge, he was amazed by the number of fresh targets popping up all around him. Enemy machine-gun and tank fire and rocket-propelled grenades came toward him in angry waves but did virtually no damage. In the darkness the Iraqis were firing wildly at muzzle flashes of American tanks shooting on the move.

Steede's tank anchored the left flank of the battalion line. He tried to pay special attention to his flank, swinging the turret around to sweep the area with his thermal sights. Burning Iraqi vehicles made the once dark battlefield so bright that Steede's thermals momentarily "whited out." The temporary blindness permitted a lone T-72 to stalk Delta 24 from amidst the burning Iraqi tanks now drifting away to his left rear.

His company commander, Captain Dana Pittard, radioed that some Iraqis were surrendering to their front. Steede groaned to himself when he spotted a group of Iraqis near a burning BMP a few hundred meters away. No tanker sergeant worth his salt wants to stay behind during a tank fight. Let the infantry deal with the prisoners when they caught up; they were better equipped to handle them.

As the Americans drew closer to the flaming BMP, the Iraqi soldiers stood sullenly together, their leader waving a weapon with a white flag attached to it over his head. To Steede's dismay, many of these would-be prisoners still carried weapons. As Delta 24 stopped, Steede used the radio to argue his way out of the prisoner detail. Just then, the nearby burning Iraqi hulk silhouetted his tank just long enough for an unseen

T-72, 1,000 meters off, to draw a bead. The Iraqi had a perfect sight on the most vulnerable part of any tank's side—the ring where the turret joins the hull.

In a white-hot flash that lasted less than half a second, a 125mm round from the T-72 blew through the turret ring and into the crew compartment. The excessive pressure generated by the exploding shock wave launched Steede out of the tank like a cork out of a bottle. Specialist John Brown, the loader, had just ducked back inside the turret, and his legs caught the brunt of the blast as jagged metal shards carved chunks of flesh from his bones. Steede landed hard on the sponson box attached to the right outside wall of the turret. He was stunned but alive. As his senses returned, he felt his arms, legs, body—all seemed intact. Numbed but feeling little pain, he turned over on his stomach and crawled back to his hatch. He knew Delta 24 had been hit by an enemy tank round, but he had no idea who or what had fired it. The Halon fire-suppressant system in the tank had activated just a fraction of a second after penetration and smothered the flash of hot gases. Although nothing was burning, Steede had to get the rest of his crew out. To his left he saw Brown struggle out of his hatch, then roll over the left side of the turret and disappear out of sight. The inside of the turret still smoldered and the danger that a fire would reignite remained very real.

Smoke was pouring out of the hatch as Steede stuck his head over the opening, swung his legs around, and slipped back into the tank. As his feet touched, he bent his knees and dropped into a crouch, coughing in the thick fumes. One of the blue internal lights burned dimly through the haze, and he saw immediately that the blast door on the main-gun ammo rack was wedged open. The floor of the tank and everything attached to the walls were trashed. Then he saw the blackened form of Sergeant James Kugler, his gunner, trying futilely to claw his way out of his seat.

Steede squatted deeper and leaned forward, grabbing Kugler's chemical suit. Straining, he dragged Kugler out of the turret, then wrapped his arms around him as the two rolled overboard, landing hard on the desert floor. Leaving Kugler where he fell, Steede went around the back of the tank. There he found Specialist Brown, lying hurt beside the track. Steede and his driver, Specialist Steven Howerton, carried Kugler and Brown to safety some 50 meters away.

Kugler and Brown were both bleeding badly. As the crew's specially trained combat lifesaver, Howerton set about examining them while Steede climbed back inside the smoking turret for the aid bag.[1] Steede moved quickly, ever conscious that the main-gun rounds were no longer separated from the crew compartment by the blast door that had been blown open. The rounds could cook off any second and turn him into a cinder. Digging around in the debris, he found the aid bag and took it to his huddled crew. Small-arms fire, which began to kick up sand around them, heightened the tension. All those would-be Iraqi prisoners had disappeared, and they still had weapons. While Howerton treated Kugler and Brown, Steede walked back around the front of his tank, hoping to restart it and drive off the battlefield. With armed Iraqi soldiers wandering around in the dark looking for targets, he didn't feel safe.

Steede swung into the driver's compartment, took his pistol out of his holster, and laid it on the slope in front of him. He was feeling very nervous about those Iraqi soldiers and his pistol was the only weapon the crew had until he could get the tank cranked up. Then he looked down at the gauges on the driver's panel. Hydraulic power, oil pressure, Halon fire suppressant, battery level, abort warning—all the warning and caution lights were lit up like a Christmas tree. He tried the starter. Although the engine turned over, it wouldn't catch. After several tries, he gave up and clambered out, then rejoined his crew, who warned him again to get down because of the small-arms fire ripping through the air all around them.

As he drew close to his crew mates, Steede peered back to the west. No more than 200 meters away was another M-1, kicking up a plume of sand as it rushed toward them. It was Sergeant Jeffrey Smith, Steede's wingman. Filter problems had stalled his tank a kilometer back, and he had only just gotten it started again when he saw Steede's tank begin to burn. Steede waved him down, then climbed up the front slope as Smith called for an ambulance to come forward to pick up the wounded. Smith reached out of his commander's hatch and shook Steede's chemical suit with both hands. He pointed toward a burning T-72 just 400 meters to the left front. "Damn, Sergeant Steede, I just popped that T-72; that's the one that fired you up." Through the dark, Steede could clearly see the burning hulk of his nemesis, its long, menacing tube pointed directly at him. Smith had saved his life.

When the ambulance arrived a few minutes later, Smith suggested that Steede join the rest of his crew en route to the rear. By now the battle had moved well beyond them. But Steede would have none of that. Like any good cavalryman with his horse shot out from under him, Steede looked for another horse—in this case, his savior's tank. Hastily demoting Smith to loader, Steede took the reins as tank commander and roared off to join the battle again.[2]

THE GROUND WAR

G-DAY: SUNDAY, FEBRUARY 24, 1991

[See Figure 5-1, "G-Day, February 24, 1991, Opening Situation," at the back of the book.]

No matter how frantically soldiers prepare for combat, at some point they can do nothing more than wait for it to begin. Time, that precious commodity always in short supply as last-minute orders are issued, inspections completed, and adjustments made, seems to stop as the moment of truth approaches. Practically all the young soldiers who waited in their assembly areas would make it through the campaign unscathed, but few shared that certainty as H-hour approached. To a person, they were gripped by a gut-wrenching fear of violent death that bound them in spirit to generations of young soldiers from Bunker Hill to Panama who had waited nervously for their first taste of battle. Because only a few officers and sergeants had combat experience, the burden faced by most leaders was made greater, for in addition to risking their own lives, they feared their lack of experience might cost the lives of their soldiers.

At 0400 on G-Day, February 24, two artillerymen hundreds of miles apart pulled the lanyards on their howitzers to begin the Desert Storm ground attack. Across the CENTCOM front, 620,000 soldiers, marines, and airmen from more than 37 nations attacked an Iraqi force then estimated at 545,000. Offshore in the Gulf, Marine amphibious forces threatened a seaborne landing as the Arab JFC-East, a Saudi-led combined Arab force, attacked up the Khafji-Kuwait City highway. On their western flank, Lieutenant General Walt Boomer's 1st and 2d Marine Divisions crossed the border to breach Fortress Kuwait. The "Tiger" Brigade with its newly issued M1A1s provided a Sunday punch for the more lightly equipped Marines. Once the Marines cleared a lane through the Iraqi defenses, the "Tiger" Brigade would take on Saddam's armored reserves. Farther west, the Arab JFC-North and VII Corps' 1st Infantry Division attacked the Iraqi security zone to clear out forward reconnaissance elements and artillery observation posts in preparation for the next day's attack against the main line of resistance. On the extreme western flank almost 400 kilometers from the coast, XVIII Airborne Corps attacked northward to seal off the theater.

XVIII AIRBORNE CORPS: G-DAY, 0400

French 6th Armored and the 82d Airborne

In the far western desert, General Luck reached out with steel fingers to strangle Highway 8. Sitting on the escarpment just across the border berm that the 82d Airborne had seized the day before, the French 6th Light Armored Division pushed north along MSR Texas with two brigades abreast. The 2d Brigade of the 82d Airborne Division followed in trucks to assist the French in rapidly clearing the road. The French-led force moved quickly toward as-Salman and the Euphrates Valley. Because the asphalt road provided the only high-speed route available to transport supplies, seizing it was critical to XVIII Airborne Corps' plan.

The French knew that a brigade of the Iraqi 45th Infantry Division waited for them at Objective Rochambeau 50 kilometers into Iraq. Therefore, at 1100 the French commander, Brigadier General Bernard Janvier, prepped the Iraqi brigade with MLRS and 155mm howitzer batteries from the American 18th Field Artillery Brigade. Gazelle attack helicopters then struck the position with HOT wire-guided missiles before AMX-30 medium tanks from the 4th Regiment of Dragoons assaulted. Already weary from pre-G-Day raids, the Iraqis quickly surrendered. Meanwhile the 82d's 2d Brigade moved up and helped clear the objective. The next goal was Objective White, the town of as-Salman, and the airfield north of it.

The French continued to move north along MSR Texas. By midday, they had destroyed a company of T-55 tanks 30 kilometers south of as-Salman. In their wake, thousands of vehicles from nearly every unit in XVIII Airborne Corps clogged the supply route trying to move supplies forward on the single hard-surface road. This logjam became so much of a problem that Janvier asked XVIII Airborne Corps to close the road to most logistic traffic so the French could mount an effective attack against as-Salman. Luck agreed and gave priority of movement on the MSR to artillery, engineers, and fuel and ammunition carriers.[3] Following this decision, the French enveloped Objective White with simultaneous flanking attacks to unhinge the Iraqi defenses oriented on the road. At 1410, the 6th French Division and the 2d Brigade, 82d Airborne Division, attacked following another massive preparation from the 18th Field Artillery Brigade. By 1800, as-Salman and the airfield were surrounded. Mounted on trucks, the 82d's 1st Brigade was prepared to clear any pockets of resistance to the south that the lead corps forces had bypassed as they attacked farther north.

101st Airborne: G-Day, 0600, to G-Day Plus 1, 1508

Meanwhile, in a valley 6 kilometers south of the Iraqi border, more than 200 helicopters, almost 1,000 vehicles, and more than 6,000 soldiers of the 101st Airborne Division waited. General Peay had assembled the largest air armada the United States had ever committed to a single air assault operation. Planning to seize a forward operating base 100 kilometers inside Iraq for his Apache attack helicopters, Peay would be the first of Luck's operational "fingers" to touch Highway 8. The air assault was to begin at 0600, but an early morning fog drifted across the desert, delaying the attack for one hour. When after a second delay a reconnaissance aircraft reported a break in the fog, Peay seized the opportunity and ordered Colonel Tom Hill's 1st Brigade to lift off.

The order began a well-rehearsed sequence of actions throughout the division. Apache helicopters took off to clear the route to the objective, then hovered in ambush positions nearby. Under the protection of other Apaches, Peay's soldiers climbed aboard UH-60 Blackhawks for a 40-minute ride into battle. The 14 to 16 soldiers combat-loaded into each Blackhawk felt as if they had been stuffed into a sardine can. Other soldiers designated as hook-up teams ran across pick-up zones to stand atop their vehicles with clevises in hand. Chinook helicopters hovered over them, each fanning a small hurricane of 100-mile-per-hour winds underneath its rotors. With sand stinging their faces and hands, the soldiers secured the HMMWVs and howitzers underneath the squatting Chinooks.

At 0727, 66 Blackhawks and 30 Chinooks lifted off carrying the first 500 soldiers of Hill's brigade to FOB Cobra. After touchdown, the infantry fanned out from multiple landing zones and quickly secured the area. Artillerymen, using well-rehearsed battle drills, soon had their 105mm howitzers ready to fire. Just two minutes after the infantry hit the ground, Lieutenant Colonel John Broderick landed the first contingent of his 426th Supply and Transportation Battalion to begin establishing refuel points. Within minutes of the first aircraft touching down in Iraq, the brigade had staked out Peay's claim to a 15-mile-diameter circle of desert just south of the east-west road to as-Salman. But the claim was tenuous. Hill had only

The second lift of 101st Airborne Division soldiers waited for the return of Blackhawks to carry them 100 kilometers into Iraq on February 24, 1991.

a portion of the four infantry battalions on the ground and the weather was not promising. Two more lifts were required to insert the remainder of the brigade.

Hill had to make the FOB a secure nest for the division's attack birds by clearing out a few nearby Iraqi positions. Shortly before 1000, Captain John Russell of A Company, 1-327th Infantry, noticed Cobra attack helicopters from the 3-101st Aviation firing on a ridge 2 kilometers to the north. The Cobras had located an Iraqi infantry unit dug in along the east-west road. Russell contacted the Cobra company commander who landed next to him to confer on tactics and to confirm friendly locations. After a short situation report to the battalion commander, the Air Force liaison officer and artillery fire support officer came on the radio and quickly coordinated an impromptu joint air attack team (JAAT) mission. Russell, his fire support team leader, and a small infantry force crawled to a position where they could choreograph the combination of available aircraft, artillery, and infantry. Within minutes, Air Force A-10s arrived and in concert with the Cobras and artillery bombarded enemy positions. After a few convincing doses of firepower, the Iraqis caved in. Before long, Russell's men had control of the Iraqi position and had taken 340 prisoners. [4]

With the Iraqis neutralized, Hill reported at 1039 that FOB Cobra was ready to support Apache operations.[5] Starting at 1330, Apaches flew north again to search for the enemy. The 1-101st Aviation (Apache) and

Apaches flew from FOB Cobra on February 24, 1991, to find enemy concentrations and the best sites for the final air assault to cut Highway 8.

one company from the 2-229th Attack took turns rotating Apache attack teams out of Cobra to take station near the Euphrates. The teams looked for the best sites for the final air assault to cut Highway 8. [6]

Peay remained concerned about the marginal weather. The forecast for the next two days was not encouraging, so he hastily moved the 2d Brigade to FOB Cobra and warned his 3d Brigade commander to be ready to attack early in the morning to seize Highway 8. That night, in buffeting wind and rain, Blackhawks inserted Team Jerry, the scout platoon from the 3-187th Infantry, in a very isolated landing zone to find a suitable spot for the brigade 80 kilometers farther north and just a few kilometers south of the Euphrates. Throughout the afternoon, Peay's soldiers built up supplies in FOB Cobra with continuous Chinook flights from supply bases along Tapline Road. Farther south, engineers worked to improve the ancient pilgrimage trail now named MSR Newmarket, clearing more than 100 miles of road in fewer than 24 hours. A long convoy began snaking slowly toward FOB Cobra. By dark its lead vehicles had reached the base, though the last of them had yet to leave the Saudi border.

An attack helicopter burns about 2.5 gallons of jet fuel per minute. Therefore, fuel is the lifeblood of the 101st, which made a ground link between Cobra and the rear supply bases increasingly important as the weather deteriorated. Seventy Chinook loads made the trip to Cobra, but the bad weather delayed 30 others until the next morning. Nevertheless, by the end of the first day the division had more than 200,000 gallons of fuel on the ground. With enough fuel on hand, attack helicopters could launch out of Cobra to maintain a continuous armed patrol along Highway 8, less than 100 kilometers away.[7]

The next step was to put troops on the ground astride Highway 8, but driving wind and rain on the afternoon of February 24 forced several delays in 3d Brigade's air assault. Team Jerry reported that the proposed landing zone was a sea of mud, so the scout platoon leader, First Lieutenant Jerry Biller, and his small body of scouts searched through the night until they found a dry spot free of enemy 10 kilometers to the west. Anxiety built as the soldiers waited for the weather to break. Finally the next day, the wind and rain abated just enough to launch, and Colonel Robert Clark ordered his brigade into the air. At 1216, 30 Chinooks carrying three antiarmor companies with TOW-equipped HMMWVs, in addition to critical communications and supply vehicles, set down in Landing Zone Sand, 40 kilometers south of the Euphrates River. At 1508 Blackhawks inserted the first 500 ground troops directly adjacent to Highway 8. The wheeled column linked up with the infantry the next day after slogging 40 kilometers through mud and sand.[8] With his 3d Brigade straddling the key Iraqi Basrah-Baghdad lifeline, Peay had cut off most support to the KTO in just 31 hours. Only an air assault division could

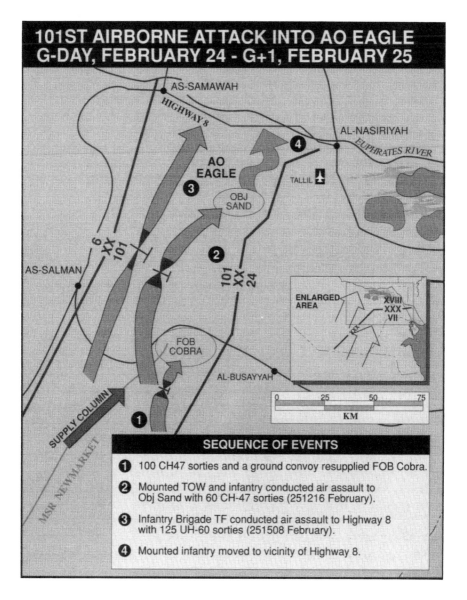

101ST AIRBORNE ATTACK INTO AO EAGLE
G-DAY, FEBRUARY 24 - G+1, FEBRUARY 25

AS-SAMAWAH

HIGHWAY 8

AL-NASIRIYAH

EUPHRATES RIVER

AO EAGLE

TALLIL

OBJ SAND

AS-SALMAN

6 XX 101

101 XX 24

ENLARGED AREA

XVIII
XXX
VII

FOB COBRA

AL-BUSAYYAH

0   25   50   75
KM

SUPPLY COLUMN

MSR NEWMARKET

SEQUENCE OF EVENTS

1. 100 CH47 sorties and a ground convoy resupplied FOB Cobra.

2. Mounted TOW and infantry conducted air assault to Obj Sand with 60 CH-47 sorties (251216 February).

3. Infantry Brigade TF conducted air assault to Highway 8 with 125 UH-60 sorties (251508 February).

4. Mounted infantry moved to vicinity of Highway 8.

have delivered such a lightning stroke. Meanwhile, the remainder of Schwarzkopf's forces were also moving with unexpected speed.

CENTCOM: G-DAY, MIDMORNING

At the other end of the CENTCOM-directed assault, the third-class Iraqi frontline troops had put up practically no resistance. Their artillery fire was sporadic and inaccurate. Friendly counterfire quickly silenced the Iraqi guns. The dreaded chemical attacks never came. Soldiers and marines found positions empty and the world-class obstacle system uncovered by fire. Tactical armored reserves, crippled by air attack, failed to counterattack in any coherent fashion. Saddam's frontline infantry divisions collapsed into disorganized rabble. Almost immediately, the problem for advancing forces was to capture and tag enemy prisoners and herd them back toward Saudi Arabia like cattle.[9]

As reports of the opening moves filtered back, Schwarzkopf formed an unexpectedly encouraging view of the battlefield. That the Iraqis had not, as yet, retaliated with chemical or biological weapons brought the greatest relief. The Iraqi operational reserves—armored forces tradition-ally held back as a counterattack force—were caught off-guard by the crumbling of the forward defenses. Schwarzkopf wanted to accelerate the attack to exploit the Iraqi weakness, but changing the basic plan would mean shifting gears in a machine with more than 300,000 moving parts. Simply sticking to the plan was easier; changing it at the last minute was infinitely more difficult. However, as Schwarzkopf consid-ered his options, electronic intelligence provided a key piece of information: confusion and disarray existed within the 3d and 4th Iraqi Corps in southern Kuwait. Armed with this information, Schwarzkopf called Yeosock and Luck to ask if they could mount their attacks on February 24 rather than February 25.

At ARCENT, General Stewart confirmed Schwarzkopf's view. JSTARS had tracked opening attacks into the Iraqi defenses. No Iraqi reaction had developed by the time the French had engaged south of as-Salman and the 101st had occupied FOB Cobra. In VII Corps, the 1st Infantry Division had penetrated and seized the Iraqi security zone without difficulty.

Yeosock relayed the question to Franks who conferred with his subor-dinate commanders. They agreed that, given minimum notice, their divisions could launch early without major problems so long as the attack occurred no later than 1400.[10] They wanted to penetrate the Iraqi 26th and 48th Infantry Divisions' main line of resistance in daylight. Thus every hour of daylight gained on February 24 was crucial.

Meanwhile, Luck had called his heavy-force commanders, General McCaffrey of the 24th Infantry Division and Colonel Starr of the 3d ACR. Both said they could attack with two hours' notice. In the next phase of the corps battle, Luck's enemies would be terrain and time. The quicker he could get his armor linked up with the 101st, the better.

A single but important exception to the confident replies came from the Egyptian commander of JFC-North on the east flank of VII Corps. Meshing operational methods between armies is a classic problem in coalition warfare, especially when significant differences exist in doctrine and equipment. Schooled in the Soviet style of regimented operations, JFC-North's combined force of Egyptians, Syrians, Kuwaitis, and Saudis was unable to react so quickly. Nevertheless, Schwarzkopf accepted the inherent risks and accelerated the attack timetable. All units would attack at 1500.

Adjustments were considerable but not impossible. Schwarzkopf told Colonel Jesse Johnson, the SOCCENT commander, to use his Special Forces advisors with JFC-North to help the Arabs. The British 1st Armoured Division had originally intended to use this last day to transport their armor into position on HETs. Having no time now to upload and download HETs, they conducted a grueling and mechanically debilitating 100-kilometer march across the desert to the breach site. Fuel tankers, previously positioned forward to top off the column just prior to the attack, had to race back to logistics bases along Tapline Road to finish the process. All across the CENTCOM front, thousands of soldiers changed plans and made adjustments as the pace dramatically quickened.

VII CORPS: G-DAY

Schwarzkopf's decision to attack early affected VII Corps more than any other unit because the corps had to move faster and farther to get into attack position. Since the breaching operation was very complex and time-dependent, any change in schedule, however small, would put considerable strain on those responsible for coordinating the overall effort. AirLand Battle doctrine, however, envisions initial combat orders as only a guide to be amended as required by the tactical situation, and the corps was accustomed to reacting to last-minute changes. The overall command intent was to strike quickly and to finish the enemy rapidly. The acceleration of the attack timetable supported that intent. Indeed, Colonel Holder's 2d ACR was already positioned 10 kilometers deep into Iraq ready to continue the advance. Administrative complications did arise, but subordinates used their own initiative to solve those problems. By 1430, the corps was on the march.

2d Armored Cavalry Regiment: G-Day

Holder's 2d ACR would be VII Corps' lead scout. Franks' mission to the regiment was twofold: to clear the zone in front of the 1st and 3d Armored Divisions and, most importantly, to discover the exact outline of the Republican Guard's main line of defense so that the two following armored divisions could aim directly toward it. For the most part only the Republican Guard possessed the T-72 tank, which meant that Holder would be able to pinpoint the center of gravity of the entire operation when his squadrons began to report engagements with T-72s.

At dawn on the 24th, the regiment was already positioned over the berm, arrayed across a 40-kilometer front. The corps screen would begin with a thin line of Bradleys and an aerial picket of Cobra helicopters from the 4th Squadron, which began to feel its way forward at 1430. Two squadrons, the 1st and 3d, followed on-line 10 kilometers behind in a thicker formation of Bradleys and M-1s. Holder's direct firepower was augmented with three additional battalions of the 210th Field Artillery Brigade, in addition to the regiment's own three howitzer batteries. Eighteen Apaches, 13 OH-58s, and 3 Blackhawks of the 2-1st Aviation, borrowed from the 1st Armored Division, augmented the aerial eyes and killing power of the 4th Squadron. To be absolutely sure that he would not be surprised or outmatched by the Iraqis in his path, Holder established a remarkably effective distant aerial screen using Air Force A-10s. The aggressive regimental air liaison officer, Air Force Captain Chris Kupko, continually vectored A-10s toward on-call targets. When the lead scouts from 4th Squadron turned up targets, Kupko immediately directed fighter bombers to engage following a drill the regiment had worked out completely in training. Iraqis in the path of the regiment found themselves continually under devastating fire, first from aerial and ground scouts, then from the A-10s, and back again to the scouts.

Once across the line of departure the regiment moved swiftly, cutting a 40-kilometer path for the divisions behind to follow. Within two hours, the lead squadrons were 40 kilometers deep and swamped by hundreds of enemy prisoners. Resistance was light, although some of the lead troops fought fleeting engagements with Iraqi T-55s and BMPs throughout the rest of the day.

At 1700, fifteen ammunition tractors carrying the regiment's ammunition reserves got bogged down in the sand as they attempted to cross the berm. Holder called VII Corps, which turned to the 11th Aviation Brigade for an emergency aerial resupply. Immediately, two Chinooks from A Company, 5-159th Aviation, flew north loaded with tank ammunition. Forced back by a sandstorm, the two aircraft made a second attempt. The company executive officer, Captain Deborah Davis, led the determined pilots in a daring rendezvous with the cavalry by descending below 50 feet and crawling the Chinooks across the desert at 30 knots. Both aircraft spent the night laagered with the 2d ACR vehicles. The company launched another flight of four more CH-47s that afternoon, but the weather forced these aircraft to abort. At dawn, a tiny crease in the weather opened just long enough for them to get through and then closed immediately afterward.[11] Despite the ammunition problem, by the end of the day the regiment had captured or eliminated the remnants of a brigade of the 26th Infantry Division.

1st Infantry Division: G-Day, Midmorning

Fortunately, when the call came to move up the attack, General Rhame had already eliminated the Iraqi border outposts. Earlier that morning he had blinded the enemy along his breach area by seizing the security zone of the Iraqi 26th and 48th Infantry Divisions. By taking the Iraqi security zone, an area south of the main enemy fortifications that contained enemy observation posts and local security patrols, he had eliminated the enemy's ability to place observed fire on the breach. At all costs, Rhame wanted to keep Iraqi artillery, particularly artillery-delivered chemicals, off his soldiers. At 0530, scouts from the 1st and 2d Brigades led their respective battalions into the security zone through 20 holes that divisional engineers had cut in the berm. 1st Brigade's TF 2-34th Armor and TF 5-16th Infantry moved forward on the left, and the 2d Brigade's TF 3-37th Armor and TF 2-16th Infantry advanced on the right. [12]

Each battalion task force spread across a 6-kilometer front, attacking north at about 0538. By the time the battle was over at 0915, Rhame's men dominated the Iraqi infantry in the security zone. If the Iraqis refused to surrender or fired on the Americans, Bradley machine gunners pinned them in their bunkers and trenches. Under cover of suppressive fire, tanks then rolled forward to collapse remaining positions with plows. Watching their comrades die in ever-increasing numbers as the morning wore on, Iraqi soldiers in the security zone simply threw up their hands and surrendered.

Like Schwarzkopf, Rhame sensed the imminent collapse of the Iraqi forward defenses. To take advantage of the situation and ultimately save American lives, he recommended to Franks that the 1st Infantry push on to attack the main Iraqi defenses without delay. Franks approved the

Preparation of the breach included an artillery bombardment that delivered more than 600,000 explosive bomblets on Iraqi positions within half an hour.

request after VII Corps received permission from Schwarzkopf and Yeosock to "go early." Rhame ordered his assault battalions to continue their advance at 1300, a time ultimately slipped to 1500.

Getting the attack off at 1500 meant compressing a three-hour fire support program into 30 minutes. Colonel Mike Dotson's 1st Infantry Division Artillery scrambled to recompute the firing program in time to begin the revised preparation at 1430. The commander of the Iraqi 48th Infantry Division later stated that "the earth shook" as the barrage struck his division. General Abrams had allocated the 75th, 42d, and 142d Field Artillery Brigades, 2 divisional artillery groups, and 10 MLRS batteries to create a Soviet-style "strike sector" over the breach area. These units fired 11,000 rounds of artillery and 414 MLRS rockets, dispersing more than 600,000 explosive bomblets into the 20x40-kilometer sector. More than 350 howitzers covered the attack with 22 artillery pieces for each kilometer of the attack zone. The gunners blasted enemy positions along the main line of resistance, crushing the Iraqis' morale with firepower. Other artillery struck command and control facilities to deny the Iraqi 7th Corps commander any vestige of control and to eliminate any possibility of responding to Rhame's attack. At the same time, the enemy's tactical reserves came under sustained attack from the air. Finally, the preparation concentrated on eliminating the threat of artillery fire against the American assault troops. An unmanned aerial vehicle had taken a last look that morning and found 13 Iraqi artillery positions that the VII Corps' artillery preparation later totally destroyed. The Iraqi 48th Infantry Division Artillery Group, 100 cannons strong on January 17, lost 17 guns during the air operation. Following the 30-minute artillery preparation, every remaining artillery piece was destroyed. The bombardment was a fitting conclusion to the carefully planned indirect fire program begun prior to G-Day. Abrams used the strengths and capabilities of cannon artillery, multiple-rocket launchers, and large tactical missiles to complement fighter-bomber aircraft, attack helicopters, and psychological warfare.[13]

In the waning minutes before 1500, soldiers in the assault battalions of the "Big Red One" composed themselves for an attack, mindful of projections that suggested 40 percent of them would be killed or wounded. Though many joked that an attack against trenches was more of the same for the "Big Red One"—like D-Day in Normandy—they still wondered who would be left. Those in the plow tanks did not wonder at all. Rhame, too, considered casualties. As early as November, before he knew when, where, or against whom the 1st Division would attack, he focused his leaders on that very problem. Rhame articulated his intent clearly: the 1st Division would mass fires and concentrate on a very narrow front. Tongue in cheek, he told commanders the idea was to win quickly with "enough of us left to have a reunion."

Success of the breaching operation depended on specialized engineer equipment. The armored combat earthmover (above) collapsed Iraqi trenches and bunkers. The mine plow (below), mounted on a standard M1A1, cleared lanes through minefields.

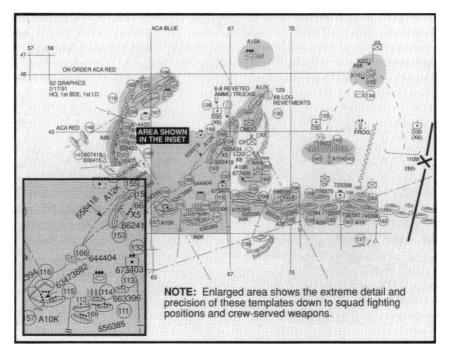

ITAC template used by the 1st Infantry Division (above) compares very closely with captured Iraqi diagram of the same position (below).

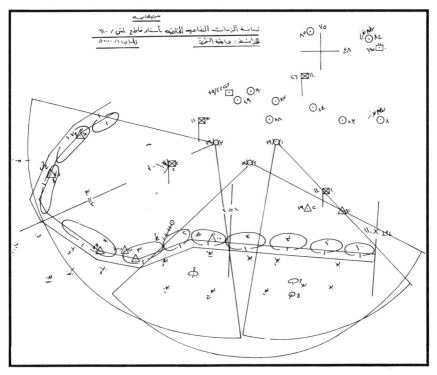

Planning focused on two problems: how to clear lanes through the obstacles and how to clear trenches quickly with minimum casualties. Tank plows and armored combat earth movers provided part of the answer. To hone its combat techniques, the division practiced supporting the ACE with fires. TF 2-34th Armor conducted the first mounted rehearsals on January 18. Rehearsing and learning continued as the intelligence picture became clearer. Eventually, the division massed 241 tanks and more than 100 Bradleys on a frontage of 6 kilometers. Simply put, battalions would attack single platoons at the points of penetration. Once a breach was achieved, units would roll out to attack adjacent platoons from the flanks and rear. Plows and blades down, tanks and ACEs would clear obstacles and flatten bunkers.

The division planned for in-depth fires to continue throughout the course of the attack. Colonel Bert Maggart's 1st Brigade targeted sections of trench using overlays built from imagery templates and UAV overflights. The scheme of maneuver and fires allowed targets within groups to be lifted so that friendlies could close within 200-300 meters of friendly artillery without shutting down a group of fires. Closing on the trenches with main guns firing and plows down, the division's troops believed they would win. Before the corps' epic bombardment ran its course, the division added its own chorus of mortar, tank cannon, and 25mm fires.

The 1st and 2d Brigades of the "Big Red One" attacked at 1500 as planned. While the artillery spectacle encouraged them, advancing soldiers were still burdened with some uncertainty. Lieutenant Colonel Daniel Fake's men in TF 2-16th Infantry, one of the assault battalions, had also been told to expect up to 40 percent casualties in rifle companies if the Iraqis used chemical weapons. Fear made the men anxious, but discipline and an unspoken resolve not to let their buddies down kept them moving forward.

2d Brigade, 1st Infantry Division: G-Day, 1500

Above the whine and clatter of his tanks and the noise of radios and shouting, Colonel Tony Moreno could faintly make out the firecracker-like sound of hundreds of thousands of artillery bomblets searching out every corner of the Iraqi defensive trenches. Moreno's 2d Brigade lay just to the south of the main Iraqi defensive line. The brigade's cutting edge, TF 3-37th Armor, TF 2-16th Infantry, and 4-37th Armor, had 76 Bradley fighting vehicles, 116 Abrams tanks, and hundreds of engineer, air defense, artillery, command and control, maintenance, and supply vehicles. At 1500, TF 2-16th Infantry and TF 3-37th Armor began the breach by clearing lanes through minefields and defensive positions.

In TF 2-16th Infantry, Fake sent A and D Tank Companies forward to cut lanes through the barrier system using ACEs and tanks equipped with plows and antimine rollers. Each tank team cut two lanes through the

Above, Bradleys carried American infantrymen into battle. Below, Marlin's 4-37th Armor pushed through the breach and moved into the rear of the Iraqi 26th Infantry.

barrier as B Mech and E Mech suppressed the Iraqi positions with Bradley 25mm chain-gun and machine-gun fire. None of the infantry had to dismount through the breach; they fought from inside their Bradleys to cover the battalion's tank teams as the tankers used mine plows to collapse Iraqi trenches. [14]

Once eight lanes were completed, Moreno committed his reserve. Lieutenant Colonel David Marlin's 4-37th Armor sped forward with 46 tanks and 6 Bradleys, passed through the cleared lanes, and fanned out on-line at 30 kilometers per hour. Beyond the breach, Marlin's D Tank Company commander, Captain Thomas Wock, noticed an Iraqi infantryman trying to surrender to the Americans. Hands up, clutching a

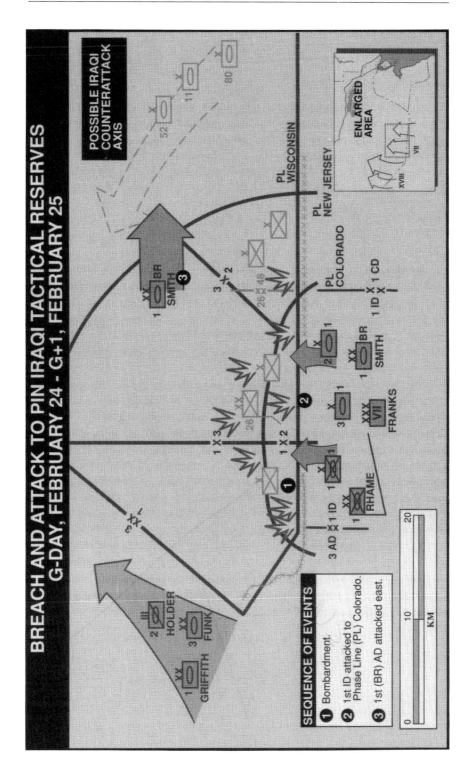

BREACH AND ATTACK TO PIN IRAQI TACTICAL RESERVES
G-DAY, FEBRUARY 24 - G+1, FEBRUARY 25

POSSIBLE IRAQI
COUNTERATTACK
AXIS

ENLARGED
AREA

SEQUENCE OF EVENTS

1 Bombardment.

2 1st ID attacked to
Phase Line (PL) Colorado.

3 1st (BR) AD attacked east.

231

surrender leaflet, the enemy soldier ran to each of Wock's tanks frantically seeking someone to take him in, but none of the tankers could stop. Tank commanders simply leaned out of their turrets and thumbed the would-be prisoners to the rear. [15]

Marlin re-formed the battalion into a diamond formation as they moved past the breach and into Iraqi artillery and logistics areas. As they picked up speed, gunners identified targets and opened fire. Wock's gunner, Sergeant Richard Yankee, destroyed an Iraqi D-30 towed artillery piece at 2,930 meters with a single HEAT round. The Iraqis' will to resist collapsed as other tanks blasted bunkers, trucks, and machine-gun nests. In three hours Moreno's brigade reached Phase Line Colorado, the limit of advance for the day. Trailing units refueled 10 kilometers beyond the breach and prepared to pass the 3d Brigade through at 0500 the next morning.

The reaction of the Iraqis to the attack varied from one position to the next. TF 2-34th took artillery fire at the line of departure where one soldier from the 1st Engineer Battalion was wounded, and desultory mortar fire fell through much of the afternoon. When Bravo 2-34th Armor attacked its objective, 4 of the 16 remaining enemy soldiers surrendered; the others fired rifles at the ACEs and plows, which ultimately collapsed the trenches.

The rapid pace and low casualties during the breach stemmed directly from effective planning and violent execution of both direct and indirect fires. Artillery destroys both physically and psychologically. Physical destruction is simple to measure: hot, jagged, tearing artillery shards kill indiscriminately. Psychological effects are more difficult to determine. Frontline Iraqis, poorly led and dazed by accurate, intense artillery, had no chance against the thoroughly professional "Big Red One." In countless past wars, a dispirited soldier's reaction to disciplined troops wielding superior firepower has always been the same. He either cowers before the firepower or runs away. The Iraqis were no exception.

Instead of needing 18 hours to break through Iraqi positions as originally calculated, the 1st Infantry Division successfully breached them in 2. During the breach operation, Rhame's division had destroyed the better part of two Iraqi divisions. The British 1st Armoured Division began passing through the breach site at 1200 on February 25.

IRAQI GHQ: G-DAY, LATE EVENING

Though battered by the Coalition for 41 days, the Iraqi GHQ had retained control of its forces in the KTO. Emergency crews swiftly repaired the communications system when it was damaged by bombing, relying heavily on the redundancy of the system to maintain contact with forces in the field. As soon as the Coalition ground attack began, GHQ reacted by repositioning forces. In Kuwait, the 3d Corps commander received orders to withdraw north through Kuwait City to avoid being cut off by the US Marines. Most disturbing were as yet sketchy reports of an undetermined threat approaching the KTO's exposed western flank. GHQ directed General al-Rawi, commander of the Republican Guard, to establish blocking positions oriented to the southwest, facing the open desert.[16] In a matter of hours and with great speed and efficiency, al-Rawi had six heavy brigades from at least four divisions moving west.

Rather than risk his own divisions, al-Rawi assumed command of the Jihad Corps adjacent to his corps in the northern KTO. Preferring to sacrifice regular army units first, al-Rawi ordered the Jihad Corps to commit a portion of its armor as part of the new blocking force. Located in northwest Kuwait astride the Wadi al-Batin, the Jihad Corps' principal mission was to defeat any Coalition thrust up the wadi by counterattacking with the 10th and 12th Armored Divisions. Like any good armor commander, al-Rawi had carefully studied his western flank as a possible avenue of approach. Now he ordered the commander of his 12th Armored Division to deploy two armored brigades south and west into the desert.

At 2130, the phone rang in Colonel Mohammed Ashad's 50th Armored Brigade headquarters. Dropping all pretense of traditional Arab phone courtesy, Mohammed's commanding general got straight to the point, asking anxiously, "Do you remember the position we reconnoitered two weeks ago?" Mohammed replied that yes, he did indeed remember the area. Despite the threat of air attack, he and the 46th Mechanized Brigade commander had gone with the division commander to the southwest part of the theater two weeks before to select possible blocking positions. Some "blockhead" at the Jihad Corps had decided that an attack by the American-led Coalition from that direction might be possible. Mohammed's combat engineers had labored nightly for two weeks to prepare tank firing positions, crew-served weapons pits, and trench works for infantry squads. Now the division commander ordered Mohammed to occupy the blocking positions they had prepared without delay. The "blockhead" at Corps headquarters had been right; Iraqi intelligence reported a column of mistakenly identified light "French armor" approaching from the west and Mohammed was to stop it. The 37th Armored Brigade would assist him. Mohammed wondered why the 46th Mechanized Brigade was not involved, but the general did not offer an explanation, nor did Mohammed ask. Orders were orders, and he quickly alerted his battalion commanders to prepare to move out.

The 50th Armored Brigade still had plenty of fighting machines. Air attacks since January 17 had caused few losses. Ninety of his original

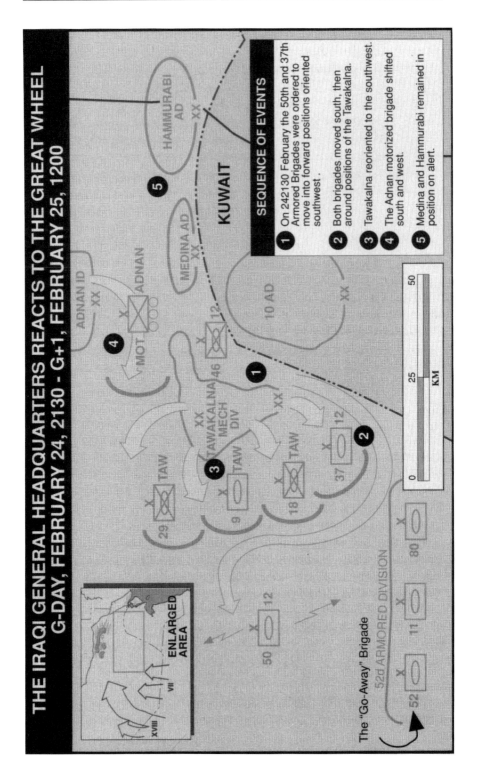

THE IRAQI GENERAL HEADQUARTERS REACTS TO THE GREAT WHEEL
G-DAY, FEBRUARY 24, 2130 - G+1, FEBRUARY 25, 1200

SEQUENCE OF EVENTS

1. On 242130 February the 50th and 37th Armored Brigades were ordered to move into forward positions oriented southwest .

2. Both brigades moved south, then around positions of the Tawakalna.

3. Tawakalna reoriented to the southwest.

4. The Adnan motorized brigade shifted south and west.

5. Medina and Hammurabi remained in position on alert.

108 tanks remained serviceable, as did most of his MTLB personnel carriers. But nothing could make Mohammed's slow Chinese Type 59 tanks go faster. He planned to place them at the end of his column, hoping beyond reason that they would reach the safety of the new fighting positions before daylight. By 2330 Mohammed and his column rolled slowly down the pipeline road, cutting through the dark, spattering drizzle. As they continued down the road, the 37th Armored Brigade fell in behind them.

While Mohammed's tired Chinese tanks chugged deeper into the desert, al-Rawi shifted his Republican Guard to meet the coming threat. His mission was to block the approaches to Basrah for as long as possible to allow the army to escape from the theater. He began constructing a layered defense using the Tawakalna Mechanized Division and portions of the Adnan Infantry Division to back up the 12th Armored. At his direction, the Tawakalna reoriented its three combat brigades to the southwest, deploying the 29th Mechanized Brigade in the north, the 9th Armored Brigade in the center, and the 18th Mechanized Brigade in the south.[17] At the same time, the Adnan moved a motorized brigade to cover the northern flank of the Tawakalna, and the 18th Mechanized Brigade in the south attempted to tie in with the 37th Armored Brigade. Each division commander placed security elements and guard force battalions even farther to the west and southwest to ensure timely warning of a Coalition advance.

By early morning, under extremely difficult conditions, al-Rawi had assembled a powerful blocking force, complete with the 50th Armored Brigade acting as a forward screen. Behind the 50th, al-Rawi borrowed from British doctrine to create a rear-slope defense along the ridges near the Wadi al-Batin using the three heavy brigades of the Tawakalna and the 37th Armored Brigade of the 12th Armored Division.

A rear-slope defense is simply a sophisticated ambush employed by a defender facing an enemy with longer-range weapons. The main defensive line digs in behind a ridge—in this instance a low rise west of the Wadi al-Batin—just far enough back so that the crest of the ridge is barely within range of the defenders' direct fire weapons. If all goes as planned, the attacking force will crest the ridge and be silhouetted on the horizon so that the defender, well dug in and camouflaged, will have every advantage in the direct firefight. To lure the attacker into the ambush, the defender places small security forces over the ridge in plain sight of the attacker. Al-Rawi directed each Guard brigade to place a company of tanks and BMPs forward, both to act as bait and to provide early warning. The rear-slope tactic also played to the strength of the

Iraqi artillery. If the security force could just slow down the attackers long enough, dense preplanned artillery concentrations could be dropped on them sequentially as they advanced. If positioned properly, a rear-slope defense could be deadly. As he would later prove, the commander of the Tawakalna was a master of the tactic. To the rear of the ambush, the Medina Division created a very strong second line of defense, while to the north the Adnan infantry attempted to protect the northern flank from envelopment. Behind this defensive line, cannon and rocket artillery units deployed and reoriented their weapons, expecting the Coalition advance from the south or southwest.

Early on the 25th, some 30 kilometers southeast of al-Busayyah in the Iraqi 7th Corps sector, Colonel Mohammed's MTLB infantry carriers already lay in their screening positions. His armor, however, was a different story. The slow Chinese tanks were still on the road somewhere behind, and in full daylight Mohammed knew their survival was doubtful. A brief air strike had caught his mechanized battalion at sunrise, destroying several MTLBs just as the unit pulled into position. No air attacks had occurred since, and Mohammed, tired from his night-long exertions, decided in the middle of the morning to take a nap. At 1230, exploding armored vehicles and screams of dying men shattered the Iraqi colonel's slumber. Within minutes, Mohammed and most of his men were prisoners of the 2-2d ACR.

ARCENT: G-DAY, MIDNIGHT

[See Figure 5-2, "Ground Operations—G+1, Monday, February 25, 0800 Hours," at the back of the book.]

Movement of the Iraqi heavy reserve units was on the ARCENT intelligence "watch for" list as VII Corps passed through the breach and fanned out across the desert. General Stewart had ensured that as the American attack unfolded, intelligence collection would be constant.

No matter how good the data, intelligence analysis always involves a subjective reading of objective information: the G2's professional assessment of what the enemy will do. Good intelligence requires the G2 to put himself in the mind of the enemy, requiring leaps of analytical faith based on a foundation of facts. Intelligence, therefore, is not a science but an art, a large part of which involves making correct assessments from partial or flawed data.

Stewart's analysts had inadvertently switched the identities of four Iraqi heavy units. As those units entered the KTO or moved around inside the theater prior to the air operation, signals intelligence analysts picked up bits and pieces of unit call signs, movement orders, and other tip-offs that said, for example, that the 12th Armored Division was moving to a new but unspecified location. If imagery showed an armor unit moving or adjusting its positions at that time, the unit was labeled the "possible" 12th Armored. As more "hits" developed on the unit's identity, the "possible" identification hardened to a "probable," and might even be confirmed by another source. The units in question were the 12th and 52d Armored Divisions in one pair and the 10th and 17th Armored Divisions in the other. Thus when General Franks slapped the map and said, "I want that unit to go away," his hand rested on the symbol of the 12th Armored rather than the 52d actually at that location.

Of the four misidentified units, the 12th and 52d Armored Divisions were most important to ARCENT because they were closest to VII Corps' breach. Late on February 24, intercept picked up orders to the 12th Armored Division's 50th and 37th Armored Brigades to move to unspecified blocking positions. Simultaneously, JSTARS detected 10 vehicles moving north along the pipeline road west of the Wadi al-Batin. It also detected a battalion-size convoy moving from the laager of what Stewart believed was the 52d Armored.[18] Stewart tracked the activity closely to determine whether the Iraqis would attempt an operational counterattack or simply move to block the US VII Corps' left-hook attack from the west. He owed that "key read" to Franks by midday on the 25th. Movement indicators in the two Iraqi divisional areas continued, reinforced by JSTARS-detected movement out of the Tawakalna laager toward Phase Line Smash.

Early on February 25, Stewart spoke to Franks about the situation, indicating that the Iraqis were not counterattacking. The 52d Armored, in conjunction with the Tawakalna, was moving less than a brigade out along Phase Line Smash. JSTARS had focused on these movements, calculating the precise number of tanks and armored vehicles, their direction, speed, and location along the phase line. The 12th Armored Division, Stewart believed, was occupying similar blocking positions west of Wadi al-Batin. None of these units, therefore, was a threat to VII Corps' attack.

Stewart projected that the Iraqis would continue to delay along the IPSA pipeline to defend Basrah. He estimated that the remaining Republican Guard divisions—especially the Medina and the Hammurabi—would reposition to defend Basrah as well.[19] Based on that assessment, Franks decided to destroy the Iraqis on Phase Line Smash. The 2d Armored Cavalry Regiment would arrive at Phase Line Smash first.

2d Armored Cavalry Regiment: G-Day Plus 1

After a relatively calm night holding in defensive positions, the regiment resumed the attack on the 25th and intensified the search for evidence of the Republican Guard. During the previous evening, the weather had worsened as winds picked up bringing in cloudy skies and rain. The winds increased as the day wore on and the ceiling dropped along with visibility due to blowing rain and sand. Continuing with the 4th Squadron leading, the regiment's progress toward the northeast eventually moved out of the way of Major General Griffith's 1st Armored Division allowing him to continue his attack to the north toward al-Busayyah and Objective Purple.

Between 1220 and 1240 the regiment engaged a mixture of T-55s and armored personnel carriers in prepared defensive positions. These proved to be part of the 50th Armored Brigade of the 12th Armored Division. Holder had yet to encounter the T-72s of the Tawakalna, but he knew he was close. Ordered by corps to develop the situation, the 2d and 3d Squadrons continued their forward progress throughout the afternoon and joined the 4th Squadron, already teamed up with A-10s, in the destruction of the 50th Armored Brigade. Late in the afternoon, Franks directed the regiment to keep contact with the enemy without becoming decisively engaged. He was already planning to move the 1st Infantry through the 2d ACR, and he wanted to pinpoint Republican Guard locations to find the best place to insert Rhame's division. That evening two of the regiment's M113 armored personnel carriers got lost in a sandstorm during an Iraqi probing action and were mistakenly taken under fire by friendly troops. Four soldiers were killed and four wounded.

By the end of the day on the 25th, the regiment shifted steadily east to give the 1st Armored's divisional cavalry squadron and the 1st and 3d Armored Divisions enough room to move north toward Phase Line Smash. There Franks would have to decide whether to continue marching northeast or turn hard right in order to collide squarely with the Republican Guard. Meanwhile, the British 1st Armoured Division still had to pin down the Iraqi 7th Corps armored reserves after passing through the 1st Infantry Division. The determined advance of the VII Corps continued.

1st Armored Division: G-Day, 1500, to Midday, G Plus 2

Under scattered clouds, Griffith moved the 1st Armored Division across the desert in a modified division wedge, with the 1st Brigade forward and the 2d and 3d Brigades to the left and right rear. Having chosen the wedge for flexibility, Griffith spread the entire formation over a 26-kilometer front. Intelligence had pinpointed enemy units of battalion strength in his sector, and Griffith planned to outflank and destroy them with his lead brigade. Out front, the brigade had room to maneuver. If the enemy put up determined resistance, Griffith could counter by ordering either the left or the right rear brigade forward. In all, the formation was very agile.

As darkness fell the first day and increasing winds created dust storms, vehicle commanders used thermal sights to scan the area around

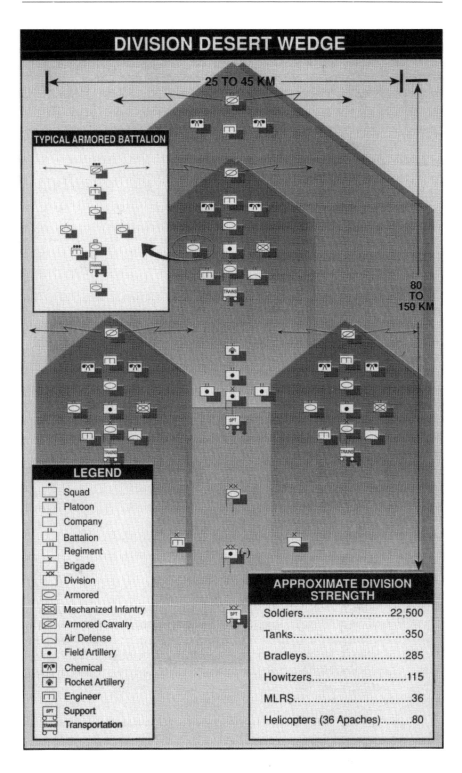

Abrams and Bradleys in a desert wedge formation.

them and drivers used night vision devices to maintain formation. To avoid fratricide and maintain position, each vehicle carried identification lights. Flank vehicles and scouts carried additional lights to mark the outline of each formation. Special infrared lights on scout vehicle antennas created a unique thermal signature. Lead vehicles carried blinking strobe lights fitted with conical shields pointed skyward so that the lights were invisible from the ground but could be seen by friendly aircraft. By 2130, all elements of the 1st Armored Division had reached their proper positions in the division wedge. The division halted for the night, and the troops saw to their equipment as leaders paused to review the next day's plans.

Shortly after the 1st Armored Division resumed its advance on the 25th, the lead brigade reached the southern positions of the Iraqi 806th Infantry Brigade, 26th Infantry Division, located some 50 kilometers south of Griffith's next objective at al-Busayyah. As the day progressed, the weather continued to worsen, eventually shutting down all close air support except Apache and Cobra helicopters. Griffith shifted the lead brigade west to bypass the Iraqi position in order to maintain momentum. He ordered the trailing 3d Brigade to attack the enemy position and catch up to the advance as soon as possible.

Months of unit rehearsals paid off as Colonel Dan Zanini's 3d Brigade conducted a hasty attack. Each task force, company team, platoon, and individual vehicle shifted into place according to long-practiced battle drills. After a short bombardment by the 3-1st Field Artillery, the brigade rolled menacingly into attack formation. As soon as the Iraqis saw the Americans approaching into direct fire range, they began to surrender.[20]

The rest of the division had continued its attack toward Objective Purple at al-Busayyah. Led by the 1-1st Cavalry, the 1st Brigade made contact with additional elements of the Iraqi 26th Infantry Division. After 2-41st Field Artillery prepped the area, TF 1-7th Infantry overran a battalion of dug-in Iraqi infantry supported by a mechanized team. The Americans knocked out eight BMPs and a T-55 tank. PSYOP loudspeaker teams convinced nearly 300 Iraqis to surrender, and at 1448 the battalion reported the area secure.

While ground units engaged in close combat, Griffith struck deep with his 4th Brigade's Apache helicopters toward the Iraqi 26th Infantry's logistics base at al-Busayyah. Shortly after 1400, two companies of Apaches launched a series of strikes that destroyed several tanks and BMPs. As a result, hundreds of enemy soldiers ran from their positions to surrender. 1st Armored Division scout helicopters simply herded them into groups as ground units from the 1st Brigade closed to within 10 kilometers of al-Busayyah and rounded up the demoralized Iraqis.[21]

The continued advance of 1st Armored Division's 1st and 2d Brigades brought them to within artillery range of al-Busayyah. In the late afternoon lead units encountered some enemy resistance from dug-in infantry, but the T-55 tanks that intelligence had reported near the town remained hidden. Griffith had two options: conduct a hasty night attack into a built-up area against infantry supported by tanks or wait until morning to conduct a coordinated attack. Griffith called Franks and

MLRS batteries laid down a carpet of explosive firepower deep behind Iraqi lines. Each launcher delivered almost 8,000 explosive bomblets in 12 seconds.

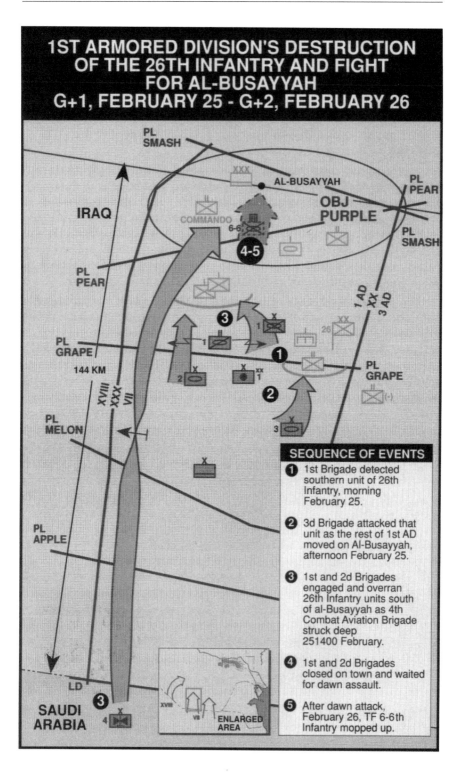

1ST ARMORED DIVISION'S DESTRUCTION OF THE 26TH INFANTRY AND FIGHT FOR AL-BUSAYYAH
G+1, FEBRUARY 25 - G+2, FEBRUARY 26

SEQUENCE OF EVENTS

❶ 1st Brigade detected southern unit of 26th Infantry, morning February 25.

❷ 3d Brigade attacked that unit as the rest of 1st AD moved on Al-Busayyah, afternoon February 25.

❸ 1st and 2d Brigades engaged and overran 26th Infantry units south of al-Busayyah as 4th Combat Aviation Brigade struck deep 251400 February.

❹ 1st and 2d Brigades closed on town and waited for dawn assault.

❺ After dawn attack, February 26, TF 6-6th Infantry mopped up.

recommended the latter. Franks agreed but told Griffith to be well beyond al-Busayyah by 0900 the next morning. Franks' design for the upcoming battle allowed no further delay. Throughout the night, Griffith pounded Iraqi defenders with 1,500 artillery rounds and 350 MLRS rockets.

At dawn on the 26th, Griffith prepared to attack al-Busayyah. Weather conditions remained dismal with wind gusts to 42 knots, ceilings as low as 200 feet, and thunderstorms intermixed with blowing sand. The Iraqi conscripts' morale was already dismally low as they huddled miserably in bunkers around the town. Griffith's artillery soon shattered al-Busayyah completely by accelerating to a maximum rate of fire 15 minutes before the ground assault began. American gunners sweated chemical suits black as they dispatched thousands of bomblet projectiles toward enemy positions. The continuous crackle of exploding submunitions began to subside at 0630 as the division's 1st and 2d Brigades pushed forward, Bradleys and Abrams on-line, to move through the Iraqi defenses.

Before the psychological shock of the artillery wore off, the 2d Brigade attacked toward the center of al-Busayyah with TF 6-6th Infantry and TF 2-70th Armor, while the 1st Brigade lanced through positions south of the town. Most of the Iraqis gave up quickly. The five missing Iraqi T-55 tanks suddenly emerged from wadis southwest of the town. Abrams and Bradley gunners immediately destroyed them at very close range. Only the 26th Infantry's commando battalion displayed any fighting spirit by refusing to leave the center of town. Griffith had issued strict instructions not to get bogged down in house-to-house fighting, and the Americans passed through quickly.

The fight around al-Busayyah was little more than a skirmish, but it was first blood for the division. The experience gave soldiers two crucial advantages. First, the fight confirmed, if only on a small scale, the superiority of Griffith's tactic of simultaneous attack in depth. To his front Griffith created a carpet of combat power that stretched 24 hours and nearly 100 kilometers ahead of his lead maneuver elements. At the greatest distance, Apache aircraft struck with company-size attacks as far as 50 to 60 kilometers forward of the advancing tanks. At 30 kilometers, MLRSs began to inundate targets uncovered but as yet undestroyed by air attack. Once within direct observation of scout helicopters and forward observers, cannon artillery joined in the crescendo of firepower. Only after these four successive waves had washed over the Iraqi defenses did Griffith carefully maneuver to achieve overwhelming tactical superiority and finish the fight with direct fire.

The second advantage of the al-Busayyah fight was that it gave the division its first combat experience since World War II. While the Iraqis at al-Busayyah were inferior to the Republican Guard, the commando battalion had been trained by the Guard and was considered its surrogate. The confidence level of the entire division rose immeasurably. Much uncertainty remained, but the 1st Armored Division had come through the shock and confusion of its preseason game a clear winner.

In addition to the enemy, Griffith faced another foe—one that he could not bend to his will—time. He had promised Franks to be rolling by 0900. While the outcome of the fight at al-Busayyah was never in question, he would not be able to meet his time line if he waited for the town to be cleared. Instead he turned the task of mopping up to Lieutenant Colonel Michael McGee, commander of TF 6-6th Infantry, and pushed the rest of the division on toward the Republican Guard.

Like his boss, McGee expended copious firepower rather than manpower to ferret out the last few commandos in al-Busayyah. He held his Abrams and Bradleys back out of antitank rocket range and attempted to entice the Iraqis to surrender. When that failed, he established a firing line east of the town with three of his companies while the fourth blocked escape routes to the north. An assault element with a Bradley platoon, two armored combat earthmovers, and a combat engineer vehicle (CEV) readied itself on the south side. After an intense 10-minute preparation from the 2-41st Field Artillery, McGee's tank and Bradley firing line opened up for 20 minutes to cover the assault force as it moved forward. The assault element still continued to receive small-arms fire. The heavy CEV with its 165mm short-barrelled gun could lob huge shells, each packed with more than 50 pounds of TNT and capable of leveling a building. The troops nicknamed the enormous shells "trash cans." Under McGee's control, Sergeant Darryl Breedlove of the 16th Engineer Battalion crept forward, halting near each suspicious building. The two ACEs with their heavy plows scraped along behind. If the defenders of a particular building or trench line did not surrender, Breedlove either leveled it with a "trash can" or the ACEs plowed it under. [22]

At 1230 on the 26th, the 72 cannons and nine MLRSs of the 75th Field Artillery Brigade caught up with the 1st Armored Division after an all-night forced march from the 1st Infantry Division breach site. During the afternoon, Griffith ordered his entire division to turn 90 degrees from a northward to an eastward orientation so that the entire formation was aligned directly toward the Republican Guard located just 50 kilometers away. Changing the direction of some 6,000 vehicles on the move was made easier by constant battle drills and by the flat, featureless nature of the terrain. Within a few minutes of the order, Griffith, flying above in his command and control Blackhawk, witnessed a sight reminiscent more of a naval than an army maneuver. While one brigade cluster of a thousand vehicles held steady, the geometrically precise dust clouds of two other brigades quickened and split gradually to the right and left as the brigades formed up on either side of each other. A 2-kilometer space between lines of tanks defined the boundary between each battalion; a kilometer or less divided companies. Once aligned, the armored tip of the three brigades again accelerated eastward. Parallel files of Abrams tanks led the formation, appearing from the air like small, single-turret battleships positioned to put maximum firepower and protection forward. The Bradleys followed behind arrayed like cruisers, spaced 50 to 100 meters apart and conforming to the movement of their more heavily armored companions. Battery-size columns of artillery followed 2 kilometers behind the armored tip. Closely behind the artillery, in hundreds of parallel columns, came a huge assortment of support vehicles: tankers and supply HEMTTs, tracked ambulances, and command posts with smaller armed HMMWVs darting in and out of the formation like destroyers keeping watch over their thin-skinned and less mobile charges.

British 1st Armoured Division: G-Day Plus 1 to G-Day Plus 2

Major General Rupert Smith was hunting for the Iraqi 52d Armored Division to prevent it from striking the exposed VII Corps flank. His overall target was a group of smaller positions, collectively called Objective Waterloo. To get at the 52d, the British 1st Armoured Division had to pass through the "Big Red One," make a sharp turn to the east, and force its way through the crumbling forward defenses of the Iraqi 7th Corps. Smith understood the need for speed. He planned to leapfrog his brigades forward to maintain momentum while his artillery struck deep against the Iraqi rear. When he received notice to move up the assault time, he marched his two combat brigades 100 kilometers to staging areas during the early morning of the 25th. All afternoon the British division negotiated lanes through Iraqi barriers just cleared by the 1st Infantry as they made their way to the line of departure, Phase Line New Jersey. By 1515, the lead 7th Brigade was attacking east along the divisional northern axis. After a long approach march, the brigade assaulted Objective Copper North, destroying a major communications facility and defeating a counterattack by a company of T-55s. The 4th Brigade began advancing on the southern axis at 1930. Traffic control problems imposed a momentary delay, but by the time the 7th Brigade secured Copper North, 4th Brigade was nearing Objective Bronze. As the attack on Bronze began at 2230, the 4th Brigade eliminated pockets of armor and infantry and overran several huge logistics sites. Asked to send loudspeakers forward to help convince the Iraqis to surrender, Smith wryly offered more MLRS fire instead. Smith pushed the 7th Brigade forward to Objective Zinc where the "Desert Rats" destroyed a weakened Iraqi armored brigade, killing 46 armored vehicles and capturing 1,800 prisoners. By daylight, Smith had his hands around the throat of the Iraqi 52d Armored Division. The hapless commander of the Iraqi division's 52d Brigade later remarked that he "did not know

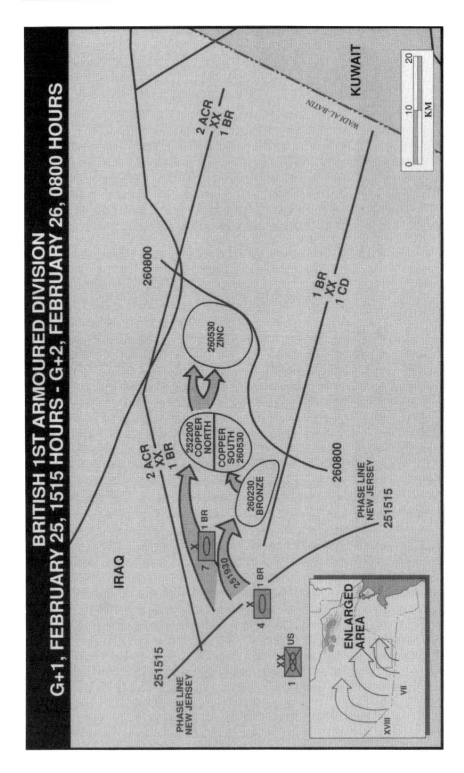

BRITISH 1ST ARMOURED DIVISION
G+1, FEBRUARY 25, 1515 HOURS - G+2, FEBRUARY 26, 0800 HOURS

what a [British] Challenger tank looked like until one showed up outside my bunker that morning." Every kilometer the British pushed eastward lessened the chance that the Iraqis could interfere with Franks' battle plan by striking VII Corps in the flank.

As dawn broke on the 26th, 7th Armoured Brigade secured its initial objective on the division's left and continued the attack against the next group of enemy armored forces farther east. On its right, the 4th Armoured Brigade continued to destroy enemy units in flanking attacks. By late afternoon on the 26th, Smith's division was ready to launch a series of attacks that would carry it across the Wadi al-Batin into Kuwait.[23]

VII CORPS: G-DAY PLUS 1, EARLY AFTERNOON

[See Figure 5-3, "Ground Operations—G+1, Monday, February 25, 2400 Hours," at the back of the book.]

1st Armored Division's order to swing east came as part of VII Corps' grand maneuver to turn directly into and destroy the Republican Guard. On the afternoon of the 25th, Franks called together his key staff members to make final preparations for the maneuver. Brigadier General John Landry, the corps chief of staff, and Colonel John Davidson, the corps intelligence officer, flew up to Franks' tactical command post from the corps main headquarters. The weather, already miserable, was growing worse. What had been one of the hottest spots on earth only weeks earlier was now near freezing. Earlier fog had turned into intermittent rain that by afternoon had increased in intensity. Howling gusts of wind mixed fine powdered sand with blowing rain and propelled the infernal muddy concoction against windshields, vision blocks, and map boards, and into every exposed corner of every vehicle on the march.[24] Visibility dropped to near zero. Thick, stinging blasts of wet sand lashed vehicle commanders straining to check compasses or global positioning systems as they struggled to maintain formation. Low clouds prevented close air support in many areas of the battlefield and high winds often grounded helicopters. Franks realized that the corps would practically have to feel its way toward the Republican Guard.

At the center of the VII Corps line, Franks' M-113A3 command track and his two M-577 command post tracks had pulled in beside the M-577 of the 3d Armored Division CP so he could maintain contact with his corps while his own TOC crew hurriedly set up. Franks and Colonel Cherrie, his operations officer, huddled with Landry and Davidson under the tarpaulin extension at the rear of the 577. The tarp could not keep out the blowing rain. Gritty brown water ran down the corps commander's map board as the shivering group of officers shouted at each other over the howling wind. Outside, a communions crew struggled to steady the multichannel TACSAT antenna to enable Franks' tactical command post

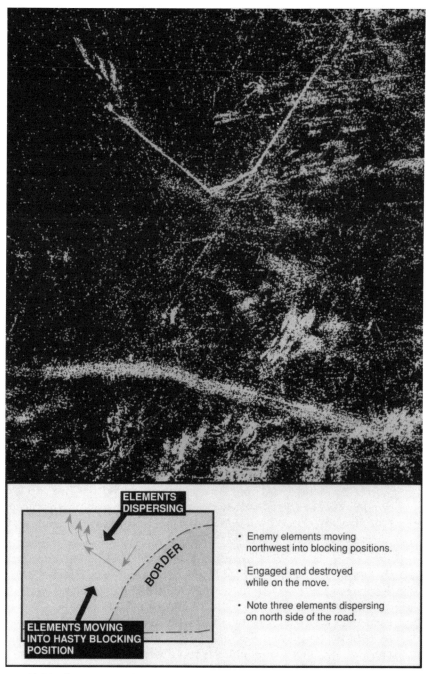

JSTARS readout, G plus 1, depicted 12th Armored Division and Republican Guard elements moving into blocking positions. This picture allowed General Stewart to track the Iraqi GHQ battle plan as it developed on the ground.

to maintain contact with ARCENT headquarters. Both Franks and Davidson had talked with Stewart at ARCENT G2 earlier that morning. Stewart told them that he believed the Republican Guard might reorient its forces but did not appear to be maneuvering against VII Corps. When Colonel Davidson reached Franks' command post in the early afternoon, he confirmed Stewart's assessment.

The time had arrived for Franks to call his audible if he was to bring the Republican Guard to battle in the next 24 to 48 hours. Turning the corps would take that long. Franks and Cherrie laid out time and space calculations on the back of a soggy envelope. Together they drew the graphics to depict the audible using a grease pencil on a dripping acetate map overlay. Franks had to make his call and then get the order out to 145,000 soldiers, most of whom were advancing deeper into Iraq with every passing second. After further deliberation, he selected FRAGPLAN 7, a contingency plan audible developed on the assumption that the Guard would remain in or near positions occupied at the start of the ground war. The plan was not a perfect fit, however. It called for three heavy divisions to make the main assault, but Franks had only two, the 1st and 3d Armored then moving side by side through the desert. The audible postulated the 1st Cavalry Division as the third finger in the armored fist but Schwarzkopf had not yet released Tilelli's unit from the theater reserve mission. Fortunately Rhame's "Big Red One" had made it through the breach relatively unscathed and was in a position to serve as the essential third division.

The decision made to turn right, Cherrie had to inform the corps. The order would be the most important and decisive of Desert Storm. In a much practiced drill, the staff quickly typed a FRAGO, or shortened version of an operations order, on a laptop computer. Cherrie's operations clerk "loaded" the order into the E-Mail system as Cherrie and Franks hovered over him to review it one last time. While the corps was no longer in Germany, the German influence remained in the corps. Cherrie, in his best Teutonic accent, ordered "Launch FRAGO!" The clerk hit the "launch key" and sounded off with "FRAGO launched!" Another staff officer then logged the order number and time in his staff journal and filed a paper copy in a binder. The VII Corps' "electronic torpedo" had just sunk the Republican Guard.

The scene illuminated Franks' personal style of command. At least once, and often twice a day, he flew directly to the divisions or separate brigades to confer with his commanders face-to-face. A quick huddle over maps spread out over the engine deck of a HMMWV or around a map board propped up by the side of an armored vehicle provided Franks the opportunity to explain his plans in detail. These trips forward allowed Franks to "smell" the battlefield and to measure his commanders: their

General Franks talked to his units via telephone. Despite the computer age, the corps commander still followed the battle with grease pencil on acetate from a canvas track extension in his tactical CP. General McCaffrey, commander, 24th Infantry Division, used a Blackhawk as his forward CP. Note the satellite antenna. TACSAT equipment kept him in touch with his widely spread and fast-moving units.

level of confidence, their understanding of his plans, and any concerns they might have about his operational intent.

With FRAGO 7 on its way, the 1st Armored Division continued to advance north on the left wing while the 2d ACR shifted south to take up station to the right of the 3d Armored Division. The cavalry would cover the ground between the 3d Armored Division and the British. Franks expected the cavalry regiment only to locate and fix the Republican Guard. Once that happened, the 1st Infantry Division would pass forward through the cavalry and form up with the 1st and 3d Armored Divisions.

VII Corps would meet the Republican Guard with the three heavy divisions on-line turning clockwise shoulder-to-shoulder to form the giant radial arm of the Great Wheel. Four heavy artillery brigades and the corps aviation brigade would support. The fourth heavy division, the British 1st Armoured, would turn more slowly at the hub of the wheel to anchor the corps' right flank by taking Objective Varsity. Traveling up the spoke away from the British 1st Armoured Division, the 1st Infantry Division would blast through Objective Norfolk and then continue east. The 3d Armored Division would attack through Objective Dorset and on toward Objective Minden. At the northern tip of the radial, the 1st Armored Division would attack and secure Objective Bonn. All of these objectives were stacked one atop the other and superimposed directly over the main fighting positions of the Republican Guard.

Franks and Cherrie calculated that the battle might begin late on the 26th, certainly by the 27th, a date still well ahead of schedule. As the evening of the 25th wore on, the calculus of battle continued to turn in VII Corps' favor. The British 1st Armoured Division's move east had allayed concerns that an Iraqi counterstroke might disrupt vulnerable supply columns or interfere with the jockeying of the heavy divisions into position for the upcoming battle. The corps had nearly completed reassigning artillery brigades to the armored divisions. Griffith would receive the 75th Field Artillery Brigade's three cannon battalions and MLRS battery. The 42d Field Artillery Brigade's one MLRS and two cannon battalions would join the 3d Armored Division in the center. The 2d ACR would pass off the 210th Field Artillery Brigade's three cannon battalions and single MLRS battery to the 1st Infantry Division.

CENTCOM: G-DAY PLUS 2, MORNING

The call from Yeosock on the morning of the 26th was a routine battle update, but he also suggested that Franks call General Schwarzkopf.[25] From his tactical command post deep inside Iraq, Franks reached Schwarzkopf at his permanent headquarters 800 kilometers south in Riyadh. Schwarzkopf wanted VII Corps to pick up the tempo of advance. Radio intercepts indicated that the withdrawal ordered by Iraqi 3d Corps in southern Kuwait had turned into a rout. Further, heavy tank transporters had been spotted moving to the assembly area of the Hammurabi Armored Division, a clear indication that Saddam might be trying to pull the Hammurabi back out of Schwarzkopf's reach. At all costs, the back door had to be shut before Saddam's best soldiers escaped. Weather remained a problem and the CINC could not count on air power to put the cork in the KTO bottle. From his distant position, Schwarzkopf had already formed an image of the ground operation as a pursuit rather than a movement to contact. In his view, the only viable course of action to prevent the Republican Guard from getting away was to increase the tempo of the ground attack and to destroy the enemy before he fled.

VII CORPS: G-DAY PLUS 2

From his forward location, Franks viewed the battle differently. Even though the Iraqi 3d Corps might be on the run, intelligence did not indicate any rearward movement on the part of the Republican Guard or the associated 10th and 12th Armored Divisions of the Jihad Corps. On the contrary, all movements thus far had been *toward*, not away from him. The Iraqi GHQ had built one solid defensive line and appeared to be assembling a second just behind it. While VII Corps senior leaders accepted the reports of feeble enemy resistance encountered by the Marines and Arabs in Kuwait, those particular Iraqi troops belonged to a different army than the Republican Guard. Should Franks simply accelerate the advance without first forming his armored fist, his divisions would bounce into the Guard sequentially and piecemeal, an open invitation to defeat in detail. In any case, only the 1st and 3d Armored Divisions, both still without their reinforcing artillery brigades, were available to attack at this stage of the battle. The Iraqis had five heavy divisions collected in a tight cluster in the vicinity of northeast Kuwait: the Republican Guard's Tawakalna Mechanized, the Medina and Hammurabi Armored Divisions, and the regular army's 10th and 12th Armored Divisions.

Pursuit of an enemy requires that he first be broken. Schwarzkopf's call to pursue clashed with the tactical reality of a stationary, dug-in, forewarned, and competent enemy. In the end, Franks simply accepted the contrast in views as the result of different perspectives. Early on the 26th, he ordered his corps to attack and destroy the Republican Guard no later than last light on the 27th. This simple message dictated the desired tempo of attack: VII Corps would press the attack without pause. Major subordinate commands received the message by 1045.

If Franks upped the tempo of the advance, he in no way changed his vision of the upcoming battle. He would smash the Republican Guard with a mailed fist before the corps shifted to the pursuit. Through the early afternoon of the 26th, Franks traveled to subordinate headquarters to receive battle updates and to issue orders to ensure that the armored formation retained its mass.

Miserable weather compounded VII Corps' communications difficulties. All corps units constantly monitored the command net on FM, but given the distance between units and the unreliable atmospherics of the region, satellite was the most reliable communication method when on the move. Unlike XVIII Airborne Corps, however, VII Corps had very few TACSAT sets on hand and these could not be used in a moving vehicle. Franks' daily trips forward partially eased the problem. When communications were out, Franks and his commanders relied on their mutual understanding of his intent.

By 1600 on the 26th, Franks' battle against the Republican Guard began to take on precisely the geometry he had envisioned. Along an 80-kilometer front, VII Corps pressed forward in the blowing sand with seven armored and mechanized brigades and an armored cavalry regiment aligned geometrically from north to south. An additional mechanized division, four heavy artillery brigades, and an attack helicopter brigade reinforced the formation. That afternoon the formation crossed Phase Line Tangerine, an imaginary control line superimposed on tactical maps along the 65 north-south grid line. The attacking brigades closed on the four heavy Iraqi brigades defending from northwest to southeast just 5 kilometers east of Tangerine. United in space, time, and purpose, the largest armored battle since the Second World War was about to begin.

With his corps approaching the first Iraqi defensive line, Franks prepared for the subsequent pursuit phase of the operation that the CINC had pressed for so emphatically. He ordered the 1st Cavalry Division, which Schwarzkopf had just released from theater reserve, to move rapidly into formation just behind the 1st Armored Division. In just 24 hours, Tilelli's "First Team" raced 250 kilometers northward in an attempt to join the fight. Franks intended to insert the division into a sweep across the northern boundary of VII Corps and attack east to Objective Raleigh. Likewise in the south, he planned to hook the 1st Infantry Division around the southern shoulder of the attacking mass to complete the envelopment by striking northeast to the coast. The British 1st Armoured Division would guard the 1st Infantry's right flank. XVIII Airborne Corps would seal the escape routes north to Basrah and across the Euphrates in front of VII Corps' enveloping armor.

XVIII AIRBORNE CORPS: G-DAY, MIDMORNING, TO G-DAY PLUS 2

The accelerated timetable on G-Day suited General Luck just fine. His biggest challenges were time and distance, and an early start would help him seize his terrain objectives and catch up with VII Corps. Luck's divisions each had independent missions and each mission was focused on terrain. The French 6th and the 82d would screen the corps' left flank. The 101st and the 24th formed the outer rim of the Great Wheel. Like the outermost skater in a line forming a whip, the 101st and the 24th would have to move faster than VII Corps divisions to maintain any semblance of geometric cohesion within the Wheel. The 101st could escape the tyranny of terrain with its helicopters, but the 24th would have to race along the outer rim while traversing some of the most inhospitable terrain in the KTO. Before either could turn east and assist in the destruction of the Republican Guard, Luck had to cut Highway 8. With FOB Cobra secure, the 101st was already patrolling the highway with Apaches, and Peay would soon place his infantry squarely across it. Getting McCaffrey and Starr's armor astride the road would complete Luck's grip on the main Iraqi lifeline into the KTO.

24th Infantry Division and 3d Armored Cavalry Regiment: G-Day, 1500, to Evening, G-Day Plus 2

Like race horses springing from the starting gate, the 24th Infantry Division and the 3d ACR sped across the border berm to begin their dash to the Euphrates. The 24th moved with three brigades abreast: the 197th Infantry on the west flank, the 1st Brigade in the center, and the 2d Brigade on the east. The 3d ACR drove north, continually stretching an arm to the east to maintain contact with the 1st Armored Division in the VII Corps sector. Both units had already eliminated Iraqi screening forces during their pre-G-Day warm-up. For the next two days, they fought time and terrain more than they did Iraqis.

General McCaffrey had to accomplish many tasks in a very short period: link up with the 101st, then cut Highway 8 by blocking it with armor, and finally, turn east and roll up the enemy's right flank. Such a complex plan demanded simple execution. McCaffrey's divisional front was almost 70 kilometers wide. By the time he reached the Euphrates his sector would stretch back nearly 300 kilometers. To simplify command and control, McCaffrey used east-west and north-south grid lines to mark limits of advance and to control fires. Key vehicles within each formation would be able to maintain precise alignment in spite of invisible boundaries and control measures, thanks to the Global Positioning System that each carried on board. Instant communication with every vehicle allowed commanders to shift formations rapidly.[26] McCaffrey used simple, well-rehearsed battle formations. Typically, each brigade moved in an upright "V" formation. Two balanced battalion task forces of 55 armored vehicles and tanks formed the tops of the "V." This formation allowed the brigade to meet an enemy from any direction with a balanced combination of tanks and infantry. The base of the "V" was a pure armor force of 58 Abrams, which also acted as the brigade reserve and formed a mobile, responsive, and massive counterattack force. The division's artillery was tucked up close behind the lead task forces. With 24 kilometers of range, the guns could conceivably have stayed farther back and still have been able to fire in front of the division's lead task force. However, when moving against an uncertain foe, McCaffrey needed his guns close so he could maintain the eye-to-eye contact between supported and supporting units that was essential to reducing response times and precluding any chance of confusion or delay in the delivery of fires. McCaffrey could have eased the problem inherent in moving less mobile artillery by echeloning or staggering battalions of guns and rockets out along the route of march, but he kept his artillery concentrated on the move to ensure that when it was needed, firepower would be applied en masse. Artillery would not be applied in penny packets; if a target was worth engaging, it would receive, as a minimum, a battalion's worth of firepower. [27]

Logistics was McCaffrey's greatest concern. To the rear, logisticians scrambled to move the 400,000 gallons of fuel, 213,000 gallons of water, and 2,400 short tons of ammunition the division would use daily. The 36th Engineer Group followed closely to smooth a path behind each brigade. Once the XVIII Airborne Corps advanced beyond as-Salman, the hard-surface roads along MSRs Texas and Virginia would ease the division's transportation problems. [28]

In the complete black of night amid blowing sand, McCaffrey's huge force of more than 26,000 soldiers and 8,600 vehicles ground steadily northward at 25 kilometers per hour. Worsening weather reduced visibility to less than 1 kilometer and rendered night vision aids useless beyond that range. Forty-five kilometers into Iraq, McCaffrey shifted the division to two brigades abreast. The 197th drove toward Objective Brown, 140 kilometers north of the border, and 2d Brigade thrust toward Objective Gray, immediately to the right of Brown. 1st Brigade shifted right behind the 2d Brigade. [29] McCaffrey employed his two lead brigades like blocking linemen to open a hole for Colonel John LeMoyne's 1st Brigade so that he could, in turn, carry the ball forward another 50 kilometers beyond the enemy's first line of defense. Colonel Ted Reid's 197th Infantry Brigade opened the assault by blocking the division's left on Objective Brown at 0300 on the 25th. He began with a bombardment from 72 guns and 27 rocket launchers, followed by deeper strikes with fighter-bombers. Colonel Paul Kern's 2d Brigade, supported by an equally heavy artillery concentration, blocked to the right at Objective Gray at 1300. By midday, the ground gained by LeMoyne's drive up the middle had carried the division into a new type of terrain. The open desert changed gradually into a series of narrowing, shallow valleys. By 2130, having met little significant opposition, McCaffrey was three-quarters of the way to the Euphrates River. [30]

McCaffrey had almost beaten his enemy—time—when the Euphrates River Valley slowed him down. His first 24 hours of movement had been along the eastern edge of the Sahra al-Hajarah (Desert of Stone), a high, rocky desert 300 to 400 meters above sea level that is covered with sharp stones and boulders. Some 60 kilometers from the Euphrates, however, the terrain changes abruptly as it begins a 290-meter drop to the river. Steep cliffs, many as high as 50 meters, flank the wadis that are the natural routes down from the high desert. Where they level out for any distance, sabkhas mark the areas flooded during the infrequent rains. The area is rough going when rain is sparse. When it rains as it had for nearly 24 hours prior to the division's arrival, the sabkhas turn into nearly impassable quagmires. During prebattle analysis in late December, McCaffrey's troops picked up the name "the great dismal bog" for the region from an Air Force pilot's survival map.[31]

Lieutenant Colonel Thomas Leney's 2-4th Cavalry, the divisional cavalry squadron, worked most of the night of February 25 to find paths through the great dismal bog. After countless stops, starts, and redirections, they found the few passable routes for the 197th Brigade. Engineer battalions following in trail began to make the routes more passable for scores of vehicles waiting on dryer ground to follow. The cavalry then turned to screen toward the division's western flank.

By midday on the 26th, the 24th Infantry Division's three brigades were ready to resume final attacks to seal the Euphrates River Valley. As McCaffrey saw the situation, the 197th Brigade had to seize Battle Position 101 on the southeastern edge of Tallil Airfield. The 2d Brigade would seize Battle Position 103 and then turn east to attack toward Jalibah Airfield. As McCaffrey's main effort, the 1st Brigade would stay in the lead and sever Highway 8 at Battle Position 102. Operating on individual axes, but in consonance with one another, the three brigades marched north at 1400.

Abrams from the 197th Infantry Brigade emerged out of the rough terrain south of Highway 8 only to encounter mud flats along the Euphrates River Valley, February 26, 1991.

The rain and blowing sand of a shamal draped the remaining daylight with a surreal shroud as the brigades wound their way up muddy wadis and sabkhas.

Prior to the operation, McCaffrey had planned to halt temporarily south of the Euphrates in order to bring his logistics forward before pressing on to cut Highway 8. But fearing that the Republican Guard might seize on his pause to begin their escape, McCaffrey pressed on. Farther south, the 24th Infantry Division's logistics system pushed supplies forward. The drive through the great dismal bog had required so many twists, turns, and diversions that fuel in the combat units was running low. Division support command soldiers set up temporary logistics bases along combat trails to the rear of the brigades. The first division support area, DSA-1, was 100 kilometers from the border in the center of the division sector. As the lead brigades moved out, the division set up DSA-2 northwest of Objective Gray to take advantage of the French seizure of as-Salman. Major Pat Shull commanded TF Shull, a convoy of 243 trucks with 95 combat loads of ammunition and 50,000 gallons of fuel that cleared MSRs Texas and Virginia and closed into DSA-2 on the afternoon of February 26.[32]

As the northernmost brigade of the 24th, LeMoyne's 1st Brigade was the first to hit its objective, BP102 astride Highway 8. The 1-41st Field Artillery and the 212th Field Artillery Brigade pummeled the objective with a 30-minute preparation. The Iraqis struck back. For the first time, the 24th met spirited resistance. Iraqi soldiers in the northern KTO were completely different from the totally ineffective infantry the 24th had overrun at their intermediate objectives. Although surprised by the Americans, the soldiers from the Iraqi 47th and 49th Infantry Divisions and commandos from the Republican Guard engaged the attackers with small arms and towed antitank guns. Soon hundreds of rounds of Iraqi artillery began to land in the midst of the Americans. As usual, however, the Iraqi gunners persisted in firing only at preselected targets, often 55-gallon drums they had evidently emplaced as reference points that LeMoyne's drivers readily learned to avoid. A Q-36 radar from C Battery, 25th Target Acquisition Battalion, was in position when Iraqi rounds came in. The radar picked up the enemy rounds in the air and electronically backplotted to a D-30 battalion immediately after it fired. Within minutes, the 1-41st and 212th Field Artillery responded with volleys of dual-purpose, improved conventional munitions (DPICM) to silence the Iraqi guns.[33]

On the northern end of BP102, Lieutenant Colonel John Craddock maneuvered his 4-64th Armor toward a canal north of Highway 8. Two 100mm rounds from an AT-12 antitank gun slammed into the main-gun mount and rear fuel cells of Craddock's tank, but the tough machine continued to roll. Craddock, shaken but none the worse for wear,

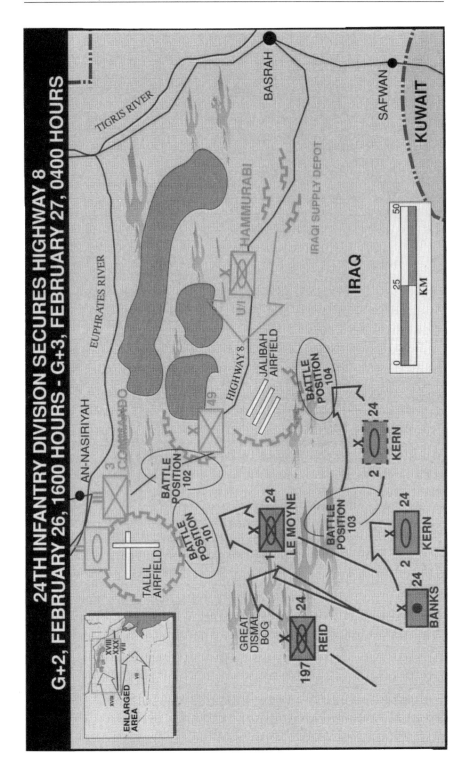

24TH INFANTRY DIVISION SECURES HIGHWAY 8
G+2, FEBRUARY 26, 1600 HOURS - G+3, FEBRUARY 27, 0400 HOURS

continued to direct his companies to overwatch positions. He used one company to block the highway and led the other two north to a canal paralleling the river. Craddock discovered several dozen Iraqi trucks and tanks on HETs, their drivers proceeding blithely along the highway, unaware that it was no longer theirs. Trucks, tanks, and HETs were quickly dispatched. Continuing north, the battalion overran a huge, untouched ammunition storage area and pushed the beaten Iraqis protecting the facility into the weeds near the canal. 1st Brigade reported BP102 secure by 0110 on February 27. Craddock later learned that his charge across Highway 8 had turned back a brigade of the Hammurabi Armored Division seeking to escape to Baghdad.

To the west of the 1st Brigade, the 197th Brigade had struggled with the terrain through the evening of the 26th. As the brigade moved north toward BP101, Reid softened his objective with A-10 strikes. Sandstorms and high winds slowed the march and obscured visibility. At 2200, elements of the Republican Guard 3d Commando Regiment attempted to ambush the lead elements of TF 1-18th Infantry, most of which were still struggling to emerge from the great dismal bog. First Lieutenant Larry Aikman's scout platoon was guiding the battalion through a particularly difficult area when one of his scouts spotted Iraqi antitank teams partially hidden around them. Acting instinctively, Aikman formed his thinly armored M113s on-line and in the midst of rocket and machine-gun fire, barreled over the commandos.

Gradually Reid pulled all of the 197th Brigade out of the bog to attack BP101. By late evening, he had massed his two mechanized infantry battalions and one tank battalion against the enemy's right flank. In a coordinated attack, the "Sledgehammers" of the 197th hit the position

Support columns stretched hundreds of kilometers back to the line of departure in Saudi Arabia.

259

simultaneously and rolled up another 300 Guard commandos. The 4-41st Field Artillery fired more than 100 rounds of improved conventional munitions and rocket-assisted projectiles ahead of the advancing infantry. By 0430, the brigade objective was secure.[34]

While the 197th struggled with the mud and the 1st Brigade slammed the door on the Hammurabi, Kern's 2d Brigade emerged from the bog and raced forward against minimal resistance to grab BP103 by early evening. Kern immediately began to prepare for the attack on Jalibah. By late evening on the 26th, McCaffrey's lead elements stood on Highway 8 while the division tail stretched 300 kilometers back to the original tactical assembly area. Not until the Hammurabi's HET-loaded tanks ran into McCaffrey's tankers did the Iraqis discover that the XVIII Airborne Corps had closed their most direct route to Baghdad.

XVIII AIRBORNE CORPS: G-DAY
PLUS 2, EARLY EVENING

Fully a day before McCaffrey reached Highway 8, General Luck realized that if he was to join the assault on the remainder of the Iraqi army gathering around Basrah, he had to swing the bulk of his corps eastward to catch up with VII Corps. By the evening of the 26th, VII Corps was far enough east to engage Republican Guard outposts, and every kilometer that Franks moved east increased the distance between the two corps. Like Franks, Luck had to call an audible to join in the fight against the Guard. CONPLAN Ridgway fit the requirement precisely. Ridgway called for the 24th to make the main effort by attacking east along both sides of Highway 8. The 101st would support with a deep attack by Apache and Cobra helicopters into an objective 10 kilometers north of Basrah.[35] Ridgway placed the 3d ACR under the operational control of the 24th Infantry Division and placed Colonel Emmitt Gibson's 12th Aviation Brigade under control of the 101st. By 2020 Luck had issued orders to reorient the corps.

The two division commanders reacted quickly in the next two hours. McCaffrey directed his brigades to continue their attacks up to the Euphrates and then to turn east. The 3d ACR would secure Objective Tim on a new boundary between VII Corps and XVIII Airborne Corps. Peay would then move his 2d Brigade from FOB Cobra to Objective Tim to create FOB Viper. Four battalions—a total of 72 Apaches—would base from Viper to screen the corps' northern flank. General Johnson, the 82d commander, established AO Bragg in the rear of the 24th Division sector to assist in clearing bypassed enemy units and to destroy abandoned Iraqi equipment. Johnson moved his 1st and 3d Brigades forward along MSRs Texas and Virginia, expecting to release them to the 24th Division to assist in clearing operations near Tallil or Jalibah. Luck's corps was prepared to synchronize its operations with those of Franks.

THE BATTLE OF WADI AL-BATIN

VII CORPS, G-DAY PLUS 2

2d Armored Cavalry Regiment: G-Day Plus 2, 1525

On midafternoon, February 26, Franks began the long awaited battle against Saddam's Republican Guard as VII Corps crossed Phase Line Tangerine on the 65 Easting, the longitude selected as the final coordination line before the corps reached the Guard. At 1525, the 2d ACR advanced past Tangerine with its three ground squadrons abreast: the 2d Squadron in the north, the 3d in the center, and the 1st in the south. Thirty minutes later at the 70 Easting, the 2d Squadron ran into the forward security outpost of the Tawakalna Division's 18th Mechanized Brigade. A task force of more than 30 T72M-1 main battle tanks and a dozen BMP infantry fighting vehicles occupied revetted firing positions, while supporting infantry manned interconnecting dugouts and trenches. The thick blowing sand and swirling mist cut visibility to less than 1,000 meters, but with thermal sights the Abrams and Bradleys still had an advantage in any weather. The cavalry advanced to the killing ground unannounced.

As the 2d Squadron pressed forward, indistinct blobs in thermal viewers grew steadily in size and clarity. Excited gunners first used low power on their gun sights to count targets, then switched to high power to pick out those with turrets rotated in their direction. A mile and a half from the Iraqis, tank commanders' fire commands broke the soft rushing noise of vehicle intercoms. Gunners answered immediately with "On the way" and pressed the firing buttons on their "cadillac" handgrips.

The boom of tank guns and the sharp "crack—crack—crack" of Bradley 25mm chain guns echoed through the fog, rolling over many Iraqi crews 10 seconds after they died. Inside American tanks, the blast of the main guns outside merely blended with the cacophony of battle. All along the firing line, the sequence in each tank was identical: a rapid-fire command to engage; the mass of the main gun slamming rearward with each shot; the blast-proof door banging open as the loader smoothly flipped another silver bullet into the breech.

Survivors in the Iraqi security force stubbornly returned fire, aiming at the muzzle flashes of the American guns. Unable to see clearly, Iraqi gunners collectively made two technical mistakes that doomed them. First, they had all zeroed their 125mm main guns at the standard Soviet battle sight range of 1,800 meters. The cavalry opened the duel at 2,400 meters, so nearly every Iraqi shot landed short. Second, they assumed that the distant muzzle flashes came from stationary tanks. Since Americans fired on the move, the Iraqi shots that came close merely skipped over the spot where the Abrams had been only seconds before. Under the

An M1A1 from the 2d Armored Cavalry Regiment just moments before meeting the Tawakalna Division.

American guns, the remaining combat vehicles in the Iraqi security force died quickly. The defending Iraqi commander later remarked that after losing 2 of his 39 T-72s in five weeks of air attack, the 2d Cavalry had annihilated his entire command in fewer than six minutes in what later became known as the Battle of 73 Easting. [36]

As flaming T-72s began to form the outline of the Iraqi firing line, the squadron's fire support teams called for artillery. More than 2,000 howitzer rounds and 12 MLRS rockets spewed 130,000 bomblets on the frontline Iraqis and targets beyond the range of direct fire weapons. When a company of T-72s threatened to overrun 3d Platoon of G Troop, howitzers fired an immediate suppression mission that stopped the Iraqis cold. Regimental gunners fired 128 DPICM rounds and 12 MLRS rockets shortly thereafter against an unseen Iraqi armored unit previously located from aerial photographs. Faint white flashes followed by dense columns of smoke stretched out horizontally by the wind proved the intelligence target to have been a good one. Later inspection verified that the strike had knocked out a company of armored vehicles, 27 ammunition bunkers, and 40 trucks. The 73 Easting fight was nearly over.

As darkness fell, the fighting in the northern zone of the regimental sector slackened, while in the southern portion of the zone the 1st and 3d Squadrons had little contact. Unfortunately, another fratricide incident occurred in 3d Squadron as a Bradley mistakenly fired at another Bradley in a neighboring troop, wounding six soldiers. Once its leaders had sorted out the friendly fire incident, the cavalry regiment halted, its job of finding the enemy completed. At the VII Corps tactical command post, reports

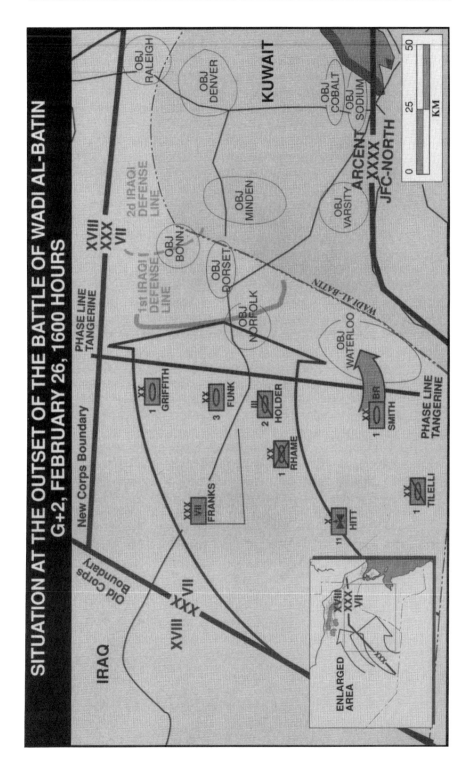

SITUATION AT THE OUTSET OF THE BATTLE OF WADI AL-BATIN
G+2, FEBRUARY 26, 1600 HOURS

The M829A1 depleted uranium round for the Abrams main gun easily cut through the T-72's thick frontal armor. Once penetrated, ammunition exposed inside caught fire and the tank exploded catastrophically. In the photo below, a silver bullet entered just below the driver's hatch.

from this engagement and others arrived almost simultaneously from across all 80 kilometers of the corps front.

VII CORPS: G-DAY PLUS 2, LATE AFTERNOON

A single glance at the corps' tactical situation map revealed that Franks' attack had achieved almost geometric precision. Because the corps approached aligned roughly north to south and the Republican Guard defenses were oriented northwest to southeast, the collision occurred at an oblique angle. As the flank divisions lapped around the dense mass of the Republican Guard, the trace of the corps front eventually formed into the horns of a bull. In the north, 1st Armored Division hooked deep around the northernmost Iraqi brigade. In the center, the 3d Armored Division pinned the Tawakalna's 9th Armored Brigade, and in the south the 1st Infantry Division prepared to pass through the 2d ACR, first to penetrate and then to envelop the southern wing of the enemy. On the corps' right flank, the British 1st Armoured Division crushed remnants of the 52d Armored Division to advance well past the left flank of the Republican Guard. The close battle now began in earnest.

1st Armored Division: G-Day Plus 2, 1300

As Griffith's 1st Armored Division rolled past Phase Line Tangerine with three brigades on-line, his aerial scouts from the 1-1st Cavalry searched across his front to confirm the latest updated templates of enemy positions from corps intelligence. At 1312 a Cobra scout team from C Troop, working the southern portion of the division sector, discovered one battalion of the Tawakalna's 29th Mechanized Brigade.

Chief Warrant Officer Gary Martin, call-sign "Snake 22," flying a Cobra in a hunter-killer team from 1-1st Cavalry, had already logged several hours rounding up prisoners, coordinating with flank units, and searching for the enemy. The weather continued to deteriorate and visibility dropped to less than a mile in the windblown sand. Martin was about to break station when he was ordered to investigate an Iraqi armored unit reported to be moving into the southern divisional sector.

"Snake 22" skimmed low over the desert beneath the overcast sky into steadily falling visibility. He closed to 1,500 meters before he saw the column of 50 T-72s. Another hunter-killer team joined Martin's as the squadron prepared a JAAT mission with two Air Force A-10s en route to the area. As the team moved into position, Martin opened fire with his rockets. His few aerial-delivered bomblets added to the hundreds of thousands being dropped on the Iraqis by MLRSs. Suddenly a loud popping noise distracted the pilot: the Cobra's compressor had stalled. A quick check of his instrument panel revealed rising engine temperature that promised an imminent forced landing. To lighten the crippled aircraft, Martin fired off his remaining rockets. He then pointed the nose of

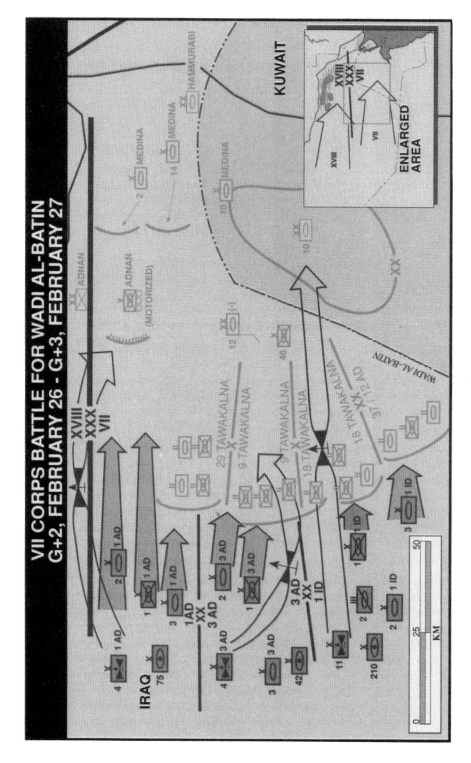

VII CORPS BATTLE FOR WADI AL-BATIN
G+2, FEBRUARY 26 - G+3, FEBRUARY 27

the Cobra toward friendly lines and called for help. Before the Cobra engine finally quit, choked by desert sand, Martin had nursed the bird along like a flat rock across a pond, skipping the Cobra off the ground four times to get out of range of Iraqi tanks.

On the ground, Martin and his gunner nervously awaited rescue as the A-10s roared overhead, pounding Iraqi positions fewer than 1,500 meters away. In minutes, Second Lieutenant Dave DeSantis, B Troop's 3d Platoon leader, careened up in an M3 Bradley scout vehicle to pick up the downed aviators. The pair quickly transferred the Cobra's crypto gear and other loose items to the scout track and mounted up. As they sped to safety, DeSantis told Martin, a highly decorated Vietnam MEDEVAC pilot, "Hey Chief, relax and enjoy the ride. You'll be safe in the back of my Brad." Martin would spend most of the rest of the war as a ground scout.[37]

After the scouts confirmed the enemy positions in 3d Brigade's zone, Griffith ordered Zanini, its commander, to destroy the Iraqis. Meanwhile, Griffith pressed forward with his center and left-flank brigades. The 1-1st Cavalry continued its reconnaissance eastward, skirting the enemy battle positions to the north.

3d Brigade, 1st Armored Division: G-Day Plus 2, 1500

Zanini returned to his command post. After reviewing the situation with his staff, he decided to add the firepower of Lieutenant Colonel Ward Critz's TF 7-6th Infantry to the assault line of Lieutenant Colonel Ed Dyer's TF 1-37th Armor. Both battalions would blast Iraqi vehicles and defensive positions with main-gun rounds, TOW missiles, and 25mm and 50-caliber fire. Zanini would hold TF 3-35th Armor in reserve under Lieutenant Colonel Ed Kane. [38]

When the enemy positions were softened up, Zanini would keep TF 7-6th Infantry in an overwatch position 3 kilometers back while TF 1-37th Armor rolled forward to crush the enemy. His intelligence showed that the Tawakalna should be arrayed within 5 or 6 kilometers to the front, so when they passed 3 kilometers they would begin to reach the range limits of TF 7-6th Infantry's covering fire. Zanini recognized that TF 1-37th Armor would be exposed, but he figured Dyer's tankers could handle the fight. Dyer's battalion was the only unit in 1st Armored Division equipped with the new heavy turret that offered the added protection of depleted uranium shielding against the powerful Iraqi T-72 125mm smooth-bore guns.

Thirteen kilometers from contact, Zanini's direct support artillery, the 3-1st Field Artillery Battalion, opened the battle. Three kilometers out, TF 7-6th Infantry opened fire as planned, soon joined by TF 1-37th Armor on its right. Along the brigade front, Abrams tanks and Bradley infantry vehicles fired at the enemy positions at ranges in excess of 2,000 meters, laying down a base of fire to cover Dyer's attack. After 15 minutes under fire from both battalions and supporting artillery, several dozen Iraqi hulks burned to the front.

It was pitch black at 1900 and the entire brigade was steering by thermals and night vision goggles. TF 1-37th Armor's line of 41 Abrams tanks charged past the right flank of TF 7-6th Infantry, leaving behind their lightly armored vehicles and attached infantry company. The tanks entered a fire storm as they closed. Iraqi machine-gun fire made a continuous slapping sound against the armor of the American tanks as red friendly and green enemy main-gun tracers skimmed across the ground and ricocheted high into the night sky. The Iraqi gunners were poor marksmen and their green sabot tracers hit nothing. The American gunners, however, were deadly. Within seconds after a T-72 had marked its position by firing its main gun, it took an American sabot in return and disappeared in a shattering set of explosions. The battleground rapidly became a junkyard of Iraqi armored vehicles.

Dyer led his three tank companies forward as he struggled to maintain the symmetry of his battle line to keep his firepower forward and thereby avoid casualties from friendly fire. They advanced toward four Iraqi battalions, two in a forward defensive line and two in a second line 1,000 meters farther back. Although he did not know it at the time, Dyer was badly outnumbered. He faced more than 150 armored vehicles on the objective, including two tank battalions. Normally assigned one tank battalion and three mechanized infantry battalions, the commander of the Tawakalna Division had removed an infantry battalion from the 29th Mechanized Infantry Brigade and replaced it with a tank battalion. The battle was to be one of quality versus quantity.

As they moved forward, what had formerly been open plains of sand gave way to vegetation. Long stretches were covered with thick, low bushes no higher than a tank. Thermals saw through the low vegetation, making it impossible for enemy soldiers or vehicles to hide. Several dozen T-72s and BMPs in the first 3,000 meters were ablaze within what seemed like seconds. Ironically, the American gunners' ability to outshoot the Iraqis began to work against them. As Iraqi tanks burned, the heat began to wash out the American thermal sights, making them difficult or impossible to use.

In Europe before the Gulf crisis began, Dyer's D Company had been training to represent the US Army in the Canadian Army Trophy Competition. The CAT gunners, as they referred to themselves, killed Iraqi vehicles with impressive speed as they rolled forward. Captain Pittard, their commander, soon found that it was extraordinarily difficult to keep his tanks on-line as they moved through the night, but he urged them on. The CAT team was living up to their advance billing as the best gunners in the Army. As he listened to his crews shout over the radio after each distant kill, Pittard knew that the extra hours of training had been worthwhile.

Pittard had started some 50 meters behind his line of 12 tanks, but like an anxious race horse at the starting gate, his own tank driver had gradually edged closer to the line as the fight intensified. Eventually Pittard shouldered aside two of his tanks to give his gunner a clear field of fire. Then they mounted a small ridge where he held his company in place on the crest.

As they waited for the other companies to catch up, many of Pittard's tanks picked up hot spots very close in the wadi below them and began methodically to knock them off. Meanwhile, Pittard monitored the battalion net, noting that B Company had fallen well behind and C Company was farther back still. He listened to Dyer urging, cajoling, even pleading with the other company commanders. Then B Company drew abreast of Pittard and joined in with their main guns at the targets in the wadi. Within 10 minutes, C Company drew up on the ridge. Once on-line, the entire battalion charged down the other side.

As TF 1-37th Armor crossed over the ridge into the heart of the Iraqi defensive zone, the Iraqi commander's carefully disposed rear-slope defense stripped Dyer's tanks of their range advantage. Within 1,000 meters, a row of dug-in T-72s and BMPs suddenly appeared below the crest. All were hull-down in prepared positions behind thick dirt walls. Now the Americans were well within Iraqi killing range, and although the Soviet-made night sights were markedly inferior, things could still get very dicey. So many Iraqi vehicles were burning around the target that areas of the battlefield were as bright as day. Again, the American thermal sights began to wash out.

The Iraqi defender was also clever enough to build his rear-slope defense behind a stretch of particularly rugged terrain, which he liberally scattered with excellent Italian-made antitank mines. After cresting the ridge, Dyer's tanks found themselves not only exposed, but considerably slowed. Dyer was trying to keep C Company on-line when Bravo 6 called to tell him that tank Bravo 23 had hit a mine and lost its engine. The tank commander still had battery power, however, and would keep fighting until the battalion trains arrived. Minutes later he got the report that Sergeant Steede's Delta 24 had been knocked out with an unknown number of casualties.

The battle had suddenly turned grim. A T-72 round had hit Bravo 23 in the rear exhaust exits. Another T-72 bypassed by D Company had killed Steede's tank. Bravo 23 took another hit from its ambusher in the back of its turret. The Iraqi sabot blew through the armor into the compartmented ammo storage area and set off an enormous explosion as many of the 30-odd main-gun rounds that were left erupted in white-hot flames. The

M-1 design came through, however. The blast escaped through the blow-out panels in the top turret, thus venting the explosion away from the crew compartment. The Halon suppression system kept fire out long enough for the crew to scramble to safety. Once they were safely away, more ammo began to cook off, and Bravo 23 started to burn in earnest.

Meanwhile, C Company had lost two more tanks to enemy fire, including the company commander's track. One of C Company's platoon leaders, Lieutenant Al Alba, killed the T-72 and BMP that had fired the lethal shots. Taking command of the company, Alba had combat lifesavers treat the wounded, then loaded both crews atop his turret and continued to attack.

Late that evening, Dyer called a halt to allow his tank crews to rearm, refuel, and rest, however briefly. He knew that the Medina Division's 14th Brigade was no more than 20 kilometers to the east, and his battalion would meet them soon. The crews of TF 1-37th Armor, though exhausted, were triumphant. Although they still had 30-odd hours of fighting before them, on that night they had utterly destroyed the best equipped and most competent force in the Iraqi army, and although they lost four tanks in the process, no Americans had died. After the war they returned to count the burned-out hulks of 76 T-72s, 84 BMPs, 3 air defense artillery pieces, 8 howitzers, 6 command vehicles, 2 engineer vehicles, and myriad trucks.

By 2300, Zanini's 3d Brigade had consolidated on the far side of its objective. TF 1-37th Armor returned briefly to the objective to sweep the trenches with infantry. Military police and engineers then took charge of the growing number of prisoners.

Griffith's division had turned the northern flank of the Republican Guard's first defensive line. Aware of enemy moves to establish additional defenses farther east, Griffith repeated his leapfrog maneuver in order to pass around the rest of the Tawakalna and the Jihad Corps and continue the fight with a fresh brigade. As he moved, Griffith again sent his attack helicopters to strike the enemy on and beyond his next objective. Franks' left horn was hooked deep in the side of the Republican Guard.

Griffith Strikes Deep

In the late afternoon of February 26, the next portion of the Iraqi defenses in Griffith's path was a defensive line occupied by a motorized brigade of the Adnan Infantry Division, located more than 20 kilometers northeast of the Tawakalna. Farther east, brigades from the Medina Armored Division began deploying in force to a previously prepared second defensive line. Griffith sent his cavalry out to pinpoint both forces. By dusk, the 1-1st Cavalry Bradleys were 50 kilometers to the front of 1st Armored when fire from BMPs and T-72s pinned them down. Griffith did not want his cavalry to get involved in a direct fire slugging match with a heavier force, so he called on the Apaches to help them disengage. As ground units continued to press forward, he called his artillery into action before ordering his forward brigades to pass through the stalled divisional cavalry squadron and pick up the close fight against the Medina.

While repositioning, the Cavalry Squadron operations center and B Troop received heavy enemy artillery fire, probably from the Adnan. Private First Class Marty Coon, a combat lifesaver, was close by the Squadron TOC when he heard the yell, "Incoming!" In moments, more than 100 enemy artillery bomblets rained down on Coon and his fellow soldiers, wounding many of them and shredding their vehicles. After the fire ceased, Coon and the other soldiers rushed about to treat the wounded, carry others to safety, and mark unexploded munitions. Helping the wounded was Private First Class Tammy Reese, a young medic from the 26th Support Battalion. She and Coon were instrumental in maintaining the cohesion of the unit. Of the 23 soldiers wounded, all but 6 were able to carry on their duties. Five wheeled vehicles were destroyed, and one Bradley and two armored command post vehicles were damaged.[39] In an ominous turn, Griffith realized that his enemy also possessed deadly bomblet artillery munitions.

Meanwhile, Griffith's 3-1st Aviation under Lieutenant Colonel Bill Hatch extracted revenge on the Adnan with their Apaches. After a quick radio call, Captain Rick Stockhausen's six A Company Apaches took off in echelon-right formation 100 feet apart and close to the deck. Each Apache carried eight Hellfires and thirty-eight 2.75-inch rockets. An unrelenting rain drummed against each canopy. The night was so black that the pilots relied on FLIRs alone to distinguish the line of Bradleys below them that marked the forward line of contact with the Adnan. Two kilometers beyond the friendlies, all six Apaches carefully eased up online, 150 meters apart and still some 50 feet above ground. Stockhausen could see 30 to 40 hot spots through his FLIR, mostly sitting still 6 kilometers to the front. He used his laser designator to divide the area into six distinct kill zones, one for each aircraft. As he methodically began to direct his Hellfires into the Iraqis, Stockhausen noticed that the dark night and the very steep angle of the missiles' trajectories completely surprised and confused the enemy. As they ran aimlessly among the burning vehicles, the hapless Iraqis obviously had no idea what was hitting them. Hatch had joined the engagement as a copilot-gunner. He was so absorbed in his Hellfire sight that he failed to notice a rumble of explosions below him until the pilot in the adjacent aircraft broke in on his radio. The pilot told Hatch that he had just chewed up about a dozen Iraqi soldiers armed with AK-47s who had collected below Hatch's Apache and were ready to shoot him down. His wingman's 30mm gun had saved Hatch's life.

After 45 minutes on station, A Company returned to refuel and rearm. Hatch's battalion made three more circuits through the Adnan during the early hours of the morning. Later, gun camera videotape confirmed that the single Apache battalion had killed 38 T-72s, 14 BMPs, and 70-odd trucks.

3d Armored Division: G-Day Plus 2, Midmorning

General Funk's 3d Armored Division formed the center of VII Corps, tightly wedged between Griffith's 1st Armored on his left shoulder and Rhame's "Big Red One" moving up steadily on his right. He had only 27 kilometers of battle front. With such limited room, Funk could only allow two brigades forward on-line and still maintain some minimal capability to maneuver. The dense formation, however, would not permit the leap-frog and bypass technique that Griffith was able to execute in the north. Instead, Funk was obliged to defeat his piece of the Republican Guard with concentrated firepower. Funk divided his supporting artillery into two roughly equal groups which he tucked up very close behind the lead task force of each lead brigade. Two distinct concentrations of artillery—as many as 50 guns and rockets apiece—were kept close so that when a major obstacle appeared, they could be immediately ordered into action to deliver an overwhelming mass of firepower. Funk's artillery practiced what could only be called a "mass hip-shoot." Given the signal, battalions of rockets and guns would halt in place and orient themselves, using GPS or the inertial locating device aboard each MLRS. Then, under the control of the brigade fire support officer, guns of all calibers would open fire in unison. The 3d Armored Division artillery and its supporting 42d Artillery Brigade could execute a hip-shoot in fewer than eight minutes.[40]

Funk pushed the artillery as far forward as possible to take advantage of every available meter of range. He kept two MLRS batteries under his direct control to work over fresh targets provided by his forward scouts, Air Force and Army pilots, or preplanned target lists derived from intelligence. Ironically, in one instance his MLRS was so close that he had to send two batteries 7 kilometers back to the rear to get the targets beyond the minimum range of the system. On Tuesday morning, February 26, Funk had driven his two-brigade phalanx within range of the Tawakalna. He initiated his drumbeat of firepower with an hour's worth of pinpoint shooting by two Air Force AC-130 Spectre gunships. As close air support A-10s and F-16s appeared over his formation, Funk established informal airspace coordination areas (ACAs) along specific grid lines to separate his artillery from his tactical air. The ACAs gave friendly aircraft a block of airspace free of friendly surface fires, especially artillery, and allowed Funk to continue attacking targets outside the ACAs. As aircraft reported on station to the division air liaison officer, he passed them to his forward brigades to allow them to work the air support as close as 5 kilometers to friendly troops. Concern for fratricide dictated that no close strikes would be flown unless the aircraft were under positive control from observers on the ground. Funk used as much air support as weather and safety allowed. He wanted to delay calling for an artillery hip-shoot for as long as possible so that the momentum of his two brigades would not be interrupted until the last conceivable moment.

Funk's two lead brigades attacked the Tawakalna's 29th Mechanized and 9th Armored Brigades on an oblique angle at 1632. As with the 1st Armored Division, he achieved total tactical surprise, appearing some five hours earlier than the Tawakalna commander expected. In the north, 3d Armored's 2d Brigade hit the southern end of the 29th Mechanized and main positions of the 9th Armored while the 1st Brigade broke into the enemy security zone in the south. Once the 2d Brigade penetrated, Funk planned to pass the 3d Brigade through to exploit the success.

1st Brigade, 3d Armored Division: G-Day Plus 2, 1630

Colonel William Nash's 1st Brigade on the right flank of the 3d Armored Division struck the enemy security forces at approximately 1630. Nash advanced with TF 4-32d Armor in the north, TF 3-5th Cavalry in the center, and TF 4-34th Armor in the south. The brigade formation was very tight. As few as 50 meters separated the fighting vehicles as they jockeyed for space and the least obstructed field of fire along the 12-kilometer line of steel. Lieutenant Colonel John Brown's TF 3-5th Cavalry pressed forward into the lead only to discover an Iraqi bunker complex supported by dug-in T-72s and BMPs 1,000 meters to its front. Sensing the imminence of a fight, more tanks and Bradleys began to elbow into the firing line.

By most accounts, First Lieutenant Marty Leners was the first tanker in the 3d Armored Division to kill a T-72. Leners led 1st Platoon, C Company, 3-5th Cavalry, and his tank, Charlie 1-1, led the brigade eastward through the dense fog and rain. At 1630 the scout platoon leader, First Lieutenant Donald Murray, reported taking a T-72 sabot round through the road wheels of his Bradley. Aware now that the enemy was very close, Captain Tony Turner, the company team commander, ordered Leners to slow a bit so that the trailing platoons could swing up on-line beside him. Just then Leners' gunner, Sergeant Glenn Wilson, spotted the T-72 through his thermal sight. The alert Iraqi tank commander picked up Leners' tank at the same time. Leners immediately dropped down to verify the target while shouting fire commands through the intercom. Wilson lased the target. A series of red digital zeros flashed below the reticle...too much dust and fog for the laser to sense a return. Leners could see the ugly snout of the T-72 main gun begin to traverse toward him. Wilson lased again. Still zeros. The tank's battle sight was set to 1,200 meters, but Leners could see that the T-72 was well beyond that range. Instantly he reached to the right wall of the turret to find the range toggle so that he could manually index a greater range. With his thumb jamming the toggle upward, the digital reading increased in 10-meter increments, slowly at first, then accelerating: 1260—1270—1280…. It seemed to Leners as if he were trying to set the alarm on a digital clock in slow motion. Wilson kept the pipper on the T-72, nervously fingering the firing button on his "cadillac" handgrips. Leners estimated a range of 1,600 meters. Both crewmen could sense that the T-72 would be on them before the new range was set. Leners commanded "Fire," and a split second later the round was gone. The round kicked a plume of sand in the air as it ricocheted just short. As Leners kept his thumb on the toggle, Specialist Leonidas Gipson loaded another sabot round. The reticle now registered 1650. Wilson fired again. Three seconds had passed between the first and second round. Leners and Wilson shouted, both in exultation and relief, as their thermal sights whited out with the explosion of the Iraqi tank.

Meanwhile, the remainder of the brigade closed on the enemy bunker complex and every gun and missile launcher seemed to open fire at once as the commander called for artillery and air support. The 2-3d and 2-29th Field Artillery delivered a concentration of 154 DPICM rounds on the fortifications at 2020. More high-explosive and white phosphorus (WP) rounds followed. Bits of burning WP found full fuel tanks ruptured by the high explosives and set off a series of gigantic secondary explosions. Using a ground laser designator, a fire support team guided two Copperhead rounds fired by the 2-3d Field Artillery onto two bunkers, destroying both.[41]

The fighting was not all at stand-off distances. For the scouts of Lieutenant Colonel John Kalb's TF 4-32d Armor, it turned into the armor equivalent of a switchblade fight. The scouts had three Bradleys forward on-line. At 1920, Sergeant Dennis DeMasters spotted a T-72 at 400 meters with infantry clinging to it closing on his Bradley from the southeast. DeMasters attempted to engage, but when his TOW test indicated a system failure, he scuttled his vehicle to the rear in an anti-Sagger drill. Meanwhile Staff Sergeant Christopher Stephens fired a TOW at the charging tank, but its guidance wire tangled and it fell short. At the same time, Lieutenant James Barker, his platoon leader, opened up with 25mm fire, shooting a few Iraqi infantry off the back of the T-72. Stephens fired a second TOW that struck the T-72's tracks, immobilizing but not killing the Iraqi tank. Then as Barker fired a third missile to kill the stubborn T-72, disaster struck. Friendly 25mm fire from the north hit Stephens' Bradley, killing him and mortally wounding another soldier. Two other scouts suffered less serious wounds. The whole frantic engagement had lasted no more than four minutes. Meanwhile, Sergeant First Class Craig Kendall from C Company rushed forward with his Abrams to cover the battered scouts as artillery and mortar fire finished the fleeing Iraqi infantry.[42]

The 1st Brigade had to pace its advance with the 2d Brigade, Funk's main effort, and keep contact with the division's 4-7th Cavalry and the 2d ACR to the south. During fighting in the southern portion of the brigade sector, 4-34th Armor, 4-7th Cavalry, and the 2d ACR became entangled with each other in the darkness and foul weather. Caught in the middle, the 4-7th Cavalry took friendly fire from its right and left rear, resulting in the deaths of two of 4-7th's soldiers and the loss of three Bradleys. Funk reconsidered continuing the night assault. He had already approved 3d Brigade's plan to conduct a deliberate attack in the north at dawn and he needed to maintain alignment of his forward brigades to prevent any chance of further fratricide. With the confusion developing on his southern flank, however, Funk decided to halt until daylight. Until then, close air support, artillery, and attack helicopters would repeatedly strike the enemy positions. Bradley gunners used 25mm cannon to mark targets for the A-10s, and the division artillery began a sustained program of fires to keep the Iraqis off-balance.[43]

Funk kept a tight reign on his attack aviation. He apportioned one Apache company to each of his two attacking brigades. At approximately 2200 a call from the corps deep battle cell informed him that a JSTARS "hit" had discovered a column of Iraqi armor moving southeast to

A TOW leaves the launcher of a Bradley fighting vehicle. The Bradley proved its ability to kill armored targets with 25mm automatic cannon as well as with longer-ranging TOWs.

northwest across his front. Documents captured later confirmed that a Tawakalna battalion task force had been alerted to conduct a shallow counterattack into the crease between the 3d and 1st Armored. The column was too far away to engage with tank fire and too imprecisely located for artillery. But if unengaged, it might disrupt the VII Corps attack at its most vulnerable moment. Funk's call to Colonel Mike Burke, his Aviation Brigade commander, brought 24 Apaches forward across the 2d Brigade sector half an hour later. The weather was abominable. Burke's helicopters moved cautiously above the 2d Brigade's line of advance, steering solely by night goggles and FLIRs. At 2300 the lead Apache spotted the distinctive heat signature of a battalion of Iraqi tanks lined up in column and closing steadily on an open area between the two divisions. The Apaches caught the column in the flank and took just three minutes to destroy 8 Iraqi T-72s and 19 BMPs. Standing in his commander's hatch 5 kilometers away, Funk could see sequential flashes of white light marking the impact of each Hellfire on the hapless Iraqi column.

Later that night, in a second effort to split the American units between boundaries, the Iraqis launched another probe with a battalion task force from the 29th Brigade of the Tawakalna. The Iraqi unit had, however, gone too far south and missed the seam. As it turned back north in the early morning light, the unit met disaster. Kalb's 4-32d Armor was in overwatch position west of the Wadi al-Batin as 3-5th Cavalry and 4-34th Armor bounded forward. At 0700 on the 27th it was Kalb's time to move. His scouts had not gone far before they spotted the Iraqi column at a great distance along the wadi, moving southeast to northwest directly across the path of the 2-34th. He had a few moments to rush his tanks into a line formation before the Iraqis spotted him. Kalb gave a task force fire order and 43 tanks opened up at once across a 2-kilometer front. The firefight ended in slightly more than a minute with 15 T-72s and 25 armored and numerous wheeled vehicles burning. Kalb had stopped the Iraqis from slicing into the southern flank of 2d Brigade.

2d Brigade, 3d Armored Division: G-Day Plus 2, 1700

As it moved into battle against the Tawakalna, Colonel Robert Higgins' 2d Brigade advanced in a wedge formation with a reinforced tank battalion, TF 4-8th Cavalry, in the lead. TF 4-18th Infantry was to its left and TF 3-8th Cavalry to its right. Supporting artillery and engineer units were tucked into the center of the formation; combat support vehicles trailed behind.[44]

The scout platoon of TF 4-8th Cavalry made first contact with the enemy defensive line at 1722 when the scout platoon leader surprised an Iraqi squad leisurely dismounting from vehicles alongside their fighting positions. After making short work of the squad with 25mm fire, the scouts moved on. Five minutes later, four hot spots on the scouts' thermal

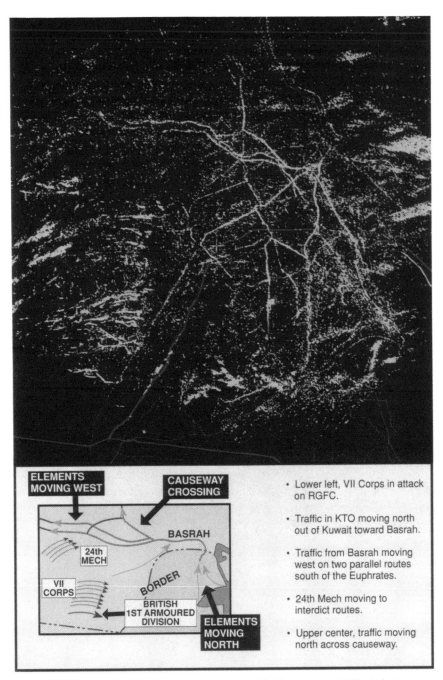

JSTARS readout, G plus 2, depicted VII Corps and 24th Infantry Division elements closing on the Republican Guard. Note that the Iraqis continued to move toward Basrah and to use the causeway over the Euphrates River.

The blast from a 120mm Abrams main gun momentarily lit up the night.

Tawakalna Division T-72 found after the Battle of Wadi al-Batin. The tanks were dug in, exposing only 2-3 feet of turret.

sights proved to be Republican Guard BMPs. After a brief fight, the "Spearhead" scouts wisely pulled back under a hail of enemy fire. Artillery air bursts, mortar rounds, and BMP shells landed throughout the formation as the scouts scuttled for shelter behind the following heavy tank companies.

TF 4-8th Cavalry commander, Lieutenant Colonel Beaufort Hallman, ordered "Action front" to his B Tank Company on the left, C Tank in the center, and D Tank on the right. B Tank moved up on-line to overwatch Charlie as Captain Ernest Szabo, C Tank commander, bounded his 1st Platoon forward to develop the situation. C Tank's wedge formation closed to within 1,500 meters of the enemy before opening fire. The 1st Platoon quickly destroyed a BRDM reconnaissance and a ZSU 23-4 anti-aircraft vehicle. After this first volley, some 100 Iraqi soldiers appeared. A few surrendered and some helped wounded comrades. Most, however, moved to cover, and as the company pressed forward, enemy rocket-propelled grenades hit them from all directions and artillery exploded randomly throughout the formation.

The increasingly intense enemy fire convinced Hallman to rein C Tank back into the center of a battalion firing line. Szabo got the call to pull back just as his tank, Charlie 66, threw a track. Under heavy fire, he dismounted and rushed over to another tank to continue the fight, only to find its radio encoding system inoperative. Again, Szabo scrambled through the hostile fire to take over his executive officer's tank, Charlie 65. As darkness fell the enemy fire slackened, but C Tank stayed to destroy enemy bunkers, infantry, and armored vehicles. By 1755, the C Tank commander had finally pulled back slightly, and B Tank shifted right to stay tied in with them. A check to Bravo's left revealed that they were still tied in with TF 4-18th Infantry.

On Charlie's left in Bravo Tank, Second Lieutenant Sean Carroll was completely absorbed in the sights and sounds of his first battle when suddenly an Iraqi BMP 73mm smooth-bore round streaked past the front of his tank and over his wingman and smashed into the heavy machine-gun mount of tank Charlie 12. Glancing off the mount, the round exploded against the left sponson box. Hit by fragments, Staff Sergeant Robin Jones, Charlie 12's tank commander, heard his driver scream as the Abrams' Halon fire extinguisher went off. Thinking the tank was on fire, Jones rolled out of the hatch and off the back deck and staggered over to Charlie 11 to get help before collapsing onto the sand. Then artillery airbursts began to explode over the formation, shredding ration boxes and duffle bags attached to the turret rails of the tanks around him. Carroll watched from his "open protected" hatch position as Charlie 12's tank commander fell in the sand behind the tank. Szabo roared up in Charlie 65 and called for his first sergeant to bring the medic track forward. After the medics recovered the stricken soldier, Szabo continued the fight. Meanwhile, Charlie 12 fought on with a three-man crew.

On the right flank, D Tank moved up into the direct firefight. As they charged forward, Delta's tank commanders observed C Tank under fire. RPGs exploded harmlessly against the armor of the Abrams, the crews inside oblivious to the hits. Enemy artillery fire continued to impact about the company. Remaining on-line with C Tank and the TF 3-8th Cavalry on its right flank, D Tank awaited further orders as the last light left the desert.

Following slightly to the rear of TF 4-8th Cavalry, Colonel Higgins was not pleased with the way his brigade's battle was unfolding. From his forward position, Higgins sensed that the enemy remained unbroken and might halt a frontal attack unless he pounded them harder. Therefore, he moved his MLRS battery back in order to strike the nearby enemy positions again. Not fully realizing his northern brigade was already into the main Iraqi defenses, Funk pressed Higgins to attack and realign with the 1st Brigade to the south. Higgins reported that the enemy positions were extensive, including battalion positions almost 3 kilometers in depth behind the main Iraqi defensive line. Higgins planned to hit the Iraqis with a hasty attack at 2200. Funk concurred and continued to blanket the vast position with masses of artillery and repeated Apache strikes.

Hallman's TF 4-8th Cavalry would again lead the attack. Hallman planned to bound forward in three phases. In the first, a single tank platoon from C Tank would rush toward the enemy, covered by fire from the rest of the task force. During the second phase the rest of C Tank would follow, coming on-line with the lead platoon. Finally, the remainder of the battalion would move forward to form on-line with C Tank. An intense artillery preparation would precede each step.

At 2247, Szabo's 3d Platoon bounded forward 500 meters, 45 degrees off the planned azimuth of advance. With a few choice words, he regained the attention of the errant lieutenant. During the second bound, a friendly DPICM bomblet fell short, killing one of the fire support NCOs. Slowly the task force advanced, firing at more and more hot spots as bunkers and dismounted infantry came into view. On the right flank, D Tank engaged reconnaissance vehicles 2,000 meters distant. Inspection of the battlefield the next morning revealed that Iraqi vehicle commanders tried to protect their machines from direct fire by hiding behind the dead vehicles. However, the 120mm sabot rounds sliced through the dead vehicles with more than enough energy to kill the live ones as well.

On the third bound, B Tank on the left flank hit heavy resistance. Bradleys and tanks engaged BMPs at ranges from 100 to 3,000 meters. The tankers used machine guns and high-explosive main-gun ammunition to disintegrate dismounted infantry and bunkers at point-blank range. For the next four hours, the tankers fought desperately in what could only be construed as a tanker's version of hand-to-hand combat.

On the brigade's left flank, TF 4-18th Infantry also encountered a thick assortment of well-hidden BMPs and tanks at ranges from 25 to 3,000 meters. In the initial fighting that afternoon, TF 4-18th Infantry's A Company got into a slugfest with an Iraqi BMP company supported by T-72s. After killing one BMP with 25mm fire, three more BMPs attacked the company but were quickly destroyed, along with one T-72. Still, the Guard infantry continued to fight tenaciously. The battalion's Vulcan section moved up to join the fight. The six-barreled 20mm cannon sprayed the Iraqi soldiers with high-explosive rounds at 2,000 rounds per minute. The rounds exploded among the Iraqis, breaking the attack. That night the enemy stubbornly continued to resist, mounting counterattacks against the boundary between the battalion and 4-8th Cavalry. The Americans destroyed enemy forces trying to hit the brigade's flank before the Iraqis could see to shoot. At 0300, Higgins reinforced TF 4-18th Infantry with an additional tank company, but by then the fighting had started to taper off. With Iraqi resistance largely broken, the Americans began regrouping. At 0345, Higgins' brigade received orders to pass the 3d Brigade forward into battle later that morning. The battle staff issued warning orders and began preparations for the battle handover that would take place soon after first light. The 2d Brigade would then become the division reserve. Funk wanted to insert a fresh brigade to maintain the tempo of the attack.

1st Infantry Division: G-Day Plus 2, 1800

To the south of 3d Armored Division, Rhame's "Big Red One" prepared to pass through the 2d ACR and pick up the battle late on the 26th. In blowing sand and rain, the division took the hand-off after a 16-hour march from the breach and lined up on the move to go into battle against a Republican Guard heavy brigade. Rhame moved his two forward brigades through the cavalry in a very delicate and risky passage-of-lines operation that came off better than many leaders had dared hope. As he formed his division to attack, Rhame took control of the 210th Field Artillery Brigade from the 2d ACR and was firmly in control of the battle by 2200. His entrance into the fight boosted the VII Corps battle line to nine heavy maneuver brigades, all attacking simultaneously across the 80-kilometer front. [45]

The Tawakalna Division commander had organized his defensive line with his tank battalions concentrated on his left and right wings with infantry entrenched between. The 1st Infantry attacked on a west-to-east axis south of the 2d ACR. As Rhame's two lead brigades, the 1st and the 3d, advanced through the enemy obstacle belt, they hit the defenders of the southern portion of the 18th Mechanized Brigade and, farther east, the

12th Armored Division's 37th Armored Brigade. The fight lasted until daybreak.

1st Brigade, 1st Infantry Division: G-Day Plus 2, 2200

In the north, Maggart's 1st Brigade attacked with two battalions abreast, TF 2-34th Armor on the left and 1-34th Armor on the right. TF 5-16th followed the remainder of the Brigade. The 1st Brigade moved against the 18th Brigade of the Tawakalna Division and mixed units from other enemy formations including the 37th Brigade of the 12th Armored Division. No longer attacking conscript infantry, the "Big Red One's" soldiers soon learned that the Guard and Army troops at Norfolk would fight with better skill and better weapons than the units they had faced at the breach.

Bone-tired after their eighth day of combat since the first shots fired in security zone fights on February 18, the 1st Brigade troops had moved up believing they would be placed in reserve. But mental agility was the order of the day. Soon after passing through the 2d ACR at the 70 Easting, both lead battalions made contact. Changing formations following the passage, two of TF 2-34th Armor's company teams turned north and broke contact with the remainder of the task force. Separated by a rise, neither of the lost companies could see the main body. Fearful of fratricide from the cavalry to the rear or between elements of the task force, TF 2-34th commander, Lieutenant Colonel Gregory Fontenot, directed Captain Juan Toro of B Company to fire a star cluster to guide the missing company teams. Toro complied, and Fontenot put two more star clusters up to mark the task force flank. The star clusters oriented the lost companies, but they also alerted the Iraqis who rewarded Fontenot and Toro by opening up with rifle fire, heavy machine guns, and RPGs. TF 2-34th Armor fought its way through one dismounted platoon position using only machine-gun and rifle fire since the enemy was between B Company and the two companies coming south. Shortly after midnight, both units were moving again, still in contact.

TF 2-34th Armor attacked with two tank teams abreast, an infantry team in echelon on the task force's left, followed by an infantry team and an engineer company. The task force identified most enemy positions at about 2,000 meters, then divided targets among companies while closing the range to 1,500 meters. At 1,500 meters, Fontenot brought his units to a short halt and engaged using volley fires when possible. When two BMPs appeared in Alpha Team's sights between them and Delta Team's trail vehicle, Captain Johnny Womack's soldiers knocked out the BMPs without waiting for orders.

To the south, Lieutenant Colonel G. "Pat" Ritter's 1-34th received fire that destroyed two Bradleys from First Lieutenant Glenn Birnham's scout platoon, killing one soldier and wounding four others. Birnham was

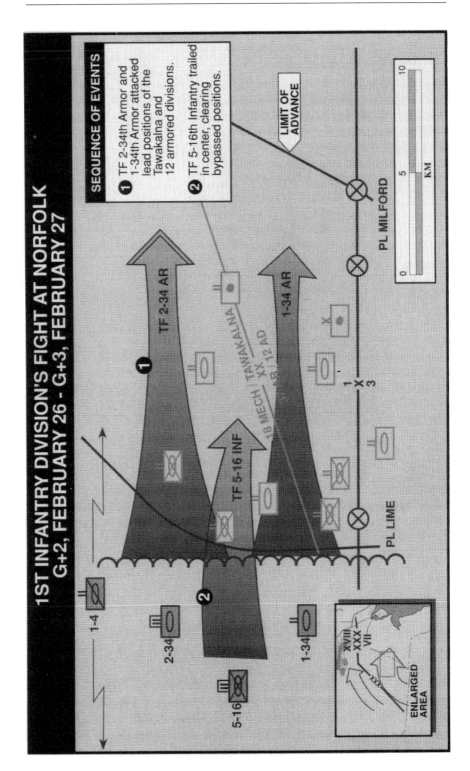

1ST INFANTRY DIVISION'S FIGHT AT NORFOLK
G+2, FEBRUARY 26 - G+3, FEBRUARY 27

SEQUENCE OF EVENTS

1. TF 2-34th Armor and 1-34th Armor attacked lead positions of the Tawakalna and 12 armored divisions.

2. TF 5-16th Infantry trailed in center, clearing bypassed positions.

TF 2-34 AR

1-34 AR

TF 5-16 INF

TAWAKALNA
18 MECH
XX
12 AD

PL MILFORD

PL LIME

LIMIT OF ADVANCE

KM
0   5   10

ENLARGED AREA

XVIII
XXX
VII

among the wounded, but he stayed with his platoon and guided in a tank company sent by Ritter to reinforce the Bradleys. Birnham continued the fight until the last of his soldiers was evacuated. Once Ritter secured the burning Bradleys, he bounded a second company forward to relieve the rest of his scout platoon. Once the scouts withdrew, 1-34th Armor broke through the initial positions of a T-55-equipped tank battalion and resumed the attack.

Ritter's battalion, attacking along the seam of two brigades, moved quickly in a diamond formation, picking off tanks and BMPs from two enemy units. The 1-34th Armor troopers dispatched both T-72s from a Guard unit and T-55s from a regular army tank battalion. By 0600 the two battalions had destroyed more than 100 armored vehicles and captured hundreds of prisoners. Lieutenant Colonel Sidney "Skip" Baker's TF 5-16th Infantry followed, gathering stragglers and destroying a logistics support area bypassed by TF 2-34th Armor.

The night settled into a seemingly endless succession of short fights against unsupported tank or infantry company positions. Across the brigade front, flaming pyres marked the destruction of the 18th and 37th Brigades, while several kilometers to the north the 1-4th Cavalry marked the horizon with pyres of their own as they attacked east protecting the brigade's flank.

By first light the brigade had swept through Objective Norfolk, and its service and combat support units were threading their way through the battlefield litter, occasionally taking fire from survivors of the night's carnage. The division interrupted refueling with curt orders to continue the attack. The brigade motored off for two more days and another night's fighting, which made them one of the few ground maneuver units that saw action on all four days of the VII Corps attack.

3d Brigade, 1st Infantry Division: G-Day Plus 2, 2200

Colonel David Weisman commanded the division's 3d Brigade from the 2d Armored Division (Forward) from Germany. He charged in the south with three battalion task forces on-line from left to right: TF 3-66th Armor, TF 2-66th Armor, and TF 1-41st Infantry. Almost at once the brigade encountered well-prepared defenses. An antitank ditch running the width of the brigade sector slowed the charge. As they crawled across the obstacle, grimly determined Iraqi antitank teams hidden in nearby trenches engaged the tanks from all sides with rocket-propelled grenades. Rockets exploded against the Abrams, blowing off gear and damaging engine doors and tracks, but causing no serious damage. Throughout the night, stubborn Iraqi antitank teams repeatedly emerged from previously bypassed positions to stalk the tanks and Bradleys. Alert and constantly on edge, the American tankers had little trouble detecting the approaching Iraqis through thermal sights, and they cut them down like wheat with long bursts of coaxial machine-gun fire. The Iraqis died never realizing how they had been detected. By remaining still and cold, a few T-55 tanks managed to escape detection long enough to open up a fanatical main-gun fusillade at point-blank range. The superior range, accuracy, and mobility of the American tanks counted for little in the ensuing tank-to-tank gunfight. Red and green sabot tracers crisscrossed and careened into the night as gunners on both sides opened fire on virtually any likely target.

American gunners relied on tube orientation and direction of movement to identify friend from foe. Any vehicle or unit not moving eastward parallel to their route of advance immediately came under fire. At 0200 tragedy struck. B Company, TF 1-41st Infantry, trailed B Company, 3-66th Armor, on the battalion's northern flank. On the south, A Company, 3-66th Armor, led C Company, 1-41st Infantry. As Bravo 1-41st moved forward to close up with Bravo 3-66th, Captain Lee Wilson's Bradley received RPG fire from his left that struck the ground in front of his track. In a tragic coincidence, the image of an Iraqi RPG exploding on or near a vehicle appeared through a thermal exactly like the image of a main tank gun firing. Almost immediately, American sabot rounds hit Wilson's and two other Bradleys. Out front the scenario was the same for A and B Tank teams. When Bravo's right front tank took two hits from RPGs, it came under friendly tank fire from the north. Three Alpha Abrams were also hit by main-gun rounds. Another Bravo tank turned toward the main-gun flashes only to be hit on the front slope. Later that morning, on the brigade's northern flank, two Bradleys from TF 3-66th Armor crossed into the 1st Brigade's sector by mistake. Clearing a bunker complex, the Bradleys came under RPG and machine-gun fire, which they returned. A Company in 1-34th Armor mistakenly identified the wayward Bradleys as T-62s and destroyed both. Fratricide had cost the lives of six soldiers and destroyed five Abrams and five Bradleys. To preclude further incidents, both brigade commanders tightened the already iron grip they had over the pace of their advancing elements. Stern orders, cross talk between units, specific instructions for opening fire, and vigilance on the part of junior leaders kept formations on-line and served to limit any further confusion on the battlefield. By 0430 on the 27th, the 1st Infantry began rounding up prisoners, regrouping units, and resupplying tanks.[46]

British 1st Armoured Division: G-Day Plus 2 to G-Day Plus 3

To Rhame's south, General Smith's British 1st Armoured Division had also pressed the attack throughout the night of the 26th. That morning, 4th Brigade attacked and seized Objective Brass. Despite the blowing sand and dust, heavy Challenger tanks and Warrior infantry fighting vehicles quickly destroyed most of two armor and mechanized infantry battalions.

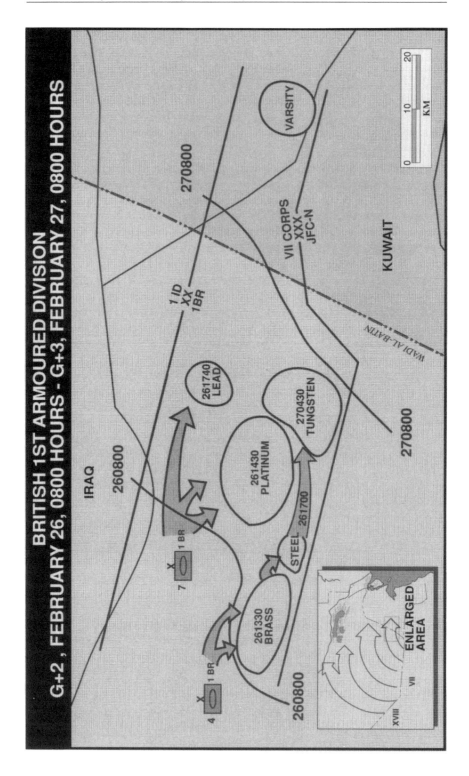

BRITISH 1ST ARMOURED DIVISION
G+2 , FEBRUARY 26, 0800 HOURS - G+3, FEBRUARY 27, 0800 HOURS

By 1330, the brigade held the objective in strength as 7th Brigade in the north launched its attack to seize Objective Platinum. In a carefully orchestrated series of one-two punches, Smith shifted his artillery back and forth in support of the alternating attacks of his brigades. By nightfall, advance British elements approached the Wadi al-Batin in the north, while 4th Brigade launched yet another attack in the south to seize Objective Tungsten by 0430. Both units then regrouped, with 4th Brigade preparing for a full-scale morning assault across the IPSA pipeline and beyond the Wadi al-Batin.

VII CORPS: G-DAY PLUS 2, 1300

11th Aviation Brigade

From the beginning, Franks had planned to fight a synchronized battle, striking the Iraqis close and deep simultaneously. One of his means for attacking deep was Colonel Johnnie Hitt's 11th Aviation Brigade, which Franks intended to launch against Iraqi armored reserves. The Air Force assumed some of the deep-strike mission, but Hitt's Apaches were more effective at precision strikes against masses of moving armor, especially at night. Franks kept his G2 looking up to 150 kilometers in front of his forwardmost units for any armored movement large enough to threaten his corps. On the afternoon of February 26 when no such movement had occurred, he decided to strike deep at the stationary Iraqi 10th Armored Division.

VII Corps' deep battle cell had developed a number of event-triggered contingency plans and had placed a series of kill boxes over areas the Iraqis would likely use to launch counterattacks. These plans were thoroughly coordinated with the staff and corps units for execution on short notice. One such plan, CONPLAN Boot, called for a deep attack to be launched from Saudi Arabia, across the breach, and into a kill box 100 kilometers inside Iraq.

Franks told Hitt to prepare for an attack that night to preempt any movement of the 10th Armored Division still in its static position near Objective Minden well inside Kuwait. Hitt issued the warning order at Forward Assembly Area Skip at 1530, then flew to the corps main command post to coordinate the plan. In order to strike so soon, Hitt was forced to change CONPLAN Boot considerably. Time was too short to plan for a detailed passage of lines as the brigade had done in the pre-G-Day feint on February 17.

Uncomfortable with some of the details, Lieutenant Colonel Roger McCauley, commander, 4-229th Attack, and Lieutenant Colonel Terry Johnson, deputy brigade commander, flew to the VII Corps Tactical Command Post to confer with Franks and his G3, Colonel Cherrie. Franks told Johnson not to launch until he and McCauley had coordinated with every

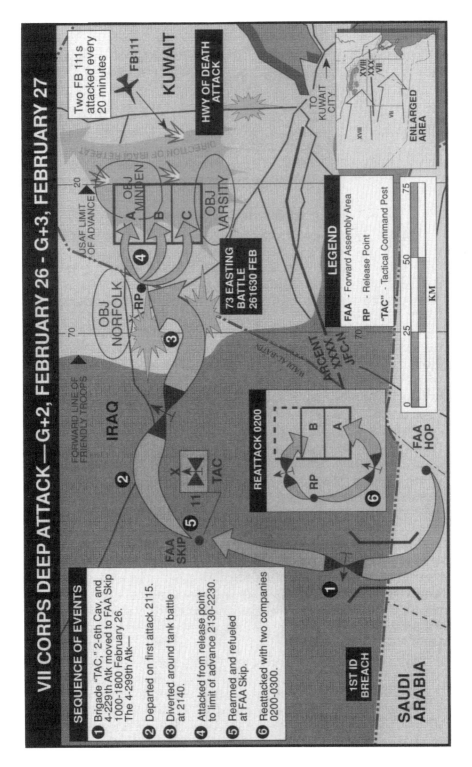

VII CORPS DEEP ATTACK—G+2, FEBRUARY 26 - G+3, FEBRUARY 27

SEQUENCE OF EVENTS

1. Brigade "TAC," 2-6th Cav, and 4-229th Atk moved to FAA Skip 1000-1800 February 26. The 4-299th Atk—

2. Departed on first attack 2115.

3. Diverted around tank battle at 2140.

4. Attacked from release point to limit of advance 2130-2230.

5. Rearmed and refueled at FAA Skip.

6. Reattacked with two companies 0200-0300.

LEGEND

FAA - Forward Assembly Area

RP - Release Point

"TAC" - Tactical Command Post

Two FB 111s attacked every 20 minutes

FB111

KUWAIT

HWY OF DEATH ATTACK

DIRECTION OF IRAQI RETREAT

USAF LIMIT OF ADVANCE

OBJ MINDEN

OBJ VARSITY

73 EASTING BATTLE 261630 FEB

OBJ NORFOLK

RP

FORWARD LINE OF FRIENDLY TROOPS

IRAQ

TAC

X 11

FAA SKIP

REATTACK 0200

RP

FAA HOP

1ST ID BREACH

SAUDI ARABIA

ARCENT XXXX JFC-N

WADI AL-BATIN

TO KUWAIT CITY

XVIII XXX VII

VII

XVIII

ENLARGED AREA

KM

0 25 50 75

division and 2d ACR. The general was particularly concerned that last-minute changes might result in fratricide when the attack passed over friendly ground units. Cherrie also told the pilots to stay in the kill boxes and not to fire east of the 20 north-south grid line. The Air Force would attack on the east side of that line.

The attack was planned to begin at 2100, but Hitt could not get through on the TACSAT to transmit the final go-ahead order until 2030. At 2100 Major Sam Hubbard, the battalion S3, took off in an Apache with A Company, and Johnson followed in the brigade command and control UH-60. A Company's six Apaches were at the point of McCauley's battalion wedge with the mission of clearing the route for B and C Companies. As Hubbard approached the friendly front line, he observed a tank battle just south of Objective Norfolk. The Apaches diverted slightly to the south. Johnson's aircraft arrived at the same point seconds later.

McCauley's battalion of 18 Apaches attacked with three companies on-line. A Company had the northern box, which included a slice of Objective Minden. B and C Companies had the center and south, respectively. After Captain Greg Vallet's A Company crossed the release point, they turned east and crossed into Kuwait. Vallet spread his Apaches about 150 meters apart and began a slow eastward movement into the box at about 30 knots. Almost immediately the Apaches received small-arms fire as they swept through, firing missiles, cannon, and rockets at anything that appeared hot in the FLIR. Friendly units were not a factor since the nearest were 50 to 80 kilometers behind them. Captain Ben Williams' B Company entered his kill box shortly after Vallet. About halfway through the box, Williams' company picked up T-62s and a mix of MTLBs and BMPs and wiped out everything in their path all the way to the 20 grid line, the limit of advance. In a moment of great frustration, McCauley, in the front seat of one of Bravo's Apaches, watched in his FLIR as hundreds of Iraqi vehicles moved steadily northward toward Basrah on the other side of the 20 grid line. He radioed Johnson to recommend a second attack across the grid line with every Apache available. Except for one engagement by one of his teams, Captain Steve Walters ran C Company all the way to the last 5 kilometers of his box before encountering the enemy. Walters' Apaches destroyed an assortment of MTLBs, T-62s, Type-59s, BMPs, and ZSU 23-4s, along with numerous trucks of all types.

Back at the corps main headquarters in the deep battle cell of the All-Source Intelligence Center, Hitt had received an updated JSTARS readout that showed thousands of moving targets on both sides of the frustrating 20 grid line. At 2230 Johnson forwarded McCauley's recommendation for a reattack and told Hitt the battalion was already rearming and refueling.

The Air Force attacked the area east of the 20 grid line with a series of single FB-111 strikes, where each dropped four 2,000-pound laser-guided bombs approximately every 20 minutes. When the air tasking order had been prepared more than 24 hours earlier, any targets east of this line were assumed to be well beyond the concern of the VII Corps commander. The methodical F-111 bombing sequence was never intended to blunt the mass withdrawal of several Iraqi armored divisions. If every bomb hit a vehicle, only 12 of several thousand would be knocked out each hour. When Hitt realized that the Iraqis were in full flight, VII Corps tried to get permission from ARCENT to attack into the Iraqi formation. Just one battalion strike with 18 Apaches could kill more than 100 vehicles in half an hour. Unfortunately, once the ATO was in the execution phase, it was almost impossible to turn off. In the limited time available, ARCENT could not portray to CENTCOM how successful Franks' deep attack had been and how devastating a strike east of the 20 grid line would have been. The missed opportunity frustrated Franks and the 11th Aviation Brigade pilots. Franks had lost a chance to attack in depth by synchronizing maneuver and air power. As for the pilots, they had had to pass up an attack pilot's dream. To salvage as much as he could from the strike, Hitt ordered another attack in the same kill box to commence as soon as McCauley rearmed and refueled. [47]

Rearming and refueling took longer than expected, but A Company was back in the air at 0130. For the second mission, McCauley ordered Vallet to attack from the south into what had been C Company's kill box while B Company reattacked in their original box. Vallet's second attack turned into a free-for-all. While his other crews systematically snaked their way through the kill box, Vallet focused on a multivehicle convoy only 2,000 meters to his front. For three minutes Vallet worked the column over from his copilot-gunner position. Using classic tactics, he knocked out the lead and trail T-62s with Hellfires and switched to multipurpose submunition rockets as he closed on the convoy. He finished off the convoy with a hail of 30mm shells in a final pass.

Even though the Apaches had swept the boxes clean on the first mission, more combat vehicles of all types continued to pour in from the south as the Iraqis rushed madly to escape Kuwait. McCauley's two companies expended all ordnance in fewer than 30 minutes. When they pulled out for the return, McCauley told Johnson he could do another attack, but it would be almost daylight before they would be finished. Johnson agreed that little was to be gained if they could not go beyond the Air Force limit line. The deep attack on Minden was over.

The raid on Minden knocked out much of the Iraqi 10th Armored Division. In the two separate 30-minute attacks, the 4-229th destroyed 33 tanks, 22 armored personnel carriers, 37 other vehicles, a bunker, and an undetermined number of Iraqi soldiers. Just 18 Apaches had broken the division's spirit and by so doing eliminated any hope that al-Rawi might have of reinforcing his Republican Guard. The men of the 10th Armored Division—the second half of the Jihad Corps—their morale shattered, blew up their personnel bunkers, abandoned their tanks, and began walking north.

[See Figure 5-4, "Ground Operations—G+2, Tuesday, February 26, 2400 Hours," at the back of the book.]

Sunrise on the 27th was a dawn for the undertaker. The morning pall lifted to reveal burned-out tanks and armored personnel carriers, crewed by corpses, scattered across the landscape. Around and in front of defensive trenches, dead Iraqi antitank ambush teams lay in clusters. At irregular intervals along the 80-kilometer front lay heaps of broken and discarded equipment: helmets, smashed automatic rifles, crushed anti-tank grenade launchers, empty boots, and blood-stained clothing—sober evidence of the night's grim events.

Clustered among the dead up and down the battle line sat stunned and morose Iraqi Guardsmen and regular army soldiers. One was Lieu-tenant Saif ad-Din of the Iraqi 9th Armored Brigade. As he sat with a group of his comrades waiting for interrogation, Saif watched the Americans methodically prepare to resume the attack. Nothing in his training had prepared Saif to fight such soldiers. When the Americans struck, Saif and his crew mates were taking advantage of the lull in fighting afforded by the blessedly atrocious weather. The attack came with such fury and suddenness that the tactics Saif had learned in fighting the Iranians proved useless. The Americans seemed to have telescoped a month's worth of fighting into minutes. First came the artillery. Thousands of exploding bomblets landed about him in such profusion that they seemed to search out every bunker and trench. Then the direct fire onslaught began. Vehicles all about him erupted in se-quence, left to right, until all were burning furiously. Within minutes the American tanks had passed his position. The terror was quickly over... and Saif, at least, was still alive.

VII CORPS: G-DAY PLUS 3, DAWN

For the soldiers of VII Corps, however, the battle was far from over. Thus far, only the 2d ACR had been pulled off-line and put in reserve, replaced by the "Big Red One." Franks' intent remained unchanged: press the fight to destroy the Republican Guard no later than sunset on Febru-ary 27. Fewer than 12 hours remained to complete the task. As the day progressed, the heavy morning fog dissipated. The theater remained under heavy cloud cover although the ceiling did lift to about 3,000 feet, allowing a greater use of close air support.

In the north, the 1st Armored Division was at least 15 kilometers ahead of 3d Armored Division. Griffith prepared to attack through Objective Bonn to Phase Line Kiwi. Already his Apaches were out forward, ranging freely about in search of the Medina Armored Division, the next and last major unbroken unit in their path.

Funk's 3d Armored Division had fought the Tawakalna's 29th Mechanized Brigade's southern battalion, as well as the majority of its armored brigade and part of its 18th Mechanized Brigade. Funk was now poised to penetrate the southern portion of the enemy defensive line with a 1st Brigade attack, while 3d Brigade passed through 2d Brigade in the north and continued the drive east.

Rhame's 1st Infantry Division's two forward brigades had destroyed the southernmost battalions of the 18th Mechanized Brigade and the majority of the 37th Armored Brigade as they clawed their way, meter by meter, through Objective Norfolk. Now they stood ready to continue the assault east across the Wadi al-Batin and into Kuwait. His lead elements were also some 15 kilometers forward of the 3d Armored Division.

In the far south at the hub of the wheel, Smith's British 1st Armoured Division, roughly on-line with Rhame's 1st Infantry Division to its north, finished a deliberate, set piece attack across the IPSA pipeline and secured their final objective on the west side of the Wadi al-Batin. Smith's lead elements then regrouped for the attack across the wadi to seize Objective Varsity, deep inside Kuwait.

1st Armored Division: G-Day Plus 3, Dawn

At first light on February 27, the 1st Armored Division with its three brigades shoulder-to-shoulder steamrolled east toward the Medina Armored Division. Griffith pulled back his Bradley scout vehicles before reaching the enemy main line. Thereafter the division front was made up exclusively of 350 M-1 tanks.[48]

2d Brigade, 1st Armored Division: G-Day Plus 3, Dawn

Five battalions would engage the Medina Armored Division's 2d Brigade and part of a brigade from the Adnan Division in the largest tank battle of Desert Storm. The fight would be remembered by those who fought it as the Battle of Medina Ridge. Colonel Montgomery Meigs' 2d Brigade marched forward on the northern end of the division. From north to south, the brigade's three battalions were TF 4-70th Armor, TF 2-70th Armor, and TF 1-35th Armor, which tied into the leftmost battalion of the first brigade, TF 4-66th Armor.

Progress that morning was slow as the 2d Brigade worked its way through an Iraqi training and logistics storage area, destroying tanks, armored personnel carriers, artillery pieces, engineering and command vehicles, and trucks. The sky was dark and brooding and a wet wind skated across the sand. The tanks had been running all night and had stopped to refuel soon after first light. Fuel was short, but each of the three tank battalions had saved enough to ensure another four hours of running time.

At about 1130, the brigade entered a wadi filled with grass-covered, sandy hillocks. As they emerged onto the clear, sandy, high ground east of the wadi, tank crews in TF 2-70th Armor began to pick up targets on their thermals. Although barely distinguishable at 3,000 meters, they appeared to be tanks and other armored vehicles buried deeply in the sand. Meanwhile, Lieutenant Colonel Bill Feyk moved his TF 4-70th Armor's tanks on-line and ordered the more vulnerable infantry Bradley company to form the reserve. Meigs moved TF 6-6th Infantry to cover the corps' open left flank. The massive tank firing line halted momentarily to request permission to engage.

Within seconds after TF 4-70th Armor had been cleared to fire, A Company opened up on Iraqi tanks at about 2,800 meters. To the right, TF 2-70th Armor had briefly stopped on the high, flat ground, and Alpha 4-70th pulled up next to them. For tank crewmen who had previously only fired on main-gun ranges, the view through their thermals was heady indeed. Hundreds of hot spots glowed from camouflaged tanks at a distance nearly impossible to see with the naked eye. Like the Tawakalna commander, the Medina's commander had established a rear-slope defense below the ridge. He had, however, made a fatal error in terrain appreciation by placing the defensive line too far from the ridge. His tanks could not reach the American tanks on the ridge, but with careful gunnery the Americans could just range his.

As they crested Medina ridge, Meigs ordered a halt when he realized the magnitude of the formation arrayed before him. To even the odds, he called for air support. Apache helicopters from 3-1st Aviation quickly took up station and hovered no more than 30 feet above TF 4-70th Armor's battle line before opening fire with Hellfires. Iraqi artillery immediately added background noise to the battle by dropping heavy fire behind Meigs' line of tanks. As usual, the artillery fired without adjustment and continued to land harmlessly in the same spot. Now Meigs' main tank guns added their own deadly tattoo to the crescendo of battle sounds. The farthest any had ever fired in training was 2,400 meters. Now, when the pressure was really on, his tankers were regularly drilling sabot rounds through T-72s at 3,000 meters and beyond. Much later Feyk recalled a particularly poignant moment. Surrounded by rotor wash, the roar of engines, and the deafening explosions of tank rounds and artillery, Feyk stopped his frenetic activity to absorb completely what his tankers were doing. Each crewman was grimly killing Iraqi tanks with calm, mechanical regularity. Excitement could be heard on the radio, but no panic—just an occasional shouted warning or a correction, or perhaps a muttered word of encouragement. It was a scene of uncanny discipline and phenomenal human control in the midst of hell. Feyk would never forget it.

Forming the 2d Brigade's right flank, Lieutenant Colonel Jerry Wiedewitsch's TF 1-35th Armor continued to shoot hot spots in their thermals while moving forward at a steady 15 kilometers per hour. D Company, TF 2-70th Armor, halted momentarily to acquire targets. The pause allowed D Company, TF 1-35th Armor, to move more than a kilometer ahead of the right flank of D Company, 2-70th. To regain realignment, Wiedewitsch ordered Delta 1-35th to stop when they got within 1,000 meters of the Iraqi defensive positions.

Sergeant First Class John Scaglione led Delta 1-35th to within 800 meters of the Iraqi lines. His platoon leader had fallen back in the formation and Scaglione had taken over the point position. He reluctantly stopped while two other tanks in his platoon fell back to cross-level main-gun ammunition. While this 20-minute operation was going on, Iraqi artillery and mortars began to fall behind them in the wadi.

In spite of increasingly accurate fire, Scaglione refused to sink into his hatch and forfeit his all-around vision. His platoon was isolated, well in front of other American forces, and he could not afford to miss anything. He stood in the turret keeping a steady watch through binoculars while his gunner continued to swing the turret and its thermal sights back and forth through a 180-degree arc. Suddenly Scaglione was just able to make out the main-gun tube of a T-72 as it rose over the top of a berm and leveled menacingly on his company commander's tank. He slipped down onto his thermal sights and twisted his override hard left, slewing the turret around. He laid his cross hairs in a spot just right and below the muzzle of the T-72. His gunner fired almost instantly and the silver bullet crossed the several hundred meters between them in less than a second, blasted through the berm, and unerringly found the steel body of the T-72. Again Scaglione popped out of the turret and continued to scan. In quick succession his crew discovered and killed three more threatening T-72s before any could get off a shot. By then his two wingmen had finished cross-leveling main-gun ammunition and were ordered to pull back 500 meters.

While the tanks slowly reversed, keeping their thick frontal armor toward the enemy, gunners continued to fire, sending Iraqi tank turrets spinning into the air like 10-ton boxes. Meanwhile, Lieutenant Colonel Steve Whitcomb, commander of TF 2-70th Armor, moved forward to retie his lines with TF 1-35th Armor. He approached D Company from

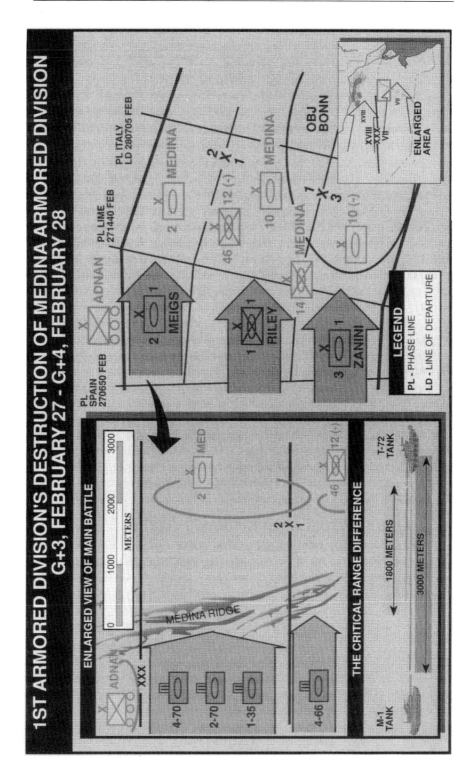

1ST ARMORED DIVISION'S DESTRUCTION OF MEDINA ARMORED DIVISION G+3, FEBRUARY 27 - G+4, FEBRUARY 28

the rear and drove forward through the company. Telling the men on the tanks to "Follow me," Whitcomb headed for the left flank of TF 1-35th, nearly 2 kilometers to the front. At this point, Meigs recognized the growing confusion within the brigade's firing line and ordered a pullback to reconsolidate.

1st Brigade, 1st Armored Division: G-Day Plus 3, 1100

As the 2d Brigade realigned, 1st Brigade units got into a fight with a mixed group of Iraqis from the Medina's 14th Mechanized Brigade and remnants of the 12th Armored Division's 46th Armored Brigade. D Company, TF 4-7th Infantry, had moved out that morning after a brief pause to rest and refuel. The company reached Medina Ridge after only a 5-kilometer march, and Staff Sergeant Charles Peters, the company master gunner, spotted several BMPs and T-72s dug in on the slope below his Bradley. Maintaining the strictest fire control, Peters destroyed one BMP with only three quick rounds of 25mm armor-piercing ammunition, then adroitly switched his ammunition selector to high explosive to engage the Iraqis as they ran from the vehicle toward some nearby trenches. He just as rapidly switched back to armor-piercing again to kill a second BMP and engaged a third, raising a cloud of dust all around the target with impacting 25mm cannon rounds. This particular Iraqi vehicle strangely did not explode like the others, and as the dust settled, Peters saw why—it was a T-72. As the tank opened fire on his company, Peters quickly raised the TOW "two-pack" launcher and switched sighting systems a third time. The sequence took only seconds, but it seemed like hours before he could launch the missile. Peters held his cross hairs steady on the tank a few seconds longer until missile impact and destruction. He finished this remarkable one-man gunnery demonstration by switching back to the 25mm a fourth time to kill a third BMP as Captain Christopher Shalosky, his amazed company commander, watched.[49]

3d Brigade, 1st Armored Division: G-Day Plus 3, 1400

Farther south, Zanini's 3d Brigade also came into contact with the southern extension of the Iraqi 14th Mechanized Brigade and elements of the 10th Armored still reeling from McCauley's devastating Apache attack the previous evening. Sergeant First Class Terry Varner led 1st Platoon of B Company, TF 3-35th Armor, toward Objective Bonn. As his platoon rolled over a series of ridges, Varner was the first to spot Iraqi armor to the front. Calling out, "Bimps! Shoot 'em—contact Bimps! Out!," Varner's first shell destroyed the lead enemy vehicle. As it exploded, a dug-in T-72 popped out of a hide position and fired at Varner's tank, missing it by 100 meters. Varner destroyed the T-72 four seconds after killing the BMP, a total engagement time of just seven seconds.[50]

Two photographs taken by LTC Jerry Wiedewitsch's TF 1-35th Armor during the Battle of Medina Ridge graphically illustrate the new dynamics of tank warfare. Above, the M-1 to the right destroyed an Iraqi T-72 at a distance of almost 2 miles. The target can be seen as a red spot on the horizon. Below, Wiedewitsch as he passed through the enemy position, marked by six burning tanks, just minutes later. The rightmost tank had just exploded, throwing its turret into the air.

2d Brigade, 1st Armored Division: G-Day Plus 3, 1300

The main fight, however, remained in the north between Meigs' 2d Brigade and the 2d Brigade of the Medina. Neither foe had much room to maneuver. The largest single tank engagement of the war would prove to be an undignified brawl. For the first 10 minutes, the main guns on the M-1s fired almost as fast as they could be loaded. Iraqi armored vehicles exploded in flames all along the line. Bradleys had also pulled up on-line in many places, and their TOW missiles added to the tank killing while 25mm guns destroyed BMPs and softer vehicles. Meigs' four armored battalions formed a shoulder-to-shoulder line of tanks and Bradleys— more than 200 armored vehicles—that stretched along a north-south line more than 10 kilometers.

The Medina's 2d Brigade was arrayed in two parallel lines of T-72s and BMPs running northwest to southeast, with each vehicle spread 100 to 150 meters apart. The Iraqis had skillfully dug in and camouflaged their firing line and placed a formidable protective ring of antiaircraft guns around it. One ZSU 23-4 managed to shoot down an American A-10 aircraft. But the distinctive signatures given off by the ZSU's four rapid-firing barrels alerted nearby tanks to its presence and it immediately disappeared in an angry flurry of tank fire. The Iraqis had also registered artillery on the wadi behind the Americans. The Iraqi plan was to kill the American tanks on the ridge with dug-in T-72s and then drive the survivors back into the wadi and finish them off with artillery. The Iraqis, however, had no idea they could be detected and destroyed at a range of nearly 2 miles.

Franks and Griffith on Medina Ridge

Some 20 minutes into the fight, Franks came up on the divisional radio. With 1st Armored Division committed against the Medina, Franks wanted to coordinate passing the 1st Cavalry around Griffith's northern flank. Griffith's aide, Captain Keith Robinson, gave Franks' pilot the coordinates of their position from the LORAN navigation device on Griffith's HMMWV, and within minutes Griffith had guided Franks to his location. Griffith was briefing his commander when one of many Iraqi artillery concentrations hit nearby, causing some concern to VII Corps staff officers, one of whom turned quizzically to Griffith's aide and asked, "What's that, some short rounds from our artillery?" Robinson shook his head and offered, "Nah, that's Iraqi artillery." He smiled at the officer's confused expression and said, "Don't worry, that's about the fifth barrage they've fired, but they don't move it. It just goes into the same place every time."

Division Artillery, 1st Armored Division: G-Day Plus 3, 1400

Initially, Griffith's counterbattery radars were looking in the wrong direction to detect the Iraqi batteries. Not long after the rounds began to impact behind the 2d Brigade firing line, the gunners reoriented two radars toward the north and east and immediately pinpointed a 122mm D-30 battalion that was firing methodically at a constant four rounds per minute. Colonel "VB" Corn ordered three full MLRS launchers to respond, but, maddeningly, the Iraqi guns were firing from across the 40 Northing grid that marked the border with XVIII Airborne Corps. Clearance to shoot took more than half an hour as the request went back to VII Corps main command post, then by satellite to XVIII Airborne Corps command post, then back again. Once received, however, the MLRS volley obliterated the Iraqi battery. Corn kept his radars illuminated continuously and within minutes his Q37 acquired nine more targets that were silenced by another 12 MLRS rocket volleys. By 1400 Corn had eliminated four Iraqi artillery battalions, using MLRSs with deadly effect. In the next 24 hours, Corn's gunners would destroy 72 Iraqi field artillery pieces. As each Iraqi battery opened fire, he retaliated in less than two minutes with a minimum of 12 rockets and a battalion's worth of 8-inch cannon artillery. The Iraqis had no hope of winning the counterbattery duel.[51] Three weeks later, Corn walked through the three firing positions occupied by the D-30s and counted 13 destroyed guns surrounded by MLRS rocket motors, fuzes, and warhead shrouds.

Beyond the impacting Iraqi artillery fire, Franks and Griffith watched Abrams tanks and Bradley fighting vehicles engage the Medina. Apache helicopters, poised above TF 2-70th Armor well to the north, added Hellfires. Smoke, dust, and communications problems between tanks and Apaches caused Griffith to send the Apaches against targets deeper in zone. A-10 and F-16 aircraft soon joined the fight. Several kilometers away, they could see friendly artillery strikes going in, the multiple explosions of distant bomblets sounding like firecrackers on the Fourth of July. Inky black clouds from oil fires created the backdrop to an incredible tableau of orange burning Iraqi tank hulks occasionally flashing white as the flames found on-board ammunition. Hundreds of intensely burning points of light spread across the horizon before them. At that moment thunder began to roll in, as if nature had decided to add its own pyrotechnics to the display. As jagged streaks of lightning stabbed the sky, the rumble of thunder and the rumble of massed artillery firing from the division rear were indistinguishable. It was exhilarating and frightening. No Hollywood director could have conceived a more dramatic panorama.

Air and artillery strikes hammered Medina Ridge for a full two hours. By 1500, everything inside or near the Iraqi defensive positions had been killed or set afire. The 2d Brigade swung forward again from the north, this time with TF 4-70th Armor on a southeast azimuth across the American front. TF 2-70th Armor, with TF 1-35th Armor following, spread behind in a giant curving tail of vehicles. As the entire mass of the brigade rolled over the Iraqi positions at an angle, engineer troops hopped aboard any Iraqi vehicles not completely destroyed and blew them up with explosives.

1st Brigade, 1st Armored Division: G-Day Plus 3, 1645

As the 2d Brigade moved forward, the scouts of TF 4-66th Armor of 1st Brigade received the mission to maintain contact. When the 2d Brigade momentarily halted, the scouts were exposed to fire from an enemy ammunition bunker complex on the flank. Within minutes an RPG struck HQ 55, a Bradley cavalry fighting vehicle, and knocked it out. To cover HQ 55's evacuation, Sergeant First Class Frederick Wiggins, the scout platoon sergeant, abruptly placed his track between the damaged Bradley and the enemy. Wiggins had just opened fire on the Iraqis when two RPGs struck his track, instantly killing the driver, Specialist Clarence Cash. Wiggins and Corporal Richard Knight were seriously wounded and several others inside were hurt. Meanwhile, the platoon leader, First Lieutenant Robert Michnowicz, maneuvered the remainder of the scouts to rescue their comrades and eliminate the Iraqis. HQ 53 moved left of Wiggins' vehicle and picked up two of the wounded. Staff Sergeant Robert Hager moved HQ 52 in close and dismounted two of his squad, Privates Timothy Wright and Matthew Meskill, to recover the others. As Wright and Meskill worked, their gunner, Sergeant David Smith, destroyed the Iraqi RPG teams. HQ 56 covered their withdrawal, killing another RPG team as the scouts moved back to regain contact with TF 1-35th Armor.[52]

Soldiers like Varner, Steede, Scaglione, Peters, and Wiggins were the cornerstone of Griffith's victory at Medina Ridge. The 1st Armored Division had one soldier killed in a fight in which more than 300 Iraqi armored vehicles, the cream of the Republican Guard, were destroyed. At 1700, VII Corps ordered Griffith's division to resume the attack as soon as possible. Significant pieces of the Medina Division were still intact on Objective Bonn, and the 1st Armored Division commander intended to continue the attack early on the 28th.

VII CORPS: G-DAY PLUS 3, 1800

Franks had intended to pass the 1st Cavalry Division around to the north of the 1st Armored Division on the afternoon of the 27th as the left wing of a double envelopment. The tank battle between the 1st Armored Division and the Medina, however, convinced him that to conduct such a maneuver any earlier than the following day would be unwise. CENTCOM had denied the corps' request for a boundary change with XVIII Airborne Corps that would have given the 1st Cavalry Division room to move around the 1st Armored Division. Without the boundary change, the risk of fratricide was too high. Therefore, Franks instructed the 1st Cavalry Division to remain behind the left wing of the 1st Armored Division, much to General Tilelli's disappointment.

The right arm of Franks' envelopment, the "Big Red One," had already crushed the Iraqi 37th Armored Brigade and had gone on the pursuit. Franks flew to the 1st Infantry Division tactical command post and told Brigadier General William Carter, Rhame's assistant division commander, to continue the attack east. Franks tapped the map where the waters of the Persian Gulf meet the sand of Kuwait and said, "See this blue... this is the way home." The division marched on all day in order to be able to cut the Kuwait City-Basrah highway by dark. Lieutenant Colonel Robert Wilson's 1-4th Cavalry had already crossed the highway shortly after 1630 and spent several harrowing hours into the evening out of contact with the rest of the division. Wilson eventually set up defensive positions astride the highway. Again, fear of fratricide intervened, and at 1930 Franks ordered the division to halt for the night to avoid any possibility of a nighttime collision with the right flank of the 3d Armored Division into whose path they were moving. Wilson's squadron spent the night processing more than 1,000 prisoners while cut off from the rest of the division by 25 kilometers.

After breaking through the armored crust of the Tawakalna, the 3d Armored Division overran the Iraqi division's artillery positions and remnants of the 10th and 12th Armored Divisions. Ahead of his division, Funk worked two Apache battalions—his own 2-227th Attack and the 11th Aviation Brigade's 2-6th Cavalry. As the division advanced, more prisoners began to appear, a sure sign that the Republican Guard's morale had finally begun to collapse. The division began to find entire battalion sets of combat equipment abandoned, some with vehicles still running, shells loaded in breeches, and radios switched on. By 2030, lead elements of the 3d Armored Division had reached Phase Line Kiwi, their limit of advance for the night.

The British 1st Armoured Division had secured Objective Varsity and was waiting for a decision on whether to continue to drive east to the Kuwait coast or to drive south and open a resupply route down the Wadi al-Batin. By 2030, Franks confirmed that the division would continue to drive east, securing its final objective between the north-south highway and the coast.

By the evening of February 27, VII Corps had broken five Iraqi heavy divisions: the Tawakalna, Medina, 10th Armored, 12th Armored, and 52d Armored. Of the Republican Guard heavy divisions, only the Hammurabi remained reasonably intact. The infantry divisions along the Saudi border, now the southern flank of the corps, had disintegrated and were joining thousands of their comrades in VII Corps POW camps. They had no coherent defense. The Iraqi GHQ had lost the battle for Kuwait and now could only concentrate on survival.

XVIII AIRBORNE CORPS: G-DAY PLUS 2, LATE EVENING

On the evening of February 26, General Luck was very pleased with his corps' progress. The attack to the Euphrates had gone faster than he expected with fortunately few casualties. However, the VII Corps' turn to the east had opened up a 50-kilometer gap between them. XVIII Airborne Corps' race was not over.

3d Armored Cavalry Regiment: G-Day Plus 2, Midnight

Colonel Starr's 3d ACR was the first unit in Luck's corps to move east. Reassigned to McCaffrey's control under CONPLAN Ridgway, the 3d ACR moved to regain contact with Franks' corps late on the 26th. During the move, Starr received an audible to attack and seize Objective Tim, the airfield at Umm Hajul along the east-west boundary between the two corps. Starr had not had physical contact with VII Corps for almost 24 hours, and he was very concerned with the proximity of the airfield to his boundary with VII Corps. He had his operations officer contact the 1st Armored Division, the left flank of VII Corps, to coordinate a boundary change to give his regiment more maneuver room. Some time later, word reached Starr that the boundary change was disapproved. The liaison officer also warned the regiment that some 1st Armored logistical units were still in the area. Starr immediately contacted his right-flank squadron commander and informed him of the disapproval. He also told him to watch for possible friendly units along the boundary.[53]

By midnight, the 3d ACR turned east toward Objective Tim. In the early morning of February 27, the southernmost squadron attacked the objective. At first they saw nothing. But as the attack progressed, the southernmost troop commander observed vehicles through his thermals on the southwestern tip of the airfield. They fired warning shots, and in the heat of the moment, one Bradley reported receiving incoming rounds from what appeared to be a building. A one-sided firefight ensued but ended abruptly when, in attempting to get the enemy to surrender, the cavalry realized their targets were fellow American soldiers. Engineers from the 54th Engineer Battalion, 1st Armored Division, were on the airfield awaiting the recovery of a disabled vehicle. Friendly fire killed one soldier and wounded another.[54]

The incident was tragic. An immediate investigation revealed that both units were on the correct side of their respective boundaries. Extreme darkness created by cloud cover made visibility possible only through night vision devices. While thermals could be used for precise targeting out to a range of 3.2 kilometers, the thermal image was so indistinct that beyond about 700 meters gunners found it difficult to differentiate between friend and foe. A square plywood tool box mounted on the back of one of the larger engineer vehicles made it appear through the thermals to be a building.

Fear of further fratricide grew as word of incidents and near misses filtered throughout the ARCENT chain of command. The corps commanders became increasingly concerned as their units began to converge in the tightly constricted battle space of Kuwait. Among thousands of units from platoons through corps, extreme caution began to work its way into the execution of the battle plan. Attacks halted more frequently to allow units to sort themselves out before advancing again. Distant targets, most surely Iraqi, were allowed to escape without engagement. Luck and Franks established a 5-kilometer "sanitary" zone between their respective corps and agreed that no target in the zone, even if positively identified as Iraqi, would be engaged. Undoubtedly all these actions saved lives, but the price paid for more safety was a substantial increase in friction and a concomitant dampening of audacity and dash throughout the remainder of the campaign.[55]

101st Airborne Division: G-Day Plus 3, 0800

Once Objective Tim—30 kilometers southwest of Jalibah airfield—was in the hands of the 3d ACR, Luck ordered the 101st to raise the curtain on one gigantic final aerial envelopment toward Basrah. The objective was to slam another door on escaping Iraqis. This time Luck would send Peay's division far to the east to cut the last remaining escape route—Highway 6 running north out of Basrah and paralleling the Tigris River. After a 45-minute flight, the first serial from 2d Brigade, with an infantry battalion, an artillery battalion, air defense, and engineers, landed at Objective Tim shortly after 0900. More than 500 infantry soldiers and 60 antitank HMMWVs spread out, immediately securing the area while field artillerymen placed 18 tubes of 105mm howitzers into action.

Within four hours, 2d Brigade converted Objective Tim into FOB Viper with enough fuel and ammunition on the ground to provide temporary support for four attack helicopter battalions. At 1430, two aviation brigades, launched from Viper, began to sequence the killing power of 64 Apaches into EA Thomas, a kill box plotted 145 kilometers farther east and directly north of Basrah. Two battalions of the 12th Aviation Brigade worked the north side of EA Thomas, while the 101st Aviation Brigade attacked the south with another two battalions. Apaches screened the northern flank of the corps sector en route to EA Thomas by shooting up anything that moved below with Hellfires, rockets, and chain-gun fire. During four hours of continuous attacks, the Apaches destroyed 14 personnel carriers, 8 multiple rocket launchers, 4 antiaircraft guns, 4 grounded helicopters, 56 trucks, and 2 SA6 radars. Significantly, the

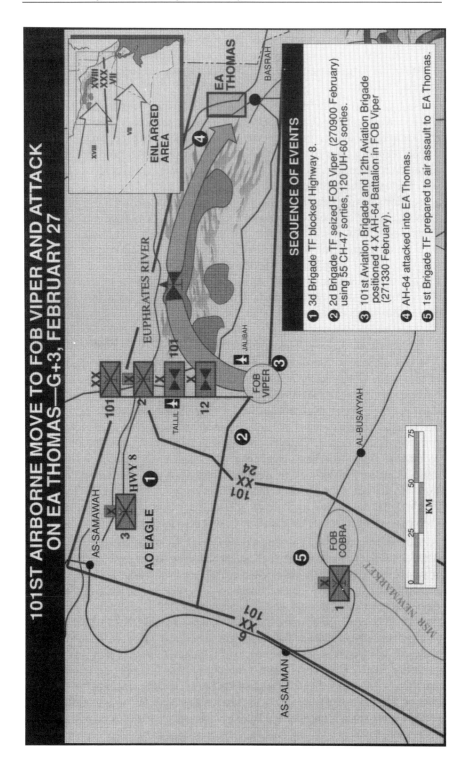

101ST AIRBORNE MOVE TO FOB VIPER AND ATTACK ON EA THOMAS—G+3, FEBRUARY 27

SEQUENCE OF EVENTS

1. 3d Brigade TF blocked Highway 8.

2. 2d Brigade TF seized FOB Viper (270900 February) using 55 CH-47 sorties, 120 UH-60 sorties.

3. 101st Aviation Brigade and 12th Aviation Brigade positioned 4 X AH-64 Battalion in FOB Viper (271330 February).

4. AH-64 attacked into EA Thomas.

5. 1st Brigade TF prepared to air assault to EA Thomas.

Apaches did not find a single tank moving through EA Thomas.[56] Either the Iraqis had not yet arrived in the EA, had already passed through it to the north, or were hiding inside the town. Later satellite and U2 imagery would show that a large number of Iraqi armored vehicles were clustered south of Basrah as late as March 2, 1991, implying that they and others arrived there after Peay's deep attack.

The pace of the operation was so intense that ammunition and fuel began to run low. Two days of bad weather had delayed the delivery of supplies forward into Iraq, so 30 cargo-carrying Chinooks were obliged to return to the main bases in Saudi Arabia for sustenance, a round-trip of more than 800 kilometers, or roughly the distance from New York City to Boston. Each Chinook ferried either 8 tons of ammunition or 2,000 gallons of fuel in a circuit of at least five flying hours. Still, the flow was barely enough to feed the hungry Apaches. As darkness fell, a ground convoy arrived with more supplies to link Viper to FOB Cobra.

The operation into FOB Viper demonstrated the overwhelming advantage accrued to the side best able to exploit the aerial dimension to support ground maneuver. By flying low and slow and by maintaining constant close-up observation of the ground, the 101st maintained control over an area of Iraq 160x380 kilometers, or roughly the size of the state of Massachusetts.

24th Infantry Division: G-Day Plus 3, 0500

With the 101st astride the Iraqis' last route of retreat, the 24th pushed eastward to eliminate Iraqi forces near FOB Viper. McCaffrey's main effort was 2d Brigade's attack on Jalibah Airfield with 1st Brigade making a supporting attack down Highway 8.

McCaffrey knew that the remainder of the campaign for his division would be a full-throttle rush eastward. Without a tight rein, momentum generated by such a huge force could get quickly out of control. To keep his force under control, he created a series of parallel boundaries aligned on Highway 8 and another series of perpendicular north-south phase lines that would allow him to dress his formation periodically before continuing. Thanks to GPS, he was able to link his phase lines to map north-south grid lines. The resulting division operational plan for the move east looked like an enormous gridiron.

At 0500, five battalions of artillery poured massed fires into the objective for an hour. While the prep was going in, TF 1-64th Armor and TF 3-69th Armor took up firing positions to the southwest and began to systematically destroy an understrength T-55 battalion from firing positions well outside the range of the obsolete Iraqi tanks. As the tanks of TF 3-69th Armor established their firing positions, C Company came under mortar and small-arms fire. In response, a tank from the company crossed the boundary into TF 1-64th Armor's sector to engage a dummy tank position. The remainder of the platoon followed, firing on what they believed were MTLBs and tanks. Although the 3-69th commander, Lieutenant Colonel Terry Stanger, called for a cease-fire to sort out the confusion, it was too late. Three Bradleys from TF 3-15th Infantry had been struck, killing two soldiers and wounding eight others. Later, TF 3-15th Infantry swept through the airfield, firing 120mm and 25mm rounds at anything that moved. The shock effect of the artillery and the speed of the American combined-arms assault overwhelmed the defenders. By 1000 the field was secure. The Iraqi armored battalion had lost all of its vehicles. The attack also destroyed 14 MiG fighters abandoned by the Iraqi air force.[57]

At 1300 McCaffrey continued the attack east with three brigades, leaving the 197th Infantry Brigade behind to clear Tallil Airfield with an on-order mission to follow and support the rest of the division. The 1st Brigade moved along the north side of Highway 8. The 2d Brigade, now past Jalibah, attacked in the center, and the 3d ACR marched on the southern flank near the VII Corps boundary. With an Apache battalion covering, the 212th Field Artillery Brigade and the division's own division artillery preceded movement with a series of planned fire strikes. The division moved out across a 50-kilometer front with more than 800 combat vehicles.

Just east of Jalibah along Highway 8, the division encountered huge logistics and ammunition storage sites. Elements of the al-Faw, Nebuchadnezzar, and Hammurabi Republican Guard Divisions continued to pop up in scattered enclaves on both sides of the highway. Whenever possible, McCaffrey's lead battalions bypassed every obstacle to maintain momentum. Drivers pushed their Bradleys and Abrams to speeds exceeding 40 miles per hour. Enemy artillery tried to react, but the attack moved so fast that the Iraqi gunners were never able to adjust fires rapidly enough to catch up to the advancing columns. Iraqis who showed no will to resist were bypassed; those who fought, died. Destroyed vehicles littered the roadway as the 24th overran more than 1,300 ammunition bunkers and nearly 5,000 Iraqi soldiers.

The fast-paced attack east strained the "Victory" Division's support structure to the breaking point. Operating out of his forward tactical command post, McCaffrey quickly outdistanced his communications. Although he could talk with his forward units on FM radio, he could reach his main command post and XVIII Airborne Corps only through TACSAT. Farther south, 24th Division logisticians attempted to keep up with the frantic pace of forward units by establishing a forward base along Highway 8 near Battle Position 102. Critical fuel and ammunition did not arrive forward until the night of February 27. Resupply vehicles, able to

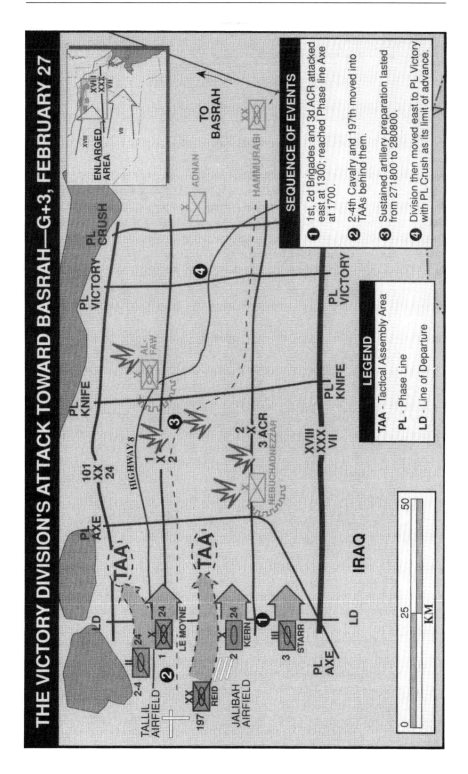

THE VICTORY DIVISION'S ATTACK TOWARD BASRAH—G+3, FEBRUARY 27

SEQUENCE OF EVENTS

1. 1st, 2d Brigades and 3d ACR attacked east at 1300; reached Phase line Axe at 1700.

2. 2-4th Cavalry and 197th moved into TAAs behind them.

3. Sustained artillery preparation lasted from 271800 to 280800.

4. Division then moved east to PL Victory with PL Crush as its limit of advance.

LEGEND

TAA - Tactical Assembly Area

PL - Phase Line

LD - Line of Departure

average about 10 to 15 miles per hour, continually fell behind. For the logisticians, the entire war had been a game of catch-up.[58]

XVIII AIRBORNE CORPS: G-DAY PLUS 3

[See Figure 5-5, "Ground Operations—G+3, Wednesday,
February 27, 2400 Hours," at the back of the book.]

General Luck moved his tactical command post forward along Highway 8 to oversee the corps' final move to seal off the KTO. McCaffrey would continue the corps' main effort and Luck gave him the additional firepower of the 18th Field Artillery Brigade. The additional artillery gave the "Victory" Division 9⅓ artillery battalions, or 4.5 artillery tubes per kilometer along its 50-kilometer front. Luck also shifted an Apache battalion from the 12th Aviation Brigade to the 24th. McCaffrey ordered the 197th Infantry Brigade east from Tallil to become the division reserve. He planned to continue the attack eastward at 0500.[59]

As for the 101st, General Peay had suspended his high-tempo Apache attacks into EA Thomas north of Basrah. He had been unable to get the fire support coordination line extended farther out and targets had proved fewer than anticipated. In any case, Peay's pilots were so exhausted from the four hours of attacks into Thomas that they could no longer fly safely. With Luck's concurrence, Peay planned to air-assault his 1st Brigade into EA Thomas the next morning. Following a proven sequence, if Peay could get forces on the ground along this highway, the Republican Guard's last escape route would be severed. The final act for XVIII Airborne Corps was put on the shelf, however, when at 0145, February 28, the corps received the first indication of a cease-fire.

CEASE-FIRE

VII CORPS: G-DAY PLUS 4, EARLY MORNING

[See Figure 5-6, "Ground Operations—G+4, Thursday,
February 28, 2000 Hours," at the back of the book.]

The on-again, off-again cease-fire order also affected VII Corps. To finish the battle, Franks had intended to execute his double envelopment at 0500, with the 1st Cavalry in the north and the 1st Infantry Division in the south. The 1st and 3d Armored Divisions would press forward in their zones, as would the British 1st Armoured Division. This plan was never fully executed. Franks informed the heavy divisions that the cease-fire would take place at 0500 and issued guidance concerning rules of engagement. Those orders soon changed when Yeosock called the VII Corps tactical command post shortly after 0200 and relayed news that Schwarzkopf had delayed the cease-fire until 0800. The CINC wanted a

General Franks, center, with three fingers of the VII Corps armored fist on March 6, 1991: Generals Funk, 3d Armored; Rhame, 1st Infantry; and Griffith, 1st Armored. Not shown are Generals Smith and Tilelli and Colonel Holder.

major offensive action mounted before that time to destroy as much of the enemy as possible. Franks alerted Colonel Hitt's 11th Aviation Brigade for another Apache strike in the direction of the town of Safwan but changed the order to retain unity of command in the 1st Infantry Division sector. VII Corps was unable to contact General Rhame directly since he was forward commanding from an M-1 tank. Instead, Colonel Cherrie called General Carter and relayed the order for the "Big Red One" to continue the attack to the east and to get Apaches to attack toward Safwan. At 0400 Franks issued an order for the divisions to continue the attack. An ARCENT order to secure the crossroads at Safwan with ground forces never reached the 1st Infantry Division, causing major frustration later when Schwarzkopf mistakenly believed the crossroads were under US control. The other divisions on or near Phase Line Kiwi would continue to use that control measure as a limit of advance.

The attack began at approximately 0600. A 45-minute preparation from 8-inch and 155mm howitzers and MLRS rocket launchers preceded the 1st Armored Division's attack. By 0615 all units were advancing, but a report of a unit receiving friendly fire froze all movement between 0645 and 0705. Even as the divisions closed on their objectives, the 1st Infantry Division would clearly not reach the crossroads at Safwan before the cease-fire. The Apaches combed the area and found some Iraqi soldiers but few vehicles. At 0723, VII Corps ordered a temporary cease-fire.

At the time of the cease-fire, the 1st Armored Division was just short of the Kuwaiti border, having destroyed more than 100 tanks and armored personnel carriers in a cataclysmic final hour of combat. The 3d Armored Division was along Phase Line Kiwi, and the 1st Infantry Division had combat units a short distance south of the Safwan crossroads and as far east as the Kuwaiti coast. The British 1st Armoured Division also succeeded in reaching the coast. The corps immediately assumed a hasty defensive posture as it began to refuel and refit the combat units.

XVIII AIRBORNE CORPS: G-DAY PLUS 4

With the order to cease fire and establish defensive positions, General Luck was now faced with a number of Iraqi military formations reluctant to withdraw behind the military demarkation line. He issued orders to avoid combat if at all possible in accordance with CENTCOM's rules of engagement, but he permitted his commanders to take whatever measures necessary to protect their forces while compelling the Iraqis to withdraw.

Commanders directed their battalions to approach Iraqi positions in battle formation. If the Iraqi units held their ground, American officers would go forward to tell the Iraqis to fall back. Sometimes the audacity of the Coalition leaders was enough.

When the menace of a massed ground attack failed to convince the Iraqis to comply with Coalition demands, commanders reinforced the threat with air power. A flight of A-10s or Apaches poised just overhead usually sufficed to deter all but the most recalcitrant Iraqi leaders. Despite their bravado, the Iraqis had witnessed more than enough destruction and were unwilling to hazard yet another dose. Nonetheless, some intrepid Iraqi Republican Guard units needed more than demonstrations.[60]

24th Infantry Division: G-Day Plus 4

The cease-fire proved particularly brief for the 24th Infantry Division. Over the next 24 hours, the 24th moved eastward to positions along Phase Line Victory with its reconnaissance elements out as far as Phase Line Crush. At Phase Line Victory, Colonel LeMoyne ordered the 1st Brigade to halt and hold a series of parallel positions running generally north to south. A parallel road only 2 kilometers to the front of LeMoyne's brigade separated his main defensive line from the bulk of the Hammurabi Division. The road was important to the Iraqis because it was the most convenient remaining route of escape for the Hammurabi north to safety deeper inside Iraq.

Tanks of the Hammurabi Division were located south of Basrah on March 1, the day before the Rumaylah Oilfield fight. Note that the unit still displayed excellent field discipline.

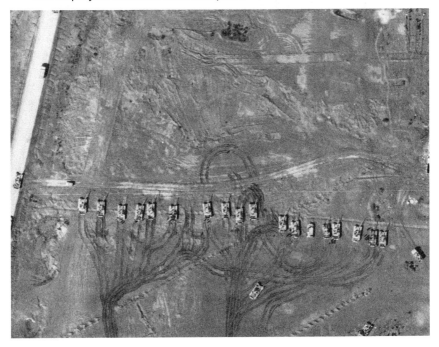

1st Brigade, 24th Infantry Division: G-Day Plus 4 to G-Day Plus 6

For the next two days, the 1st Brigade continued to receive sporadic artillery fire. Most of it fell among the scout platoons of TF 2-7th Infantry, the most forward of the brigade positions. The isolated fire was little more than a nuisance, and at first LeMoyne believed it was just coming from Iraqi artillery units that had not gotten the word to cease fire. But early in the morning on March 2, scouts reported receiving RPG and Sagger fire. This direct fire was a clear violation of the cease-fire terms and LeMoyne did not hesitate to respond in kind. After a short firefight, TF 2-7th Infantry scouts captured an enemy infantry squad responsible for some of the mischief.

Any doubt concerning Iraqi intentions was erased later in the morning when LeMoyne's scouts reported an endless column charging northward across the division front and deliberately firing at 1st Brigade forward elements as it moved. More than 200 T-72s and BMPs, accompanied by an equal number of support vehicles, clearly told LeMoyne that the Hammurabi were making a run for the causeway, the most direct route out of the Rumaylah oil fields and the Basrah pocket. Saddam needed his best armor to crush the spreading rebellion inside Iraq.

LeMoyne held every tactical advantage. If he could block off the narrow 2.5-kilometer causeway with artillery-fired mines, he could then call in Apaches to ravage the stalled column and finish off the enemy with an armored assault. Helicopters from 2-4th Cavalry took up aerial battle positions on the north end of the causeway, blocking escape. Meanwhile, Lieutenant Colonel John Floris, the brigade fire support coordinator, called on three M-109 self-propelled 155mm howitzer battalions, an 8-inch battalion, and an MLRS battalion to fire a combination of scatterable mines and DPICM on the causeway and main body of the Iraqi column. As the artillery began to fall on the convoy, the Iraqi vehicles scattered in all directions.

Those who fled west on Highway 8 ran smack into LeMoyne's two mechanized infantry battalions where they were killed or captured or forced to scurry back to the causeway. The cavalry and artillery destroyed many of the Hammurabi vehicles fleeing north. At the rear of the stalled column, Iraqi vehicles tried to break away back to the south only to be crushed by a continuous and impenetrable wall of artillery. To the east, about 200 Iraqi armored vehicles that had not yet crossed the cease-fire line remained unengaged. Another 200 enemy combat vehicles were already safely across the Euphrates River outside the division's protective zone.

At 0900, McCaffrey reassigned Lieutenant Colonel Tom Stewart's 1-24th Aviation to LeMoyne's control. In less than an hour, Stewart's 18

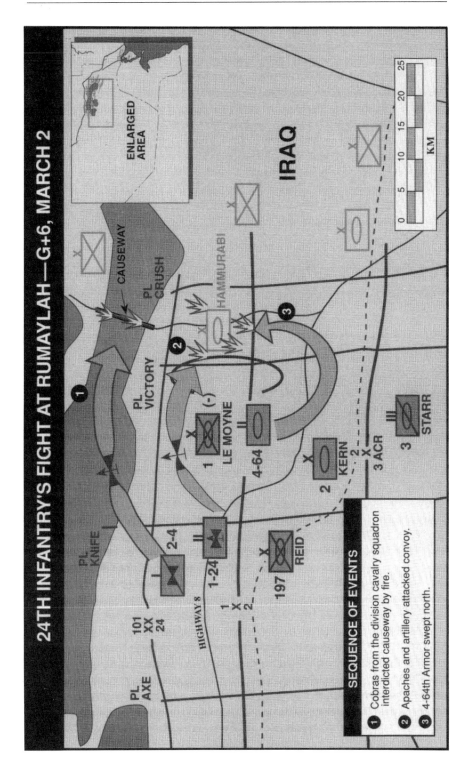

24TH INFANTRY'S FIGHT AT RUMAYLAH—G+6, MARCH 2

ENLARGED
AREA

IRAQ

PL
AXE

101
XX
24

PL
KNIFE

HIGHWAY 8

PL
VICTORY

PL
CRUSH

CAUSEWAY

HAMMURABI

2-4

1-24

197

REID

LE MOYNE

4-64

KERN

3 ACR

STARR

SEQUENCE OF EVENTS

1 Cobras from the division cavalry squadron
   interdicted causeway by fire.

2 Apaches and artillery attacked convoy.

3 4-64th Armor swept north.

KM
0   5   10 15 20 25

Apaches approached on-line from the east and methodically destroyed 102 vehicles with 107 Hellfires.

The entire Iraqi column was a mass of desperate Guardsmen. Some had fled when the artillery and the Apaches arrived. Others steadfastly remained at their vehicles, stalled along a 15-kilometer stretch of road, and continued to fight. To end the fight, LeMoyne ordered Lieutenant Colonel Craddock's 4-64th Armor to swing well to the south of the column and then attack up the road, rolling up the Hammurabi all the way to its lead element at the tip of the Fish Lake Causeway. As the Abrams advanced, they slammed silver bullets into every undamaged armored vehicle. The toll was devastating. Over 185 armored vehicles, 400 trucks, and 34 artillery pieces lay burning in the swath cut by the 24th Infantry. Only 40 armored and 200 wheeled vehicles limped to the east toward Basrah while LeMoyne's brigade policed up hundreds of prisoners. Certain they would no longer threaten the Coalition, LeMoyne let these vehicles go. Thousands of footprints in the killing zone were evidence that most of the Iraqis had escaped before their vehicles were destroyed.

MILITARY VICTORY

A military force reaches its culminating point when continued combat operations—offensive or defensive—risk defeat in detail because of losses, resupply shortfalls, simple exhaustion, or growing enemy strength. Campaign plans strive to force the enemy to pass beyond his culminating point first. It can be a close-run race as it was in the October '73 War, with the outcome hanging in the balance to the last bloody moment, or it can be more distinctly linked to a catastrophic event such as the bombing of Japan in World War II. In the Gulf, CENTCOM never reached its culminating point. Despite the fact that many combat units were nearing exhaustion after days of uninterrupted fighting and moving, CENTCOM could have sustained operations considerably longer. The Iraqis, on the other hand, reached their culminating point when the Republican Guard was destroyed. Without the Guard's power and mobility, Saddam could not stop the Coalition. Schwarzkopf's correct assessment of the Guard as the Iraqi center of gravity assured overall victory once the Guard was eliminated as a viable threat. That moment was reached by midnight, February 27, when al-Rawi realized the magnitude of his defeat at the battle of Wadi al-Batin and ordered an immediate withdrawal of the remnants of the Republican Guard out of the KTO to positions designated for the defense of Iraq.[61] With the exception of the Hammurabi Armored Division, the majority of the remaining Guard armor had already reached or passed through the Basrah sanctuary en route to positions well inside Iraq. The 24th Infantry Division's blocking action along Fish Lake Causeway eliminated a brigade of the Hammurabi. After that fight, the remainder of the Hammurabi would slip away through Basrah. As many as one-third of the Guard's T-72s made it out of the KTO. The same was generally true for the regular army.

To some extent the Iraqis benefitted from the gap that grew between the two corps as VII Corps swept east and XVIII Airborne Corps reduced enemy resistance in the Euphrates Valley. The two-corps attack against the Republican Guard that ARCENT envisioned turned into a sequential affair with the XVIII Airborne Corps trailing Franks' VII Corps. By 1300 on the 27th, lead elements of the 1st Armored Division were almost 50 kilometers ahead of XVIII Airborne Corps. But the Adnan, Nebuchadnez-zar, and al-Faw Republican Guard Infantry Divisions north of VII Corps were little threat to VII Corps' flank, and as XVIII Airborne Corps turned east, most of their units escaped north across the Euphrates or turned back to Basrah.

The time to kill Saddam's armor was before it reached the Basrah pocket, but once al-Rawi ordered a withdrawal, the chance to do so was fleeting. The night of the 26th, when the 11th Brigade Apaches worked over the 10th Armored Division, presented the best window of opportu-nity to eliminate the bulk of the Iraqi armored forces that eventually escaped. Both VII and XVIII Airborne Corps worked Apaches as deep as allowed on the 27th. Significantly, Peay's Apaches did not destroy a single tank in four hours of daylight attacks on EA Thomas just north of Basrah, suggesting that the bulk of the Iraqi tank elements had not yet reached that far north. Meanwhile, Franks' Apaches took a steady toll of Iraqi tanks through most of the day on the southern and western approaches to Basrah. The decision to leave everything east of the 20 Easting to air power rather than mount a series of Apache attacks against the retreating armor gave the Iraqi tanks the opportunity to run a rather porous gauntlet and seek sanctuary within the Basrah pocket. Close examination of the "Highway of Death," created by the Coalition air forces along the main road from Kuwait City to Basrah, showed the vast majority of the de-stroyed vehicles to be trucks, cars, and buses looted from the Kuwaitis, none of which were capable of off-road movement. Saddam's armor, able to fan out across the desert, merely sidestepped to the east and retreated into Basrah.[62]

Given the Coalition's need to minimize civilian casualties, the Repub-lican Guard and regular armored forces were safe from air attack once inside Basrah. The only way to have stopped the escape of Iraqi armor at that stage would have been to completely seal the theater by closing all exits by air or by blocking them with ground troops. An air assault by ground combat forces into EA Thomas was not tactically feasible until the 28th. With more than 20 bridges and causeways leading out of the KTO, cutting them all and keeping them cut from the air proved impossible. By

March 1, Republican Guard armored and mechanized units had reached as far north as al-Quarnah, almost 100 kilometers north of Basrah. These units were not fleeing in disorder; their march order was disciplined. As they halted, tanks dug dispersed revetments with 360-degree security. They were leaving one fight to join another against the Shia and Kurds. To have reached so far north on the 1st, the Guard armor had to have moved into Basrah on the 27th, if not the 26th.

The weather played a hand by interfering with air interdiction against the bridges. During the ground operation, the weather was the worst the area had experienced in 14 years. Even before the air operation began, the Iraqis had pre-positioned pontoons, barges, and extension bridges to offset the effects of bombing against their transportation network. Once the war began, Iraqi engineers worked furiously and effectively. Under cloud cover and rain, they quickly built by-passes around damaged bridges or bulldozed causeways across the relatively shallow rivers. On March 1, the Rumaylah Causeway was operational as was at least one bridge inside Basrah. Given the poor weather and inability to see them with overhead systems, the bridges were probably in service during the night of the 27th. Only that would explain the Republican Guard's presence at al-Amarah, 200 kilometers north of Basrah, on March 2.

That said, the Iraqi military machine that sputtered out of the Basrah pocket was still a beaten army. In the next few weeks, its fight against the Shia and Kurdish insurgents proved to be a close-run race. As in the past, Saddam's Republican Guard proved its loyalty to the regime by leading the fight to crush the rebels. However, the Republican Guard was but a shadow of its former self. Forced to reconstitute, the Guard stripped its regular army brethren of the best equipment, reducing even many regular heavy divisions to shells. Six months after the campaign, the 5th Mechanized Division, the Iraqi attacker at Khafji, surrendered in mass to Kurdish rebels in northern Iraq. As for the Republican Guard, some of its units were beyond help. Obliterated by Franks' VII Corps, the Tawakalna Mechanized Division was deactivated.

In 41 days of air operations culminating in a lightning 100-hour ground battle, the Coalition had utterly crushed the Iraqi military machine, liberating Kuwait from its occupiers. While the Marines, the "Tiger" Brigade, and the Arab Coalition forces had rolled over Fortress Kuwait, ARCENT had unhinged the Iraqi defense of the KTO with the XVIII Airborne Corps and VII Corps' Great Wheel. General Luck had reached out and strangled the Highway 8 lifeline to Saddam's forces. General Franks had ridden roughshod over the Republican Guard, destroying the center of gravity of Saddam's defense of the KTO in a ground war that was all but over as General Griffith closed on Medina Ridge.

Notes

1. Combat lifesavers are soldiers with other duties who have received training in advanced first aid. They are not intended to replace combat medics, but serve to stabilize injured soldiers until they can receive medical attention. Once trained, combat lifesavers are issued the same medical kit bag used by medics.

2. Tom Carhart, *Iron Soldiers*, to be published by Pocket Books. Copyright 1993 by Tom Carhart. All rights reserved.

3. XVIII Airborne Corps Operations Log, February 25, 1991.

4. Sean D. Naylor, "Flight of Eagles," *Army Times*, July 22, 1991.

5. 101st Airborne Division (Air Assault) After-Action Command Report, Operation Desert Shield/Storm, June 13, 1991, pp. 45-47.

6. 101st Airborne Division Commander's Narrative, February 24, 1991, pp. 1-5.

7. 101st Airborne Division After-Action Report, pp. 49-50.

8. *Ibid.* pp 50-52.

9. VII Corps Command Report, Volume 11A, Annex A-G. Contains the Executive Summary of 1st Infantry Division's participation in the campaign. See also Lieutenant Colonel Gregory Fontenot, "The 'Dreadnoughts' Rip the SADDAM Line," *Army*, January 1992, pp. 28-36, for a battalion commander's view of the ground war.

10. VII Corps Command Report, Volume I. Although the Executive Summary and the Historical Narrative describe events, a better source is Enclosure 2 to the Executive Summary which contains a "Combat Operations" briefing that describes, by day of battle, the plan for the day, the read on the enemy, and the decisions taken at the end of each period.

11. Colonel Johnnie Hitt, "Desert Storm Tactical Vignettes: Emergency Resupply of 2d ACR," undated, p. D-3.

12. A task force is a temporary combat organization established under a normal battalion headquarters that has a mix of combat arms, usually armor and infantry. For example, an armor battalion and an infantry battalion in the same brigade might swap two companies, creating two balanced task forces each with two armor and two infantry companies. In contrast, a battalion composed of a single combat arm is never referred to as a task force. A task force might have two companies with the same alphabetical designation. To avoid confusion, such companies are usually identified in full, giving their alphabetical letter and type unit as in Bravo Tank or Bravo Mech. If a battalion commander so desires, he can cross-attach platoons at the company level to create "teams."

13. VII Corps Artillery After-Action Review, undated; VII Corps Artillery, "Concept of Fires, Operation Desert Saber."

14. Jim Tice, "Coming Through, The Big Red Raid," *Army Times*, August 26, 1991, p. 20.

15. Lieutenant Colonel David W. Marlin, "History of the 4th Battalion, 37th Armored Regiment," unpublished manuscript, April 12, 1992, pp. 249-279.

16. VII Corps Battlefield Reconstruction Study, "The 100-Hour Ground War, The Failed Iraqi Plan," April 20 1991, pp. 101-103, 108-109.

17. *Ibid.* pp. 110-111.

18. *ARCENT MI History,* Chapter 8, Section VII, Annex A, Appendix 3, Desert Read 007-91, 513th MI Brigade message 242300Z February 1991.

19. *Ibid.* Desert Read 009-91, 513th MI Brigade message 250900Z February 1991; Stewart memorandum.

20. HQ 1st Armored Division, "1st Armored Division in Operation Desert Storm," April 19, 1991, hereafter cited as *1st Armored Division.*

21. Colonel Daniel J. Petrosky and Major Marshall T. Hillard, "An Aviation Brigade Goes to War," *Aviation Digest,* September/October 1991, p. 56.

22. *Ibid;* Carhart.

23. Inspector General for General Doctrine and Training, Ministry of Defence, *Operation Granby: An Account of the Gulf Crisis 1990-91 and the British Army's Contribution to the Liberation of Kuwait* (London: Ministry of Defense, 1991); Operation Desert Sabre-Objective Summary, Tab 1 to Appendix 3 to Annex J to HQ 1st (UK) Armoured Division 202/26/22 G3 Plans, March 25, 1991.

24. Armored vehicles are equipped with a number of vision blocks, which are similar to periscopes in function. They allow drivers, gunners, and vehicle commanders to see outside in several directions while "buttoned up."

25. This timing is according to Major Toby Martinez, General Franks' aide, who personally booked the call.

26. 24th Infantry Division (Mech) After-Action Report, June 19, 1991, JULLS Report No. 52154-15005, p. 14.

27. *Ibid.,* JULLS No. 52155-37544, p. 19.

28. 24th Infantry Division History, pp. 9-10.

29. *Ibid.* p. 17.

30. *Ibid.* pp. 17-18.

31. Interview with Major General Barry R. McCaffrey, February 27, 1992.

32. 24th Infantry Division History, pp. 9-10; 24th Infantry Division, *The Victory Book, A Desert Storm Chronicle,* ed. Margot C. Hall (Fort Stewart, GA: December 1991), p. F5.

33. Telephone interview with Major Kent Cuthbertson, fire support officer, 1st Brigade, 24th Infantry, June 19, 1992.

34. 24th Infantry Division History, pp. 19-20.

35. XVIII Airborne Corps, "Phase IIID Operations to Destroy the RGFC Positional Defense in Place (CONPLAN Ridgeway)," undated, distributed on February 26, 1991, p. 3.

36. This information, quoted in *Soldiers* magazine, was from the debrief of the luckless commander.

37. Major Mark Hertling, "Downed Pilot," 1st Armored Division Vignettes, undated.

38. Carhart; 1st Armored Division.

39. Hertling, "Combat Lifesaver"; Private First Class Tammy Reese, "Combat Medic," 1st Armored Division Vignettes.

40. Interview with Major General Paul Funk, June 1992; Historical Overview of the 3d AD in the Persian Gulf War.

41. 1st Brigade, 3d Armored Division, "History of the Ready First Combat Team, 1st Brigade, 3d Armored Division, November 1990 thru 22 March 1991."

42. Lieutenant Colonel John F. Kalb, "Investigation Into the Combat Action Involving TF 4-32 Armor Scouts on 26 February 1991"; Steve Vogel, "The Tip of the Spear," *Army Times*, January 13, 1992, p. 16.

43. Major General Paul Funk, "Investigation of Possible Fratricide by 3d Armored Division Units," 16 March 1991; Vogel.

44. 2d Brigade, 3d Armored Division, "Operation Desert Shield, December 1990 thru 27 February 1991."

45. HQ 1st Infantry Division, "Chronological Summary of Events," March 26, 1991.

46. Colonel David Weisman, "Informal Investigation of the Night Attack Conducted by 3d Brigade on 26-27 February 1991," March 10, 1991.

47. Interviews with Colonels Stan Cherrie and Johnnie Hitt and Lieutenant Colonel Terry Johnson.

48. Carhart; 1st Armored Division.

49. Captain Christopher Shalosky, "Bradley Master Gunner," 1st Armored Division Vignettes.

50. Lieutenant Colonel Edward Kane, "Tanker Perfection," 1st Armored Division Vignettes.

51. 1st Armored Division; interview with Colonel V.B. Corn, June 23, 1992.

52. "Scout Platoon," 1st Armored Division Vignettes.

53. Major Mark W. Maiers' written statement, March 2, 1991, AR 15-6 Investigation directed by Colonel Douglas H. Starr, investigated by Captain David Jacquot, SJA, February 27, 1991.

54. AR 15-6 Investigation Information Paper, June 17, 1991.

55. AR 15-6 Investigation.

56. 101st Airborne Division (Air Assault) After-Action Report, p. 57.

57. 24th Infantry Division, *The Victory Book*, pp. 98-100. BDA figures came from XVIII Airborne Corps battle log dated February 27, 1991.

58. 24th Infantry Division History, p. 20.

59. *Ibid.* pp. 22-23.

60. CENTCOM ordered a suspension of offensive operations with instructions to establish defensive positions along a line of demarkation in occupied

Iraq. Nonhostile Iraqi forces were to be allowed to withdraw, but under the rules of engagement, Coalition forces could defend themselves if attacked.

61. Ala Lafta Musa, "Why Was the Ground Attack Against the Republican Guard Moved Up a Whole Day?" *Al-Quadisiyah* (Iraqi army newspaper), March 9, 1992, p. 4.

62. *AUSA Green Book*, October 1991, p. 290, shows a JSTARS scope image of the Iraqi withdrawal routes parallel to the north-south highway from Kuwait City to Basrah, the "Highway of Death."

Chapter 6

RESTORING CALM AFTER
THE STORM

First Lieutenant Craig Borchelt's scout platoon, having led his battalion, the 3-37th Armor, through the ground war, now had orders to secure Safwan for the cease-fire talks between General Schwarzkopf and the defeated Iraqis. As Borchelt drove into the town, his senses, sharpened and on edge after five days of combat, were almost overwhelmed by the surreal and foreboding scene that greeted him. The town's silence was a dramatic counterpoint to the recent violence evidenced by devastated buildings and the deathly company of corpses strewn among destroyed T-62 tanks and MTLB armored personnel carriers. The only signs of life were occasional wild dogs and ravenous farm animals attacking garbage, bodies, and abandoned food rotting on the cluttered roads. Curiously bright metal objects, some cylindrical and others shaped like silver softballs, beckoned to the unwary. Each was an unexploded but fully fuzed bomblet requiring only a careless touch to add more carnage to the macabre scene.

Borchelt and his scouts, picking their way cautiously through the deadly obstacles, emerged on the northwestern edge of the town. Across a mile-wide expanse of onion and tomato fields, they could make out the familiar shape of Republican Guard T-72 tanks poised with main gun tubes pointed toward Safwan. Through binoculars, Borchelt could see Iraqi crewmen clad in undershirts leisurely smoking and pointing indifferently at the unexpected sight of American armor emerging from the outskirts of town.

Borchelt's contemplation of the bizarre standoff was suddenly interrupted when his radio operator reported that the mortar platoon had located a lone remaining family consisting of a woman and her four nephews and nieces. As the news was reported, Borchelt's somber mood changed; out of this wasteland, a sign of hope still existed. From the hardened warrior emerged a powerful instinct to preserve life.

The repulsion of war often transforms instincts from killing to compassion. Soldiers, who just hours before had destroyed a half-dozen Iraqi tanks in close combat, "adopted" the frightened Iraqi family. The woman explained that the children's mother had been brutally beaten, raped, and killed because the father, who was eventually murdered, had refused to join the Iraqi army. Iraqi soldiers had also beaten the aunt so badly that she suffered multiple contusions and a badly fractured arm. Captain Craig Simons, the battalion surgeon, set the woman's broken arm and treated the children while the battalion executive officer, Major Thomas Connors, and the mortar crewmen scrounged food, water, and clothing from on-board supplies.

Word of humanity in the midst of war spreads quickly. These simple humanitarian acts soon began to multiply as townspeople reappeared, first in ones and twos, and later by the thousands, all seeking help from these least expected benefactors. Such scenes were to be repeated in the days ahead as the Iraqi regime's war against the Kurds in the north and the Shiites in the south forced the US Army into humanitarian operations for which it was ill-prepared yet quite willing to perform. Meanwhile, just 7 kilometers northwest of Borchelt's scout platoon, VII Corps units worked feverishly to set up the airfield for the forthcoming peace talks.

CEASE-FIRE TALKS AT SAFWAN

Just before 1100 on March 3, Schwarzkopf landed at Safwan airfield in a flight of three Blackhawks escorted by six Apaches. Schwarzkopf jumped from the Blackhawk with General Franks in trail, and as they strode briskly to the tents set up for the cease-fire talks on the northeast edge of the airstrip, they passed a big sign that said, "Welcome to Iraq, Courtesy of the Big Red One." General Rhame's division had set up the negotiation site with an array of Apaches, Abrams, and Bradleys to represent the might of the Coalition. Cameramen ran to catch up with the fast-paced CINC as he pushed his way through the crowd of soldiers and civilians lining his path. Multicolored flags, a wide variety of uniforms, and civilians in Arab garb lent something of a carnival air to the bright Sunday morning. Two Apaches hovered overhead as the Iraqi delegation, riding in American vehicles flying white flags emblazoned with the Moslem red crescent, inched toward the tent.

Negotiations began across a wooden table with Schwarzkopf and Coalition officials on one side and the Iraqi contingent sitting uncomfortably on the other. After a perfunctory hour, the Iraqis emerged smartly

General Schwarzkopf confronted Iraqi representatives with Coalition cease-fire demands.

and departed more quickly than they had arrived. Schwarzkopf then took up a position on the strip where he could address the crowd. Raising his booming voice over their murmurs, Schwarzkopf announced that the Iraqis had accepted all of the cease-fire terms and that Coalition prisoners would be repatriated in the next several days. After praising Coalition soldiers for their decisive victory, he fielded a couple of questions, but the excitement of the moment drowned out most of his responses.[1]

The war was technically over. No further fighting would occur within the boundaries of Coalition-held territory behind the newly established line of military demarkation. However, until the details of the UN armistice were resolved, Coalition forces would remain in Iraq and Kuwait to protect and defend against any further Iraqi aggression. As Schwarzkopf's flight took off to return to the Kuwait City Airport, the hard work of keeping the victims of war alive continued.

Wars never end cleanly and this one was no exception. The cease-fire occurred more quickly than anyone had expected. The postwar process that had existed only in concept was now imminent. Literally overnight the Army found itself flexing an entirely different set of operational muscles. Staffs still exhausted from 100 hours of combat were suddenly inundated with the details of enforcing the cease-fire provisions. Combat soldiers from forward divisions formed demolition and search teams to find and destroy hundreds of thousands of tons of Iraqi ammunition, abandoned vehicles, and pieces of equipment scattered across thousands of square miles of desert. Even before Schwarzkopf and the Iraqi delegation had finished at Safwan on March 3, troops had begun "smelling the barn," while the media, politicians, and loved ones in the United States picked up the drumbeat to return their soldiers home. Conditions at Saudi ports and airfields complicated the situation. While some units were still unloading in Dhahran, many others were unsure if they even had a redeployment destination. VII Corps units were variously told they would disband, return to Germany, or transship as a complete unit back to the United States. The same dilemma applied to equipment. No one was sure at the time what would remain in theater or what would be processed for return. International events further confused the situation when a full-scale rebellion in Iraq and Saddam's subsequent brutal repression of the Kurds and Shiites caused a mad scramble to improvise assistance programs to address the terrible circumstances.

HUMANITARIAN ASSISTANCE

Humanitarian assistance is not a new mission for the Army, nor is it confined to wartime. During World War II and in Korea and Vietnam, soldiers provided humanitarian aid to those in need, often at considerable personal sacrifice. In the mid-seventies, the Army played a major role in the reception and resettlement of thousands of Vietnamese boat people. During the early eighties, the Army helped to resettle Cuban refugees. Later in that decade, soldiers provided such diverse humanitarian assistance as firefighting in the national forests of the American northwest and disaster relief in the 1989 Loma Prieta earthquake, and in Hurricanes Hugo, Andrew, and Iniki.

Civil affairs (CA) units, both Active and Reserve, are composed of soldiers who possess the skills necessary to organize humanitarian assistance operations. They assist military commanders in establishing temporary military government, including administration and assistance in restoring the basics essential for survival in occupied or conquered territories. This rather unique specialty started formally during the World War II occupations of Germany and Japan. By the early sixties, most civil affairs units were assigned to the Army Reserve because most of the skills needed by civil affairs units, such as public education, utilities engineering, and city management, are more closely related to civilian than military professions.[2] This fortuitous fit between military needs and civilian means has produced part-time CA soldiers who are also full-time school principals, fire chiefs, waste management engineers, foreign service officers, lawyers, and police officers.

The only Active CA battalion, the 96th from Fort Bragg, North Carolina, arrived in theater between August and November 1990. Lieutenant Colonel Ted Sahlin, its commander, organized his soldiers into CA teams of about five soldiers each. These soldiers put their valuable

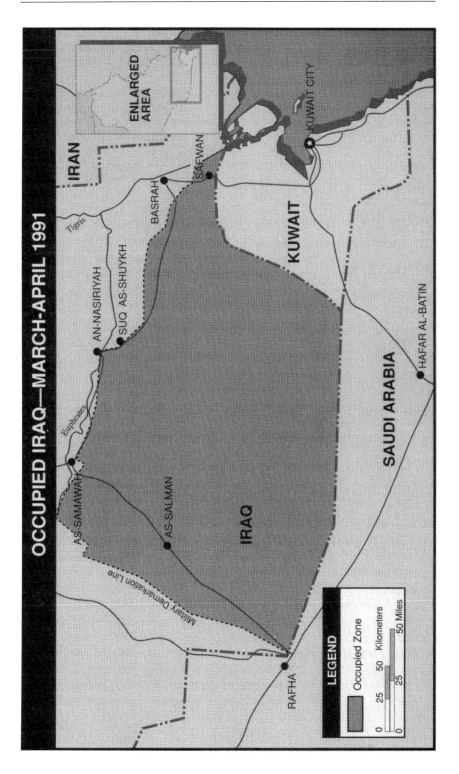

OCCUPIED IRAQ—MARCH-APRIL 1991

ENLARGED AREA

IRAN

KUWAIT CITY

BASRAH

SAFWAN

Tigris

AN-NASIRIYAH

SUQ AS-SHUYKH

KUWAIT

HAFAR AL-BATIN

Euphrates

AS-SAMAWAH

AS-SALMAN

SAUDI ARABIA

IRAQ

Military Demarkation Line

RAFHA

LEGEND

Occupied Zone

Kilometers

0   25   50

0   25   50 Miles

cultural skills to work by assisting the Saudis with host-nation support, tactical reconnaissance, and liaison between Arab and US headquarters.[3]

As ARCENT planning transitioned to the offensive, the civil-military needs, and subsequently the civil affairs troop list, changed dramatically. The liberation of Kuwait under the best of circumstances would require substantial recovery assistance for an undetermined period. Even if Coalition forces planned to attack through sparsely populated areas, dislocated civilians were sure to be in the battle area. Therefore in early December, Colonel James Kerr, Jr., the ARCENT civil-military operations officer, asked for a full slate of civil affairs units for ARCENT forces. He requested that the first CA units to deploy be those with a Southwest Asia regional focus.[4] Mobilization of Reserve civil affairs units continued into January, but because much of their equipment arrived late, many did not join their assigned tactical units until just before G-Day. Considering the fact that the 352d Civil Affairs Command, ARCENT's CA headquarters, would not fully close in theater until January 24, Yeosock made the decision to decentralize most civil-military operations down to corps level or below.

Soon after hostilities ended, Shiites in unoccupied southern Iraq revolted to depose Saddam's Baathist supporters. North of Baghdad, the Kurds reignited their centuries-old struggle against the Baghdad government. After some initial setbacks, Saddam's forces regrouped and began a brutal program to repress both revolts. In full view just across the military demarcation line, American forces watched helplessly as Republican Guard soldiers killed thousands of their countrymen. In northern Iraq, the Kurds fled north to seek refuge from the marauding Iraqis in the mountains of eastern Turkey and western Iran. In the south, refugees fled to Kuwait and Saudi Arabia, toward the Americans.

SOUTHERN IRAQ

Refugees fleeing an-Nasiriyah, near the military demarcation line in the Euphrates River Valley, began a steady migration toward the sanctuary of the 82d Airborne Division in the XVIII Airborne Corps area of operations. They had heard that in addition to food, water, and medical treatment, the Americans would provide protection from Iraqi reprisal. The refugees settled at an abandoned Polish construction camp near Suq as-Shuykh, about 35 kilometers southeast of an-Nasiriyah. Soldiers named the settlement Camp Mercy. Depending on the intensity of the fighting north of the military demarcation line, Camp Mercy's population ranged from as few as 200 to as many as 6,000. In wide-eyed horror, the refugees recounted Saddam's atrocities against his own people. Stories emerged of mass executions, of family members dragged through the streets lashed behind tanks, and of patients and doctors murdered in hospitals.[5] From February 28 until March 24 when the 82d departed

Iraq, doctors and medics treated more than 1,100 refugees for maladies ranging from minor illnesses to gunshot wounds. Airborne soldiers distributed more than 35,000 meals. Army trucks and helicopters returned several hundred dislocated Kuwaitis to the border near Safwan and transported non-Kuwaiti and non-Iraqi refugees to a camp established by the Saudis in Iraq, just across the Saudi border near the town of Rafha. Although they encouraged the refugees to return to their homes in Iraq, the paratroopers' kindness and aid continued to attract many thousands to the American sanctuary.[6]

In VII Corps the story was similar. At Safwan, the family that the 3-37th's mortar platoon had adopted was quickly joined by refugees who began to trickle in on March 3. Safwan was the first safe town refugees encountered as they fled from the horrors of the fighting in Basrah, 45 kilometers to the north. As the Republican Guard became more brutal, the refugee problem became more acute. At first his superiors could not provide Lieutenant Colonel David Gross, the battalion commander, much help. He had not received orders to establish a permanent refugee center, so he had to improve the efficiency of his temporary sites with the few soldiers he could spare.

Many of the refugees were residents of Safwan and its surrounding area, but some were former residents, though not necessarily citizens, of Kuwait. In addition, numbers of Egyptians, Pakistanis, and Palestinians had been trapped in Iraq since August and wanted out. Kuwaitis manning border checkpoints south of Safwan would not allow non-Kuwaitis to flee Iraq to the relative sanctuary of Kuwait and Saudi Arabia. Thus, thousands of refugees who had lived in Kuwait before the war were trapped in the Safwan limbo. Among the saddest cases were the Kuwaiti dissidents who, after escaping the horrors of Basrah prison, walked barefoot from Basrah to Safwan. For six months, they had subsisted on one bowl of rice and a cup of water per day. Malnourished, dehydrated, and sick, they arrived in Safwan to recount horrific stories of torture and cruelty. Some of their friends and families had been hanged from electric wires thrown over utility poles. Others had been beaten, starved, or tortured with electric shocks for not cooperating with their Iraqi captors.

The task of providing even basic necessities soon began to overwhelm the battalion. Realizing the enormity of the growing problem, Gross instructed Doctor Simons to move his battalion aid station forward to Safwan. He also requested and received additional food and water from his forward support battalion. At that point, ARCENT's Mobile Command Post was located in Kuwait City under the command of Brigadier General Robert Frix who dispatched his G5, Lieutenant Colonel Don Saffold, to Safwan to assess the situation. Clearly, the refugees' most pressing need was for food and water, and Frix directed Saffold to purchase a large quantity of basic foodstuffs and bottled water and push it forward to the hastily established camps. Prior to receiving civil affairs support, Gross had to exploit talent where he found it. He used Captain Ernest Marcone, one of his operations officers who had prior experience in Special Forces, to assess, screen, and organize the refugees into manageable groups of about 20 to 30 each at two sites established by the scout and mortar platoons. Whenever possible, Marcone arranged the groups around a single extended family or nationality. One of his primary tasks was to teach these city dwellers how to maintain basic outdoor sanitation.[7]

As the Safwan population grew, the number of injuries caused by unexploded ordnance rose alarmingly. Hundreds of thousands of Iraqi mines remained buried throughout the area, many in unmarked mine-fields. Time after time, unsuspecting children who wandered in the fields to play stepped on the small, hard-to-detect plastic antipersonnel mines. Equally threatening were the artillery- and air-delivered bomblets that had landed in soft sand at odd angles and had failed to detonate. Highly unstable, these enticingly shiny and palm-sized bomblet munitions attracted curiosity. A child needed only to touch a bomblet for it to explode. The terrible sight of dead and maimed children was devastating to the soldiers. They distributed flyers warning residents of the danger and instructing them to report the locations to Coalition linguists at the food or medical sites. Explosive ordnance disposal soldiers and engineers then located and destroyed as many of the mines and bomblets as they could.

Despite their best efforts, the soldiers in Safwan could not eliminate the problem. On March 19, four Iraqi children were the victims of yet another detonated cluster bomb. A nearby ground surveillance radar team from the 101st Military Intelligence Battalion hastily mounted their M113 armored personnel carrier and tore through the bomb-cluttered streets to aid the children. Although two of the children had died almost immediately, it looked as if the other two could be saved. The radar team, consisting of Sergeant Lynn Wey, Specialist Richard Trevino, and Private First Class Paul Harmon, concentrated their combat lifesaving skills on those two. Despite their efforts, another died. But once stabilized, the surviving child was treated by Doctor Simons and evacuated to an American hospital in Saudi Arabia.[8] Nor were Iraqi civilians the only casualties of the mines and unexploded ordnance. On March 2, Major Mark Connelly, an Army doctor, was killed when he stepped on a land mine.

The number of refugees at Safwan continued to grow. In March more than 3,000 dislocated civilians crowded into Safwan and more were on the way. ARCENT quickly directed the establishment of a more permanent camp nearby.[9] On March 19, the 1st Brigade, 3d Armored Division, commanded by Colonel William Nash, replaced the "Big Red One" in the Safwan area and assumed the mission of humanitarian relief, this time with more authority and resources. Nash divided his humanitarian assistance operation into three phases: initial relief, sustainment and program enhancement, and site closure once the last refugees were taken to Saudi Arabia. Nash's soldiers focused on distributing food and water, providing emergency medical care, and getting organized for the rest of the mission. Lieutenant Colonel John Kalb, who commanded 4-32d Armor, secured a site inside the town for a second medical facility. The 404th Civil Affairs Company, commanded by Lieutenant Colonel Kenneth Brier, an insurance executive in civilian life, organized a bulk-food distribution site in a nearby school and enlisted the help of town leaders in Safwan to induce the locals to assist in the distribution effort. Additional military police, doctors, and interpreters augmented the brigade.[10]

Refugees quickly overwhelmed Safwan's original refugee sites and by late March the armor battalion had to establish another. They located it south of the town at an abandoned Indian construction camp compound about a kilometer north of the Kuwait-Iraq border. As Kalb's battalion led the way, Brier's soldiers assisted in running the site since none of the regular soldiers had any experience in such work. As additional refugees flooded the new site, soldiers searched and registered them and provided food, water, tents, blankets, shoes, and clothing. Camp organization was a continuous problem because many refugees were unwilling or unable to help themselves. Local elders, assisted by civil affairs soldiers, established eight subvillages within the site, each of which contained groups of refugees of similar status. All single males lived in one subvillage and widows without families in another. Most subvillages were occupied by groups of extended families. Life support consisted of a medical aid station and water and food distribution points. A trash pit and slit-trench latrines completed the site. Soldiers from the 22d Chemical Company and the 12th Engineer Battalion combined efforts to repair a pump, which eventually allowed more than 20,000 gallons of water to be pumped into storage tanks at Safwan. Military police and Kalb's soldiers patrolled the area to keep law and order among potential troublemakers. Although conditions were not what anyone desired, the refugees were grateful for the Americans' care. Chief Warrant Officer Ben Beaoui, an Arabic-speaking physician's assistant with the 122d Main Support Battalion of the 3d Armored Division, told of his astonishment when an Iraqi woman knelt down and kissed his foot after he treated her seriously ill baby. He recalled later that as each patient left his makeshift facility: "They all said thank you and thank God for the Americans."[11]

The growing refugee problem at Safwan was being repeated elsewhere in occupied Iraq. The population of as-Salman, the largest village in west-central Iraq, numbered about 4,000 during better times. Its water well and its position astride a major paved north-south highway allowed the village to prosper. On G-Day, B Company, 96th Civil Affairs Battalion, arrived on the trail of the French 6th Light Armored Division and found the town virtually empty. The townspeople began to trickle back after the cease-fire, but many key citizens whose services were essential to restore the town to normal operation, such as doctors and engineers, did not return right away. Therefore, Major Jack Knox, commander of B Company, became "mayor" of as-Salman. One of his CA soldiers, Captain Joseph Lindland, got the as-Salman water system working. By no means an expert, Lindland traveled more than 100 kilometers to Rafha to learn from the waterworks supervisor how water pumps and generators worked. When as-Salman's non-Iraqi itinerant workers returned to their jobs, trash collection and street cleaning resumed. By mid-March the town, under the leadership of its American mayor, was running as well as could be expected.[12]

On March 23, VII Corps assumed the occupation mission for all of southern Iraq. The 11th Aviation Brigade picked up the French 1st Combat Helicopter Regiment and relieved the French 6th Light Armored Division on the western flank. The 11th's civil affairs team, led by Army Reserve Lieutenant Colonel John Meyers, took charge of the as-Salman humanitarian effort. Just as Safwan provided a funnel for refugees in the east, as-Salman and Rafha provided a conduit in the western area of the occupation zone. Meyers and his civil affairs team organized a program to deliver food, water, and medical treatment each day to a series of temporary checkpoints spread along 200 kilometers of the north-south highway between the Saudi border and the military demarcation line at the Euphrates River in the north. The checkpoints moved often to keep up with the shifting flow of refugees. Meyers borrowed a brigade helicopter to overfly the highway daily to count refugees and to coordinate delivery of supplies.[13]

The as-Salman endeavor, born of necessity, was never intended to be a permanent solution. CENTCOM knew that sooner or later the Saudi government would have to shoulder more responsibility as VII Corps soldiers began to leave. By the end of March the Saudis had established a large, semipermanent refugee holding facility, known as Rafha I, just inside the Iraqi border. Before the end of March, Rafha I contained more than 17,000 refugees. All were non-Saudis denied entry into Saudi Arabia. The funnel of refugees was controlled by a government wrestling with itself to establish a mechanism to accept more foreigners where no mechanism had previously existed.

The permanent cease-fire agreement with Iraq called for Coalition forces to depart Iraq by the end of April and for the United Nations to assume responsibility for occupied Iraq. However, before Coalition forces could withdraw, thousands of dislocated civilians in Safwan, as-Salman, and Rafha I had to be moved out of Iraq to protect them from Iraqi retribution. After General Yeosock's personal intervention, the Saudi

"Help on Wheels," HQ 2d Armored Division (Forward), Rafha, Saudi Arabia, April 1991.

government agreed to build and operate a permanent refugee camp just inside Saudi Arabia.[14] It was not indifference to the plight of their fellow man that motivated the Saudis, but rather their desire to avoid the creation of a "Gaza Strip" inside their border. Construction of the permanent camp would require about six months, but by then American soldiers would be gone. To get the refugees out of Iraq sooner, Brigadier General Gene Blackwell's 2d Armored Division (Forward) built a temporary camp, Rafha II, just inside Saudi Arabia adjacent to the proposed site of the permanent Saudi refugee camp.

Rafha II was a large facility, about 1 by 1.5 kilometers, surrounded by a concertina barbed wire fence and capable of accommodating 30,000 refugees. Engineers placed 13 rubberized 3,000-gallon fabric tanks known as SMFTs (semitrailer-mounted fabric tanks) on top of sand berms around the perimeter of the camp. Gravity-fed water flowed from the SMFTs to faucets and shower facilities inside. A perimeter road ringed the camp and another bisected it. On each side of the bisecting road, refugees were grouped by family and organized into subcamps known as "counties." Each county had its own water, showers, and latrines.

The Saudis insisted that dislocated civilians be registered and resettled in Rafha II before they would assume responsibility for camp operations. The International Committee of the Red Cross, the Red Crescent, and the United Nations High Commission for Refugees were among the nongovernmental organizations ready to assist the Saudi government in camp administration. Dislocated civilians began arriving at Rafha II almost immediately upon its completion. Some drove cars, but most traveled by military and civilian trucks and buses. American military police

331

3d Armored Division soldiers assisted refugees from a Safwan camp as they arrived by Air Force C-130 at Rafha.

registered the refugees and gave each an identification card and an MRE with a bottle of water on arrival.

Soldiers from the lst Brigade, 3d AD, moved dislocated civilians from Safwan to Rafha II in late April and into early May. Safwan refugees who chose to go to Saudi Arabia were making a lifelong decision never to return to Iraq. Those who wished to return to their homes in Iraq were offered gasoline and all the food and water they could carry. When Safwan closed on May 7, the "Ready First" soldiers had registered more than 24,000 people and distributed more than 979,000 meals, 173,000 cases of bottled water, and 1,136,000 gallons of water. In addition, division doctors and medics had treated more than 23,400 patients.

Blackwell's soldiers processed a total of 20,000 civilians into Rafha II—4,000 a day at the peak of the operation.[15] When the flood of refugees threatened to overwhelm Rafha II, Blackwell built a smaller camp, Rafha III, to provide a short-term holding area. On May 10, Blackwell handed over responsibility for the camps to the Saudis.

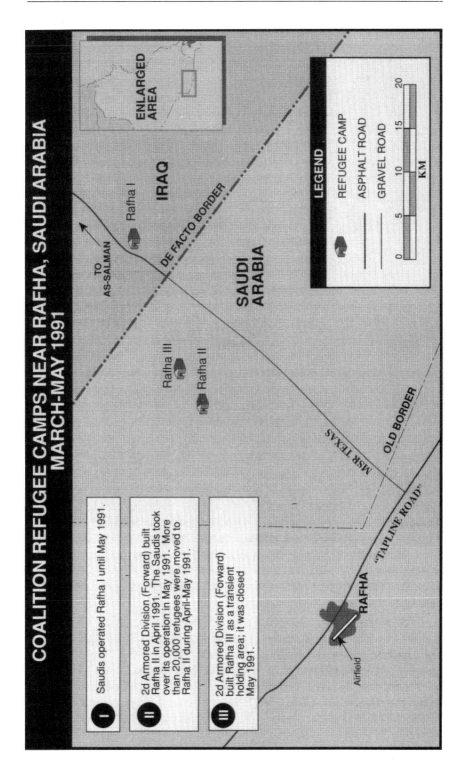

COALITION REFUGEE CAMPS NEAR RAFHA, SAUDI ARABIA
MARCH-MAY 1991

I Saudis operated Rafha I until May 1991.

II 2d Armored Division (Forward) built Rafha II in April 1991. The Saudis took over its operation in May 1991. More than 20,000 refugees were moved to Rafha II during April-May 1991.

III 2d Armored Division (Forward) built Rafha III as a transient holding area; it was closed May 1991.

ENLARGED AREA

IRAQ

Rafha I

TO AS-SALMAN

DE FACTO BORDER

Rafha III

Rafha II

SAUDI ARABIA

MSR TEXAS

OLD BORDER

"TAPLINE ROAD"

RAFHA

Airfield

LEGEND

REFUGEE CAMP
ASPHALT ROAD
GRAVEL ROAD

0 5 10 15 20
KM

More than 20,000 refugees occupied Rafha II, May 1991.

KUWAIT CITY

By its nature, the effort to save lives in occupied Iraq was an evolution-ary affair based on emerging needs. On the other hand, bringing Kuwait City back to life required a much more structured effort. A cornerstone of the President's Gulf War objectives was to restore the legitimate govern-ment of Kuwait. Once it became apparent that Saddam would not leave Kuwait without a struggle, the Bush administration accepted the reality that much of Kuwait City would be damaged, either by retreating Iraqis or by the liberating Coalition. Naturally, no one was more concerned about restoring Kuwait after the war than the Kuwaitis themselves. Other ▸than the "tanker" war with Iran in 1988, Kuwait had never faced such disaster.

In September 1990 the Kuwaiti government in exile had established the Kuwait Economic Recovery Program (KERP) in Washington under the direction of Fawzi as-Sultan, a Kuwaiti official of the World Bank. In October, the Emir had formally requested the President's support for the recovery effort. As a result, the Defense Department, in November, estab-lished the Kuwaiti Task Force (KTF) led by Army Reserve Colonel Randall Elliott. Elliott was particularly well qualified for the job. A career foreign service officer and an expert on the Middle East, Elliott was a personal friend of Edward Gnehm, the newly appointed American ambassador to Kuwait. As operations officer for the 352d Civil Affairs Command, Elliott had compiled a computerized data base with the names and civilian skills of each of the command's members. When the KTF was still a concept, Elliott had used his data base to identify 57 of its 63 potential members based on their particular civil-military skills. When it was time to organize his task force, Elliott had already located most of its eventual members and informally alerted them.

The KTF received planning assistance from the American-educated, mid-level officials of the Kuwaiti government assigned to the KERP. The Kuwaiti-American team calculated that after the war they would be required to care for 600,000 residents. Before deploying to the desert on January 26, Elliott's citizen-soldiers assisted the KERP in obtaining more than $558 million in contracts for goods and future services. More than 70 percent of the dollar value of these contracts went to American firms.[16] Once in Saudi Arabia, the KTF concentrated on organizing their short-term recovery efforts. The KTF and the KERP located their previously purchased supplies and organized a program for distributing them to Kuwait City residents. Kuwaiti officials then turned to the US Army Corps of Engineers because of its experience in responding to natural disasters. The Corps established the Kuwait Emergency Recovery Organization (KERO) under Colonel Ralph Locurcio to conduct damage surveys and administer reconstruction contracts. On January 14, 1991, DOD signed a $46.3 million foreign military sales agreement with the Kuwaiti government to assist in the restoration of facilities and systems controlled by the Ministry of Public Works, the Ministry of Electricity and Water, and the National Guard.

On February 15 Colonel Kerr and newly arrived Brigadier General Howard Mooney, commander of the 352d CA Command, briefed Yeosock and Frix on the plan for civil-military support in liberated Kuwait. To supervise the recovery effort, they proposed a combined civil affairs task force with Mooney in command. Yeosock agreed with the task force concept, but he placed Frix and the ARCENT Forward Command Post in command of the overall Kuwait recovery mission. Having been on the ground since August 1990, Frix was the right choice to coordinate the effort. Frix task-organized military units, such as engineers and logisticians, with Mooney's Combined Civil Affairs Task Force to form Task Force Freedom.

Lead elements of Task Force Freedom entered Kuwait City by ground and air in the early afternoon of February 28, immediately on the heels of the retreating Iraqi troops. The drive up the coastal road to the city past the destruction of the ground war and the burning oil-well fires in the darkened midday reminded them of Dante's description of the journey into the "ninth circle of hell."[17] Frix had elected to move the ARCENT

Forward Command Post, "Lucky Tac," and its signal, security, and support staff to Kuwait City as his base of operations. The KERO team entered Kuwait on March 4. Frix established his headquarters at Camp Freedom, a warehouse complex near the Kuwait International Airport. Relief efforts kept Task Force Freedom decisively engaged for more than two months. In addition to commanding the task force, Frix also directed the humanitarian assistance operations in southern Iraq.

Kuwait City was badly damaged but not destroyed. Although enemy soldiers looted everything movable, most of the buildings and infrastructure remained intact. Mooney and the KERO's damage assessment and survey teams conducted more than 1,260 inspections of hospitals, schools, and telecommunications centers to determine the extent of damage and to estimate the time needed to return them to normal operation. Based on Frix's priorities, soldiers first repaired essential facilities and functions, like food distribution centers and hospitals. They left other, less crucial facilities to be fixed later. Fortunately, food was not an immediate problem because residents had hoarded sufficient quantities to last until the local food distribution system got going again. Using contracted trucks, the Kuwaiti Task Force delivered bulk food and bottled water to neighborhood food centers where Kuwaitis then distributed it to families.

The Iraqis had stolen most of the equipment and supplies from medical facilities, but the buildings were intact and structurally sound. Kuwait City medical personnel received an unexpected bonus, compliments of the civil affairs soldiers working with VII Corps units in southern Iraq. First Lieutenant William Burke of the 418th CA Company, a police officer in civilian life, had led a small team into a bunker complex near Safwan. Moving cautiously and constantly checking for booby traps, Burke had stumbled onto an underground field hospital only recently vacated by the Republican Guard, complete with beds and equipment for about 60 patients. They found several bunkers loaded with medical supplies of every sort, including crutches, X-ray machines, wheelchairs, and literally tons of bandages. Burke had spent 12 of his childhood years in Saudi Arabia and could read the Arabic markings on the equipment and supply containers. He realized that most had been looted from Kuwaiti hospitals. For the next four days, Burke and his team made more than 20 round-trips by truck moving the precious supplies to the Ministry of Health building in Kuwait City.

The biggest problem Frix faced was to return Kuwait City to normal, and the first step toward this objective was to turn on the street lights. Smoke from burning oil fires had turned day into night and the resulting pall added to the pervasive sense of despair that gripped the city. For months the Kuwaitis had suffered the terror of rampaging Iraqis kicking in doors to loot and kill in the middle of the night. Lighted streets would symbolize an end to that terror. By March 27 the 416th Engineer

Command and KERO had restored enough generating capacity to produce more than 150 megawatts of power and the lights went on. Reluctantly at first, Kuwaiti citizens began to emerge from their homes to walk about freely at night. With lights and power on, the combined civil affairs task force turned its attention to restoring the city's electrical grid system, which had suffered significant damage.

To restore order, Major General Jaber al-Kahlid, the military governor of Kuwait City, immediately established martial law. Kuwaiti units that assisted in liberating the city were assigned among the 16 police stations, providing control and stability to the chaotic situation. Colonel Jesse Johnson, commander of CENTCOM's Special Operations forces, became Jaber's military advisor. US Special Forces soldiers who were still with Kuwaiti units began to expand their role beyond that of advising. With the help of Kuwaiti resistance fighters who remained in the city during the entire occupation, SOF soldiers cleared areas of booby traps and minefields and otherwise assisted in the recovery. Resistance members also guided Special Forces teams to key Iraqi headquarters buildings and torture sites. The teams collected and evacuated five truckloads of documents indicating possible violations of the Geneva Convention.[18]

Task Force Freedom, which operated until the end of April, was a tremendous success. During its tenure, not a single Kuwaiti died from lack of water, medical care, or food.[19] As the *New York Times* reported, "It is the American Army that has turned the electricity back on here, got the water running, cleared the highways of shrapnel and wrecked cars, hooked up those telephones that work, dredged the main port of Shuaiba and unloaded the ships, brought the drinking water and food, fixed the police cars, and fed the animals in the zoo."[20] Mooney's damage assessment and survey teams allowed Frix to focus his soldiers' efforts on the most pressing needs, and soldiers of both Active and Reserve components worked together to bring relief to the residents of Kuwait City.

The KERO surveyed and restored major infrastructure systems and facilities in Kuwait. It also worked on electrical substations, water mains, two seaports, the international airport, and more than 160 public schools and buildings, including police, fire, medical, ministerial headquarters, and defense facilities. In the first 10 months after liberation, the KERO managed $300 million in repair work done by major American and foreign construction firms. On April 8, Colonel Glenn Lackey, the Task Force G3, traveled to Riyadh to brief Schwarzkopf on Task Force Freedom's accomplishments. He passed on Frix's recommendation that the executive agency for restoration of Kuwait be shifted from CINCCENT to the Secretary of the Army fully 30 days ahead of the originally projected date. Schwarzkopf and the Secretary of Defense endorsed that action and set April 30 as the end date for the emergency phase of the restoration of Kuwait. Army Major General Patrick Kelly, commander of the Defense

Recovery Assistance Office, assumed responsibility for long-term reconstruction efforts in the city.

REDEPLOYMENT: RECOCKING THE FORCE

The ARSTAF, at the direction of Lieutenant General Reimer, the DCSOPS, had directed the 22d Support Command to start working on redeployment in December 1990. At the same time, Reimer directed the ARSTAF to draft a redeployment plan entitled "Reshaping the Army." The plan would preserve General Vuono's three vectors and provide for a comprehensive rearming and refitting of the Army's contingency force. It would maintain worldwide readiness while reshaping the Army. Continuing to shore up FORSCOM, Reimer assigned his assistant, Major General Tom Fields, to lead the ARSTAF effort. A team led by Colonel Randy Medlock briefed the blueprint for reshaping the Army to its 1995 base force endstate in theater and at FORSCOM in late February-early March.

On March 2, 1991, before the cease-fire talks and the restoration of Kuwait, CENTCOM issued ARCENT initial redeployment orders. The redeployment of US forces from Saudi Arabia would require 10 months to complete. According to Schwarzkopf's policy of "first in, first out," the first priority was to get XVIII Airborne Corps out of Iraq and back to the US to resume its worldwide contingency corps mission. The ARCENT plan was for VII Corps to relieve XVIII Airborne Corps until the final UN accords were complete. Luck's corps pulled out of Iraq and returned to Saudi Arabia to begin redeployment while Franks extended his forces to take over the entire occupied sector in Iraq.

ARCENT had to locate and gather all supplies and equipment in the theater for preparation and shipment to appropriate destinations. When VII Corps eventually cleared out of Iraq and redeployed, ARCENT would shut down the theater. The soldiers of the 22d Support Command had to close buildings, seaports, and airport facilities and turn them over to the Saudis. ARCENT established five redeployment assembly areas near seaports and airports in Saudi Arabia where Army units could prepare their equipment for storage and shipment and process their soldiers for flights back to the United States or Europe. Assembly areas at KKMC, Dhahran, King Fahd International Airport, al-Jubayl, and Doha, Kuwait, each had wash sites and provisional units to help soldiers clean and repair equipment. Once the equipment was ready, US Agriculture Department and US Customs inspectors certified that it met United States entrance requirements.

From the start the redeployment was not without problems. Inspectors contributed to the confusion among the soldiers preparing equipment for shipment, resulting in delays in loading. When the Department of Agriculture finally did begin certification on March 24, 1991, two weeks after

The homecoming parade in New York City rivaled World War II ticker-tape extravaganzas.

redeployment began, inspectors certified equipment for shipment one day, only to have different inspectors reject the same equipment the next day. The urgency displayed by government agencies in getting the troops back home was not matched in getting the equipment back. With the war over, USTRANSCOM reimposed peacetime rules for loading equipment in ships. Transportation operators at Saudi Arabian ports organized the loading to make maximum use of space rather than to meet unit load plans. As a result, some critical equipment, particularly things packed in shipping containers, did not arrive for months. All of these factors slowed the return of units to full combat readiness at their home stations.

Nevertheless, the same technology, management techniques, and inspired efforts of soldiers during the buildup also prevailed during redeployment. Military Airlift Command sent aircraft schedules and numbers from the United States to the 22d Support Command staff; they in turn planned and sent passenger schedules to affected units via satellite. At its peak, the command shipped 5,000 passengers out of Saudi Arabia each day. From March 2, 1991, to January 2, 1992, ARCENT shipped 541,429 soldiers and 1,928,000 tons of equipment and supplies back to Europe and the United States in 2,500 aircraft and 420 ships.[21] The last XVIII Airborne and VII Corps soldiers left Saudi Arabia on June 14 and August 15, 1991, respectively. The 22d Support Command, which Yeosock charged with running the redeployment, left Saudi Arabia on January 2, 1992.

Despite the challenges and interminable waiting, going home was filled with excitement for the returning troops. The first contingent, representing all Army units in the theater, boarded planes for the United States and Europe after a short departure ceremony in Dhahran on March 8, beginning a cycle of homecoming celebrations that would be repeated for many months. In a cathartic outpouring of national pride and appreciation, millions turned out for the welcome-home parades held in Washington, D.C., on June 8 and New York City on June 10. While these redeployment and homecoming events unfurled before the American public, humanitarian assistance continued unabated in the theater.

NORTHERN IRAQ

With Desert Storm headlines fading from the front pages of the newspapers, world attention focused on the plight of the Kurds in northern Iraq and southern Turkey. The Pesh Merga, a loose confederation of 10,000 Kurdish guerrillas, grasped the opportunity offered by Saddam's preoccupation with the more dangerous Shia rebellions in the south. In a matter of days, the Kurds seized the key cities of northern Iraq, including the oil production center in Karkuk, ousting the few Iraqi military left in the those towns. Their successes, however, were fleeting. They could not stand up to Saddam's Republican Guard, the remnants of which had escaped from Basrah to deploy to the north, fully supported by helicopter gunships and artillery. The Iraqi counterattack was at once vicious and indiscriminate, pushing the Kurds out of villages and onto the few roads through northern Iraq. Some fled because their homes were destroyed; most simply left out of fear of reprisal and mass extermination, sparked by memories of the recent past. The Iraqi army pushed these people north like cattle, packing them against the Turkish border.

The picturesque mountain region on the Turkish border with northern Iraq can be one of the most inhospitable areas in the world. High elevations, steep slopes, narrow, mostly unpaved roads limited to mountain passes and ravines, and a restricted water supply join the unforgiving climate, with its extremes of hot and cold, to create incredibly harsh conditions. Many Kurdish refugees forced to exist in the open on the

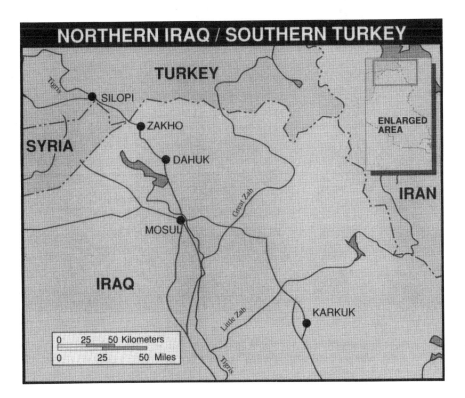

exposed mountainsides along the international boundary were dying at a rate of nearly 2,000 per day from exposure, starvation, dysentery, and Iraqi-inflicted gunshot wounds.

On April 5 President Bush announced that relief supplies would be sent to the area. Two days later, US Air Force MC-130 cargo planes began air-dropping the first relief supplies into the mountainous areas of northern Iraq. Within days, additional air and ground forces from the United States and a dozen other countries, along with more than 45 private relief organizations, moved to southern Turkey and northern Iraq. Many units in Saudi Arabia were alerted to assist; some, who were about to board planes for the United States, were simply diverted to Turkey. In Europe, other units were ordered to deploy from Germany and Italy to augment the force.

American soldiers played a prominent role in relieving the misery. On April 18, when the humanitarian mission's emphasis changed from air-drops to on-the-ground relief, Lieutenant General John Shalikashvili, deputy commanding general of US Army Europe, assumed command of Combined Task Force Provide Comfort. Shalikashvili's most immediate task was to stop the dying and stabilize the situation. He then needed to secure a safe area and assist the refugees in returning to their homes.

View from northwest to southeast near Zakho, Iraq, May 1991. Transit Camps 1, 2, and 3 were located in the broad valley beyond the nearest foothills.

Shalikashvili faced three major problems as he set about organizing the relief effort. First, despite the cease-fire, a large hostile Iraqi force presented a significant threat to Coalition troops in the area. Shalikashvili worked out informal rules of engagement to prevent armed conflict between the various Coalition forces and the Iraqis. In 17 recorded incidents when they were fired on by Iraqi troops, Coalition forces showed great discipline and restraint in not returning fire. Second, interoperability posed a major problem. Incompatible communications equipment and language differences would be overcome by extensive liaison, much as they had been during the war with Iraq. Third, Shalikashvili's planners were even more strapped for information about that region of northern Iraq than Schwarzkopf's were about southern Iraq when planning the Great Wheel. They would need to rely heavily on the British whose experience in the region was extensive.

Shalikashvili immediately set to work designating two task forces. Joint Task Force Alpha, commanded by Brigadier General Richard Potter, worked with civilian relief organizations to dispense humanitarian assistance to Kurds in the mountains. Joint Task Force Bravo, commanded by

Major General Jay Garner, opened the towns and cities of northern Iraq to provide a safe haven so refugees could go home.

Parachute drops got supplies to the mountain camps quickly but not very efficiently. Some bundles were lost on the steep slopes or damaged when dropped, and, unfortunately, some fell on the desperate refugees, killing or injuring them. Delivery was more precise by helicopter, but helicopter delivery required someone to build landing zones, coordinate ground transportation, and control distribution of the supplies. Within the next two weeks, three battalions of American Special Forces soldiers, part of Joint Task Force Alpha, moved into the mountain refugee camps to organize the resupply effort, improve the refugees' sanitation conditions, and provide basic medical care.[22] One of those soldiers was Major Lloyd Gilmore, commander of C Company, 2-10th Special Forces, whose company moved to the rugged mountains near Pirincinken along the Iraq-Turkey border.[23] Their camp was in a river valley about 4 kilometers long astride the border, wedged between two towering mountains. For eight months each year, including April, the area was completely inaccessible by road. Twenty thousand people, disorganized and dispirited, were crammed from the valley floor to the highest points in the surrounding mountainsides.

Described by the Green Berets as "Woodstock without music," the valley was almost too crowded to walk without stepping on someone. Dead animals, garbage, and human waste had turned the ground into a quagmire, fueling outbreaks of dysentery and cholera. A hastily dug graveyard, located at one end of the valley, grew steadily as 50 or more people a day were buried. Refugees were desperate for any form of shelter. The more fortunate threw blankets, plastic sheets, or used American parachutes over tree limbs to create primitive lean-tos and tents. The less fortunate lived in the open. To get the situation under control, Gilmore called the camp elders together as soon as he arrived. His team leaders met with the people, drank tea, and got to know them personally. Gilmore established a parallel hierarchy with the Kurdish elders by matching each of his team leaders with a Kurdish counterpart. Slowly, he added structure and organization to what had been a helpless mob.

A United Nations High Commission for Refugees representative monitored camp activities and provided expertise on refugee management. Nevertheless, the various nongovernmental agencies residing in the camp came to consider Gilmore as mayor of the project and leader of the total relief effort. Although their initial contacts were reserved, soldiers and civilian relief workers soon recognized that they were both dedicated to the same cause and eventually established a solid working relationship.

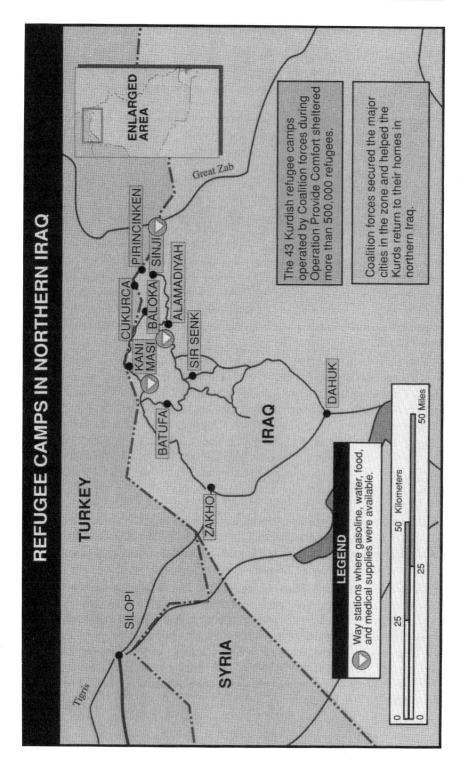

REFUGEE CAMPS IN NORTHERN IRAQ

The 43 Kurdish refugee camps operated by Coalition forces during Operation Provide Comfort sheltered more than 500,000 refugees.

Coalition forces secured the major cities in the zone and helped the Kurds return to their homes in northern Iraq.

LEGEND

Way stations where gasoline, water, food, and medical supplies were available.

Gilmore had to get the refugees to improve sanitation conditions, the cause of most of the health problems in the valley. The younger, weaker children, as well as older adults, were the most susceptible to disease and death, with 40 to 50 children dying each day, mostly from dysentery caused by impure water. The river that ran through the valley provided the only water for washing, cooking, drinking, personal hygiene, and sewage disposal. The farther downstream in the valley that a family lived, the greater the risk of disease. While some soldiers spent their first days in the camp building landing zones for delivery of supplies, others immediately began to teach the refugees rudimentary sanitation requirements such as boiling water and digging latrines.

By mid-April, additional supplies began arriving to support Gilmore's efforts. A key item was the World Health Organization kit, designed for disaster relief and refugee assistance missions. The kit contained enough medical supplies to treat about 10,000 people. For Gilmore, the most important item in the kit was the rehydration fluid. A very bad-tasting potion similar to a "super Gatorade," this liquid provided needed salts and minerals for the children, allowing them to survive the dehydration induced by dysentery. Complying with Potter's determination "to stop this dehydration of the kids," Gilmore directed his medics to begin treating the most severe, life-threatening cases.[24] A British doctor and nurse from the organization "Save the Children" focused on the most serious medical cases while acting as general consultants to the Special Forces medics. The doctor, long used to working with Third World medical staffs, soon gained respect for the diagnostic skills of the medics and began to treat them as colleagues of equal competence. Gilmore's medics found one three-year-old boy who was so small and malnourished that he hovered near death. Because he was too weak to swallow, the medics provided a dose of the "magic" fluid by introducing a tube into his stomach. The boy not only regained his strength within hours but lived to return to his family.

The combination of rehydration fluids, antidiarrheal medicines, boiling water, and the use of latrines seemed magically to stop the dying. The soldiers' morale rose as the horrors of the camp abated. American soldiers have always had a weakness for kids, and within days they became green-clad pied pipers walking about the camp with tiny, chattering entourages in tow. The soldiers knew that without their help most of the kids would have died. "It's a good feeling," said Sergeant Mike Conlon. "We know we're doing some good. We come back [to our base camp] at night, we're tired, we're smoked. But it's real, we can see the effect."[25]

Soldiers fed the refugees MREs, which, like most soldiers, the Kurds did not much like. Unfamiliar with the contents and not very thrilled with the taste, most Kurds refused to eat them once they were beyond the risk of starvation. About the same time as sanitation and health conditions

Medical supply delivery in northern Iraq during Operation Provide
Comfort, May 1991.

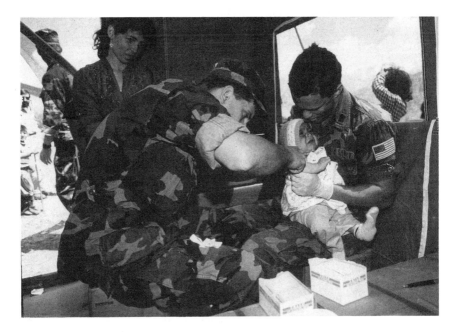

Army medics inoculated infants during Operation Provide Comfort.

improved, the soldiers began receiving and distributing bulk food such as potatoes, flour, sugar, rice, and cooking oil. The refugees could then prepare their own meals.

Potter's Joint Task Force Alpha soldiers, sailors, airmen, and marines, working with the nongovernmental organizations, performed organizational and medical miracles. Within 10 days of their arrival, most of the refugees in the mountains were healthy enough to go home. Conditions in the camps, although somewhat stable by late April, would only get worse as temperatures climbed and water sources dried up. So far the weather had cooperated. The moderate April climate kept the Kurds from freezing while snow melting in the higher elevations continued to feed water to the river. Although contaminated, water was at least plentiful and would remain so until the end of May. Insects, major carriers of disease, were not a significant problem. However, as the temperature rose, so would the potential insect problem. Gilmore realized that time was his greatest enemy.

Most refugees, however, were not willing to go home until they could feel safe from the hated Iraqi army. Refugees repeatedly told Gilmore that they would rather risk death through exposure in the mountains than return to certain death in their hometowns. While working to stop the dying and to reestablish stability, Shalikashvili simultaneously turned his

347

attention to establishing a security zone and getting the refugees safely to their homes. He tasked General Garner with securing areas of northern Iraq so that he could begin repatriation.

Garner arrived in Silopi, Turkey, on April 17 with five hand-picked officers. The American 24th Marine Expeditionary Unit (MEU), already at Silopi, provided the baseline organization for him to build Joint Task Force Bravo. The MEU had an aviation squadron, a battalion landing team, and a marine service support group. Also attached were a battalion each of British Royal Marines and Royal Dutch Marines. Joint Task Force Bravo grew, and within days Garner was commanding a combat force of soldiers, marines, airmen, and sailors from nine countries with the firepower of an army division. His staff, built upon the marines and his five American soldiers from Germany, represented a multinational and multi-Service collection of combat forces.

On April 19 Shalikashvili met with Iraqi military representatives in Zakho, Iraq, where he issued a rather dramatic demarche: Coalition forces would enter northern Iraq to create a security zone in order for the Kurds to return to their homes. Shalikashvili told the Iraqis that Coalition forces were on a humanitarian mission and were not looking for a fight. The Iraqis were ordered to withdraw their armed forces 30 kilometers south of Zakho, where their artillery would be beyond the range of the town. On the morning of April 20, American Marines airlifted into the vicinity of

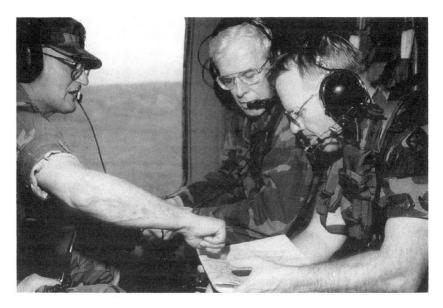

Lieutenant General Shalikashvili (left) discusses Provide Comfort security plans with SACEUR, General John Galvin (center), and Major General Garner (right) during a helicopter flight over northern Iraq.

Zakho and after careful negotiations between Garner and the Iraqi commander, the Iraqi soldiers withdrew. But playing a sly game of bait and switch, 350 Iraqi special police quickly showed up in town to replace them. The Kurds did not want the special police in their town, so Garner sent his British Royal Marines, supported by the American and Royal Dutch Marines, into Zakho to chase them out. Fresh from a tour of duty in Northern Ireland, the British commandos were most familiar with operations in urban areas. Although the situation was tense, the special police realized that the British had called their bluff and withdrew without incident. Dutch marines set up checkpoints around the town, allowing Iraqis to leave but denying non-Kurds entry into the town.

As more combat units arrived in Silopi, Garner expanded the security zone. Coalition forces under the command of British Brigadier Andrew Keeling extended Coalition control to the east by securing the town of Batufa on April 28. Four days later, Keeling's soldiers and marines secured Sirsenk and al-Amadiyah, both key Kurdish towns in the northeast portion of the security zone. A French brigade secured Suri on May 6, and by mid-May Joint Task Force Bravo controlled most of the Kurdish areas of northern Iraq, an area 70 by 160 kilometers in size. The major exception was Dahuk, normally populated by about 500,000 people. After a series of tense negotiations with Iraqi military officials in Dahuk, Shalikashvili, Garner, and the Iraqis agreed to a compromise, allowing both the Coalition and the Iraqis to occupy Dahuk. The Iraqis could maintain a small police presence there, but not the special police, and all Iraqi military forces would have to withdraw at least 6 kilometers south of the city. The Coalition agreed to provide 81 soldiers, most of whom would be engineers or civil affairs or explosive ordnance demolition specialists. These soldiers would provide a degree of security for international relief workers in the town and for the Kurds upon their return. By then foreign relief organizations were very comfortable working with the military and insisted that Coalition forces provide security in most areas.

Garner employed his own version of psychological warfare to keep the Iraqis honest. One of his commanders, Lieutenant Colonel John Abizaid, who had led A Company, 1-75th Infantry (Rangers) during Urgent Fury, drove his 3-325th Airborne Battalion Combat Team over hundreds of miles in the security zone. Encountering an Iraqi formation menacing the Kurds he was protecting, Abizaid told the Iraqi commander to withdraw or face destruction. Two A-10's roaring overhead punctuated his demand and the Iraqis hastened to withdraw. Garner, taking a page from such experiences, directed every aircraft, both rotary- and fixed-wing, to fly low and slow to produce as much noise as possible when in the security zone. Every day Coalition forces conducted overly dramatic rehearsals of their actual contingency plans, carefully staged to impress their Iraqi audience. Vehicles rushed about to generate all the noise and dust they could, and radio operators eschewed net discipline to keep up a steady stream of transmissions. The Iraqis, always prone to theatrics themselves, were impressed by this tremendous effort and chose to stay away.[26]

Once Zakho, Dahuk, and the other towns in the security zone were under Coalition protection, the Kurds felt safe enough to begin the long trip home. Although coordinating movement for 500,000 very eager people proved to be a challenge, the refugees made the journey in only a few weeks. To encourage the refugees to leave the mountain camps, Potter created a series of transient way stations along the Turkey-Iraq border. In his zone, Garner established a series of temporary refugee camps to be used by the Kurds as they traveled south.

Coalition engineers, under the command of Colonel Steve Winsor, helped provide for the refugees' basic need for sanitation and shelter by building latrines and other facilities, often using contractors for construction. Winsor sent a team into southern Turkey and northern Iraq to help establish relocation camps for Kurdish refugees coming down from their mountain sanctuaries. A corps contractor built 4,000 latrines on-site at Zakho and put them in service. Through $3 million in contracted projects, a small contingent of contractor personnel provided latrines, water, tanks, and workhouse tents to three refugee camps in the Zakho Valley.

In northwest Iraq, soldiers from the 418th Civil Affairs Company ran one of three transient refugee camps in the area. One of the CA specialists was Major Ronald Jelks, in civilian life a sales executive from Kansas City, Missouri. Jelks was the American mayor of Coalition Transit Camp Three, located in a yawning valley about 10 kilometers southeast of Zakho. As soon as they arrived on May 13, Jelks divided his group into sections responsible for camp administration, food distribution, water and sanitation management, camp security, and civilian labor coordination. Jelks had a diverse assortment of Coalition military units to assist him in running the subcamps he eventually established. One came under the control of US Marines, another under Army military police, and a third under an Italian airborne infantry battalion. A Dutch engineer battalion ran the fourth subcamp, and a Spanish airborne infantry battalion ran the remaining one. In 48 hours, Jelks had transformed a northern Iraqi wheat field into a functioning tent city. Dutch and American engineers constructed a road network and laid out the camp dimensions. Other Coalition soldiers began to dig latrines and mark locations for tents where Jelks expected the refugees to pitch their own temporary lodging. Jelks divided each subcamp into four "blocks," each containing 64 "zozans," with each zozan holding 12 tents.[27] The camp setup was something like an American KOA campground, so Jelks inevitably chose "Kampground of Iraq," or "KOI," as his logo. His men encouraged refugees to come to the camp, to stay as long as they liked, and then to move on toward their homes. The camps were not intended to be permanent.

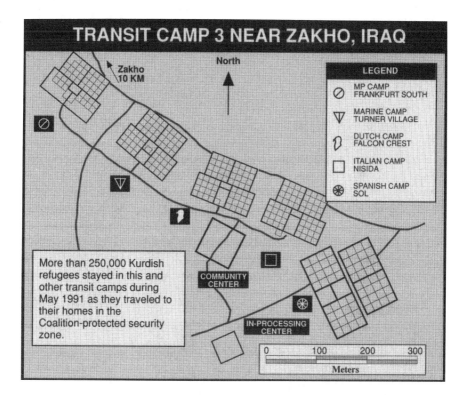

TRANSIT CAMP 3 NEAR ZAKHO, IRAQ

Zakho
10 KM

North

LEGEND

⊘ MP CAMP
FRANKFURT SOUTH

▽ MARINE CAMP
TURNER VILLAGE

⌂ DUTCH CAMP
FALCON CREST

▢ ITALIAN CAMP
NISIDA

✴ SPANISH CAMP
SOL

More than 250,000 Kurdish refugees stayed in this and other transit camps during May 1991 as they traveled to their homes in the Coalition-protected security zone.

COMMUNITY CENTER

IN-PROCESSING CENTER

0   100   200   300
Meters

Once the refugees began to arrive, Jelks' soldiers counted, medically screened, and placed them in one of the subcamps with members of their extended family or regional group. No fences surrounded the camp and the people were free to come and go. The work was grueling for the soldiers tending the campground, requiring usually 12 to 16 hours a day to take care of the 20,000 refugees living there.

Jelks established control by keeping communications open with both his Kurdish and Coalition partners and by holding daily meetings with the camp's leaders. He wanted to incorporate the Kurdish leadership and people as much as possible in day-to-day camp operations. When needed, French and Dutch military field hospitals provided medical support for Transit Camp Three, but by mid-May earlier epidemics had been checked. Only two refugees died during the three weeks that Transit Camp Three was open: a little girl from nonvirile meningitis and a 70-year-old man from a heart attack.[28]

By late spring the people in Gilmore's Pirincinken camp had started to return to their homes as well. The camp was remote, requiring most people to make a day-long walk down the rugged mountains to the main road in order to find cars and tractors that they had abandoned on the Iraqi side of the border. Those without cars rode in trucks driven by locally contracted drivers. Gilmore used helicopters to transport those who could not walk. Because some refugees feared Iraqi reprisals upon their return, United Nations representatives took several Kurdish leaders into the towns and villages to show that the Iraqis had departed and would not soon return. The word spread quickly and the exodus from the refugee camp, which started as a trickle in late April, turned into a flood within a week. By early May most of the 20,000 refugees had departed the Pirincinken camp.

Operation Provide Comfort was a success by any measure. American military organization and leadership held together a Coalition of forces even more disparate than that of Desert Storm. It consisted of armed forces from more than a dozen nations, along with thousands of civilians

Picture drawn by Umer-a-Sindi, a 10-year-old Kurd, in May 1991 and presented in gratitude to Major General Jay Garner, commander of Task Force Bravo.

from more than 60 organizations. The operation was executed with no prior planning or preparation. Civilian relief organizations, loosely organized under the auspices of the United Nations High Commission for Refugees, worked within areas secured by military units from many nations. Time was not available for fancy formal agreements, a fact recognized by military and civilians alike. Everyone focused on the tasks at hand: to stop the dying, to secure a safe haven for the Kurds, and to get them back to their homes before summer heat dried out the mountain streams and cut off the water supply.

GREAT SOLDIERS, GREAT PROVIDERS

Many of the skills and capabilities that make a great military force successful in waging brutal battle paradoxically serve equally well in relieving large-scale human suffering. Whether created by war itself or by natural disaster, the requirements to handle mass casualties, to feed, protect, and transport large numbers of people, and to restore order are adjuncts of military operations. Yet the transition from war to humanitarian relief is anything but automatic. In the absence of discipline, leadership, and moral restraint, soldiers, themselves brutalized by battle, have often terrorized the helpless populace of a defeated foe. Such is not the American way.

In the Gulf, consistent with the American way of war, soldiers fought the enemy tank-to-tank one day and then actively provided that same enemy lifesaving assistance the next. From chaotic Safwan to the choked camps of Rafha to the pathetic plight of the Kurds in the mountains of northern Iraq, Coalition forces fought to save thousands of lives in an effort that lasted much longer than the war. In some ways—certainly in the hearts of those served—the effects of this humanitarian support will also last longer than those of the war.

Notes

1. Lieutenant Colonel Terry Johnson, 11th Aviation Brigade, the air mission commander for General Schwarzkopf's flight to Safwan.

2. John R. Brinkerhoff, *Waging the War and Winning the Peace: Civil Affairs in the War with Iraq* (Washington: Office, Chief of the Army Reserve, August 1991), p. 10.

3. Interview with Lieutenant Colonel Carl T. Sahlin, commander, 96th CA Battalion (Airborne), November 20, 1991.

4. Interview with Colonel James T. Kerr, February 27, 1992.

5. John Kifner, "Iraqi Refugees Tell US Soldiers of Brutal Repression of Rebellion," *The New York Times*, March 28, 1991, p. A-1.

6. Interview with Major Randy Kolton, April 7, 1992.

7. Interviews with Lieutenant Colonel David Gross and Captain Ernest Marcone, 3d Battalion, 37th Armor, 1st Infantry Division, February 12, 1992.

8. Interview with Major Thomas Connors, executive officer, 3-37th Armor, 1st Infantry Division (Mech), February 12, 1992.

9. Interview with Major David Estes, S3, 4-32 Armor, 3d Armored Division, April 23, 1992.

10. Captain James P. Aiello, "History of the Ready First Combat Team (1st Brigade), 3d Armored Division, 20 March through 11 May 1991," and memorandum, AETV-TFC, "Humanitarian Relief Operations, HQ 3d Armored Division," undated.

11. Staff Sergeant C. Randy Piland, "American Troops Answer Iraqis' Call for Help," *Jayhawk*, April 9, 1991, p. 5.

12. Interview with Major Douglas Nash, B Company, 96th Civil Affairs Battalion (Airborne), November 20, 1991.

13. Interview with Colonel John Meyers, 354th Civil Affairs Brigade, March 27, 1992.

14. Interview with Colonel Joseph Molinari, March 9, 1992.

15. Meyers interview.

16. Brinkerhoff, p. 58.

17. Interviews with Major General Robert Frix, DCG, Third US Army, February 27, 1992, and Brigadier General Howard Mooney, CG, 352d Civil Affairs Command, July 14, 1991.

18. Interview with Colonel Jesse Johnson, commander, Special Operations Command Central, May 15, 1992.

19. Frix interview.

20. John Kifner, "US Army Doing the Work in Kuwait," *New York Times*, April 5, 1991, p. 10.

21. 22d Support Command After-Action Report, January 2, 1992, Vol. XII, p. 13.

22. Lieutenant Colonel Gordon W. Rudd's *Operation Provide Comfort, One More Tile on the Mosaic* (Washington: The US Army Center of Military History, undated) provides most of the overview material for this portion of chapter 6.

23. Interview with Major Lloyd Gilmore, commander, C Company, 2-10th Special Forces Group (Airborne), March 5, 1992.

24. John Kifner, "Green Berets Bring Food and Discipline to Kurds," *The New York Times*, April 25, 1991, p. A-13.

25. *Ibid.*

26. *Ibid.*

27. Interview with Major Ronald Jelks, 418th Civil Affairs Company, April 8, 1992.

28. *Ibid.*

Chapter 7

CONTINUITY AND CHANGE

Specialist Fourth Class Steven Slocum, his khakis rumpled after the 17-hour flight from Tan Son Nhut, looked pensively through the window of his "freedom bird" as it dropped low over Travis Air Force Base, California. Twelve months earlier and only one month after his eighteenth birthday, he had joined the 1st Battalion, 327th Airborne Infantry, near Phan Rang, Vietnam. After five months in the jungle, he had taken two AK rounds in the groin in an ambush outside Chu Lai. His best friend, Corporal Robert Groom, had been killed. Instead of returning to the States, Slocum had insisted on recuperating in Japan so that, after recovering, he would be sure to return to his buddies in Charlie Company. He caught up with them in the A Shau Valley in February just in time for the 1968 Tet Offensive. The company's mission was to block Highway 547, which ran east out of the valley toward Hue, and to prevent the NVA from reinforcing the city. Troops called this muddy jungle path "the yellow brick road." Charlie Company's 110 paratroopers collided with an NVA regiment there late one February morning. After a day-long firefight, Slocum was the senior of 32 paratroopers who were still alive and unwounded.

Slocum deplaned at Travis and was moved with a herd of soldiers through the usual lineups and tiresome debriefings. Still in his khakis, he picked up a few hundred dollars travel money and caught a cab to San Francisco International Airport for the trip home to Panama City, Florida. A few passengers watched curiously as he stood in line to buy his ticket. No big deal. He was one of the lucky ones; he wasn't accosted or hassled...he was just ignored.

Twenty-three years later, on March 18, 1991, Command Sergeant Major Slocum returned from another war. The big Pan American 747 broke through the overcast as it lined up to land at Pope Air Force Base, North Carolina. Slocum's 2d Brigade, 82d Airborne Division, the

DRB-1, had been the first American combat unit to deploy to Saudi Arabia. Eight grueling and uncertain months of digging fighting positions and humping 80-pound rucksacks in up to 120-degree heat followed. The discomforts of living in holes for months at a time with no showers, no latrines, and no hot food were as bad or worse than Vietnam. But more than years separated the experience in Desert Storm from that in Vietnam. For one thing, Slocum took 2,000 young paratroopers to the Gulf and brought them all back. Throughout the assault on as-Salman and the clean-up operations that followed, he watched the young infantrymen he had trained go about their business with a professionalism and self-confidence far different from what he had seen on the yellow brick road.

This homecoming was also a great deal different from his return from Vietnam. Ten minutes out, the flight attendants moved through the cabin checking seat belts and occasionally high-fiving the raucous crowd of cocky young infantrymen, who by now were hooting and grunting and pushing each other back and forth in their seats. The attendant in Slocum's aisle was about his age, maybe a year or two older. As she walked by, she put her hand gently on his shoulder and leaning over just a bit to look him squarely in the eye, said, simply, "Thank you, Sergeant Major."

Far from being ignored when they arrived, the troops could see thousands of people with fluttering flags and banners, shouting and waving madly. The hangar was dressed in bunting, and the band was barely audible above the shouts of the crowd. As Slocum formed up his planeload of infantrymen, he scanned the crowd, hoping to spot his wife, Faith, and son, Steven. The speeches lasted only a few moments, but they seemed interminable. As Slocum stood at restless attention, his thoughts drifted to the yellow brick road and then to the flight attendant's kind words, which summed up what all these people were really trying to say.

Nearly a quarter century separated Slocum's return from the two wars—about the same interval that separated two distinctly different armies. A product of both, Sergeant Major Slocum was witness to a revolutionary era of institutional reform. He represents many thousands of selfless professional soldiers who remained with the Army through the tough years and committed their professional lives to making General Abrams' vision of reform a reality. That vision was founded on a unique melding of traditional values with the changing strategic and technological environment that followed Vietnam. The Army's subsequent performance in Grenada, Panama, and during Desert Storm would testify to the completeness of that transformation.

The photo above was taken in November 1967 just days before Specialist 4 Steven Slocum (left) was wounded and his best friend, Corporal Robert Groom (right) was killed. Below, Command Sergeant Major Slocum and his wife, Faith, March 18, 1991.

CONTINUITY

Command Sergeant Major Slocum's story reaffirms this book's central tenet that Army reform began not with a narrow focus on new equipment or doctrine, but with a holistic view of the Army as an institution. Realizing that wars are won by quality soldiers, the Army committed itself to developing them.

Two themes of continuity emerge from this story. The first lies in the paradox that change itself is constant. Armed forces in the past have had to change their doctrine in order to respond to new technologies. Both sides in World War I, for example, fell into the trap of attrition warfare while leaders adjusted to the new dimensions offered by machine guns, tanks, and airplanes on the battlefield. In Desert Storm, however, quality soldiers and leaders at every echelon, well-grounded in solid doctrinal foundations, modernized on the move. They harnessed the sometimes unknown or untested capabilities of their weapons systems to great advantage in the worst of weather and under the most violent combat conditions. The American Army's ability to operate at such a tempo and depth demonstrated a second enduring truth: that in joint operations, land combat plays a decisive role in winning wars with minimum casualties. Indeed, in an age of unprecedented technological advances, land combat is now, more than ever, the strategic core of joint war fighting. Despite 41 days of almost continuous aerial bombardment, the Republican Guard remained a cohesive and viable military force able to fight a vicious battle and survive to fight insurgents in northern and southern Iraq. Driving the Guard from Kuwait and rendering most of its units combat-ineffective took the joint and combined efforts of all Coalition forces.

Other equally immutable truths inherited by the Army from past wars were also reaffirmed in the Gulf. The Army's recommitment after Vietnam to traditional soldierly values of moral and physical courage and discipline was vindicated in full by the performance of numerous leaders and soldiers. Captain John Abizaid, who pushed his company up the hills surrounding Port Salines in Grenada, and who later, as a lieutenant colonel, confronted and backed down Iraqi formations in Northern Iraq during Provide Comfort is one example. Captain Szabo and Sergeant First Class Steede, both of whom refused to permit a damaged tank to keep them from leading their soldiers against the enemy, are two more. The accounts of soldiers and leaders in these pages demonstrate the discipline and mental agility that derive from mutual respect and confident, competent leadership, not from fear of punishment.

The Army's aggressive program to provide for soldier welfare served as an essential catalyst for unit bonding and coalescence. Frontline Iraqi soldiers fought poorly because they were neglected. On the other hand, the Republican Guard—better led and well supplied—fought well, even ferociously. Soldiers fight best when led by effective, caring leaders. Modern combat demands, to an unprecedented degree, creative, adaptive leadership. It also requires a love of soldiers and of soldiering that has been a hallmark of the American Army for more than two centuries. Though American soldiers suffered great hardships in the Gulf, officers and noncommissioned officers shared their discomfort. Leaders provided thorough training and set high standards by their example. Moreover, American soldiers were assured that their families were secure and well cared for in their absence. The Army in the field held itself together under trying and dangerous circumstances because units from squad to corps maintained a sense of cohesion and teamwork that had been nurtured over the years by constant exercise and realistic training. The long established value of placing soldiers on the ground to stake out America's national interests was demonstrated convincingly during Desert Shield.

Whether or not Saddam planned to continue his attack into Saudi Arabia, American paratroopers blocked his path. The rapid deployment of heavy armored units and attack helicopters caused Saddam to dig in and hide behind a formidable barrier in order to protect his gains from attack. The presence of soldiers on the ground during Desert Shield and the decisive joint air and ground operations that ultimately ejected Saddam from Kuwait during Desert Storm again demonstrated that determined enemies can only be defeated with certainty by decisive ground action. Nevertheless, the success of any maneuver depends on the ability of land, sea, and air forces to make conditions as favorable for the ground combat soldier as possible. The more an enemy is battered, blinded, and deceived, the more surely a ground force can end the conflict at the lowest possible cost. The Gulf War again demonstrated that wars can best be ended decisively by occupying our enemy's territory.

Aggressors are often driven to conflict by intangibles such as greed, ideology, or hatred. Once committed, a leader like Saddam Hussein stakes his political and physical existence on standing up to international pressure, and he is not likely to be deflected from that course just because he witnesses the destruction of his hastily mobilized, third-line forces. Likewise, competent armies in the field can be remarkably adaptive and resilient when subjected to physical attack and can, in fact, be tempered and hardened by such adversity. As these pages have shown, Iraq's operational center of gravity, the Republican Guard, and to a lesser extent, the heavy divisions of the regular army, remained a viable fighting force in spite of significant physical damage caused by air attack because their will to fight was not broken. Only by vanquishing an enemy and displacing him on the ground can a military force break the enemy's will and ensure ultimate victory. *Maintaining an immediately deployable capability for decisive land combat to end a conventional conflict successfully is the single most enduring imperative of the Gulf War.* It is a lesson that has been repeated with unbroken fidelity through all of America's wars. Writing after the Korean War, T. R. Fehrenbach dealt with exactly the same reality when he wrote:

> *You may fly over a land forever; you may bomb it, atomize it, pulverize it, and wipe it clean of life—but if you desire to defend it, protect it, and keep it for civilization, you must do this on the ground, the way the Roman legions did, by putting your young men into the mud.*[1]

CHANGE

The partner of continuity is change. Every war is unique because the variables that influence the conduct of war, such as the strategic environment, technology, and the global factors of METT-T, change continuously. The cardinal sin of any military organization is planning to fight the next war like the last.

Many aspects of Desert Storm may not apply directly to future conflicts. The combat dynamic in desert terrain differs markedly from that in jungles and mountains. Sorting through the catalog of nations likely to cause mischief or threaten our national interests, it seems unlikely that the United States will again face an enemy as poorly led as the Iraqis. It is equally unlikely that the United States will find such willing allies unless a vital strategic commodity like oil is at risk. Neither can we count on a wealth of regional logistics facilities like Saudi Arabia's, nor expect as much time to prepare for combat.

While specific insights into the future cannot be derived from a single snapshot—even one with the exceptionally fine resolution of Desert Storm—some distinct and powerful threads of continuity begin to emerge from a collage of all post-Vietnam conflicts. From this collage surfaces the outline of a fundamental change in the nature of American wars since Vietnam and a concomitant shift in the manner in which these wars have been fought. While its character remains indistinct, a few tentative generalizations can be made about what increasingly appears to be a new and unique style of fighting wars.

The new style of war fighting is marked first and foremost by relatively small groups of carefully selected, carefully trained, tightly disciplined, and skillfully led fighters equipped with state-of-the-art equipment. They achieve dominance on the battlefield not through numbers but through a continuously high tempo of operations and the skillful employment of superior weapons. Second, in the new style, forces from around the world are concentrated along global lines, using air and sea transport to overwhelm a distant enemy with speed and violence. Third, the enemy is blinded and bewildered by the use of technologically sophisticated means of deception, an unprecedented knowledge of his capabilities, and, to an increasing degree, of his intentions. Perhaps the trait that most distinguishes the new method of war fighting is the competent conduct of joint and coalition operations. While much has been aired publicly about the problems experienced in orchestrating the various Service components in recent wars, other militaries of the world recognize the United States for demonstrating an exceptional ability to meld land, sea, air, and space components to achieve a synergistic power on the battlefield that far exceeds individual Service capabilities.

As Desert Shield and Desert Storm demonstrated, the American Army has effectively adapted to the evolving character of American war fighting. That ability to adapt is the foundation that will continue to undergird our country's unparalleled military excellence. Inherent in this ability are those sinews or solid, resilient strengths that must be identified and nourished if the Army is to continue to provide a decisive land power dimension in future wars.

Quality Soldiers

Neither two decades of Army reform nor the desert victory it spawned could have occurred without quality soldiers like McMaster, Reagan, Stephens, Lloyd, Steede, Jones, O'Neal, and Purvis in company with the many others whose accomplishments are portrayed here. They vindicated reformers like Abrams and DePuy who rejected the notion that our lessons on the battlefield should be bought in blood and commemorated by monuments to our dead.

Quality soldiers are smart, healthy, fit, and resilient. Only carefully conditioned and disciplined soldiers could have functioned effectively when inserted into the 120-degree heat of Saudi Arabia with less than a day's warning. Early deploying forces like Slocum's paratroopers not only acclimated themselves quickly but were ready to march and fight on arrival. They maintained themselves for months in the most primitive conditions imaginable. Not one of the 315,000 soldiers deployed to Southwest Asia died of heat injury, and the overall sickness rate was the lowest of any Army in history.[2] On the battlefield, well-trained crewmen, aviators, and infantrymen demonstrated steadfastness, tenacity, and propensity for action in close combat. A telling mark of their discipline was their self-control and reluctance to kill Iraqi soldiers who could do them no harm and their overnight metamorphosis from warriors to humanitarians after the cease-fire.

Successful application of AirLand Battle doctrine relies on quality soldiers. Complex equipment cannot be transported to a theater and flung across a battlefield with the velocity and intensity of Desert Storm unless it is crewed by soldiers who understand how it works and how to keep it going when established procedures fail. AirLand Battle demands flexibility, creativity, and individual initiative of leaders from sergeant to general—traits that can only be developed within a body of exceptional human talent.

Quality soldiers permit developmental technology to be inserted directly on the battlefield. The bold decision to modernize the Abrams and Bradley fleets in theater was made mainly because the Army leadership recognized that exceptional combat arms crewmen could exchange the equipment quickly without any loss in fighting ability. The appearance of GPS during Desert Shield obliged combat units to change tactics and operating procedures in order to realize the full potential of precision-locating devices. The successful employment of prototypes and nondevelopmental items such as TROJAN, JSTARS, ATACMS, and aerial drones was due in large measure to soldiers and leaders who quickly grasped how to operate the equipment after only rudimentary familiarization and then, on their own, devised tactics and techniques to employ it to best advantage.

In a volunteer army, quality soldiers are a precious commodity. In peace, they have the option of voting with their feet and will do so if they are not rewarded adequately for their service or sufficiently challenged in their jobs. When committed to a distant theater, they must receive the best possible care that limited infrastructure and transportation will support. Better field feeding, clothing designed for specific climates, proper hygiene facilities, temporary shelter, and in-country recreation constitute the most pressing requirements. In war, soldiers deserve, and American society increasingly demands, extraordinary efforts to limit the human cost of conflict. While the soldiers are deployed, their families must be cared for at home. Recent history has shown that quality soldiers, led by caring, competent, confident leaders, are better able to cope with the stress imposed by close combat—an edge honed by realistic force-on-force training at combat training centers—and are thereby able to survive longer.

Training, Education, and Leader Development

The Army was prepared to fight in Desert Storm because it made the commitment through two decades of reform to train realistically, and it willingly paid the price in dollars and sweat to fulfill that commitment. Leaders were prepared to lead because the Army invested in schools that developed officers and noncommissioned officers by motivating them to pursue self-development, rewarding competence, and giving them the confidence to lead. Units fought well in the desert because they had been bonded and exercised realistically in the field during deployments, ARTEPs, and live-five exercises. Most importantly, combat units had undergone the necessary combat inoculation that can only come from realistic force-on-force mock combat at the NTC at Fort Irwin, California, JRTC recently relocated to Fort Polk, LA, CMTC at Hohenfels, Germany, maneuver exercises, and simulation. War gaming and command post exercises using BCTP had supplemented live-fire and maneuver exercises and honed the less tangible skills of decision making and coordination that are so critical to higher-level commanders and their staffs.

If wars are to be won at the lowest possible cost in the future, soldiers must learn to fight realistically before deployment. Despite the luxury of more than two years' predeployment training, some World War II units such as General DePuy's 90th Division suffered terribly once exposed to the realities of combat. In a force projection army, units may have only hours' notice before they find themselves engaged in direct combat. In times of shrinking budgets, the temptation will always exist to reduce training expenditures because the tangible value of training dollars is difficult to measure—difficult, that is, until a force inadequately prepared for the realities of combat is again sent into harm's way. General Abrams' warning is clear. The price paid for unpreparedness will not be in dollars but in blood and sacrifice.

A common view among military writers following Vietnam was that the Army exhibited a singular inability to adapt its doctrine and training to the unique character of that war. A perception emerged of Army leaders who continued to emphasize larger-scale operations using massive amounts of firepower while only a few chose to fight the insurgent on his own terms. Whatever the fairness of this accusation, the perception of intellectual ossification that lingered after the war compelled the Army to change fundamentally the way it trained and educated soldiers and leaders.

The battlefields of Iraq and Kuwait demonstrated the completeness of the Army's training revolution. The officer and NCO educational systems not only improved the professional skill of leaders, but inculcated and nourished in them the initiative and confidence to extend themselves beyond the bounds of set procedures and doctrine. Leaders from corps commanders to squad and section leaders demonstrated an unprecedented ability to focus their intellectual energy to solve thorny problems and to adapt themselves to a completely foreign combat environment. In October 1990 no procedures existed for moving a European-based corps 5,000 miles and transforming it into a contingency force on the fly. Yet within three months, General Franks' VII Corps deployed, with some units moving almost immediately after debarkation directly from port to attack positions. While an armored division commander might command a 90-degree turn on the move, smooth execution demands that tens of thousands of soldiers respond quickly and solve among themselves an equal number of problems and unforeseen difficulties that inevitably accompany such a complex maneuver. To succeed, an operation as complex and dangerous as the passage-of-lines executed by the 1st Infantry Division through the 2d ACR demands exceptionally well-trained units.

In another example, only confident, self-reliant soldiers like Lieutenant Jerry Biller's "Team Jerry" could have pressed on without orders through the darkness and mud of the Euphrates Valley to locate landing zones for the helicopters of the 101st. Major Lloyd Gilmore's transformation of a helpless mob of Kurdish refugees into an organized hierarchy is yet another example of initiative and adaptability—one that helped save thousands of lives in the process. A future contingency-based Army will continue to place a premium on soldiers who are flexible, adaptive, and self-reliant—traits that can only be engendered by a system of education and training that continues to be progressive, innovative, and adequately resourced.

Dominant Overmatch in Weapons Technology to Achieve Quick Victories with Low Casualties

In 1942 the M-4 Sherman was a fine tank, but by the time the European campaign started in earnest two years later it had been seriously outclassed by German Panther and Tiger tanks. In an often told story, a German antitank officer who was captured after a particularly bloody engagement with American armor during the Italian campaign professed that his unit lost the fight because it ran out of projectiles before the Americans ran out of tanks. This perhaps apocryphal story makes the point that in the conscripted army of World War II, to have many more of a lesser weapon was acceptable because America could always produce enough men and materiel to inundate an enemy with quantity if not quality.

That ethos no longer applies. With each post-World War II conflict, the patience to suffer through a protracted conflict of attrition warfare and to tolerate combat deaths has decreased dramatically. In fact, the tremendous success of Desert Storm may have created unrealistic expectations in the public's mind concerning the American Army's conduct of ground operations. Only fortuitous circumstances of enemy and location might allow the Army to repeat a victory won so quickly and so cheaply. The challenge to do as well next time will be complicated by future antagonists learning from the egregious mistakes of Saddam Hussein.

If our nation's armed forces are to win quickly at low cost, they must begin to control an enemy's movements and to defeat him psychologically and physically well before the eye-to-eye, direct fire battle begins. Desert commanders used air operations and deception to lay down a deep carpet of destruction to mask attacking units and to break the Iraqis as early as possible. General Peay's technique for deep attack focused on mobility. The surprise appearance of a substantial combat force 180 kilometers into Iraq unhinged Iraqi forward defenses and created an obstacle whose destruction would require an immediate and complete reorientation of substantial enemy ground forces—a task beyond the Iraqis' capabilities.

Generals Griffith, Funk, Rhame, and Franks struck deep with firepower and mobility. Successive waves of tactical air power and missiles, followed by Apaches and finished with MLRS, fixed the enemy in place and weakened him for subsequent destruction.

In the new style of war, simultaneous attack in depth will be accomplished expeditiously and more cheaply using long-range tactical missiles. Capable of killing point targets with smart precision munitions guided by millimeter wave and infrared seeker technology, these missiles can selectively destroy critical targets. Such technologies, indeed, have already changed the dynamics of the battlefield. Yet, ATACMS will only be effective against fleeting targets if a UAV or JSTARS or a clandestine Special Operations team can track the target and send a mission directly to the firing unit within minutes.

In addition to threatening the enemy throughout his operational depth, the desert commanders sought simultaneously to eliminate all Iraqi capabilities that might impede the positioning and maneuver of Coalition forces. The process took three forms. First, the Iraqis were blinded, principally by being denied use of the air. They could not get high enough to see into the Coalition sector, nor could they exploit their own aerial mobility to insert special operations forces into Coalition rear areas. XVIII Airborne Corps and VII Corps pre-G-Day raids into the security area robbed Iraqi frontline commanders of their ability to see over the berm. Fear of certain detection and destruction also kept most of Iraq's state-of-the-art electronics surveillance, detection, and jamming devices off the air. Second, air and artillery specifically targeted the Iraqi reserves capable of counterattack to fix them in place for later destruction by maneuver forces. The annihilation of the "go-away brigade" during the air phase of the operation is an example of how effective air power, concentrated and relentlessly applied to a single operational objective, can be in paving the way for a ground maneuver force. Third, longer-range Iraqi artillery was detected and destroyed by immediate counterbattery fire. The war clearly demonstrated the success of the side that fully integrates its intelligence, fire control, and communications with devastating effect. With modern target acquisition means such as UAVs and counterbattery radars, any artillery unit that fires can be detected instantly, no matter how well emplaced or hidden. The Iraqi experience confirmed that if artillery is to survive, it must move quickly and continuously about the battlefield between missions. Although the Iraqis were never able to adjust fires to capitalize on the superior range of many of their artillery cannon weapons, they did highlight the pressing need to increase the reach of American cannons from the present 30 to at least 40 kilometers or more.

Regardless of our estimates of how successful the firepower system has been in weakening the physical strength and breaking the psychological will of an enemy, decisive victory—the achievement of the given objective to destroy the Iraqi army—was only achieved when the enemy was engaged in ground combat. The unstoppable Coalition ground attack destroyed the Iraqis along the barrier line, physically ejected them from Kuwait, and forced them to retire from the field of battle in the face of certain death. In previous conflicts, most American casualties occurred in close combat, largely from artillery and mortar fire. In Korea, 82 percent of all Army combat deaths were infantrymen. In Vietnam, a war supposedly without fronts, the figure was 65 percent. Infantrymen, in fact, accounted for more than half of all combat deaths from all Services in Vietnam even though they comprised less than 4 percent of the armed forces. Close combat deaths were proportionately much lower in Desert Storm because combat soldiers, infantrymen, tankers, artillerymen, and Apache pilots collectively possessed a pre-dominant "overmatch" in weaponry and mobility and because the Iraqi chemical threat failed to materialize. Precision killing power, protection, and mobility were so superior that even the Republican Guard units, equipped with the best that the Soviets could provide, were unable to exploit any technological edge they possessed.

Army combat forces did possess some vulnerabilities that the Iraqis could have exploited. As mentioned previously, light forces still do not have sufficient means to defeat the best Soviet-design tanks. Had Saddam seized the opportunity to attack through to ad-Dammam in late August, the 82d might have held off his tanks with TOWs and Dragon missiles, but the cost may have been unacceptably high. Incomplete modernization left some combat arms units with many armored fighting vehicles that were a generation out of date. Older versions of the venerable M113 personnel carrier used to carry TOW launchers, mortars, and artillery forward observers (or FISTs) were often left behind in battle because they could not keep up. The Vietnam-era AH-1 series Cobra attack helicopter could not join Apaches in fighting at night and remained extremely vulnerable to ground fire. Soldiers still need surer protection against chemical and biological threats that will permit them to fight efficiently and survive in a chemical environment. Had Saddam defended his barriers more resolutely, the mines he sowed and the obstacles he constructed could have caused many more casualties. The Army must continue to institutionalize all it has learned about negotiating barriers and crossing minefields and train to the highest standards so it can maneuver through or around them successfully.

Casualties were kept low in the direct firefight in large measure because American combat forces owned the night. Thermal and infrared sights permitted combat vehicles and helicopters to engage Iraqi armor while completely masked by darkness. However, the thermal imaging technology employed in Iraq and Kuwait did not give high enough resolution for gunners to differentiate friend from foe at extreme ranges. Most incidents of fratricide occurred because gunners and pilots mistook American for Iraqi equipment in the heat and confusion of combat. The Army must improve the resolution of night sights and night vision devices.

Overmatch in the direct firefight was achieved largely by three of the Big Five weapons systems. The Apache striking from ranges of up to 8 kilometers was seldom seen by the enemy. It proved to be both lethal and survivable on a mid-intensity battlefield, especially at night. Similarly, the Abrams achieved great stand-off detection and engagement ranges. Both the Abrams and the Bradley also achieved remarkable results in crew protection and, though not tested, would also have saved lives in chemical warfare.

The other two Big Five systems acquitted themselves equally well. The Blackhawk has become a true workhorse, shouldering the load once carried by the older UH-1. With its greater range and speed, larger loads, and improved survivability, the UH-60 gave the 101st Airborne its unprecedented mobility. While the final count on Scuds downed by the Patriot may never be determined, the missile clearly provided an umbrella of security immensely appreciated by those it protected. Perhaps more importantly, the Patriot played a significant role in keeping the Israelis out of the war.

Even though the American Army possessed a distinct technological lead in direct fire systems, most of the technology that gave the Abrams its superiority was already 30 years old. In fact, many of the basic technological advances incorporated into the Abrams, the Bradley, and the Apache had already been purchased by the Iraqi army on international arms markets. The lessening of the great powers' arms race will likely slow the pace of developing new weapons technology, but it will not stop the proliferation and replication of existing technology throughout the developing world.

Decisive victory in the direct engagement is not enough. The Army has a moral obligation to the American people to lessen the cost of the battle in American blood. To honor such an obligation, there can be no such thing as a fair fight. An eye-to-eye battle is not a boxing match or a football game. An even match in either quality or quantity only serves to prolong the horror with needless casualties on both sides. The object of future wars, therefore, will be to collapse an enemy by maneuvering an overwhelming joint force against him so that his will to resist is broken and close-in killing becomes a coup de grace rather than a bloody battle of attrition.

Combined Air and Ground Forces Employed in Synergy to Achieve a Single Operational Objective

In modern war, the new high ground belongs to the side that controls the air—and space. The United States has been fortunate to achieve and maintain air superiority in every war it has fought in this century, and it has been more successful in exploiting the advantage of air superiority than any other warring power. Since the end of World War II, the sure possession of the new high ground has changed fundamentally the way the American Army fights. After every war, the Army has sought better ways to exploit the third dimension in joint operations. In every case, the Air Force has been drawn more deeply into joint prosecution of land operations: first, following World War II and Korea with close air support and then, after Vietnam, with battlefield air interdiction.

The Coalition bombing of the Iraqi army, prosecuted with great tenacity and professionalism, was terribly destructive. Iraqi losses from the air may never be truly known but, while less than the CINC's 50-percent objective, were sufficient to demoralize and disrupt all but the best of the Iraqi ground forces. Lower-quality, recently drafted frontline troops were so demoralized from the unrelenting day-and-night bombardment that as many as half of some units fled before the ground attack began. Interdiction of road resupply was so effective that supplies to frontline troops were drastically curtailed. Coalition air forces so dominated the air that enemy ground units were largely prohibited from maneuvering and only dared to reposition at night or in bad weather. Yet the air operation, even though it lasted 41 days, failed to break the will of the Republican Guard, to stop it from responding to the Great Wheel, or to prevent it from retiring some of its elements to safety. The traditional rule of thumb says that if a unit suffers 30 percent casualties in close combat it is no longer combat-effective. On the other hand, a first-rate unit with high morale and good leadership can reconstitute its fighting strength if the destruction occurs gradually through attrition rather than suddenly through decisive, unrelenting close-in combat. Fighting units fail when their will is broken, not when some of their equipment is destroyed. The Iraqi battalion that lost 37 tanks in six minutes in its fight with the 2d ACR clearly demonstrated that good units can only be broken in direct combat.

The ATO with its characteristic 72-hour cycle seemed unresponsive to battlefield commanders, particularly to corps commanders, in both the early air operations and in the frustrating last-day effort to destroy the Republican Guard inside Kuwait. In World War II, Korea, and Vietnam, the preplanned mission cycle against deep targets required 24 hours to complete—one-third the time required in Desert Storm. Fortunately, the Iraqis were obliging enough to remain relatively static during most of the air phase of the campaign. Prior to G-Day, however, whenever they did move, even if just to reposition slightly, the decrease in target kills was significant. Generals Luck and Franks were continually frustrated by their inability to influence target selection for the ATO. Franks in particular was concerned because he had developed an elaborate program for attack in depth. He intended air power to play a key role by destroying operational reserves that might strike his corps in the flanks before it closed on the Republican Guard. As the ground war drew nearer, Franks received more sorties and managed indeed to crush the "go-away brigade" with concentrated air power. Nevertheless, frustration with the rigidity of the air support system increased as the war of movement began. The 20-grid-line restriction imposed by CENTCOM air planners kept 11th Aviation Brigade helicopters from preventing the escape of Iraqi armor. As a result, the Coalition was unable to exploit the synergy of deep attack with the unique ability of Apache helicopters to kill large numbers of moving targets at night in conjunction with integrated airpower attacks.

The launch of 32 Army tactical missiles during the air phase went largely unnoticed. Too few missiles were available to cause extensive damage and the complex clearance procedures necessary before each launch made them relatively unresponsive. Likewise, the missiles were so new that targeteers in the corps deep battle cells and at ARCENT often did not know how best to employ them. Yet ATACMS demonstrated its potential for assuming many of the more difficult and crucial time-sensitive, deep-strike missions. Unlike fighter-bombers, the missile needs no ATO to program its launch, no elaborate penetration aids, refueling tankers, AWACS command and control aircraft, ELINT jammers, or HARM missiles to penetrate and hit the target. Nor are pilots' lives put at risk. In fact, because an ATACMS rocket pod is interchangeable with an MLRS pod, deep attack missions can be accomplished with a simple fire mission to the corps artillery deep battle cell.

The "flow" close air support system worked quite well in practice. The A-10 in particular was devastating once the ground war began and once the aircraft dropped low enough to provide effective 30mm cannon support. However, CAS seldom descended below 10,000 feet due to the still effective Iraqi antiaircraft defenses. Nor did CAS fly closer than 5 kilometers to friendlies because the armored forces were moving too quickly for ground FACs to work with any less separation. Also, after Khafji, the fear of further aerial fratricide caused most ground commanders to employ close air very cautiously if they used it at all. In any case, the weather was so bad on February 25 and 26 that most tactical aircrews could not see to bomb accurately. Most significantly, the presence of substantial organic aerial firepower in the form of Apaches and Cobras lessened greatly the traditional Army reliance on close-in delivery of tactical air power. The impromptu JAAT operation that the 101st Airborne Division performed on G-Day illustrates that only an organic attack helicopter unit could have spotted the dug-in Iraqis, landed next to the infantry company commander to coordinate the attack, and then immediately participated in the destruction of the target. As in past wars, once tactical aircraft arrived over the battlefield, pilots provided supporting fires to advancing troops with great tenacity and skill. The task for the future will be to shorten the ATO cycle and streamline the system of control between air and ground forces so that pilots can get to the battlefield more quickly and, once on station, keep track of the swirling, fast-paced battle below.

Problems with procedure and philosophy, however, should not diminish the fact that in Desert Storm the United States raised the execution of joint warfare to an unprecedented level of competence. In land combat, the term "joint" centers almost exclusively on the integration of ground and air combat forces. In years to come, the single most distinguishing characteristic of joint land combat will be the presence of aerial vehicles from every Service and in support of every battlefield function. It is essential that all aerial and ground platforms, regardless of the Service of origin, be blended together into an effective, seamless striking force.

An Unblinking Eye to Provide A Continuous and Unambiguous Picture of The Battlefield

Just as the Army must achieve and maintain a dominant overmatch in the direct firefight, it must also do so in intelligence, achieving a more complete understanding of the foe while rendering the enemy blind. Field Marshal Erwin Rommel's defense of Fortress Europe rested ultimately upon divining where and when the Allied main landing would occur. Rommel sought to defeat the invasion at the water's edge. Similar to Desert Storm, the success of the invasion of France—Operation Overlord—depended upon the ability of the Allies to deny the Germans that critical piece of intelligence until a solid beachhead had been established. The Allies successfully kept the veil of secrecy drawn around the invasion plan by conducting the most intensive deception ever mounted up to that time. The Enigma code-breaking machine that allowed them to read the Germans' most sensitive traffic, assured them that the secret was safe. The absolute dominance of the air over France in 1944 allowed daily reconnaissance flights to study the German defenses. The striking difference between the two campaigns was that the preparation for Overlord required more than two years, that for Desert Storm only six months.

The high-technology intelligence-gathering capability of the United States today is without equal. Yet the burgeoning technologies of surveillance, data processing, and global communications offer even greater technological leverage for future exploitation. The level of intelligence support for Desert Storm should be viewed as a starting point, not a model for the future. The technology traditionally devoted to strategic intelligence must be turned downward and adapted to a tactical focus. In any future contingency, the Army will require detailed intelligence before the arrival of an intervening force. Particularly in the case of early arriving light forces, commanders need a clear picture of what awaits them on the ground. As the Army shifts increasingly to a force projection Army, the ability to observe, analyze, and understand potential enemies and the operational environment in any area of the globe must be enhanced and adjusted to better support such operations.

Our efforts must seek an unblinking eye, constant in its watch over the battlefield and guided by the needs of the theater commander. Failure to do so carries great risk. The ability of intelligence at times to plot Iraqi tactical deployments down to individual weapon systems before the ground operation began benefited from a cooperative enemy and a benign environment. The Iraqi military machine moved into the desert of the Kuwaiti theater of operations and turned it into the world's largest parking lot. For months, most units remained in place, making only minor positional adjustments as they worked feverishly to create Fortress Kuwait. Once the Great Wheel began to turn, the severe weather and smoke meant that JSTARS became the cornerstone for both situational development and targeting. Future enemies and battlefields may not be so easy to examine. The answer to supporting a contingency force is to maintain a blend of tactical and strategic surveillance systems like satellites, JSTARS, U-2, RF-4, and UAVs that can readily be adapted to the situation. Those systems must, however, be positioned early enough to maintain coverage over the theater, wherever it may be.

Tactical forces have specific intelligence requirements that joint national agencies cannot satisfy. Organic Army intelligence proved absolutely necessary to meet the needs of ground tactical commanders in Desert Storm. Only intelligence professionals with a background in land warfare could have made the key estimates that allowed commanders to decide on the correct course of the campaign. An example is Saddam's operational center of gravity. Very early in the crisis, Army intelligence developed an accurate assessment of his military strategy and correctly forecast that ground operations would have to target the Republican Guard before Saddam would withdraw from the KTO. That assessment drove campaign planning, which ultimately arrived at the concept of the Great Wheel. Once that plan was formulated, only Army intelligence professionals had the cultural experience to devise the "key read" series of assessments that allowed General Franks to slam his armored fist into the Republican Guard at the optimum time and place.

Dissemination proved to be the Achilles heel of the intelligence system in Desert Storm. Combat commanders demanded an unprecedented volume of precise hard-copy imagery. Intelligence was generated in such great quantity that existing communications proved incapable of pushing the required hard-copy imagery and information down below division level. The demand also reinforced the need for a responsive tactical imagery collection system that includes JSTARS, UAVs, and a method to provide wide-area, high-resolution imagery that can both "freeze the battlefield" and provide targetable data. While pictures of the battlefield are important, they can be misleading without analysis. Graphic intelligence displays, either in hard copy or transmitted by electronic means, are the way of the future. Carefully written intelligence estimates are useful for long-term analysis, but commanders need something they can read at a glance. The highly accurate templates provided by the ITAC showed the way to achieve that goal. But the capability to update such templates locally in a moving battle must be further developed.

Closely related to the dissemination problem is the issue of obtaining off-the-shelf "nondevelopmental" items and prototypes that have yet to be fielded. In Desert Storm, JSTARS, UAVs, TROJAN, and a host of other systems gave US Army intelligence an overwhelming edge in the intelligence battle. The intelligence problem is particularly suitable to nondevelopmental, off-the-shelf technological solution because intelligence collection and dissemination demand low densities of highly complex equipment that can be placed in the field very quickly. Although a great tribute to the mental agility of our soldiers and their leaders, the process for putting nondevelopmental systems in the field should be institutionalized and streamlined to maintain the tactical intelligence overmatch. The "Big Red One" should not have had to learn to use TROJAN just 24 hours before the ground war.

The focus and design of US intelligence organizations is shifting from the cold war defense of Europe to a force projection Army capable of supporting offensive operations. The intelligence units that deployed in Desert Storm were largely designed to support the Army in a defensive battle in Europe over completely familiar terrain. Intelligence units at division and below must focus on providing targetable data to field commanders in offensive operations over terrain which is in all likelihood totally unfamiliar. To do so requires a more balanced collection capability within military intelligence units and instant and reliable communications to firing units. Moreover, military intelligence units must be able to keep up in a fast-paced action. Combat units that outrun their intelligence coverage face increased risk just as they do by outrunning their fire support. Even so, collection means like UAVs and JSTARS will always be limited. They will have to satisfy both targeting and situational development needs in accordance with tactical commanders' requirements. Experience in Desert Storm indicates that the targeting function should be first priority for those systems capable of producing target-quality intelligence.

Desert Storm leaders often expected too clear a picture of the enemy, in part because the capabilities of the intelligence system were oversold.

Battle staffs in peacetime exercises, conditioned by their focus on Europe and the Warsaw Pact, had grown accustomed to deriving from available data a clear and distinct picture of the enemy that could not be reasonably matched in Desert Storm. Future battle staff training at BCTP and elsewhere should inculcate a sense of uncertainty in the enemy situation so that commanders are accustomed both to dealing with uncertainty and risk as an inherent component of leadership in battle and to placing a demand on national systems to provide operational and tactical intelligence. The intelligence challenge is to catch up with and ultimately get ahead of the escalating demand for high-quality, targeting-level tactical intelligence.

Operational Agility to Permit Movement About the Battlefield with Unprecedented Speed and Surprise

A commander introducing a different war-fighting style for the first time can fatally upset the psychological equilibrium of his opponent. The French corps commander responsible for the defenses of Sedan on May 13, 1940, knew that Guderian's XIX Panzer Corps was coming. Yet the French commander was ejected from his strong river-line defense in large measure because he was simply never able to adjust his own internal clock to match the accelerated pace of the German advance. From his post atop the Heights of Marfee, the French commander could observe Guderian's bold daylight river crossing perfectly, and he had more than 200 guns available to crush the attack. Guderian was outnumbered and most of his artillery was snarled behind him along roads leading out of the Ardennes. Yet he and a force comprised mostly of engineers and infantry crossed to the far bank of the Meuse successfully in rubber boats. Any staff college student doing a simple correlation of forces would have given Guderian little chance of success. He succeeded because he always arrived at unexpected points of crisis before the French could set their defenses. Then he employed unconventional tactics that psychologically unhinged his enemy and fractured his will to resist.

In Desert Storm the story was much the same. The Great Wheel surprised the Iraqi high command because from their own experience they believed that such a grand maneuver was impossible. The Iraqi commander who opposed General Funk's 3d Armored Division declared later that even though he knew the Americans were near, he believed that he had another five hours before they could begin an assault. The Hammurabi Division was still sending tanks to the rear loaded on HETs after the 24th Division obstructed their route of escape on Highway 8. The 2d ACR caught elements of the Tawakalna facing in the wrong direction, and Griffith's deep Apache strikes surprised and decimated the Adnan, which had survived extensive attempts at aerial attack. The Iraqis completely misjudged the ability of American crewmen to maneuver at night and kill at extremely long ranges in darkness, rain, and blowing sand.

The psychological dominance of American land combat forces came from their agility—the ability to rush forward quickly, yet maintain the overall pace of the advance without interruption and react with lightning speed to unexpected threats or opportunities. In the American style of war, agility is as much a mental as a physical quality. The American soldier's ability to "think on his feet" has been enhanced by a military educational system that emphasizes mental flexibility and self-confidence rather than learning by rote. Realistic force-on-force training at combat training centers and other areas has embedded in a generation of commanders the lesson that battles are won when subordinate commanders possess an intuitive propensity to act and when their authority to do so is limited only by the commander's general intent. A generation of officers has grown up in the Army sharing a common cultural bias and the ability to translate that bias into operational plans and "audibles" that can be instantly understood and acted upon by field commanders.

The physical side of agility was enhanced by technology that provided unprecedented air and ground mobility. No other army in the world could have moved over such vast, inhospitable terrain so quickly. Collectively, four of the Big Five weapons systems developed during the past 20 years offered a quantum leap ahead in the ability to outmaneuver an enemy.

The 180-kilometer aerial vault to the Euphrates made by the 101st again proved that the helicopter remains our most agile all-weather platform for fire support and maneuver. It also proved that the American Army remains preeminent in helicopter employment. The psychological dislocation that occurs from placing and sustaining a major maneuver force in the enemy's backyard more than justifies an air assault operation's complexity, tactical risk, and high cost. The Desert Storm air assault also demonstrated the reliance of such operations on joint fighter-bomber and airlift support. Weather plays an uncertain hand in aerial combat, and Desert Storm was no exception. Throughout the first few days of the assault, marginal weather continually delayed movement and hindered resupply. While fixed-wing aircraft might have been able to interdict Highway 8, assault landings by the 101st cut it off completely and controlled the surrounding terrain both day and night.

The Abrams and Bradley fighting vehicles effectively doubled the cross-country speed and range of the older M60 and M113. Yet as Desert Storm demonstrated, a serious gap in ground mobility still exists between direct fire combat systems such as the Abrams and Bradleys and systems that make up following echelons. Self-propelled cannon artillery can accompany the general pace of the advance but lack the "dash" speed to conform to the close-in maneuver of modern direct fire fighting vehicles. Likewise, the older combat engineer vehicles cannot keep up. The experience of the 24th Infantry Division in the "great dismal bog" graphically demonstrated the problems experienced by the Army's road-bound tactical truck fleet. The operational agility of ground forces was seriously impaired by a shortage of heavy equipment transporters necessary to move tanks quickly across long distances. Until the end of the war the Iraqis still possessed more HETs than the American Army could scrape up worldwide.

To exploit the agility of the force completely, the Army must be able to move freely at night. General Funk's 3d Armored Division gained its five-hour advantage over the Tawakalna by maintaining the tempo of its advance during darkness. The 101st overcame Iraqi antiaircraft defenses by exploiting darkness for cover. While the armored tip of the combat spear possesses excellent night vision capability through the use of night vision goggles and thermal sights, the rest of the spear, including fire support, logistics, and transportation, requires extensive additional night equipment in order to maintain the tempo of night movement. Since many potential adversaries already possess comparable night vision capabilities, all Services must continue to exploit and expand night fighting doctrine to retain the advantage.

Modern command, control, and communications technology forms the neurons and synapses that make agility possible by tying together the brains and muscles of a field army. Although much of the command and control structure that the Army took to the Gulf was originally designed for defensive operations in Europe, it was extraordinarily successful in fast-paced, continuous, all-weather ground operations. To accommodate sustained faster-paced offensive operations, command posts and battle staffs must be made leaner and more agile. The Army tactical communications system was also structured to support defensive operations in Europe. The wider fronts, greater maneuver depths, and tremendously greater tempo of movement associated with desert offense hampered the ability of General Franks' corps to maintain contact while on the move. The problem was lessened to some degree by subordinate commanders' thorough understanding of Franks' intent, the ability of VII Corps units to operate with considerable autonomy, and the availability of some tactical satellite terminals. The image still lingers in the minds of many senior tactical commanders of radio operators trying to punch through to adjacent units using 30-year-old FM radios and of operations sergeants drawing grease-pencil graphics on acetate overlays much as their grandfathers did in World War II. Agility should be limited only by the mental and physical capacity of the force, not by the communications that link them together. The technology is available and, in many cases, on hand to provide the necessary degree of control a commander needs to exploit the intrinsic agility of his force.

Logistics as the Engine of Global Envelopment

As any Latin student who has read *The Battle for Gaul* will recall, in 55 B.C. Julius Caesar constructed a bridge across the upper Rhine in 10 days. He built the bridge not to conquer but to intimidate. As the restless German tribes on the far bank watched the soldiers complete an engineering feat far beyond their comprehension, they realized the futility of resisting the power of Rome. After 18 days of marching about on the opposite shore, Caesar, having never fought a battle, recrossed the Rhine and dismantled the bridge behind him. He had made his point.[3]

The global air and sea bridge constructed by the transporters and logisticians in Desert Shield served the same purpose. The Iraqi army stood by and watched on television as the American Army assembled a sophisticated combat force in front of them with efficiency and dispatch. The act of building the logistics infrastructure during Desert Shield created an atmosphere of domination and a sense of inevitable defeat among the Iraqis long before the shooting war began. In the new style of war, superior logistics becomes the engine that allows American military forces to reach an enemy from all points of the globe and arrive ready to fight. Speed of closure and buildup naturally increases the psychological stature of the deploying force and reduces the risk of destruction to those forces that deploy first. In contrast, dribbling forces into a theater by air or sea raises the risk of defeat in detail. XVIII Airborne Corps' first three weeks' buildup prior to the arrival of heavy armored forces by sea were the most critical of the campaign. A sea bridge can only be built as quickly as the availability and steaming speed of ships will allow.

Sealift is the weakest link in today's global bridge. Not only are there too few high-speed ships, but experience in Desert Shield indicates that maritime forces must become far more responsive, flexible, and accommodating if heavy Army forces are to close quickly in theater in shape to fight. The 24th Division would have found it very difficult to fight on arrival in ad-Dammam had they loaded to maximize efficiency or had they adhered to established regulations and procedures intended for a NATO-like contingency prior to departure. As our Army is increasingly based in the United States, more fast sealift ships are needed. At the same time we must modernize our "fort-to-port" infrastructure to handle the demands of a crisis-response Army. The ability to carry two full armored divisions and part of a light division to any point on the globe within 30 days is both prudent and necessary.

Once the sea bridge is complete, the theater campaign must quickly begin to exploit the psychological leverage gained from rapid deployment. In Southwest Asia, much of the theater infrastructure had to be built from scratch. General Pagonis and his team of logisticians refined the model for theater building to support the new style of warfare. Limited shipping space and the demand to build combat power quickly impeded the establishment of a theater structure using methods that had sufficed in World War II and for most of the Cold War. Nor will logisticians of the future be able to build a plan of support based only on concrete, predictable factors of METT-T. Although uncertainty may demand ad hoc solutions, Pagonis' adaptive use of building blocks for theater building in distant regions should be streamlined and institutionalized. Once the decision to deploy has been made, essential support may have to be assembled on the fly, projecting just what is needed when it is needed to preserve as much space as possible for combat forces. Decisions made on the front end concerning what to send will directly affect fighting effectiveness on the other end. Not enough stevedores and ship-handling equipment forward early enough in building the theater might delay the unloading of combat vehicles and ultimately defeat the intended purpose of putting the vehicles on the ground first.

Disciplined and controlled improvisation in theater building can be greatly enhanced by technology that will provide more effective communications, better and more compatible data processing systems, and more responsive sea and air transportation. Technology, in fact, will allow a fighting CINC to build and sustain a theater while carrying with him to the theater significantly less of the logistics needed to support the campaign. Most of what in World War II was termed the communications zone, or the theater rear area, can be moved back to the United States or perhaps positioned in a forward region. The CONUS COMMZ concept to support the new style of war has several intrinsic advantages. Technology exists today in modern coding techniques and satellite communications to supply spare parts and critical items of supply from depots in the United States across an aerial bridge directly to the foxhole. Many if not all administration and housekeeping chores can be accomplished from a CONUS COMMZ, including personnel, administration, finance, and other record-keeping, as well as depot-level repair and major medical services. Present technology also offers a solution to the problem of tracking supplies that so seriously plagued logisticians in the Gulf as they tried to identify the contents of shipping containers.

The concept depends for success on strategic stockpiles of bulk items such as ammunition, both in POMCUS sites overseas and afloat aboard maritime pre-positioned ships. The flexibility and mobility of strategic stockpiles would be greatly enhanced if they could be reconfigured into discrete modular units. Modularity gives the logistics commander the option of mixing and matching support packages to conform to the particular crisis and the regional environment. The Army must efficiently use what is already available in theater. Pagonis' logisticians did this through aggressive pursuit of host-nation support wherever they could find it. Quick exploitation of host-nation support in the future requires early deployment of contract representatives and survey and liaison officers to organize and begin procurement of indigenous supplies. The Army must lighten the load of deploying forces. As previously mentioned, much can be left behind, such as base support structure. Modern packaging technology developed by civilian industry should be incorporated for most commodities, particularly ammunition.

Logistics planners must ensure that a future contingency can be supported throughout the campaign either from stockages on hand or from civilian off-the-shelf sources. Increasingly, off-the-shelf technology must be incorporated into Army materiel not just because it is potentially cheaper, but because the commodities in the civilian economy greatly increase existing sources of supply.

Wrangler's switch from jeans to DBDUs and Raytheon's doubling of Patriot production are evidence of civilian industry's ability to meet the needs of a wartime crisis. But the more complex the technology, the longer it takes to gear up to increased production rates. Fortunately, Raytheon was already producing the PAC-2 in August 1990 and could, by extraordinary measures, build and ship 600 missiles by January 1991. Other ordnance, such as the 25mm penetrator round, could not be produced so quickly. Clearly the industrial base must be kept in a state of readiness for future contingencies.

Logistics has always assumed a degree of importance far beyond that of merely sustaining the force in the field. As the previous chapters have shown, the strength of the logistics engine determines the pace at which an intervening force makes itself secure. In distant regions like the KTO, the length of a CINC's operational reach will be determined largely by his logisticians. Finally, the act of building the global bridge begins the process of moral intimidation against a waiting enemy. As they watched the inexorable pace of the American buildup in the Gulf, the Iraqis, like the German tribesmen in 55 B.C., must surely have asked themselves, "If they can do this so well, how much better can they fight?"

Reserve and Regular Units Able to Deploy Quickly and Arrive Prepared to Fight

The performance in Desert Storm of units like the 212th Engineer Company from Dunlap, Tennessee, and the 352d Civil Affairs Command that helped to restore civil government in Kuwait testify to General Abrams' commitment made 18 years before to a fully integrated force of Active and Reserve forces. By war's end, more than 70 percent of all theater combat service support would come from the Army National Guard and the Army Reserve.

While the Reserve component combat service support structure tailored for the reinforcement of Europe proved to be too large and too cumbersome for the Gulf War, at times the logistics manning was too thin. Had more supply soldiers been available earlier at ports and supply points, the Army would certainly have done a better job of accounting for materiel and moving it forward. While General Pagonis' 38,000-soldier infrastructure might have been too small for the campaign, that number, substantially reinforced, would still fall far short of the doctrinally "correct" 120,000 originally projected for deployment. If required to deploy on short notice into a theater where METT-T factors are indistinct, the Army must retain the flexibility to draw from the available pool of predominantly Reserve component combat support units. It must call forward those whose capabilities are needed most to form discrete logistics building blocks. Once on the ground, the building blocks should be assembled using a minimum of overhead to keep pace with the needs of arriving combat forces.

The greatest practical leverage to be gained from the Reserves will come from Reservists who perform tasks in war similar to those they practice daily in peace. Sergeant Ken Stephens' years of practical experience as a plumber and heavy equipment operator could not be replicated by an 18-year-old engineer soldier just out of high school and advanced individual training at Fort Leonard Wood.

Desert Storm demonstrated several significant structural shortfalls where civilian skills could easily be exploited. The shortage of long-haul truckers was almost a war stopper. One air defense battalion was converted to a battalion of truck drivers and sent to Saudi Arabia. Yet, had the Saudis not provided thousands of trucks and drivers, Schwarzkopf would not have been able to shift two corps westward in three weeks. Civilian communications workers would speed up transcontinental satellite linkages between a theater and bases in the United States. Supply and inventory control clerks, as well as stevedores, computer operators, and transportation management specialists of all varieties, had they been available in greater numbers earlier, would have greatly eased General Pagonis' difficult job of theater building. A less well developed theater would have required many more soldiers with construction and engineering skills to build ports, airfields, and roads.

While Reservists accounted for the majority of support troops in Desert Storm, very few Reserve component combat troops fought in the war. Those who did fight, fought well. The 142d Field Artillery Brigade, Arkansas National Guard, went into combat from the docks at ad-Dammam and acquitted themselves well in support of the 4th Mechanized Brigade, 1st British Armoured Division, on February 27. However, while three roundout brigades—the 48th Infantry Brigade (Mech) from Georgia, the 155th Armored Brigade from Mississippi, and the 256th

Infantry Brigade (Mech) from Louisiana—were activated for 180 days, for several reasons none made it to the desert. With no comparable civilian skills, the Guardsmen have to learn the complexities of fire and maneuver in close combat during their meager 39 days of training per year. The combat skills that Desert Storm soldiers and units had to master in order to be combat-ready were far more complex and demanding than just a decade before. Long-range tank and TOW gunnery, rapid maneuver, and complex electronic equipment all require skills that take a great deal of time to learn and maintain.

Leader training is most complex in the combat arms. The incomplete preparation of combat arms officers and NCOs in Reserve component combat units presents the greatest obstacle to combat readiness. Ground combat is extraordinarily complex and mentally challenging. Commanders must synchronize thousands of disparate pieces, each moving at higher and higher velocities and engaging at greater and greater distances while avoiding damage to friendly forces. In addition to dexterity and technical competence, a leader must inspire confidence in his soldiers so that they will trust him with their lives. In addition, he must be able to perform flawlessly with little sleep, under extremely uncomfortable conditions, and in significant personal danger. Notwithstanding the proven abilities and great patriotism of our citizen-soldiers, skills such as these are best developed over many years of schooling, daily training, and practical application.

Army leaders like General Vuono insisted that the lives of young National Guardsmen not be placed at risk until they and their leaders had been exposed to the stresses of war in training to the same degree as regular units. As a minimum, Reserve combat maneuver units at battalion level and higher deserve the opportunity to train at the National Training Center or other suitable combat training centers prior to combat. The time required to become combat-ready may be shortened through liberal use of simulations, but the remarkable combat skills demonstrated in the Gulf can only be honed to sharpness through realistic field exercises. Combat units in particular require more time to coalesce and harden into tight, confident fighting teams. While unit building can be accelerated, it must not be done at the peril of soldiers' lives.

An Army Prepared to Form the Center of a Fighting Coalition

In Desert Storm, the Army was prepared to provide the institutional glue that held together a remarkably disparate yet effective Coalition. Special Forces soldiers like Master Sergeant Joseph Lloyd proved just as adept at training Kuwaitis and building confidence in the Coalition as they were in providing the chain of command the unadulterated ground truth concerning the fighting prowess of their charges. The success of the

US-led Coalition provided the world a hopeful example of how future aggression might be defeated. With the decline of great power influence, collective bodies, particularly the United Nations, may offer threatened states a variety of political alternatives for deterring aggression. Nevertheless, as the Gulf War again demonstrated, active participation of the US in any global system of collective security will be essential. Future alliances, however, may have few of the assurances and foundations of NATO. Few, if any, formal treaties or standardized agreements may exist. Any similarities in military culture or commonalities of equipment could be coincidental, especially in light of the proliferation of military technology since the Berlin Wall came tumbling down.

While the composition of a future coalition effort will most certainly be joint, the central nature of ground operations in achieving decisive victory will inevitably thrust the US Army into a leading role. American soldiers must be prepared to deal successfully with unfamiliar strategic arrangements. As in Desert Storm, partnerships are formed to meet the partners' agendas. While each nation has an agenda, each also brings value to the coalition even if it does nothing more than add legitimacy to the enterprise. Soldiers will have to tread carefully in such environments. As the CINC's principal agent, the Army must be able to assess the practical value of each coalition member while building as much rapport and instilling as much competence as the partner will permit.

General Yeosock's C³IC in Riyadh served as a model for future coalition-building efforts. The team acted as both a conduit to report military information to the CINC and as an informal sounding board for allies to make themselves heard within CENTCOM headquarters. At the same time, officers carefully selected from throughout the Army established a series of liaison teams with every major Coalition partner. The new style of war, therefore, demands a new set of guidelines for doing business with allies. The guidelines should be as flexible as the prospective coalition. Those selected to act in a crisis as regional liaison officers should be groomed to possess a balance of solid military experience and knowledge of a particular region.

The Army's experience with the Patriot 2 missile deployment to Israel in January 1991 demonstrated how a tactical weapon can have both strategic and political influence on a campaign. The Patriot's antiballistic missile capability demonstrated tangible evidence of US resolve to defend Israel against Iraqi Scud attacks. Such resolve served in large measure to forestall an immediate counterstrike by the Israelis against Scud-launching sites in western Iraq and, in the process, averted a possible collapse of the anti-Saddam Coalition.

The Army must continue to maintain a meaningful presence abroad. Security assistance not only equips potential allies with common hardware, but through the infusion of mobile training teams and nation-assistance exercises establishes bonds with them, while at the same time exposing soldiers to unfamiliar regions. Large-scale exercises such as BRIGHT STAR flex the deployment muscles of larger units and establish solid army-to-army relationships. In the post-Cold War world, the US Army will find itself increasingly engaged in peacekeeping and humanitarian operations similar to Provide Comfort and CENTCOM's efforts in southern Iraq. Such efforts are useful, not only because the Army is uniquely qualified to accomplish them effectively, but also because such experiences continue to enhance the image of the Army abroad as an institution for fostering international cooperation and goodwill.

The challenges inherent in leading temporary alliances will be daunting, encompassing differences in equipment, training, and culture. In Desert Storm, the Egyptians, Syrians, Kuwaitis, and others possessed some equipment identical to that of the Iraqis. The Iraqis, in turn, flew F-1 fighter aircraft and Gazelle and Puma helicopters, built and also flown by the French. General Schwarzkopf and the CENTCOM staff devoted a great deal of energy to keeping the Coalition together and focused on the task at hand. Some tasks involved the establishment of an elaborate liaison and integration structure that sought to rationalize and synchronize as much as possible the myriad of languages, radio sets, encryption equipment, and styles of warfare that the 37 Coalition partners brought with them.

THE LEGACY OF DESERT STORM

To those familiar with Vietnam and other major American wars of the twentieth century, the image of certain victory that emerges from the Gulf War stands in dramatic contrast to the performance of American arms in previous conflicts. This time, the American Army was clearly better prepared to fight the first battle than its adversary. It took to war a doctrinally based, modernized force trained to a standard of excellence the Iraqis could never comprehend, much less match. The Army went to war with a war-fighting, training, and leader development doctrine that not only withstood the initial clash of arms but emerged substantially intact and completely vindicated.

The United States projected a major land force directly into a combat theater with unprecedented speed and efficiency. Often with little in-theater preparation, soldiers went into battle fully prepared to fight in one of the world's most inhospitable climates. Not only did US forces win the first battle, they won the campaign with an operational concept that sought in a single climactic operation to destroy the enemy's center of gravity. For the Total Army the first battle proved to be the last battle of the war.

In Desert Shield the Army created a military metropolis half a world away in less than 90 days. Soldiers operated and maintained advanced weaponry in desert sand yet kept more than 90 percent of it in action throughout the campaign. The Great Wheel proved to be the largest single land battle in American history won in the shortest time. In 100 hours of combat, American forces destroyed or captured more than 3,000 tanks, 1,400 armored carriers, and 2,200 artillery pieces. The Great Wheel swept over and captured almost 20,000 square miles of territory. The conflict terminated with a loss of only 140 soldiers in direct combat, roughly equivalent to the deaths suffered by US forces in two days of combat during the peak of the war in Vietnam.

The Army that went to Desert Storm represented the resurgence of an institution crippled both by the Vietnam War and the subsequent period of societal neglect. No victory so complete and unprecedented could have been achieved without an even more fundamental metamorphosis within American military institutions. A young 1st Armored Division soldier charging into the Tawakalna had very little save bravery, patriotism, and tradition in common with his grandfather who last took "Old Ironsides" into battle against the Germans nearly half a century before. In fact, Desert Storm represents the culmination of a more gradual process of change that has emerged from all the conflicts fought by the American Army since Vietnam. Our nation was fortunate indeed to have an army that produced leaders not only of extraordinary wisdom in successfully preparing for war in peacetime, but also leaders with great politico-military acumen such as General Schwarzkopf and the Chairman of the Joint Chiefs of Staff, Colin Powell.

To fight similar wars successfully in the future demands, more than ever, a trained army ready for combat on a moment's notice. The experience of the American Army in post-World War II conflicts has shown time and time again that an army can be effectively dismantled in months or allowed to atrophy through neglect in a few short years. Although easily lost, a trained and ready army takes a great deal of time to rebuild. Fifteen years are needed to develop a competent, confident battalion commander or platoon sergeant or to design, build, and field a new tank. Desert Storm demonstrated conclusively that an army kept sharply honed can win quickly at minimum cost. Other, less sanguine experiences show that the only alternative to peacetime readiness is to gain combat proficiency through bloody practical experience on the battlefield. The second alternative might be cheaper in peacetime, but the cost in war, particularly among the nation's soldiers who must pay the price, will surely exceed what the American people are willing to spend in the blood of their sons and daughters.

Certain Victory is the Army's story—a story of extraordinary success wrought by men and women better prepared than any before for the demands of war. Backed by the American people in a righteous campaign, the Army joined its sister Services and Coalition allies in a massive response against aggression. The campaign, like the victory itself, has many parents, and the lasting legacy is a credit to all of them. As the world order changes and the American Armed Forces reshape to face an uncertain future, *Certain Victory* will be a lasting touchstone for generations to come.

Notes

1. Fehrenbach, T. R., *This Kind of War: A Study in Unpreparedness* (New York: Macmillan, 1963).

2. Office of the Surgeon General, Department of the Army, briefing slides entitled "Non-Battle Injury Rates from Desert Shield and Desert Storm, September 1, 1990 to June 3, 1991."

3. Julius Caesar, *The Battle for Gaul*, trans. by Anne and Peter Wiseman (Boston: D. L. Godiva, 1980), pp. 78-79.

EPILOGUE

August 1993

Two and one-half years after Desert Storm, the Army continues to evolve to meet the challenges of the post-Cold War era. General Gordon R. Sullivan succeeded General Vuono as Army Chief of Staff in the summer of 1991. Soon after assuming his duties, General Sullivan expressed his guidance and focus for the Army in his fiscal year 1992 Posture Statement:

> *The Army of tomorrow will be significantly different from the Army that won Desert Storm and the Cold War. It will be smaller and more CONUS-based, more versatile and responsive, and it will be a trained and ready force capable of decisive victory. It will operate across the continuum of military operations, and it will continue to reflect the United States' will and commitment at home and abroad. Just as they have for two centuries, the men and women of America's Army will be there to answer the call when needed.*

Under Sullivan's direction, the Army transformed itself from a forward deployed force postured to contain global Soviet power and fight a major war in Europe into a CONUS-based force projection Army. As such, it reaffirmed its role as an integral member of the joint team that protects vital national interests worldwide.

In the months following the Gulf War, the Army leadership carefully studied all aspects of the war and subsequent operations. The lessons derived from these studies were then incorporated into the latest revisions of doctrinal literature. At the head of this body of literature is the Army's keystone manual, FM 100-5, *Operations*. The most recent edition, published on the Army's birthday, June 14, 1993, was updated over a two-year period to address the changing needs of a force projection Army.

This Army capstone doctrine bridges technological, physical, and intellectual change. It synthesizes and harmonizes the outlook of the profession of arms about future military operations, while linking individual Army soldiers and leaders more closely to the institution. As a result, all Army personnel are better able to understand the nature and reasons for changes that are taking place around them. FM 100-5 retains a central focus on decisive land combat through greater operational flexibility, improved force projection, and improved incorporation of technological warfare. It refines the focus of AirLand Battle on the linkage of the strategic, operational, and tactical levels of war into an operational concept of simultaneous, continuous, all-weather joint and combined land combat operations across the depth of the battlefield. At the same time, it acknowledges the full range of military operations from war to operations other than war and the Army's role in multiservice and coalition military operations worldwide. The doctrinal principles of depth, simultaneity, continuous operations, and clearly defining the conditions for success are found to be appropriate not only in war, but also in operations other than war, such as hurricane relief in Florida, Louisiana and Hawaii. This updated doctrine requires versatile leaders and will touch all aspects of America's Army, from operational concepts and organizational structure to modernization of equipment, leader development, and training.

Declining budgets and extreme personnel turbulence have exacerbated the process of institutional metamorphosis. When the Berlin Wall fell in 1989, Army planners anticipated an operating budget of $87 billion for fiscal year 1992. The actual allocation of $67 billion represented a loss of almost one-quarter of planned funding. Active force strength dropped from a Desert Storm high of 930,000 to 640,000 as the Army released 180,000 soldiers—70,000 as a result of reshaping initiatives. The Army also moved 457,000 people and replaced nearly every soldier in Europe in less than a year with the deactivation of one corps, two divisions, and an armored cavalry regiment and their associated Active component support units. At the same time, modest reductions were made in the Army National Guard and the US Army Reserve, and hundreds of installations and facilities were closed. Under the FUTUREUR Program, the Army began transferring thousands of pieces of modern equipment from Europe to the Reserve components or war reserves. An important but unheralded aspect of the turbulence and an important chapter in Army history passed quietly in July 1992 with the safe removal of the last Army nuclear weapons from overseas, marking the end of the Army's Cold War nuclear mission.

Quality soldiers and confident, competent leaders remain the Army's most valuable, yet perishable resource. Thus, training and readiness continue to garner top priority in the Army's 1993 budget and multiyear programs. Leader development is ultimately the overmatch capability that will ensure that America's Army remains the world's dominant land power and our nation's strategic force. The Army continues to invest in long-term programs to groom future leaders. Today's focus on more opportunities for schooling at every level—noncommissioned officers, warrant officers, officers, and Department of the Army civilians—is intensifying as it did during the interwar period of the thirties. Operational assignments are paralleled by opportunities to study the profession of arms, the relevancy of our doctrine to a changed and changing world, and the role of land combat power in service to our nation in the twenty-first century. To further enhance training, the Army has tied ammunition procurement more closely to unit requirements and increased reliance on cost-effective simulations at every organizational level. Most importantly, the Army ensured sufficient funds for operations, exercises, and flying hours to sustain a high operational tempo and state of readiness.

Inspector General and Government Accounting Office reports on Reserve component readiness reinforced the Army's commitment to a single high standard of preparedness for the Total Army. If the Army's full contingency corps were deployed today, the Reserve components would comprise fully 60 percent of the combat support and combat service support units deploying with it—more than 100,000 soldiers. In the first 30 days of deployment, more than 10,000 Reserve component soldiers would be required to deploy with or support their Active counterparts. This inextricable link argues for the same mission readiness for Reserves as their Active counterpart in a truly Total Army. The Total Army will go to war as a team on Day One. To ensure that it is trained and ready, the Army has developed leader and training development plans for officers and noncommissioned officers of the Active Army, the Army Reserve, and the National Guard. By the end of 1993, 2,000 Active component officers and noncommissioned officers will be in direct support of Reserve training in the field. Operations BOLD SHIFT and STANDARD BEARER focus on the readiness of the contingency force pool for rapid, no-notice deployments. Increased overseas deployments for training support Total Army readiness and forward-presence missions in Europe, Africa, the Pacific Rim, and Latin America.

The Army is currently studying two new organizational concepts that will work in tandem to enhance Total Army readiness. The Future Army Schools Twenty-one (FAST) Study will integrate the efforts of the Active and Reserve components to establish common standards for all Army schools in curriculum, instructor certification, and student selection and performance. A second innovation will be peacetime training divisions, consisting of all three components. Their missions will be premobilization training, mobilization, and postmobilization validation and deployment of Army National Guard and Reserve combat units.

In the aftermath of the war, the Army implemented a series of quick fixes on low-cost, immediately correctable materiel shortcomings identified during Desert Shield and Desert Storm. Given its shrinking budget, the Army decided to upgrade current systems rather than develop completely new ones, placing the focus of selective research and development efforts on aging equipment requiring near-term replacement.

The Army published a new equipment modernization strategy in the fall of 1992 designed to maintain dominance on future battlefields through superior weaponry. In a departure from the Big Five systems-acquisition strategy of earlier years, the Army chose to modernize entire functional areas rather than concentrate solely on individual pieces of equipment. The functional areas include projecting and sustaining the force, winning the information war, providing precision fires throughout the depth of the battlefield, protecting the force, and dominating the maneuver battle. Force protection and projection include investment in domestic transportation networks, strategic airlift and sealift, and equipment such as the family of modern tactical vehicles. To protect the force, the Army will invest in more reliable means for identifying friendly forces; nuclear, biological, and chemical defense; air defense; and counterfire systems. Continued development of aerospace and ground-based systems to better see the battlefield, to improve communications, and to blind the threat will help win the information war. The fusion of sensors with attack means through decision support systems like the Advanced Field Artillery Tactical Data System will enable instantaneous precision strikes deep in the enemy's rear. The Army will continue to develop the Armored Gun System, the Paladin—a semiautonomous cannon artillery system—and the Comanche helicopter to replace the aging reconnaissance helicopter fleet.

In 1941, General George Marshall and Lieutenant General Leslie J. McNair recognized the near certainty of American involvement in the war in Europe. Their situation was far grimmer than ours today. They organized and conducted a massive training exercise called the *Louisiana Maneuvers* for an Army suffering from 20 years of neglect and diversion to domestic missions. By contrast, the Army of 1993 has benefited from years of investment in leader development, training, and modernized equipment. It has demonstrated that it is a force trained and motivated to succeed in military operations on the battlefield, as well as a number of operations other than war, with capabilities that inspire the admiration or envy of every other Army in the world. The intent of the Louisiana Maneuvers of 1995 is to sustain our world-class Army; to energize and guide the intellectual and physical change in the Army while simultaneously keeping it ready for any contingency operation. LAM serves as a laboratory for the Army to think about its profession and responsibilities to the nation, to practice its roles and missions, to develop and explore options to assess and direct progress, and to provide a framework for decisions about people, equipment, force structure, and doctrine.

Advanced technology will help move the Army through this era of dramatic change. Newly organized battle labs are helping to define capabilities, identify requirements, and determine priorities for the force projection Army of the future. Early Entry, Mounted Battlespace, Dismounted Battlespace, Command and Control, Depth and Simultaneous Attack, and Combat Service Support battle labs are networked together to accomplish this mission.

Desert Storm confirmed that the nature of war has not changed. At its heart is control of resources, people, and territory, and the strategic core of joint warfare is ultimately decisive land combat. The nation's means to wage war changed with the advent of advanced long-range weapons and communications systems. Both gave a clear edge to the Coalition in land combat with a concomitant increase in the importance of joint operations in generating decisive combat power. Since 1991, the Army has worked closely with the Joint Staff and the other Services to develop recommendations for the Chairman's Triennial Roles and Missions Report, joint doctrinal concepts, and the Congressionally mandated Mobility Requirements Study. The Army will continue to support and participate in joint exercises like REFORGER, ULCHI FOCUS LENS, TANDEM THRUST, and OCEAN VENTURE. Further, in November 1991, Army and Air Force senior uniformed leaders launched a series of annual conferences when they met for two days to harmonize inter-Service operational concepts, doctrine, and organization. A similar series of staff talks with Navy and Marine Corps leaders, begun in November 1992, produced initiatives such as linking Army air defense weapons with AEGIS cruiser radars to improve our joint force protection and projection capabilities and to clarify procedures for operating Army helicopters on Navy ships. Follow-up meetings attest to all the Services' commitment to continuing this process. Currently, the Army and the Department of Defense are engaged in a "bottom-up" review to determine the total requirements for each of the armed services. The results of this study will be the basis for the Army force structure of the twenty-first century.

Certain Victory's call for quickly establishing a global bridge is echoed in the results of the Mobility Requirements Study. For the first time, the nation has a blueprint for strategic airlift and sealift funded with strong Congressional and administration support. The American armed forces' ability to execute the National Military Strategy in far-flung regions will be further enhanced by consolidating worldwide war reserve stocks under Departmental control and by creating a global system of pre-positioned unit equipment sets for the war-fighting CINCs to use in crisis response operations. A major step forward was signaled with the Air Force's acceptance of the first operational C-17 on June 14, 1993. The keel for the first of 20 large US-built medium-speed roll-on/roll-off (RO-RO) ships will be laid in October 1993.

America's changing Army continues the intellectual growth and physical transformation from a forward deployed Army to a strategic force for the next century. The 125,000 soldiers and their families permanently stationed overseas in Germany, Korea, and Panama represent approximately 20 percent of the force—down from a Cold War high of more than half of our Active Army units. Yet, America's Army sustains its continuity of purpose with an average of 20,000 soldiers deployed in more than 1,100 operational missions in 50-60 countries every day of the year. That is almost a 100-percent increase from just a year ago and there is little likelihood that these operational requirements will decrease. These soldiers are performing humanitarian operations in Somalia, northern Iraq, Guantanamo, and the Pacific; peacekeeping in the Sinai, Cambodia, the western Sahara, Syria, and Macedonia; training exercises in Italy, Saudi Arabia, and Kuwait; counterdrug and nation assistance operations in Latin America and the Pacific Rim; and medical support for UN forces in Croatia. In addition to conducting military operations other than war, soldiers also establish personal and professional relationships with the predominant military forces in the world—armies. Finally, our combat units and their support forces are training to go to war at home stations and at our combat training centers at forts Irwin, Polk, and Leavenworth and Hohenfels, Germany. With little fanfare and little attention, America's Army executes these missions daily to secure our interests and to control conflicts in ways that no other military organization can.

Since 1991, the Army has been called upon to support hurricane victims in Florida and Louisiana, to quell riots in Los Angeles, and to repair flood damage in Chicago. At this writing, soldiers and marines are working together with coalition partners and humanitarian organizations to "Restore Hope" to the starving masses in Somalia and "Provide Comfort" to repressed minorities in northern Iraq. Soldiers are also working with their sister Services and counterparts in Central and South America to fight drug traffic while demonstrating the positive and legitimate role of a professional army in a democratically elected government.

During these efforts the Army has maintained the uncompromisingly high standards that Americans have come to expect. The turmoil of today's world events both threatens our national interests and cries for our humanitarian intervention. Fragments of the bipolar world smolder in hundreds of potential flash points. Continued instability has accelerated the proliferation of conventional arms and weapons of mass destruction to a degree unimaginable before the fall of the Berlin Wall. Since the truce, the Army has kept faith with General Vuono's three vectors and with General Sullivan's vision. Despite the hardships, both institutional and personal, the Army simultaneously recovered from Desert Storm and maintained an immediately ready land combat capability to serve our nation. As it has reshaped, the Army has preserved more than 20 years' investment in the nation's treasured resources: people and property.

Certain Victory's exciting story of renaissance, growth, initiative, leadership, and courage in the Gulf War must not be read as an end point or even a high point in the Army's history. Despite diminishing resources and the perceived lack of serious military threats, the nation simply cannot afford to allow the Army's newly honed edge to be dulled or corroded through neglect. America's Army accepts this challenge and enlists the American public's continued support of the military with the same warmth it demonstrated during the crisis in the Gulf. Let the Specialist Slocums of 1991 look back in 2016 at 25 years of the same support and appreciation they felt as they stepped off the planes following their return from Desert Storm.

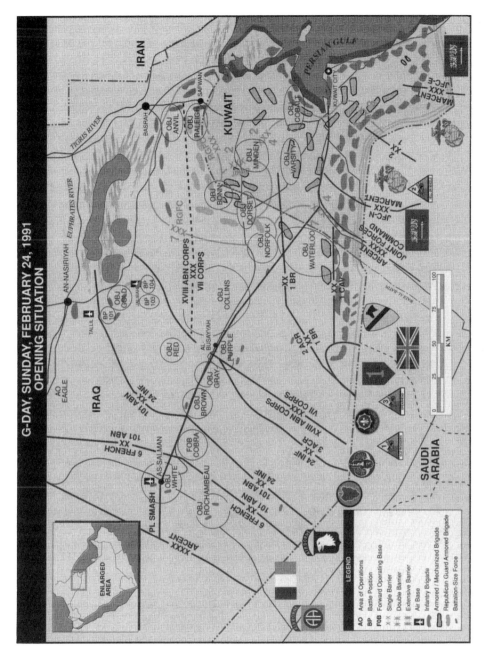

G-DAY, SUNDAY, FEBRUARY 24, 1991
OPENING SITUATION

Figure 5-1

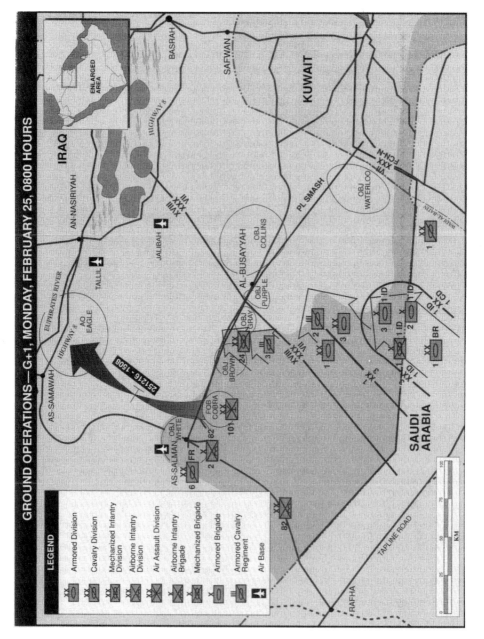

GROUND OPERATIONS—G+1, MONDAY, FEBRUARY 25, 0800 HOURS

Figure 5-2

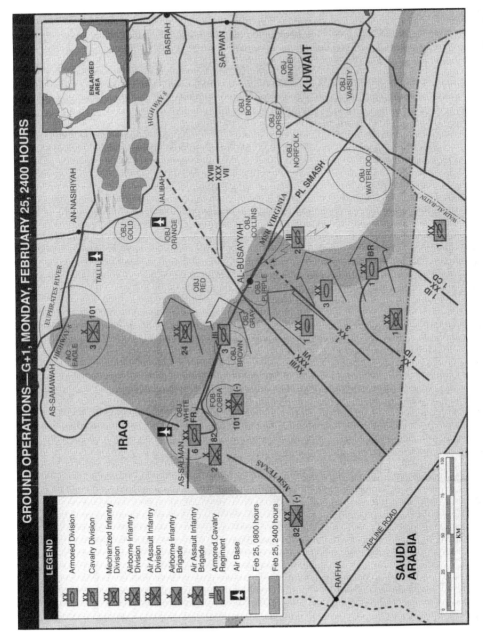

GROUND OPERATIONS—G+1, MONDAY, FEBRUARY 25, 2400 HOURS

Figure 5-3

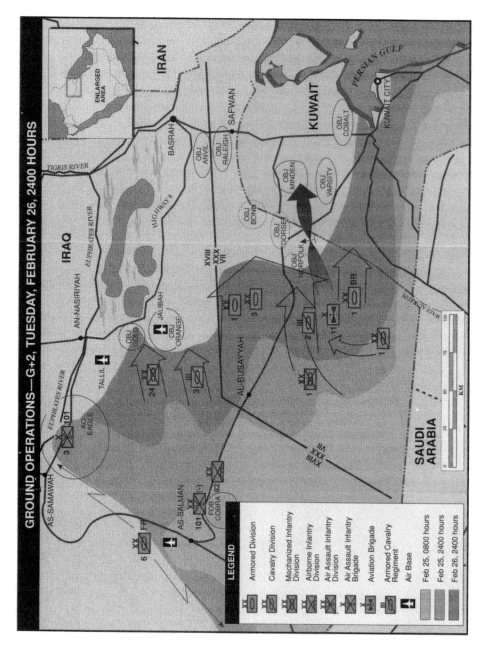

GROUND OPERATIONS—G+2, TUESDAY, FEBRUARY 26, 2400 HOURS

LEGEND

Armored Division
Cavalry Division
Mechanized Infantry Division
Airborne Infantry Division
Air Assault Infantry Division
Air Assault Infantry Brigade
Aviation Brigade
Armored Cavalry Regiment
Air Base

Feb 25, 0800 hours
Feb 25, 2400 hours
Feb 26, 2400 hours

Figure 5-4

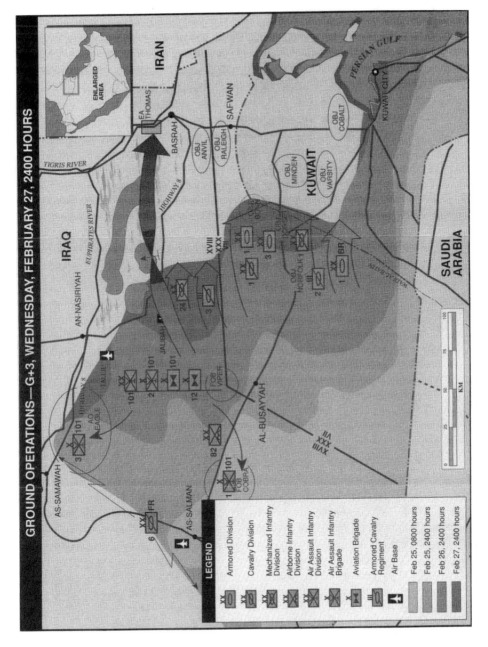

GROUND OPERATIONS—G+3, WEDNESDAY, FEBRUARY 27, 2400 HOURS

Figure 5-5

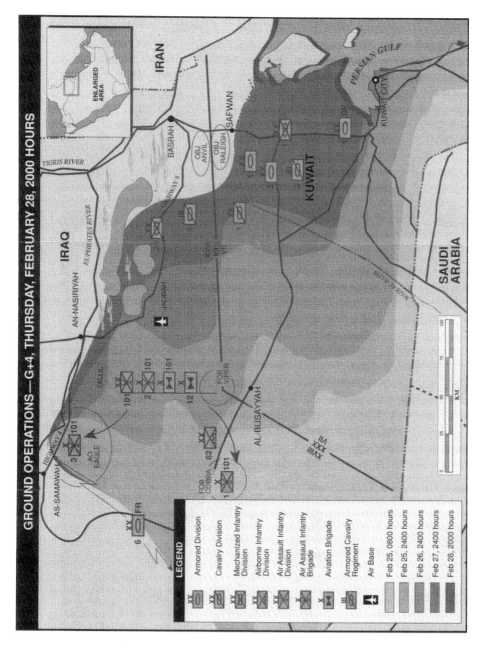

GROUND OPERATIONS—G+4, THURSDAY, FEBRUARY 28, 2000 HOURS

Figure 5-6

CHRONOLOGY OF EVENTS

August 2, 1990[1] — Iraq invades Kuwait.

August 6 — Saudi Arabia requests US assistance in its defense.

August 7 — Operation Desert Shield begins (C-Day).

August 8 — Lead Air Force elements from the 1st Tactical Fighter Wing arrive in theater.

August 9 — Lead Army elements from the 82d Airborne Division arrive in theater.

August 10 — Secretary of the Navy activates Ready Reserve force.

— First fast sealift ship reaches Savannah and begins loading.

August 13 — First ship—*FSS Capella*—departs Savannah with the 24th Infantry Division (Mech) equipment.

August 14 — 82d Airborne DRB-1 closes at the KTO and moves to secure ports.

August 15 — First Marine MPS-2 arrives in Saudi Arabia.

August 17 — First Army prepositioned ship arrives in Saudi Arabia.

— Civil Reserve Air Fleet 1 activated.

August 22 — Presidential Executive Order #12727 authorizes first use of 200K Selected Reserve call-up and limited implementation of Stop Loss Program.

August 23 — Secretary of Defense authorizes call-up of 25,000 Army National Guardsmen and Army Reservists in combat and combat service support units.

---

1   Dates reflect Greenwich Mean (ZULU) Time.

August 27	— Army activates first Reserve units.
	— First FSS arrives in Saudi Arabia and begins off-loading; first M1 Abrams tanks arrive in theater.
August 29	— 82d Airborne Division closes in theater.
September 1	— Stop Loss Program goes into effect.
September 2	— I Corps designated to replace XVIII Airborne Corps as primary contingency corps for worldwide operations.
September 6/7	— Marine MPS 2 and 3 complete off-loading.
September 7	— First Army RC units deploy to Saudi Arabia.
September 12	— Major combat elements of 24th Infantry Division (Mech) close in theater.
October 6	— 101st Airborne Division (Air Assault) closes in theater.
October 22	— 1st Cavalry Division closes in theater.
November 2	— M1/M1A1 tank replacement program begins.
November 8	— VII Corps and 1st Infantry Division alerted for deployment.
November 13	— Presidential Executive Order #12733 extends selected Reserve call-up to 180 days.
November 14	— Secretary of Defense increases Army selected Reserve call-up authority to 80,000 and authorizes call-up of Reserve combat units.
November 21	— VII Corps begins deployment to Saudi Arabia.
November 30	— First Army National Guard roundout brigades called to active duty.
December 1	— XVIII Airborne Corps closes in theater.
	— Secretary of Defense increases Army selected Reserve call-up authority to 115,000.
December 6	— First ship carrying VII Corps equipment arrives in theater.
January 15, 1991	— UN deadline for Iraqi withdrawal.
January 17	— Operation Desert Storm begins (D-Day).

January 18	— Presidential Executive Order #12743 declares partial mobilization.
January 18/19	— Iraq fires first Scud missiles at Israel and Saudi Arabia.
January 20	— XVIII Airborne and VII Corps begin movement to forward assembly areas for ground phase of the campaign.
February 3	— XVIII Airborne and VII Corps (minus elements of 3d Armored Division) complete movement to forward assembly areas.
February 6	— VII Corps closes in theater with the arrival of last elements of 3d Armored Division.
February 24	— Coalition forces begin ground phase of campaign (G-Day).
February 28	— 48th Infantry Brigade (Georgia Army National Guard) validated for deployment.
	— Temporary cease-fire initiated.
March 1	— Task Force Freedom begins emergency recovery operations in Kuwait.
March 3	— Cease-fire terms accepted by Iraq at Safwan Airfield.
March 8	— Redeployment of Army units begins.
April 7	— Iraq accepts UN cease-fire conditions and resolutions.
	— Operation Provide Comfort begins.

SELECTED BIBLIOGRAPHY

Interviews

General William DePuy
General Frederick Franks, Jr.
General Colin Powell
General Dennis Reimer
General Jimmy Ross
General Gordon Sullivan
General (Retired) Maxwell Thurman
General (Retired) Carl Vuono

Lieutenant General Ronald Griffith
Lieutenant General (Retired) Thomas Kelly
Lieutenant General Gary Luck
Lieutenant General Glynn Mallory
Lieutenant General Barry McCaffrey
Lieutenant General William Pagonis
Lieutenant General Binford Peay, III
Lieutenant General (Retired) Calvin Waller
Lieutenant General John Yeosock

Major General Steven Arnold
Major General Paul Blackwell
Major General Robert Frix
Major General Paul Funk
Major General John Landry
Major General Thomas Rhame
Major General Rupert Smith, UK
Major General John Stewart
Major General John Tilelli
Major General Richard Timmons

Brigadier General Creighton Abrams, Jr.
Brigadier General Morris Boyd
Brigadier General Leonard Holder, Jr.
Brigadier General Patrick Hughes
Brigadier General Howard Mooney

Colonel (Retired) Roy Alcala
Colonel David Blodgett
Colonel Stanley Cherrie
Colonel V.B. Corn
Colonel John Davidson
Colonel Gregory Fontenot
Colonel Gary Goff
Colonel James Hill

Colonel Johnnie Hitt
Colonel Jesse Johnson
Colonel James Kerr
Colonel Thomas Leavitt
Colonel John LeMoyne
Colonel Lon Maggart
Colonel John Meyers
Colonel John Molinari
Colonel Robert Noonan
Colonel James Pardew
Colonel Joe Purvis
Colonel David Schulte
Colonel Richard Sinnreich
Colonel Ray Smith
Colonel James Solimon
Colonel Richard Swain
Colonel John Sylvester

Lieutenant Colonel Paul Barb
Lieutenant Colonel Terry Buettner
Lieutenant Colonel Dick Cody
Lieutenant Colonel William Doyle
Lieutenant Colonel David Gross
Lieutenant Colonel Bryant Hamaker
Lieutenant Colonel William Harrison
Lieutenant Colonel Terry Johnson
Lieutenant Colonel David Marlin
Lieutenant Colonel Toby Martinez
Lieutenant Colonel Douglas McGregor
Lieutenant Colonel George Oliver
Lieutenant Colonel Michael Quirk
Lieutenant Colonel Carl Sahlin
Lieutenant Colonel C. Lane Toomey
Lieutenant Colonel Michael Velten

Major Thomas Connors
Major Kent Cuthbertson
Major Ronald Dade
Major David Estes
Major Dan Farley
Major Steven Finch
Major Lloyd Gilmore
Major Richard Hablieb
Major Ronald Jelks

Major Randy Kolton	Chief Warrant Officer David Jones
Major Douglas Nash	Chief Warrant Officer Thomas O'Neal
Major Thomas Odom	
	Command Sergeant Major Steven Slocum
Captain Eric Kennedy	Sergeant Major John Whitten
Captain Ernest Marcone	Master Sergeant Joseph Lloyd
Captain H.R. McMasters	Sergeant First Class Anthony Steede
Captain Joseph Sartiano	Staff Sergeant Ken Stephens
Captain Ernest Szabo	
	Mr. Dick Manning, Raytheon Corporation
First Lieutenant Steve Daigle	Mr. Dick Slaughter, Patriot Project
First Lieutenant Timothy Gauthier	Manager's Office

Documents

British Ministry of Defence, Inspector General, Doctrine and Training. "Operation Granby: An Account of the Gulf Crisis of 1990-91 and the British Army's Contribution to the Liberation of Kuwait." United Kingdom, 1991. A straightforward account of the British role in the war.

Central Intelligence Agency, National Intelligence Council (NIC) Papers, dates various. Collection of NIC information papers and nationally coordinated intelligence estimates (NIEs and SNIEs).

——Near East South Asia (NESA) Papers, dates various. Collection of finished intelligence papers produced by NESA on topics associated with the Gulf War.

——Persian Gulf Crisis Task Force "Spot Commentaries," August 1990- May 1991. Published thrice daily for most of the crisis. Included all significant events since the preceding report.

Defense Intelligence Agency. Defense Special Assessments and Defense Intelligence memoranda, dates various. Special reports on specific subjects, i.e., the status of the Iraqi Air Force's training or Iraqi logistic vulnerabilities. Of related interest to the crisis.

——Iraqi Task Force (ITF) and Joint Intelligence Center (JIC) Military Situation Summaries, August 1990-April 1991.

——ITF Defense Special Assessments: Persian Gulf Crisis, July 1990- June 1991. Twice-daily intelligence summaries that incorporated the Military Situation Summary with political intelligence.

Department of Defense. *Conduct of the Persian Gulf War: Final Report to Congress Pursuant to Title V of The Persian Gulf Conflict Supplemental*

Authorization and Personnel Benefits Act of 1991 (Public Law 102-25). Washington, DC, April 1992. Available in classified and unclassified versions, this comprehensive report is dry reading at best.

——Inspector General. Memorandum for Assistant Secretary of Defense (Force Management and Personnel), "General Accounting Office Draft Report, Operation Desert Storm: Army Encountered Problems in Providing Ready Support Forces—*Preparation of the Proposed DOD Response to the GAO Draft Report.*" December 26, 1991.

Department of the Army

——ODCSINT, DAMI-FI, Bomb Damage Assessment Records, dates various. Collection of ARCENT, USAF, DIA, and CIA bomb damage assessments issued during the war.

——ODCSINT, DAMI-FI, Chief of Staff Briefs, August 1990-April 1991. Briefs on the Iraqi crisis presented daily to Army senior leaders. Include military and political analyses.

——ODCSINT, DAMI-FI, Enemy Prisoner of War Debriefs. Two-volume collection. Provides Iraqi perspective on the Gulf War from the senior officer level.

——ODCSINT, DAMI-FI, Estimates, dates various. Collection of DA internal information papers and drafts for external coordination with the intelligence community.

——ODCSINT, DAMI-FI, 12-Hour Situation Summaries, August 1990 through the end of postwar rebellions.

——ODCSLOG, Operation Desert Storm Sustainment Brochure. Washington, DC, December 1991. Provides logistics analysis of the theater of operations, equipment modernization, Army support group operations, supply, transportation, maintenance, and automation.

——ODCSOPS, Concepts Analysis Agency, "Desert Shield/Desert Storm After-Action Review." September 1991. Multivolume mobilization study.

Headquarters, 1st Armored Division. 1st Squadron, 1st Cavalry. Memorandum for the G3, 1st Armored Division, "Operation Desert Storm." Saudi Arabia, undated.

Headquarters, 1st Brigade, 2d Armored Division. "Actions of the 'Tiger' Brigade during Operation Desert Shield/Desert Storm, August 10, 1990-March 1, 1991." Fort Hood, TX, undated. Contains a commander's summary with unit chronologies.

Headquarters, 1st Cavalry Division. Chronology covering period January 13-March 13, 1991. Includes subordinate unit logs.

——Executive Summary on the Gulf War. Saudi Arabia, undated.

Headquarters, 1st Corps Support Command. "1st COSCOM Observations and Lessons Learned: Operations Desert Shield/Storm." Fort Bragg, NC, February 3, 1992. Provides a good account of the automation and Class IX problems at corps level.

Headquarters, 1st Infantry Division. Operations Desert Shield and Desert Storm Command Report. Saudi Arabia, 19 April 1991.

Headquarters, 2d Corps Support Command. 2d COSCOM briefing on Lessons Learned: Operations Desert Shield/Storm. Undated. Provides corps supply statistics without narrative.

Headquarters, 3d Armored Division. Briefing. Saudi Arabia, undated. Summary of 3d Armor's role in war, with an especially useful template of enemy forces at 71 Easting.

——Chronology. Saudi Arabia, undated. Contains overall division chronology as well as individual reports for the 1st and 2d Brigades.

Headquarters, 5th Special Forces Group. Collection of Operational Orders and Reports, January 17-February 28, 1991. Fort Bragg, NC. Includes a summary of operational phases, mission orders, operations maps, and task organizations for JFC-North and JFC-East.

Headquarters, 6th Theater Signal Command. Desert Shield/Storm After-Action Report. April 25, 1991. Very good account of the deployment and operations of theater signal units.

Headquarters, 11th Air Defense Brigade. Desert Shield/Desert Storm After-Action Report. Fort Bliss, TX, undated.

Headquarters, 24th Infantry Division. After-Action Report. Fort Stewart, GA, June 19, 1991.

——Desert Shield and Desert Storm Operations Overview: Testimony of MG Barry R. McCaffrey to the US Senate Armed Services Committee, May 9, 1991.

——Operation Desert Storm Initial Impressions Report. Fort Stewart, GA, 10 March 1991.

Headquarters, 101st Airborne Division (Air Assault). Lessons Learned from Operations Desert Shield and Desert Storm. Fort Campbell, KY, June 27, 1991. Two-volume set of JULLS-formatted reports on the division's operations.

Headquarters, VII Corps. After-Action Review. Saudi Arabia, March 11, 1991. A transcript of an after-action review conducted soon after the war.

——Artillery After-Action Brief, Operation Desert Saber. Saudi Arabia, undated. Covers the preparation of the breach, offensive operations, deep attack operations with ATACMS and Apaches, and Army-Air Force cooperation re BAI, AI, and CAS.

——Artillery Commander's Report, Operation Desert Storm. Saudi Arabia, March 15, 1991. Excellent overview of corps artillery operations during the war and salient lessons.

——Battlefield Reconstruction Study: "The 100-Hour Ground War, The Failed Iraqi Plan." Saudi Arabia, April 20, 1990. Based on EPW reports, battlefield studies, and documents, this report provides the best analysis of the Iraqi defensive plan.

——Command Report. Saudi Arabia. Multivolume set constitutes the Corps' after-action report to ARCENT. Volume I includes an Executive Summary and historical narrative with an extensive index.

Headquarters, XVIII Airborne Corps. After-Action Brief for Operation Desert Shield and Desert Storm (Updated). Fort Bragg, NC, 25 September 1991.

——Desert Storm Brief. December 9, 1991. General Luck's notes for a formal presentation.

——Executive Summary—Operations Desert Shield/Storm. Fort Bragg, NC, June 24, 1991.

——Joint Committee Report: XVIII Airborne Corps Desert Shield Deployment. Pope Air Force Base, NC, undated.

——OPLAN Desert Storm. Saudi Arabia, January 13, 1991. Includes General Luck's concept of the operation and commander's intent.

Headquarters, US Third Army. Compendium of Fratricide Reports. Fort McPherson, GA, 1992. One-volume collection of fratricide investigations conducted after the war.

Luck, LTG Gary. "Issues of Concern to the Defense Science Board Lessons Learned Task Force." November 26, 1991. Talking points for briefing to the Defense Science Board.

Purvis, COL Joe. Purvis Diary. Unpublished. Located in the Combined Arms Research Library at Fort Leavenworth, this diary covers the Purvis planning group's actions from October 2, 1990 to February 24, 1991.

Schulte, COL David. 1st Battlefield Coordination Detachment, "Desert Shield/Desert Storm After-Action Review: Executive Summary." Riyadh, Saudi Arabia: 1st BCE, March 26, 1991. Schulte's contributions provide an inside view of targeting and Army-Air Force cooperation during the war.

——Memo to BG Scales on Air Force Doctrine. March 31, 1992.

——Responses to questions on BCE Issues.

Sylvester, COL John. "Tiger" Brigade Papers. Undated. Collection of unit reports on the "Tiger" Brigade while attached to the USMC during Desert Storm.

Tait, MG Thomas. Desert Storm Lessons Learned. January 8, 1992.

The US Army's official after-action review of Desert Shield and Desert Storm.

US Army Armor Center. Desert Shield and Desert Storm Emerging Observations. Fort Knox, KY, October 7, 1991. Contains a complete set of battle summaries from each of the US divisions and armored cavalry regiments.

US Army Central Command Military Intelligence History. COL Donald Kerrick, committee chairman. Approximate date April 1991. A three-volume, 13-chapter history that catalogues the establishment and expansion of ARCENT G2 during the Gulf War.

US Army Intelligence Agency. *AIA Intelligence Encyclopedia Operation Desert Shield.* Washington, DC, dates various. A multivolume encyclopedia assembled by the intelligence centers under AIA: the Intelligence and Threat Analysis Center, the Missile and Space Intelligence Center, the Foreign Science and Technology Center, and the Armed Forces Medical Intelligence Center, as well as ODCSINT, DAMI-FI.

US Army National Guard Bureau After-Action Review Briefing. Undated. Provides statistics on Guard units that deployed.

US Army Transportation School. "Transportation and Distribution Observations and Lessons Learned for Operation Desert Storm." Undated. A summary of 20 transportation-related issues that surfaced during the war.

US General Accounting Office. Draft report: "Operation Desert Storm Army-Encountered Problems in Providing Ready Support Forces." Chairman, Subcommittee on Readiness, Committee on Armed Services, House of Representatives, December 18, 1991.

US National Guard Bureau After-Action Report: Operation Desert Shield and Operation Desert Storm Executive Summary. Arlington, VA: October 1991.

Articles, Books, Manuscripts, Periodicals

"Army's Patriot: High-Tech Superstar of Desert Storm." *Army*. March 1991, pp. 40-42.

Bird, Julie, and Tom Donnelly. "Friendly Fire." *Army Times*. September 19, 1991, pp. 3-4, 11.

Blank, Stephen J. *The Soviet Military Views Operation Desert Storm: A Preliminary Assessment*. Carlisle, PA: Strategic Studies Institute, US Army War College, September 23, 1991.

Brinkerhoff, John R. "US Army Reserve in Desert Storm, The Case of the Unit That Was Not Called—The 377th Theater Army Area Command." Undated. Analysis of the decision not to deploy the 377th TAACOM.

Burba, GEN Edwin H., Jr. "Training, Quality, Decisive Factors in Desert Victory." *Army*. October 1991, pp. 63-69.

Carr, COL John J. "Logistics Planning for Desert Storm." *Army Logistician*. September-October 1991, pp. 23-25. Provides an account of the 22d Support Command's planning cell.

Chapman, Anne. *The Army's Training Revolution: 1973-1990, An Overview*. Fort Monroe, VA: Office of the TRADOC Historian.

de la Billiere, GEN Sir Peter. "The Gulf Conflict: Planning and Execution." *Military Science: RUSI Journal*. Winter 1991, pp. 7-12. The British perspective on coalition warfare, the escalation of British participation in the war, and the actions of the British 1st Armored Division.

Detterline, Donald. "History of the 1185th Transportation Terminal Unit (TTU)." August 1991. An account of the unit's role in supporting the deployment in the US.

——"Desert Shield/Desert Storm CSS." *Military Review*. April 1991.

Dunnigan, James F., and Austin Bay. *From Shield to Storm*. New York: William Morrow and Company, Inc., 1992. A good account of weapons, tactics, and techniques, although its account of the war, especially the ground operations, is inaccurate.

Edmond, MAJ Rick J., and Captain Kermit E. Steck. "M1A1 NETT in Southwest Asia." *Armor*. March-April 1991, pp. 14-15.

Flanagan, LTG (Ret) Edward. "100-Hour War." *Army*. April 1991, pp. 18, 21-26.

——"Special Operations—Hostile Territory Was Their AO in Desert Storm." *Army*. September 1991.

Floris, LTC John. "1-41 in Desert Storm: A Test Bed For Doctrine and Equipment." *Field Artillery*. December 1991, pp. 37-41.

Foley, MG Thomas. "Desert Shield Deployment Rivals Patton's Rush to the Bulge." *Armor*. January-February 1991.

Foss, GEN John W. "Building the United States Army for the Twenty-First Century." *Military Science: RUSI Journal*. Winter 1991, pp. 13-17.

Franks, GEN Frederick, Jr. "After the OPFOR, the Medina Ain't Nothin'." *Army*. October 1991, pp. 73-77.

Fulgham, David. "US Special Forces Advisors Integrate Armies from Arab Nations." *Aviation Week & Space Technology*. February 25, 1991.

Gass, COL James M. "1st Cav Div Arty." *Field Artillery*. February 1991, pp. 26-27.

Gibson, COL Emmitt E. "Insights of Commander, 12th Aviation Brigade." *Aviation Commander*. April 6, 1992.

Grier, Peter. "Joint Stars Does Its Stuff." *Air Force Magazine*. June 1991, pp. 38-42.

Griffin, LTC Gary B. *The Directed Telescope: A Traditional Element of Command*. Fort Leavenworth, KS: The Combat Studies Institute, US Army C&GSC, July 1991.

Hall, Margot C. "HASC Targets Gulf War Intelligence Shortcomings." *Aerospace Daily*. May 17, 1991.

Hellen, 1LT John. "2d Armored Cavalry: the Campaign to Liberate Kuwait." *Armor*. July-August 1991, pp. 8-12.

Herbert, MAJ Paul. Leavenworth Paper No. 16, "Deciding What Has to Be Done: General William E. DePuy and the 1976 Edition of FM 100-5, *Operations*." Fort Leavenworth, KS: US Army C&GSC, Combat Studies Institute, 1988. The best single work re DePuy's influence on the doctrinal revolution.

Hooker, Richard D., Jr. *The Land Warfare Papers #8: 21st Century Doctrine and the Future of Maneuver.* Washington, DC: The Institute for Land Warfare, AUSA, October 1991.

Kidd, SMA Richard A. "Where Our Soldiers Stand." *Army.* October 1991, pp. 37-39.

Kindsvatter, LTC Peter S. "VII Corps in the Gulf War." *Military Review.* January 1992, pp. 2-16. First of a three-part article on the VII Corps in the Gulf War.

Kirkpatrick, Charles E. *The Land Warfare Papers #9: Building the Army for Desert Storm.* Washington, DC: The Institute for Land Warfare, AUSA, November 1991.

Langford, CPT Gary D. "Iron Rain: MLRS Storms Onto The Battlefield." *Field Artillery.* December 1991, pp. 50-54.

Lionetti, MG Donald M. "Air Defense: No Road To Basrah." *Army.* July 1991, pp. 16-26.

Merritt, GEN (Ret) Jack N. *Special Report: Operation Desert Shield/Desert Storm: The Logistics Perspective.* Washington, DC: Institute of Land Warfare, September 1991.

Nordwall, Bruce. "US Relies on Combination of Aircraft, Satellites, UAVs for Damage Assessment." *Aviation Week & Space Technology.* February 4, 1991.

Peay, LTG Binford, III, and COL Jack LeCuyer. "Gearing the Force for Crisis Response." *Army.* October 1991, pp. 152-158.

Puryear, CPT A. A., and LT Gerald R. Haywood, II. "Ar-Rumaylah Airfield Succumbs to Hasty Attack." *Armor.* September-October 1991, pp. 16-20.

"Redlegs in the Gulf." *Field Artillery.* October 1991.

Rolston, COL David. "Victory Artillery in Operation Desert Storm." *Field Artillery.* April 1991.

Ross, LTG Jimmy D. "Victory: the Logistics Story." *Army.* October 1991, p. 128.

Scales, COL Robert H., Jr. "Accuracy Defeated Range in Artillery Duel." *International Defense Review.* May 1991, pp. 473-481.

Schemmer, Ben F. "USAF MH-53J Pave Lows Led Army Apaches Knocking Out Iraqi Radars to Open Air War." *Armed Forces Journal International.* July 1991.

Schubert, Frank N., and Theresa L. Kraus, eds. *Whirlwind War: The United States Army in Operations Desert Shield and Desert Storm.* Draft, Washington, DC: US Army Center of Military History, January 31, 1992.

Schwarzkopf, GEN H. Norman, with Peter Petre. *It Doesn't Take a Hero.* New York: Bantam Books, October 1992. Schwarzkopf's account of the details of the ground war and of his frustration with GEN Franks needs to be considered in context with the author's personality and distant perspective from Riyahd. The tactical maps used in his book contain numerous errors.

Scicchitano, J. Paul. "Eye of the Tiger." *Army Times.* June 10, 1991, pp. 12-13, 16, 18, 61. *Army Times* reports on the "Tiger" Brigade.

——"Night Strikes: The Secret War of the 1st Cavalry Divison". *Army Times.* September 23, 1991, pp. 8, 14-16.

Scott, William. "USAF Officials Explain How War Altered Joint-STARS Requirements." *Aviation Week & Space Technology.* October 14, 1991.

Siffry, Micah, and Christopher Cerf, eds. *The Gulf War Reader: History, Documents, Opinions.* Random House, 1991. Mainly a political treatise on the war.

Starry, GEN (Ret) Donn A. "To Change An Army." *Military Review.* March 1983.

Steele, Dennis. "100-Hour War." *Army.* April 1991, pp. 19-20.

——"Tanks and Men: Desert Storm From The Hatches." *Army.* June 1991.

——"155 Miles Into Iraq: The 101st Strikes Deep." *Army.* August 1991, pp. 30-35.

Stewart, BG (P) John, Jr. "Operation Desert Storm, The Military Intelligence Story: A View From The G2, 3d US Army." Riyadh: ARCENT HQ, April 1991. Firsthand narrative on the challenges, successes, and failures encountered during the Gulf War. The narrative makes a positive but frank appraisal of Army intelligence during the war.

Stone, Michael P.W. "The Challenge: To Reshape, Remain Army of Excellence." *Army.* October 1991, pp. 12-20.

Sullivan, GEN Gordon R. "Maintaining Momentum While Accommodating Change." *Army.* October 1991, pp. 24-32.

Summers, COL (Ret) Harry G., Jr. *On Strategy II, A Critical Analysis of the Gulf War.* New York: Dell Publishing, February 1992. Follow-up to Summers' earlier work on Vietnam; compares the Vietnam experience to the success of Desert Storm.

Sun Tzu Wu. *The Art of War: The Oldest Military Treatise in the World*, trans. Lionel Giles, Harrisburg, PA: The Military Service Publishing Company, 1949.

Swain, COL Richard. "ARCENT History." Draft. Washington, DC: US Army Center of Military History, undated. Provides the best view of General Yeosock's role in the war.

"The 3d Armored Division Fought Saddam's Toughest Troops Through Rain and Wind." *Armor*. March-April 1991.

Tuttle, GEN William G.T. "Operation Desert Storm Demonstrates AMC's Mission Framework." *Army*. October 1991, p. 80.

US Army Intelligence Center. *Military Intelligence Desert Storm: The MI Experience*. Fort Huachuca, AZ: PB 34-91-4, October-December 1991, Vol 17, No 4. Contains a special collection of articles on MI units and operations in the Gulf War.

US News & World Report Staff. *Triumph Without Victory: The Unreported History of the Persian Gulf War*. Random House, 1991. Although the best account of the war outside of military sources, the work has numerous errors of fact that contribute to questionable analysis.

Vogel, Steve. "A Swift Kick, 2d ACR's Taming of the Guard." *Army Times*. August 5, 1991, pp. 10-13, 18, 28, 30, 61.

——"Fast and Hard, The Big Red One's Race Through Iraq." *Army Times*. March 25, 1991, pp. 12-13.

——"Hell Night—For the 2d Armored Division (Forward) It Was No Clean War." *Army Times*. October 7, 1991, pp. 8, 14-15, 18, 24, 69.

——"VII Corps Soldiers Describe Incidents." *Army Times*. September 19, 1991, p. 3.

Yeosock, LTG John J. "Army Operations in the Gulf Theater." *Military Review*. September 1991, pp. 2-15.

GLOSSARY

Terms

AA	Assembly area.
AAA	Antiaircraft artillery.
AAR	After-action review.
ABCCC	Airborne command and control center.
ABN	Airborne.
ACA	Airspace coordination area.
ACE	Armored combat earth mover.
ACR	Armored cavalry regiment.
AD	Armored division.
ADA	Air defense artillery.
AI	Air interdiction.
AIA	US Army Intelligence Agency.
AK	US designation of Russian/Chinese Kalishnikov-model automatic rifles.
ALO	Air liaison officer.
AMC	US Army Materiel Command.
AMX	French model designation for family of armored vehicles.
AO	Area of operations.
AOC	Army Operations Center.
APC	Armored personnel carrier.
ARAMCO	Arabian-American Oil Company.
ARCENT	Army Central Command; also US Third Army.
ARSOTF	Army Special Operations task force.
ARSTAF	Army Staff.
ARTEP	Army Training and Evaluation Program.
ASP	Ammunition supply point.
ATACMS	Army Tactical Missile System.
ATO	Air tasking order.
audible	Option play that commanders can call on the move to accommodate the enemy's reactions.
AUSA	Association of the United States Army.
AWACS	Airborne Warning and Control System.

BAI	Battlefield air interdiction.
BCE	Battlefield coordination element.
BCTP	Battle Command Training Program.
BDA	Battle damage assessment.
BDE	Brigade.
BDU	Battle dress uniform.
BG	Brigadier general.
"Big Red One"	Nickname for the 1st Infantry Division (Mech).
"Bimp"	Nickname for BMP.
Blackhawk	UH-60 utility helicopter.
BMP	Russian-design infantry fighting vehicle.
BN	Battalion.
BR	British.
Bradley	M-2 infantry fighting vehicle or M-3 cavalry fighting vehicle.
BRDM	Russian-design armored wheeled reconnaissance vehicle.
C^3IC	Coalition, Coordination, and Communications Integration Center.
CA	Civil affairs.
CAB	Combat aviation brigade.
Capstone	Term for Reserve units aligned with Active component units.
CAS	Close air support.
CAT	Crisis Action Team.
CAV	Cavalry.
CD	Cavalry division.
C-Day	Commencement of deployment, August 7, 1990.
CENTAF	Central Air Force Command.
CENTCOM	Central Command; one of six United States multi-Service commands.
CEO	Chief executive officer.
CEP	Circular error probable.
CEV	Combat engineer vehicle.
CFA	Covering force area.
CFE	Conventional Forces in Europe Treaty.

CG	Commanding general.
CGSC	US Army Command and General Staff College.
Chinook	CH-47 cargo helicopter.
CINC	Commander-in-Chief.
CINCCENT	Commander-in-Chief, Central Command.
CINCFOR	Commander-in-Chief, Forces Command.
CIS	Core Instrumentation System.
Closes	The arrival of a unit's deploying personnel and equipment at a specified destination.
CMTC	Combat Maneuver Training Center.
COL	Colonel.
COMMZ	Communications zone.
Composition A3	A type of explosive filler for ammunition.
CONPLAN	Contingency plan.
CONUS	Continental United States.
COSCOM	Corps Support Command.
CP	Command post.
CPT	Captain.
CSA	Corps support area.
CSAR	Combat search and rescue.
CUCV	Commercial utility cargo vehicle.
DA	Department of the Army.
DBDU	Desert battle dress uniform.
DCSINT	Deputy chief of staff for intelligence.
DCSOPS	Deputy chief of staff for operations and plans.
Desert One	Site of failed 1979 rescue attempt in Iranian desert.
"Desert Rats"	Famed British 7th Armored Brigade.
DIA	Defense Intelligence Agency.
DMA	Defense Mapping Agency.
DOD	Department of Defense.
DPICM	Dual-purpose improved conventional munitions.
DPSC	Defense Personnel Support Center.
DRB	Division ready brigade.

EA	Engagement area.
EAC	Eastern Army Command.
EG	Egypt.
ELINT	Electronic intelligence.
ENCOM	Engineer Command.
EPW	Enemy prisoners of war.
FAA	Forward assembly area.
FAC	Forward air controller.
FEBA	Forward edge of the battle area (foward limit of the main battle area).
FID	Foreign internal defense.
Firefinder	Countermortar, counterartillery radar.
"First Team"	Nickname for the 1st Cavalry Division.
FIST	Fire support team.
FISTV	Fire support team vehicle; a modified M113 APC.
FLIR	Forward-looking infrared.
FM	Field manual.
FOB	Forward operating base.
FORSCOM	US Army Forces Command.
FR	French.
fragging	Attacking unpopular leaders with grenades.
FRAGO	Fragmentary order.
FRAGPLAN	Fragmentary plan.
FROG	Free rocket over ground.
FSCL	Fire support coordination line.
FSE	Fire support element.
FSS	Fast sealift ship.
G2	Intelligence staff officer/section.
G3	Operations and plans staff officer/section.
G4	Logistics staff officer/section.
G-Day	February 24, beginning of the ground phase of the campaign.
GEN	General.
GHQ	General headquarters.

"go-away brigade"	Iraqi 52d Armored Brigade.
GPS	Global Positioning System; AN/PSN-9.
HAM	Hammurabi.
HARM	High-speed antiradiation missile.
HEAT	High-explosive antitank.
Hellfire	Laser-guided antitank missile.
HEMTT	Heavy expanded mobility tactical truck.
HET	Heavy equipment transporter.
H-Hour	The specific hour on D-Day at which a particular operation commences.
HMMWV	High-mobility, multipurpose wheeled vehicle.
HNS	Host-nation support.
HOT	A French-built wire-guided antitank missile.
HQ	Headquarters.
Huey	UH-1 Iroquois utility helicopter.
HUMINT	Human intelligence *or* human resources intelligence.
HWY	Highway.
ICBM	Intercontinental ballistic missile.
ID	Infantry division.
IMINT	Imagery intelligence.
IN	Infantry.
INTERNAL LOOK 2	A joint training exercise.
IPSA	Iraqi Pump Station, Arabia
"Ironsides"	Nickname for 1st Armored Division.
IRR	Individual Ready Reserve.
ITAC	US Army Intelligence and Threat Analysis Center.
J2	Intelligence staff officer/staff section at joint headquarters.
J5	Operations and plans staff officer/section at joint headquarters.
JAAT	Joint air attack team.
"Jayhawk"	Nickname for VII Corps.

JCS	Joint Chiefs of Staff.
JFACC	Joint forces air component commander.
JFC-E	Joint Forces Command-East.
JFC-N	Joint Forces Command-North.
JIC	Joint Intelligence Center.
JLO	Joint Liaison Organization.
JRTC	Joint Readiness Training Center.
JSOTF	Joint Special Operations task force.
JSTARS	Joint Surveillance Target Attack Radar System.
JTF	Joint task force.
Just Cause	December 1989 operation in Panama.
KARI	French-built air defense radar integration center.
KERO	Kuwait Emergency Recovery Organization.
KERP	Kuwait Economic Recovery Program.
KFIA	King Fahd International Airport.
KKMC	King Khalid Military City.
KM	Kilometers.
KTF	Kuwaiti task force.
KTO	Kuwaiti theater of operations.
KU	Kuwait.
LAR	Logistics assistance representative.
LCC	Land component commander.
LD	Line of departure.
LORAN	Long-range navigation system that operates on very low frequencies using signals from globally positioned ground transmitters.
LT	Lieutenant.
LTC	Lieutenant colonel.
LTG	Lieutenant general.
M1	Abrams tank.
MACH III	Three times the speed of sound.
MARCENT	Marine Central Command.
MAZ	Soviet model truck or tractor.

MBA	Main battle area.
MBB	Messerschmidtt-Boelkow-Blohm.
MEB	Marine Expeditionary Brigade.
Mech	Mechanized.
MED	Medina.
MEDEVAC	Medical evacuation.
METT-T	Mission, enemy, terrain, troops, and time available.
MG	Major general.
MHD	Material handling device.
MI	Military intelligence.
MiG	Common model designation for Russian- or Chinese-built fighter planes.
MILES	Multiple Integrated Laser Engagement System.
MLRS	Multiple-Launch Rocket System.
MP	Military police.
MPS	Maritime prepositioning ships.
MRE	Meals, ready to eat.
MSR	Main supply route.
MTLB	A Soviet-style armored personnel carrier.
NBC	Nuclear, biological, chemical.
NCO	Noncommissioned officer.
NCOES	Noncommissioned Officer Education System.
NDI	Nondevelopmental item.
NEB	Nebuchadnezzar.
NEO	Noncombatant evacuation operations.
NTC	National Training Center.
NVA	North Vietnamese Army.
OBJ	Objective.
OCS	Officer Candidate School.
ODCSLOG	Office of the deputy chief of staff for logistics.
OPFOR	Opposing force.
OPLAN	Operations plan.

PAC-1	First version of Patriot missile modified for antitactical missile mission.
PAC-2	Improved antitactical missile version of Patriot.
PDF	Panamanian Defense Force.
PL	Phase line.
PM-SANG	Project manager, Saudi Army National Guard.
POG	Psychological Operations Group.
POMCUS	Prepositioned materiel configured in unit sets.
POTF	Psychological operations task force.
POW	Prisoners of war.
PSYOP	Psychological operations.
Quickfix	Electronic warfare system mounted in Army aircraft.
RC	Reserve component.
"Ready First"	Nickname for the 1st Brigade, 3d Armored Division.
REFORGER	Return of forces to Germany.
RES	Reserves.
RGFC	Republican Guard Forces Command.
RP	Release point.
RPG	Rocket-propelled grenade.
RPV	Remotely piloted vehicle; unmanned aerial vehicle (UAV).
RVTS	Revetments.
SA	Saudia Arabia.
sabkha	A coastal salt flat.
sabot	Type of armor-piercing projectile.
SACEUR	Supreme Allied Commander, Europe.
sagger	Soviet-manufactured wire-guided antitank missile.
SAMS	US Army School for Advanced Military Studies.
"Sandcrabbers"	Nickname for MI units that operate Sandcrab radio-intercept system.
SANG	Saudi Army National Guard.
SATCOM	Satellite communications.

Scud	Ballistic missile.
SF	Special Forces.
shamal	A seasonal windstorm often associated with blowing dust and rain.
SIGINT	Signals intelligence.
"silver bullet"	Nickname for tank sabot round.
SJA	Staff Judge Advocate.
SLAR	Side-looking airborne radar.
"Sledgehammers"	Nickname for 197th Infantry Brigade.
SMA	US Army Sergeants Major Academy.
SMFT	Semitrailer-mounted fabric tank.
SO	Special Operations.
SOC	Sector Operations Center.
SOCCENT	Special Operations Command Central.
SOCOM	Special Operations Command.
SOF	Special Operations forces.
"Spearhead"	Nickname for 3d Armored Division.
Spectre	Air Force AC-130 aircraft.
Stinger	Antiaircraft infrared missile.
Stop Loss Program	Presidential authority to suspend laws relating to separations and retirements in order to retain in the Services a sufficient pool of immediately available, fully trained manpower to meet operational requirements.
SY	Syria.
TAA	Tactical assembly area.
TAACOM	Theater army area command.
TAC	Tactical command post.
TACSAT	Tactical satellite (communications).
TAW	Tawakalna.
TENCAP	Tactical exploitation of national capabilities.
TF	Task force.
"Tiger" Brigade	Nickname for 1st Brigade, 2d Armored Division.
TOC	Tactical operations center.

TOW	Tube-launched, optically tracked, wire-guided antitank missile.
TPFDD	Time-phased force deployment data.
TRADOC	US Army Training and Doctrine Command.
TROJAN	Intelligence high-frequency radio terminal.
TSA	Theater support area.
UAV	Unmanned aerial vehicle; remotely piloted vehicle (RPV).
UHF	Ultrahigh frequency.
UK	United Kingdom.
UPS	United Parcel Service.
USAF	United States Air Force.
USAREUR	US Army Europe.
USASG	US Army Support Group.
USTRANSCOM	US Transportation Command.
VHF	Very high frequency.
VIC	Vicinity.
"Victory" Division	24th Infantry Division.
VOLAR	Volunteer Army.
VULCAN	Model designation for 20mm antiaircraft cannon/gun system.
WP	White phosphorus.
XO	Executive officer.
ZSU	Model designation for Soviet-style antiaircraft gun system.

Symbols

Coalition Forces	Combat Service Support Supply Units
Iraqi Forces	Airborne Units
Republican Guard Forces	
Infantry Units	Coalition Support Units
Mechanized Infantry Units	Iraqi Motorized Units
Armor Units	Temporary Grouping of Units Battalion Company Teams or Task Force
Armored Cavalry Units	Platoon
Air Defense Units	Company
Field Artillery Units	Battalion
Chemical Units	Regiment
Engineer Units	Brigade
Attack Helicopter Units	Division
Air Assault Units	Corps
Motorized Units	

Single arrowhead for supporting direction of attack and supporting axis of advance

General movement for aircraft

Proposed axis of advance

General movement for aircraft with assaulting troops

Double arrowhead for direction of main attack and axis of advance for the main attack

Movement of Army attack aircraft

417

INDEX

Abizaid, Captain/Lieutenant Colonel
John, 30, 349, 358

Abrams
General Creighton, 7, 15, 18-19, 28,
361-62
General Creighton, Jr., 201, 205-06,
225-26
tank(s), 19, 77, 80-1, 93, 151, 261,
264, 267, 278, 299, 306, 362,
367, 374

active defense, 13-14, 25

Active strength, US Army, 386

ad-Damman, 57, 82, 132

ad-Din, Lieutenant Saif, 210, 291

Advanced Field Artillery Tactical
Data System, 387

Afghanistan, Soviet invasion of, 42

after-action reviews (AARs), 21-23

agility, 374-75

Aikman, Lieutenant Larry, 259

air attack, 125-26

airborne
forces, 128
radars, 178
Warning and Control System.
See AWACS.

Air Force, US
1st Tactical Fighter Wing, 391
363d Tactical Fighter Wing, 195
and combat search and rescue
missions, 194
and destruction of Iraqi equipment,
145
and interdiction, 26
and JSTARS, 167-68
and psychological operations,197
and relief supplies, 341
and the one-corps concept, 126

and the 20 north-south grid line,
289-90
close air support, 85, 92
doctrine, 174
friction with the Army, 180
in Grenada, 29-30
in Panama, 33
Ninth Tactical Air Control Center,
44
Tactical Air Command, 26, 167
time estimates, 124

air interdiction (AI), 26, 174-75, 178

AirLand Battle doctrine, 14-15,
25-26, 53, 106-08, 121-22, 132,
154, 174, 223, 361, 385

airmobility, 14

air
offensive, 122, 124
operation(s), 106, 111, 128, 145-46,
174, 180-81, 188, 206, 209
power, 107, 126, 145, 175-76, 178,
192, 310
Staff, 167

Alba, Lieutenant Al, 270

al-Busayyah, 238, 240-43

al-Jahra, 65, 126

al-Jubayl, 57, 66

al-Kahlid, General Jaber, 337

All-Source Intelligence Center, 289

al-Masoud, Colonel Salam, 102

al-Rawi, General Ayad Futayih, 44-5,
114, 233, 290, 314-15

al-Wafrah, 190

American industrial base, 71

America's First Battle, 22

ammunition, 81, 89, 305-06

Amos, Colonel Granville, 30